T0202932

Natural Language Understanding in a Semantic Web Context

Caroline Barrière

Natural Language Understanding in a Semantic Web Context

 Springer

Caroline Barrière
Computer Research Institute of Montreal (CRIM)
Montreal
Canada

ISBN 978-3-319-82327-0   ISBN 978-3-319-41337-2   (eBook)
DOI 10.1007/978-3-319-41337-2

Printed on acid-free paper

This Springer imprint is published by Springer Nature
The registered company is Springer International Publishing AG Switzerland

Preface

I hope for this book to serve as a good starting point for students and researchers in Semantic Web (SW) interested in discovering what Natural Language Processing (NLP) has to offer. At a time when Open Data is becoming increasingly popular, there is a pressing demand for tools to help the SW community transform those data into a shareable, normalized format, making all these data accessible as Linked Open Data. But a large portion of the data held by organizations seeking to make their data openly accessible are not stored in tables, but in much less structured forms, that is, textual forms such as reports, notes, memos, and articles. Manually generating structured information from them seems like an insurmountable task. Certainly, NLP can help uncovering the information held in text, thus augmenting the real content of the Semantic Web in a significant and lasting way.

My main goal is not just to foster interest in NLP in the readership, but awareness of how useful it can be to the Semantic Web community. I will not delve very deeply into linguistic principles, but instead focus on how NLP approaches different kinds of problems and provides solutions to them. My aim is also to show how, for the past 40 years, researchers in NLP have been interested in problems closely related to the ones faced by the Semantic Web community. Problems such as ambiguity and linking of knowledge are not specific to one field or the other, but central to both.

This book covers the basics of Natural Language Processing (NLP), with a focus on Natural Language Understanding (NLU). Here, understanding refers to semantic processing, Information Extraction, and knowledge acquisition, which I see as the key links between the SW and NLP communities. Much emphasis will be placed on mining sentences in search of entities and relations. In our quest in NLU, we will encounter challenges for various text analysis tasks, including part-of-speech tagging, parsing, semantic disambiguation, Named Entity Recognition, and Relation Extraction. I will present the standard algorithms associated with these tasks so as to provide an understanding of the fundamental concepts. Furthermore, I chose to emphasize the importance of experimental design and result analysis, and for doing so, most chapters show small experiments on corpus data with quantitative and qualitative analysis of results.

I assume that readers are familiar with the Semantic Web and are looking to learn about NLP in order to expand their horizons. That being said, the book provides enough information for a reader new to both fields to understand their underlying principles and the challenges they face. Also, the reader should be familiar with algorithms and simple programming principles, as this book will often use algorithms to describe problem-solving approaches.

Since I chose to cover a small number of simple algorithms in details, I do include a *Further Reading* section in most chapters for links to relevant state-of-the-art research in which readers can find more complex algorithms. I believe that understanding the fundamentals within basic algorithms is the best preparation for understanding more complex algorithms. I hope that through this book, important challenges in NLP will become familiar to the reader and that the book will stimulate the reader's interest in investigating them further.

Montreal, Canada   Caroline Barrière

Acknowledgements

I would like to acknowledge the contribution of the Centre de Recherche Informatique de Montréal (CRIM) for the writing of this book. During the time of writing, CRIM was very supportive and encouraging of this ambitious project.

I specially acknowledge the editing work of Amanda Bon, good friend of mine, and such a talented person, who performed a first editorial review of the entire book. Amanda performed more than simple editorial changes, and she pointed out unclear passages, learning gaps, and confusing parts. This allowed me to perform a thorough review of the material in the hope of making it clearer. Without Amanda's reading, suggestions, and corrections, this book would not have seen the light. I cannot thank her enough.

Thank you as well to my parents, Fernand and Fernande, for their constant encouragement throughout the long (even longer than expected) writing process.

And finally, thank you to Cyril, who patiently heard me talk about this book, day after day, from beginning to end. Thanks for the late-night dinners waiting for me. Thanks for being so supportive of everything I do.

Contents

Acronyms

AI	Artificial intelligence
BOW	Bag of words
IE	Information Extraction
IR	Information retrieval
KB	Knowledge base
KR	Knowledge representation
LOD	Linked Open Data
MT	Machine Translation
MWE	Multi-word expression
NED	Named Entity Disambiguation
NER	Named Entity Recognition
NLP	Natural Language Processing
NLU	Natural Language Understanding
OOV	Out-of-vocabulary
POS	Part of speech
RDF	Resource Description Framework
SW	Semantic Web
URI	Uniform Resource Identifier
WSD	Word Sense Disambiguation

URI Prefixes

PREFIX foaf: http://xmlns.com/foaf/spec/
PREFIX rdf: http://www.w3.org/1999/02/22-rdf-syntax-ns#
PREFIX rdfs: http://www.w3.org/rdf-schema/
PREFIX dbr: http://dbpedia.org/resource/
PREFIX dbpedia-fr: http://fr.dbpedia.org/resource/
PREFIX dbo: http://dbpedia.org/ontology/
PREFIX dbp: http://dbpedia.org/property/
PREFIX owl: http://www.w3.org/2002/07/owl
PREFIX yago: http://dbpedia.org/class/yago/
PREFIX wikidata: http://www.wikidata.org/entity/
PREFIX schema: http://schema.org
PREFIX wordnet: http://www.w3.org/2006/03/wn/wn20/instances/
PREFIX dct: http://purl.org/dc/terms/
PREFIX umbel-rc: http://umbel.org/reference-concept/
PREFIX nlusw: referring to made-up examples in the current book

Chapter 1
Introduction

Natural Language Processing (NLP) is a large research field, and although it has evolved over recent decades, many of the fundamental difficulties being tackled today are similar to those people were grappling with fifty years ago. The introduction of electronic corpora in the early 1990s, combined with the rise of internet accessibility in the later part of the decade, caused NLP to take a sharp statistical turn toward corpus analysis, increasing its overlap with the fields of machine learning and information retrieval. These changes led to the surfacing of new challenges, such as question-answering using large corpora, as well as new data-oriented statistical views on linguistic problems, such as measuring distributional similarities between words. Although these changing tides have had positive effects on the field of NLP, some underlying problems related to the understanding of language remain to this day.

In my view, **language understanding** implies the transformation of text into a deeper representation, one on which reasoning can occur. Admittedly, this view is more in line with the traditional view of artificial intelligence (AI) than with current trends in NLP, but this is not to say that the content of this book will be old-fashioned. On the contrary, it is intended to introduce current available resources and up-to-date algorithms, and to revisit the fundamental goal of Natural Language Understanding (NLU) from the point of view of the research field as it is today.

1.1 Scope

Since this book is primarily concerned with exploring what NLP has to offer to the **Semantic Web** community (and other research communities interested in knowledge representation), there are many subfields of NLP that will not enter into the discussion. These include Machine Translation, text summarization, text categorization, and others. The subfield that will be central to this book is **Information Extraction** (IE). It is through the study of IE that this book can show the important contribution that NLP can make to the Semantic Web community that of providing methods toward the transformation of unstructured data (e.g., textual information) into struc-

© Springer International Publishing Switzerland 2016
C. Barrière, *Natural Language Understanding in a Semantic Web Context*,
DOI 10.1007/978-3-319-41337-2_1

tured data (e.g., the Semantic Web datastore), being particularly helpful for **ontology population**.

IE is a well-established area of study in NLP, with important research results dating back to the Message Understanding Conferences (MUC) of the 1990s. IE is also quite wide reaching, ranging from the acquisition of structured information from text involving company mergers to text presenting biographical facts about people. It even has modern-day commercial applications, such as the extraction of dates from e-mail messages for the purpose of automatically suggesting calendar events.

Common to all research in IE is the need to extract two important types of information: **entities** and **relations**. Each of these is important and complex enough in itself to have an entire subfield of NLP research devoted to it. In the study of entities, the fields of Named Entity Recognition and Entity Linking are highly active today. The primary focus of **Named Entity Recognition** is searching for dates, locations, organizations, and other types of entities in text. **Entity Linking** involves linking particular mentions of entities in text back to their definitions. These definitions of entities are often taken from Wikipedia, an incredibly vast and openly accessible source of knowledge. As for the study of relations, the task of **Relation Extraction** is concerned with attempting to find occurrences of relations in text, in order to better link entities. For example, Relation Extraction could find information in text that would lead to the conclusion that a particular person is the director of a movie, not its leading actor.

This book will focus on both entities and relations. Through the use of IE methods, we will aim to extract both from text, in order to express them within a structured representation.

1.2   Approach

Although we have reduced the scope of this book to focus mainly on Information Extraction (IE), this subfield is itself quite large and diverse, and attempting to capture both its depth and its breadth in a single book would be ambitious to say the least. For this reason, we will adopt a **breadth coverage approach** in this book, meaning we will complete a general investigation of most areas of the field, but will not delve into the finer details of any one. The reader will be introduced to several problems facing IE and will learn a few simple algorithms for approaching each one.

For each topic that is covered, rather than providing the details of the multiple algorithms in current research, I will focus on the intuitions that inform them. It is crucial to grasp the underlying principles, general trends, and baseline algorithms if we hope to gain a solid general understanding of the field of IE. This will also provide us with the knowledge necessary for informed consideration of current research. That said, for the reader who is interested in learning more about particular topics, each chapter will include a **Further Reading** section to gather pointers to research surveys and relevant research articles. These sections will also serve to consolidate all references for the algorithms and elements of discussions presented within their corresponding chapter, making this information easier to find at a later date.

An important feature of this book is a focus on experimentation and analysis of results. Much current research in NLP is experiment-driven, an approach that is promoted by the various international competitions that have emerged in recent years (these cover various NLP tasks including Word Sense Disambiguation, Question Answering, and Machine Translation). This book will follow this trend and emphasize the **design of experiments**, as well as the **analysis of results**, even when it comes to the simplest of approaches. During our analysis of experiments' results, emphasis will be put on the importance of performing both **qualitative analysis** and **quantitative analysis**, so as to both understand the reasons for which algorithms succeed or fail, and provide measures of their performance.

Another commonality among the various chapters is the use of **Wikipedia** as a source of textual information. In order to perform Information Extraction, we require text to analyze, and from which to extract information. Being free, accessible and of considerable size makes Wikipedia the ideal resource for the learning examples presented in this book. That being said, we will discuss throughout the book how Wikipedia only covers one genre of text (informative texts) which might not be appropriate for all extraction tasks.

1.3 Prerequisite Knowledge

This book promotes a very hands-on approach to the study of Natural Language Processing, which rests on the assumption that readers have a certain amount of previous knowledge of algorithms and software programming. Most NLP strategies will be explored through the use of algorithms, and as such, the reader is assumed to be capable of reading and understanding individual steps of algorithms, and of programming them for analysis of results.

No knowledge of NLP is assumed on the part of the reader. This book is intended to take the reader from an initial introduction of the basic concepts of NLP, gradually toward an eventual understanding of the more advanced concepts that appear in its later sections.

A certain amount of knowledge about the Semantic Web will be assumed. As such, I steer readers less familiar with the Semantic Web to Appendix A, which provides a concise overview of the required material. Appendix A also introduces the query language SPARQL, which is useful for finding information within the Semantic Web.

Being that the focus of this book is on language analysis as opposed to mathematical models, it is accessible to a large audience and does not assume any preexisting knowledge of advanced mathematics. As a consequence of this, machine learning approaches are excluded (except for mention of word embeddings in Chap. 10), even though they have a large influence on current research methods. This is not to say that these machine learning approaches are unimportant. On the contrary, they are highly relevant in today's world of NLP, and those readers who are interested are strongly encouraged to complement the knowledge contained within this book with additional knowledge of machine learning. Here though, the only statistical models we will consider are those that are required for corpus analysis. Furthermore, when considering these models, details of the mathematical processes involved will be explicitly provided, in order to accommodate the range of mathematical backgrounds among the readership.

1.4 Structure

This book is divided into four parts, each containing three chapters.

Part I, Searching for Entities in Text, is dedicated to the search for entities in textual data. It begins with *Chap.* 2, *Entities, Labels, and Surface Forms*, which discusses the fundamental many-to-many relationship between concepts and lexical units, as well as the multiple ways language has of referring to concepts. Then *Chap.* 3, *Searching for Named Entities*, expands the search for individual entities to the classes of entities. This chapter also introduces a common and essential tool of NLP, regular expressions. Finally, *Chap.* 4, *Comparing Surface Forms*, presents two algorithms (Edit Distance and Soundex) used for discovering surface forms in text that have been altered by typographic errors.

Part II, Working with Corpora, is dedicated to an investigation of corpora as valuable resources for NLP work. *Chapter* 5, *Exploring Corpora*, discusses the various types of corpora and provides a sense of how words behave inside them. It takes us through both a quantitative exploration of corpora using word frequency measures and a qualitative exploration using a concordancer. Secondly, *Chap.* 6, *Words in Sequence*, provides a brief introduction to probabilistic modeling of word sequences, revealing the often predictable nature of words' occurrences in text. The ideas presented in the first two chapters are transposed to a bilingual context in *Chap.* 7, *Bilingual Corpora*, toward applications of automatic language detection and term equivalent search.

Part III, Semantic Grounding and Relatedness, is focused on the process of linking surface forms found in text to entities in resources. Its first chapter, *Linguistic Roles* (*Chap.* 8), introduces NLP processes of tokenizing, part-of-speech tagging, and parsing, in order to shed light on the linguistic nature of words. Determining the linguistic nature of a word can be thought of as the first step toward its disambiguation (e.g., *to cook* versus *a cook*). Next, *Chap.* 9, *Definition-Based Grounding*, tackles the problems of Word Sense Disambiguation and Entity Linking, which occur within a particular part of speech (e.g., *mouse* as a computer device versus a small animal, or *Paris* as the city in France or the name of a person). This chapter adopts a definition-based approach, since it considers the similarity between the context of occurrence of a surface form and the definitions of all the possible word senses or entities it can be linked to. In order to help disambiguation, additional contexts of occurrence in a text can be discovered through coreference analysis, which is a very difficult NLP task of which we only skim the surface. Finally, *Chap.* 10, *Relatedness*, takes us back into the realm of statistical corpus analysis, in order to discover relatedness between words. Knowledge of words' relatedness can be beneficial in many different NLP tasks, and we show one example of this by revisiting the definition-based grounding algorithm from the previous chapter and use word relatedness to increase its performances.

Part IV, Knowledge Acquisition, delves into the world of relations and Relation Extraction. First, *Chap.* 11, *Pattern-Based Relation Extraction*, looks into pattern-based approaches to Relation Extraction in text. It revisits regular expressions as possible implementations of lexical and lexico-syntactic pattern searches. The underlying purpose of the task will be ontology population, also called knowledge base expansion. *Chapter* 12, *From Syntax to Semantics*, first introduces dependency grammars for performing syntactic analysis, then moves on to an exploration of semantic frames as providing a structured representation for the semantic interpretations of sentences. The path from dependency graphs to semantic frames is a challenging one and is the focus of the remainder of the chapter. In *Chap.* 13, *Semantic Types*, we consider the constraints that semantic relations or semantic frames impose on their participants. For example, when defining a relation between an employee and an employer, that relation requires that the employee be of type PERSON and the employer of type ORGANIZATION. Named Entity Recognition will be introduced as one possibility for identifying standardized semantic types in text, such as LOCATION, PERSON and DURATION. As for less standardized semantic types (e.g., FOOD or CONTAINER), we will investigate their presence in various resources, as well as strategies for automatically discovering instances of these particular types through searches in text.

This book also includes three appendices. *Appendix A, A Look into the Semantic Web*, provides a brief overview of the Semantic Web. It is intended to bring readers less familiar with the Semantic Web up to speed, so that they too can fully benefit from the material of this book. *Appendix B, NLP Tools and Platforms*, provides information about NLP platforms and tools. *Appendix C, Relation Lists*, gathers lists of relations under different categories, showing how relations can be varied and serve different purposes.

Finally, this book provides an extensive *Glossary of terms*. The glossary consolidates the definitions of all the NLP-related terms used over the course of the book and is to be used as a reference whenever necessary. Throughout the text, the reader will find terms emphasized but not necessarily completely defined when first mentioned, perhaps because they refer to concepts explained in a later chapter. In such cases, the reader can minimally use the glossary to find short definitions to help his/her comprehension of the material.

1.5 Learning Paths

This book is structured to comprise an incremental study of NLP. We will construct the more advanced knowledge found toward the end of the book out of the simpler pieces of knowledge we gather over the beginning sections. This means that later chapters will often refer back to material from earlier chapters. However, so as not to force a linear reading of the book, many references to previously learned knowledge will be made explicit, allowing the reader to seek out the missing pieces of information when desired.

I recognize that goals, aims, and reasons for approaching this book can vary among readers. While one person may be looking for a thorough, all encompassing understanding of Information Extraction, someone else may desire a shorter, more concise overview of only the key elements, perhaps to complement their studies in another area. For this reason, I have outlined various **learning paths** one could follow through this book. The shortest path covers only crucial chapters, while the longer ones include additional chapters that deal with particular interests or niche areas of NLP. The hope is that, in this way, each reader can get out of this book what he or she is seeking.

For the reader seeking to work through the material of this book in a more concentrated fashion, the **short path (7 chapters)** may be the best option. Begin with Chaps. 2 and 3, to grasp the fundamentals of searching for entities in text. Next, move on to Chap. 5, to learn about corpora. Corpora provide the source material (text) for IE to apply its algorithms on. Then, skip right to Chaps. 8 and 9, which together will provide the basics of linking surface forms found in corpora to entities described in resources. Lastly, Chaps. 11 and 12 will provide important knowledge about Relation Extraction and semantic interpretation of sentences.

A slightly more thorough route would be to take the longer **semantic exploration path (9 chapters)**. This path adds Chaps. 10 and 13, which provide additional insight about **word relatedness** and **semantic types**, both quite important for Entity Linking and semantic interpretation of sentences.

Then, there are three additional chapters, corresponding to more specific interests.

The reader interested in applying IE on **noisy texts** (e.g., e-mails, sms, and blogs) would do well to add Chap. 4 to their reading. This chapter provides algorithms for comparing words that are similar sounding, as well as those that contain orthographic errors.

The reader wanting to learn basics in **statistical models of language** can additionally read Chap. 6, in order to gain an understanding of sequence models, commonly used in word prediction, error correction, and even Machine Translation.

Finally, Chap. 7 contains pertinent information for those interested in **bilingual corpora** as it provides the statistical tools for finding information in a bilingual parallel corpus, such as term equivalents, which are terms in different languages linking to the same concept.

Part I
Searching for Entities in Text

Our starting point is a knowledge base within the Semantic Web that contains a certain amount of information about select entities. Our objective will be to search in text for further information about those entities.

Below are three entities, provided by three URIs (Uniform Resource Identifiers) taken from DBpedia.[1] All three refer to specific instances of people or places.

http://dbpedia.org/resource/Mount_Everest
http://dbpedia.org/resource/Wolfgang_Amadeus_Mozart
http://dbpedia.org/resource/Ireland

We will also see the term *entity* used to refer to generic objects, such as those seen below. These do not refer to a specific *mobile phone* or one particular *Chinese cabbage* bought on a certain day, but rather to any *mobile phone* or *Chinese cabbage*.

http://dbpedia.org/resource/Mobile_phone
http://dbpedia.org/resource/Chinese_cabbage

The information we seek regarding specific and generic entities can be quite varied, as demonstrated by the following questions:

What is the height of *Mount Everest*?
When was *Wolfgang Amadeus Mozart* born?
What is the capital of *Ireland*?
When were *mobile phones* invented?
What is the typical color of a *Chinese cabbage*?

Answers to these questions may very well be somewhere in the Semantic Web datastores, but they may not be. For example, answers to the first two questions are available within DBpedia, but answers to the last three are not.[2] In cases where DBpedia (or any other datastore) does not provide the answer, we hope that textual data will contain an answer which can be uncovered through the process of **Information Extraction**.

---

[1] DBpedia is an important resource of the Semantic Web and can be accessed at http://dbpedia.org.
[2] The inclusion of these predicates in DBpedia was validated in the summer of 2015.

In Information Extraction, the first step toward finding answers to questions like the ones above is to find mentions of the relevant entities in text. Given that entities often have multiple names; however, our quest into text should account for this by searching them in their various **surface forms**. For example, if we are searching for information about *Mozart*, we might also search his other names, such as *Wolfgang Amadeus Mozart* and *W.A. Mozart*. Likewise, a search for *Chinese cabbage* should include synonyms such as *bok choy*. Entities and their multiple surface forms will be the focus of *Chap. 2, Entities, Labels, and Surface Forms*.

Certain information in text is better searched for based on the type of information it has. For example, a search for when Mozart was born would involve searching for textual information corresponding to the specific entity type DATE. On the other hand, a search for the capital of Ireland would seek information corresponding to a LOCATION, or more precisely a CITY. There are various entity types that are quite common, such as PERSON, DURATION, and ORGANIZATION, and other less common ones, such as POLITICIAN and SYMPHONY. Furthermore, certain entity types such as dates have particular, predictable formats (i.e., May 2 2015 or 15 June 2014), which make them easier to find in text relative to other, less predictable ones. To search for entities with predictable formats, we can use **regular expressions**, a very powerful text search tool that is commonly used in Natural Language Processing. One goal of *Chap. 3, Searching for Named Entities*, will be to demystify regular expressions.

In *Chap. 4, Comparing Surface Forms*, we will learn how to address instances of surface forms that contain typographic errors, for example, *musician* misspelled as *misicien*, by matching them to existing words in our vocabulary. This matching can be accomplished via an **Edit Distance** algorithm, looking at letter deletion, insertion, and substitutions. Another algorithm, called **Soundex**, relies instead on the sounds of words for resolving cases of typographic error. We will also explore Soundex in this chapter and compare it with Edit Distance.

The knowledge we acquire over the course of the following three chapters will provide us with the necessary tools for *Searching for Entities in Text*.

Chapter 2
Entities, Labels, and Surface Forms

The starting point for Information Extraction (IE) is textual data in the form of a document, a set of documents, or even a set of individual sentences in which we will search for information. For now, let us refer to any such textual data as a **corpus**.[1] Let us set our first IE goal as to find all sentences from a corpus in which a particular entity is mentioned.

In this chapter, we will look into a first obstacle toward this seemingly simple IE goal: the fact that entities do not have normalized names. Instead, entities can be referred to by many different **surface forms**. For any entity searched (e.g., dbr:Wolfgang_Amadeus_Mozart), there could be various associated surface forms present in the corpus (e.g., *W.A. Mozart, Amadeus Mozart, Mozart*), and knowledge of these surface forms is necessary to achieve our goal. We will introduce a measure called **recall measure** to evaluate the extent to which a set of known surface forms suffices for retrieving all of an entity's textual mentions.

The search in the corpus for a particular surface form is likely to output sentences unrelated to the entity we are looking for. That is due to **polysemy**. Polysemy is the word used to describe the fact that a surface form (e.g., *Mozart*) can be associated with many entities (e.g., *Wolfgang Amadeus Mozart, Café Mozart, Mozart Street*). We will introduce a second measure called **precision measure**, to evaluate the extent to which the sentences retrieved from the corpus actually lead to the desired entity.

Which surface forms are available to the IE process largely influences its precision and recall. We will explore DBpedia as a resource in which surface forms can be found and further provided to the IE process. DBpedia contains surface forms explicitly stated through the standard naming predicates (e.g., rdfs:label, foaf:name). But we will shift our attention toward a non-standard naming predicate, the predicate dbo:wikiPageRedirects, as to explore a larger, but more eclectic set of candidate surface forms. Studying this eclectic set reveals semantic variations (e.g., quasi-

---

[1] We will further discuss definitions of the word *corpus* in Chap. 5, Sect. 5.1.

© Springer International Publishing Switzerland 2016
C. Barrière, *Natural Language Understanding in a Semantic Web Context*,
DOI 10.1007/978-3-319-41337-2_2

synonym, related word), lexical variations (e.g., plural, singular), and orthographic variations (e.g., capitalization of the first letter, use of hyphen) as surface forms to be expected to occur in text.

We will suggest **generative rules** to construct some of an entity's associated surface forms automatically, as to provide the IE process with an even larger set of surface forms. We will then briefly look at surface forms from a multilingual point of view, as provided by DBpedia. Finally, we will discuss the most problematic surface forms: **pronouns**. Mentions of entities in text through the use of pronouns such as *it*, *them*, or *he* make it very difficult for IE.

2.1 A First Surface Form: Entity Label

I am interested in the composer *Ludwig van Beethoven*. I find an entity referring to him in DBpedia under the URI dbr:Ludwig_van_Beethoven. The Semantic Web provides a network of Universal Resource Identifiers (URIs) to uniquely identify concepts.[2] Such normalization is necessary for the sharing of information and is ideal for communication among machines. In IE, on the other hand, the source of information to analyze textual data has been written by humans for human consumption. In such human-to-human communication channel, there is no notion of normalization, quite the opposite actually, as creativity is usually valued in such communication. Therefore, for an IE process to search in text, it requires knowledge of the **surface forms** likely to be used by the writers of text to refer to various concepts, surface forms that are also likely to be understood by readers of these texts.

The Semantic Web contains a certain number of naming predicates that provide alternate surface forms for entities. Some commonly used naming predicates are foaf:name or rdfs:label as in the following examples[3] providing two different names for the desired entity:

(dbr:Ludwig_van_Beethoven, rdfs:label, "Ludwig van Beethoven")
(dbr:Ludwig_van_Beethoven, foaf:name, "Beethoven, Ludwig van")

These surface forms can be provided to the IE process to search for their occurrences in the BEETHOVENCORPUS, which contains 12 sentences, as shown in Table 2.1.

The IE process finds the first surface form *Ludwig van Beethoven* in sentences {1,4,8}. We can then assume that this set of sentences contain information about our entity of interest. If we provide the second surface form *Beethoven, Ludwig van* to the IE process, it leaves us with an empty set. Although a valid surface form, it is not one commonly used in text and no sentences of the BEETHOVENCORPUS contains it.

So, how successful is the IE process so far? It might seem early in our quest to think of evaluating our method, but it is not. It is never too early.

---

[2]An introduction to the Semantic Web is provided in Appendix A.

[3]Prefixes associated with various Semantic Web data provider sites are listed at the beginning of this book.

Table 2.1 The small BEETHOVENCORPUS

No.	Sentence
1	The Andante favori is a work for piano solo by *Ludwig van Beethoven*.
2	The other great passion of the young Mirabehn was the music of *van Beethoven*.
3	*L.V. Beethoven* spent the better part of his life in Vienna.
4	Charles Munch conducted the symphony no. 9 of *Ludwig van Beethoven* in 1962.
5	Among the few composers writing for the orphica was *Ludvig von Beethoven*.
6	*Betthoven*, too, used this key extensively in his second piano concerto.
7	Naue went to Vienna to study briefly with *von Beethoven*.
8	Bonn is the birthplace of *Ludwig van Beethoven* (born 1770).
9	Johann van Beethoven joined the court, primarily as a singer, in 1764.
10	Camper van Beethoven were inactive between late 1990 and 1999.
11	Beethoven, meanwhile, runs after a loose hot dog cart and ends up on a merry-go-round.
12	Beetehoven hit theaters in april 1992.

2.2 Experiment — Searching for *Beethoven*

Evaluation is a major focus of NLP, and new methods presented by researchers are always regarded relative to other methods or established baselines. So far, we can consider that we have defined a **baseline algorithm**, meaning a first simple method. Our baseline algorithm for finding information about a particular entity consists of searching in text using the surface form provided by the predicates rdf:label and foaf:name. Once we have evaluated the performance of this baseline algorithm, we will move on to suggest new ideas and hope these will lead to improvements.

The most common evaluation measures are based on a comparison between a **gold standard** and an algorithm (or system). The gold standard defines what is correct and incorrect, and our system tries to mimic it.

A **contingency table**, as shown in Table 2.2, summarizes the system's various possible results in relation to the gold standard. If the system turns up a correct answer, we have a **true positive** (TP). If the system thinks an answer is correct but it is not, then we have a **false positive** (FP). If the system thinks the answer is incorrect when in fact it is correct, we have a **false negative** (FN). Lastly, if the system rightly identifies an answer as incorrect, then we have a **true negative** (TN).

Table 2.2 Contingency table

		Gold standard	
		correct	incorrect
System	correct	true positive (TP)	false positive (FP)
	incorrect	false negative (FN)	true negative (TN)

Typical evaluation measures derived from the contingency table are as follows:

$$Recall = \frac{TP}{TP + FN}$$

$$Precision = \frac{TP}{TP + FP}$$

$$F1 = 2 * \frac{Precision * Recall}{Precision + Recall}$$

$$Reject = \frac{TN}{TN + FP}$$

$$Accuracy = \frac{TP + TN}{N}$$

$$N = TP + TN + FN + FP$$

In Natural Language Processing, the first three measures, **recall**, **precision**, and **F1**, are the most commonly used. As you will see throughout this book, we constantly try to balance the precision and recall of algorithms as we search for information in text. We hope for high recall as an indication that our algorithm did not miss important information and we hope for high precision as an indication that the algorithm did not dilute the important information among many irrelevant candidates. Sometimes, an application dictates whether high recall or high precision is more important, but if that is unknown, then the F1 measure is a good compromise, since it combines both measures by calculating the harmonic mean between recall and precision.

In our example, assuming we use the BEETHOVENCORPUS to define our gold standard, the entity dbr:Ludwig_van_Beethoven is referred to in sentences 1 to 8, making these sentences positive examples. Sentences 9 to 12 are negative examples referring to three other entities with very similar names. We compare our baseline algorithm, searching using the surface form *Ludwig van Beethoven*, against this gold standard. Since our algorithm identifies only the three sentences {1,4,8} as correctly relating to the entity dbr:Ludwig_van_Beethoven, it provides 3 true positives. The full contingency table is shown in Table 2.3, and the derived precision/recall measures follow.

Table 2.3 Contingency table for baseline algorithm of *Ludwig van Beethoven* search

		Truth (Gold standard)	
		correct	incorrect
Baseline search	correct	3	0
	incorrect	5	4

$$Precision = \frac{3}{3} = 100\%$$

$$Recall = \frac{3}{8} = 37.5\%$$

$$F1 = 2 * \frac{100 * 37.5}{100 + 37.5} = 54.5\%$$

These results show that our baseline algorithm provides a high degree of precision, but unfortunately it comes at the expense of recall, which is low. We missed many of the positive sentences from the gold standard in which the entity's full surface form was not used. Let us see in the next section how recall can be improved, hopefully without loosing in precision.

2.3 Looking for Additional Surface Forms

As in any search problem, the goal is to improve on our precision and recall. So far we have a good level of precision in our baseline algorithm, because our query is very specific. To obtain higher recall, we will have to relax the query somewhat, or add alternative names. The predicate `dbo:wikiPageRedirects` found in DBpedia is a good place to find alternative names, since it provides all the redirect links used in Wikipedia to access a desired page. It shows us the various ways humans attempt to find a particular Wikipedia page, and we can assume that the same ones would apply to text.

Through the DBpedia SPARQL endpoint, we can find the redirect links using the following SPARQL query, which returns 53 variations[4]:

```
PREFIX dbr: <http://dbpedia.org/resource/>
PREFIX dbo: <http://dbpedia.org/ontology/>
select ?X where {
    ?X dbo:wikiPageRedirects dbr:Ludwig_van_Beethoven .
}
```

Table 2.4 Examples of redirect links to `dbr:Ludwig_van_Beethoven` and matching sentences from BEETHOVENCORPUS

No.	Redirects	Sentences retrieved
1	Beethoven	1, 2, 3, 4, 5, 7, 8, 9, 10, 11
2	Beethovens	
3	Baytoven	
4	Beeethoven	
5	Beetehoven	12
6	L.V. Beethoven	3
7	Ludvig von Beethoven	5
8	Ludwig van Beitoven	
9	van Beethoven	1, 2, 3, 8, 9, 10
10	von Beethoven	5, 7

The second column of Table 2.4 shows a sample of these variations. As you can see, these surface forms vary in their nature. Some are **abbreviations**, some are **short**

---

[4]Information about SPARQL can be found in Appendix A. The DBpedia SPARQL endpoint is at the address http://dbpedia.org/sparql. The number of variations returned by the query is likely to vary depending on the date you access the site, as DBpedia is expanding every day.

forms, and others include **orthographic errors**. We will look more closely at these variations in the next section, but for now let us focus on the impact of using them in our search on the BEETHOVENCORPUS.

Assuming we include all variations in our search, how does this influence our results? The third column of Table 2.4 shows the sentences retrieved by each surface form. We can summarize the results in the contingency table shown in Table 2.5, and the equations that follow show the new precision, recall, and F1 results.

Table 2.5 Evaluation of search using surface forms provided by the redirect links

		Truth (Gold standard)	
		correct	incorrect
System	correct	7	4
	incorrect	1	0

$$Precision = \frac{7}{11} = 63.6\%$$

$$Recall = \frac{7}{8} = 87.5\%$$

$$F1 = 2 * \frac{63.6 * 87.5}{63.6 + 87.5} = 73.7\%$$

Using all variations, our recall is now at 87.5%, but our precision has dropped to 63.6%. This is typical of a query expansion process in information retrieval, which is precisely the process we have engaged in. This trade-off between precision and recall is often the struggle in searches for information in text, whether they involve entities, as seen here, or relations, which we will investigate in later chapters. Our strategy will therefore depend on our ultimate purpose. If the goal is really to *not miss anything*, assuming a human reviewer will later filter the results, we should aim for high recall. On the other hand, if we are less concerned with capturing every possibility and more with presenting tailored, quality results to a user, then we should aim for high precision.

In our example, the surface form *van Beethoven* leads us to include sentences about the rock band *Camper van Beethoven*, as well as one about *Johann van Beethoven*, Ludwig's father. The surface form *Beethoven* included sentences about the movie *Beethoven*, which features a dog named Beethoven. This could be problematic if we intend to use these results as the basis for a later fact extraction algorithm. Including sentences about the rock band and/or the movie is bound to lead to errors or even ridiculous facts.

We are now confronted with the significant problem of **polysemy**. Surface forms, especially those that are made up of single words, have multiple meanings. The longer form *Ludwig van Beethoven* ensured that we were finding relevant sentences. Relaxing our query to *Beethoven* also returned relevant sentences, but with them many other, less relevant ones which we will have to somehow filter out. One important approach to dealing with polysemy is to develop disambiguation algorithms, something we will look at in Part III of this book, investigating *Semantic Grounding and Relatedness*.

Before moving on, there are a couple of things we should take note of. First, notice that when we apply an all encompassing pattern such as *Beethoven*, all the more precise variations are subsumed by it and defining them becomes less useful. Also, although we had many variations to search for, sentence 6 is still missing from our results. That sentence contains the misspelled form *Betthoven* which was not included in the known variations. We will further explore misspelling errors in Chap. 4.

For now, let us continue on our exploration of name variations.

2.4 Categorizing various Surface Forms

As we search for information in text, we may be interested in **specific entities** (e.g., *Ludwig van Beethoven*) as we have seen thus far, or our interest could be geared more toward **generic entities** (e.g., *garden, laptop computer*). Similar to specific entities, the surface forms provided by naming predicates for generic entities are usually insufficient for searches in text. For example, if we want to know about mobile phones, the only label provided in DBpedia is *Mobile phone*.

However, people tend to be very creative in how they refer to particular concepts. To demonstrate this point, Table 2.6 shows a subset of the results returned by the following SPARQL query:

```
PREFIX dbr: <http://dbpedia.org/resource/>
PREFIX dbo: <http://dbpedia.org/ontology/>
select ?X where {
    ?X dbo:wikiPageRedirects dbr:Mobile_phone .
}
```

Table 2.6 Examples of `dbo:wikiPageRedirects` for the URI of Mobile_phone in DBpedia

Cell_phone	Cellular_mobile	Cellular_telephone
Celluar_telephone	Cellular_Radio	Cellular_phones
Mobile_cellular	Handphone	Mobile_Phones
Cell_telephones	Cell_phones	Hand_phone
Cell_phone_carrier	Cellular_radio	How_mobilephones_work?
Mobile_telecom	Cell_Phone	Cellphones
Cell-phone	Cellular_telephones	Mobile_phones
Mobile_communications	Mobile_Phone	Cellular_phone
Flip_phones	Mobile_telephone	Wireless_phone
Mobile_telephones	Cellular_Telephone	Cell_Phones
Cell_phone_dance	Cellphone	Cellphone_video

To be sure, not all the variations in Table 2.6 are proper synonyms for *mobile phone*. So what are they? Should we include them all in our search, or not? Let us begin to answer these questions by characterizing the variations found in the table.

Real synonyms Many of the variations are real synonyms of *mobile phone*, meaning the two surface forms are completely interchangeable in a sentence. Many variations also show that *mobile phone* has a compositional meaning, formed by the individual meanings of *mobile* and *phone*. Being that it is compositional, *mobile phone* allows for variants of both components of the expression. The first word, *mobile*, has the variants *cell* and *cellular*, and the second word, *phone*, has the variant *telephone*. Together, these variants lead to multiple possible combinations.

Quasi-synonyms *Flip phone*, *hand phone*, and *wireless phone* are loose extensions of *mobile phone* and could probably be used interchangeably with *mobile phone* in certain contexts, but not always. Quasi-synonyms are very common in language, much more so than real synonyms.

Uppercase variations Many variations simply come from using the uppercase for the first letter of either or both words, such as in *Cell phone* or *cell Phone*.

Orthographic variations Different ways of combining the words lead to orthographic variations. Examples here include the use of a hyphen in *cell-phone*, the use of a space in *cell phone*, and even the two words being combined into a single word in *cellphone*.

Plural form Some variations come from the use of the plural, such as *cell phones* and *mobile phones*.

Typographic error Some variations included in the redirect links are simply to ensure that the Wikipedia entries are reached even if the user makes a typographic error, such as in *celluar telephone*.

Related topics Variations such as *How mobile phones work?*, *Cell phone carrier*, *cellphone video*, *cellular radio*, and *Mobile telecom* are certainly related to *mobile phone*, but they are neither synonyms nor quasi-synonyms.

Given all of these variations, which one(s) should we use to expand our search in text? As we have seen, anything we add will increase recall but runs the risk of decreasing the precision of our results.

It is safe to say that real synonyms should be used in a search. The more precise the synonym, the less likely it is to introduce noise and lower the overall precision of our algorithm (e.g., *cellular phone*). On the other hand, introducing a synonym like *mobile* in our search is very likely to create noise, given its polysemous nature.

As for quasi-synonyms, they can be tricky. There are times when we should include all of them in a single search, especially if our goal is to search for information at a general level. Other times though, we will want to understand the difference between quasi-synonyms, in which case they should be searched for individually.

Typographic errors are fairly important for searches in noisy corpora (e.g., Web, e-mails, etc.), but much less so for searches in books or Wikipedia. ***Chapter*** 4, ***Comparing Surface Forms***, looks at algorithms to automatically evaluate the distance between two strings, such as *Celuar* and *Cellular*. Such algorithms are very helpful in analyzing text, since predicting all possible typographic errors ahead of time is not possible.

When it comes to uppercase and plural forms, as a rule we should probably include them in our search. The exception would be in searches for company names (e.g., *Apple* versus *apple*), where the differentiation lies in the first letter being capitalized. Contrarily to typographic errors, variations such as plural or uppercase forms are predictable, which makes it possible to write algorithms for generating these variations ahead of time. That is the topic of the next section.

2.5 Expanding the Set of Surface Forms with a Generative Approach

Despite being listed as *wikiPageRedirects*, certain surface form variations of entities can be generated automatically, and doing so will allow us to obtain a more complete list of variations. For example, if *Mobile phone* and *cell phones* are included on our list, why should not *Cell phones*, *Cell phone*, *Mobile phones*, and *mobile phones* also be there? It would be possible to generate all of these variations with only two rules, one for changing the first letter to uppercase and another for adding the plural marker '*s*'.

Rather than listing all variations, we can write **generative rules** in order to derive all variations from a subset of elements. These generative rules are most valuable since they can be applied generally, to all Wikipedia entries (not just *mobile phone*). A rule for first letter capitalization is a good example of one that would be generally applicable. Other examples are rules for orthographic variations (hyphens, spaces, single word) as well as ones for plural variations, even though plural rules must be adapted to word endings (e.g., story/stories).

Since rules can be applied systematically to generate all forms, using them is likely to lead to more reliable coverage of a larger number of variations. This is much more straightforward than attempting to compile an exhaustive list one form at a time, where we could easily forget to include one or several forms.

Table 2.7 provides examples of generative rules for different types of variations. Some of these rules can be combined to generate further variations. Then, Table 2.8 takes us back to our example of *Ludwig van Beethoven* and suggests some generative rules for proper nouns.

Table 2.7 Examples of generative rules applied to *cell phone*

Variation type	Rule	Derived form
plural	Add 's'.	cell phones
capitalization	Put first letter of first word in uppercase.	Cell phone
capitalization	Put first letter of all words in uppercase.	Cell Phone
orthographic	Put hyphen between words.	cell-phone
orthographic	Remove space between words.	cellphone

Generative rules can be put in opposition to **normalization rules**, perhaps more commonly used in NLP. A typical example of a normalization rule is **lemmatization** which tries to find a word's base form, called a **lemma**. For example, lemmatization would transform *chosen* and *choosing* into a single base form *choose*. This will be part of our exploration into linguistic processes in *Chap.* 8 looking at *Linguistic Roles*.

Table 2.8 Examples of generative rules applied to *Ludwig van Beethoven*

Variation type	Rule	Derived forms
abbreviation	Gather the first letter of each word separated by periods.	L.V.B.
spaced abbreviation	Apply abbreviation rule and add space in between letters.	L. V. B.
first names initials	Apply abbreviation rule except on the last word.	L.V. Beethoven
skip middle noun	Remove the middle name.	Ludwig Beethoven

Generative rules derive multiple surface forms which are then stored in a resource as possible variations for an entity. At search time, all forms can be used to find relevant sentences in text. Normalization rules take the opposite approach of going through the text at search time and attempting to map all encountered forms onto a limited number of normalized forms held in the resource. Both of these processes will be useful at different times, depending on our application.

2.6 Multilingual Surface Forms

Let us now make a small incursion into multilingual surface forms and look at labels and surface forms provided in the Semantic Web for languages other than English. As an example, we discuss the multilingual DBpedia, defining a conceptual system in each language, and then relating concepts using the `owl:sameAs` predicate. In theory, the `owl:sameAs` should be used to establish an equivalence between concepts (URIs). If two concepts are equivalent, then we could assume that their respective labels, as provided by the usual naming predicates, would correspond to translations of each other.

The problem, though, is that the same variations seen in Sect. 2.1 exist in every language. There are even languages that would contain more variations based on **grammatical case**, for example, having a different form of a word corresponding to its accusative case (direct object of the verb) or dative case (indirect object of the verb). These variation types, similar to differentiation between plural forms, verb forms, or even abbreviations, cannot be captured with a `rdfs:label` naming predicate and would require an encoding format able to capture linguistic information about words. I encourage the reader to follow the pointers to the **lemon model** and the initiative of Linguistic Linked Open Data in Sect. 2.9, for more information about encoding linguistic information in the Semantic Web.

Besides variations within languages, there are problems related to the linking of information between languages. For example, things become quite complex with the spilling over of some English information into the naming information of other languages. If we follow the `owl:sameAs` link for `dbr:United_Kingdom` to the French DBpedia, we find different labels, as shown below.

```
(dbr:United_Kingdom, owl:sameAs, dbpedia-fr:Royaume-Uni)
(dbpedia-fr:Royaume-Uni, rdfs:label, "Royaume-Uni")
(dbpedia-fr:Royaume-Uni, rdfs:label, "United Kingdom")
(dbpedia-fr:Royaume-Uni, rdfs:label, "Regne Unit")
(dbpedia-fr:Royaume-Uni, rdfs:label, "Reino Unido")
...
(dbpedia-fr:Royaume-Uni, foaf:name, "United Kingdom")
(dbpedia-fr:Royaume-Uni, dbo:frenchName, "Royaume Uni")
```

The same predicate, `rdfs:label`, leads to different surface forms, corresponding to different languages, but without explicit indication of which language. Then, how could an automatic system find the French name assigned to UK, given all this information? The `dbo:frenchName` predicate could help select the correct label, but this predicate is not consistently used to name entities. Unfortunately, the lack of coherence within this multilingual labeling will cause this information to be very difficult to use in NLP, if we wish to expand, for example, our entity search to texts written in different languages.

Ensuring resource coherence is a challenge in itself, either for experienced **lexicographers**, **terminologists**, or **domain experts** in the case of curated resources, or for community contributors in the case of collective resources such as Wikipedia. From an NLP point of view, it is important to be aware that resource coherence will have an impact on any automatic process that tries to use it.

2.7 The Most Ambiguous Surface Form: Pronouns

In the last section of this chapter, I wish to introduce the most ambiguous surface forms: **pronouns**. Below is a short made-up text in which I highlighted the use of pronouns.

Lora Bruntelli earns income from publication of *her* works and from public performances. *She* also depends on the generosity of a particular patron, Mr. Zelig, for income. Lora is lucky that *his* wife, Clara, especially loves *her* music. *He* often commissions *her* compositions to be played in private performances to which *they* invite friends.

Pronouns are short surface forms most often used in text to refer to previously mentioned entities. Once the entity *Lora Bruntelli* is established in the first sentence, the following mentions of *she* and *her* can be associated with *Lora Bruntelli*. Then, once the entity *Mr. Zelig* is introduced in the second sentence, the pronoun *his* and *he* can be used to refer to *Mr. Zelig.* The use of pronouns allows for fluidity in text, avoiding the repeated use of names of people, location, or objects. But fluidity for human consumption of text adds an additional heavy burden on NLP, since pronouns quickly become very ambiguous in who or what they refer to.

In our example, when the entity *Clara* is introduced in the third sentence, it also permits the use of *her* to refer to *Clara.* Now, having two entities *Lora* and *Clara* possibly referred to by *her* creates ambiguity. Seemingly easy for humans, disambiguating the reference of a pronoun is one of the most difficult tasks in NLP, called **anaphora resolution**. In anaphora resolution, we try to automatically find the entity previously mentioned in the text to which a pronoun corresponds.

The use of **coreferences** is a related language phenomenon also included in the example above. The use of *Lora* in the third sentence links back to *Lora Bruntelli* in the first sentence. Automatically finding such links is called **coreference resolution**, perhaps a slightly more approachable task than anaphora resolution, but still in the realm of the research NLP world. We will come back to the task of coreference resolution in Chap. 9.

Another related but much less frequent language phenomenon is called **cataphora**, as shown in the following example:

Knowing he tends to be late, Brandon always sets his clock fifteen minutes early.

Notice how the pronoun *he* is used before the name *Brandon* is mentioned. The associated NLP task is called **cataphora resolution**, but it is not studied as much as anaphora resolution given the much less frequent use of cataphora in text.

Some NLP tasks that will be mentioned throughout this book are considered *mature problems*, meaning that they have implementations in software packages that are usable, out of the box, with reasonable performances. Anaphora and cataphora resolutions are not among those tasks, as they are still very much in the realm of NLP research. Most IE systems do not attempt to perform those tasks and simply ignore sentences in which pronouns occur (except for the very easy cases of non-ambiguity). Not dealing with sentences containing hidden forms (e.g., his, him, he) is most often compensated by using a larger corpus, in which we hope to find sufficient explicit mentions.

2.8   In Summary

- Both specific entities and generic entities are referred to by multiple surface forms in text.
- Precision and recall of an entity search process will be influenced by which surface forms were used in the search.
- Not all the variations found through the `dbo:wikiPageRedirects` are to be considered as valid surface forms for entity search.
- Many variations of lexical units can be generated automatically (e.g., plural, capitalization).

- Generative rules can also be developed for proper nouns (e.g., generating initials from a person's name).
- In a multilingual setting, we should use with care the predicate `rdf:label` as indicative of surface forms for each language.
- Pronouns are the most ambiguous surface forms, making Information Extraction difficult on sentences containing them.

2.9 Further Reading

Beyond labels: In this chapter, we have used `foaf:name` and `rdfs:label` as naming predicates, but the Semantic Web contains many other predicates used for labeling purposes (see Ell et al. (2011)). Still these various predicates do not provide an integrated and agreed-upon model in which entities are related to surface forms. But, in recent years, there has been various efforts toward a "linguistically aware" Semantic Web. One such major effort, called *lemon—The Lexicon Model for Ontologies*, is worth paying special attention to. This suggested model for encoding lexical information is quite rich, allowing us not only to link word forms to word senses, but also to express variations in word forms (see http://lemon-model.net, McCrae et al. (2012)). I also encourage the reader to look into efforts in Linguistic Linked Open Data, as there is growing interest in formalizing linguistic information as part of the Linked Open Data cloud (http://linguistic-lod.org/). There is also effort in standardization of linguistic processes and resources, through the Natural Language Processing Interchange Format (NIF) described in Hellmann et al. (2013).

DBpedia/Wikipedia: DBpedia will often be referred to in this book. The article by Lehmann et al. (2012) describes its extraction process from Wikipedia, another resource largely used in this book. In *The People's Web Meets NLP*, Gurevych and Kim (2013) show various usages of the community resource Wikipedia for NLP, and vice versa.

Anaphora resolution: It is interesting to compare an early survey on anaphora resolution (Mitkov 1999) to a recent one (Poesio et al. 2010). For a survey on coreference resolution, see Elango (2006).

2.10 Exercises

Exercises 2.1 (Entity search evaluation).

a. Among all the possible surface forms provided by the `dbo:wikiPageRedirects` predicate for *Beethoven*, ten are listed in Table 2.4. Can you find the remaining ones? If you use all of them, what is the impact on precision/recall of the entity search applied to the small BEETHOVENCORPUS provided in Table 2.1.

b. Reflect on why *precision and recall* are favoured in NLP for reporting on search experiments, rather than the other measures of *reject and accuracy*. All the equations are given in Sect. 2.2.

Exercises 2.2 (Variations in surface forms).

a. Look up DBpedia for the generic entity *Cat*, at dbr:Cat. Go through the list of its dbo:wikiPageRedirects and classify the entries, provided the classification from Sect. 2.4. You will notice that some variations do not quite fit within our classification. Identify new categories of variations, give them a name, and provide examples for them.
b. Look up DBpedia for the specific entity *Paris*, at dbr:Paris. Again, go through the list of its dbo:wikiPageRedirects and classify the entries according to the classification in Sect. 2.4 enriched with the new categories you defined in the previous exercise.

Exercises 2.3 (Generative rules).

a. Write a software program that can take a word as an entry and generate variations implementing the rules from Table 2.7. Which ones are easier to program? Why?
b. Adapt your code from exercise *(a)* to work for noun compounds. A noun compound is composed of two or more words, such as *kitchen appliance*, *Japanese rock garden*, or *laser printing*. Does your program work for all of these examples? What are its limitations?
c. Moving on to specific entities, implement the rules in Table 2.8 and add a few more rules of your own. Test your rules on the names of ten famous people, companies, or organizations of your choice. Are the rules generating likely-used surface forms? How would you test if a surface form is actually a likely one to exist in text?

Exercises 2.4 (Multilingual surface forms).

a. Go to the Spanish DBpedia, following the owl:sameAs predicate from the *United Kingdom* entry in the English DBpedia, found at dbr:United_Kingdom. In terms of use of naming predicates, does it resemble what we saw in the French DBpedia, in Sect. 2.6? Discuss. Try another language of your choice and observe again.

Exercises 2.5 (Use of pronouns).

a. Take a news article at random from a newspaper of your choice. Find the pronouns. Do you find them easy to solve to earlier mentions? How would you quantify their use: frequent or infrequent? For a single explicit mention, are there many further anaphoric mentions?

Chapter 3
Searching for Named Entities

In the previous chapter, we searched for the specific composer *Ludwig van Beethoven*. But what if we wanted to find sentences about *any* classical music composer, or even more generally, about any composer? So far our strategy has consisted of starting with a URI, finding possible alternative surface forms, and looking for sentences in which they occur. If we follow the same strategy in the case of *composers*, we can find the URI dbr:Composer in DBpedia and discover some of its surface forms (e.g., *music composer*, *musical composer*, and even *author*) through the predicate dbo:wikiPageRedirects.

Would a search in a corpus for sentences containing these surface forms be likely to lead us to information about composers? Perhaps it would, but it is certain that the recall performance of such approach will be quite low. For example, if we attempt the above strategy on the BEETHOVENCORPUS from the previous chapter (see Table 2.1 in Sect. 2.1), we find a single sentence (sentence no. 6) among the 10 sentences about composers, which explicitly uses the word *composer*.

An alternative approach, presented in this chapter, is to consider COMPOSER as an **entity type**, also referred to as **entity class**. An entity type, or entity class, represents a set of individuals, and we will develop **text mining** strategies for finding the individuals which belong to this class.

The first strategy is using a list of the individuals in the class. For example, we can gather a list of composers, such as *L.V. Beethoven*, *W.A. Mozart*, and *J.S. Bach*, and search for them in text. In NLP, such list is often referred to as a **gazetteer**.

The second strategy is to search for regularities in the way of expressing the individuals in the class. The type COMPOSER is likely not the best candidate for this strategy, although being a subclass of PERSON, we can expect the same regularity in a composer's name than in a person's name. Such regularity could be a sequence of two capitalized words (e.g., *[F]rank [Z]appa*), although we can imagine such regularity leading to many other entity types than PERSON, such as CITY (e.g., *[N]ew [Y]ork*) or COUNTRY (e.g., *[S]ri [L]anka*). Other entity types, such as DATE or TIME, are better candidates for this regularity detection strategy.

© Springer International Publishing Switzerland 2016
C. Barrière, *Natural Language Understanding in a Semantic Web Context*,
DOI 10.1007/978-3-319-41337-2_3

We will look at various entity types in this chapter, as well as the use of gazetteers and the detection of regularities through a very powerful tool, **regular expressions**. We will also continue with the experiment-based learning approach promoted in this book, by defining an experiment to test the precision and recall of regular expressions in search of DATE in a corpus.

3.1 Entity Types

COMPOSER is simply an example of an **entity class**, also called an **entity type**, a **semantic type**, or a **category**. SYMPHONY would be another example, as would be AUTHOR, COMPANY, and CITY. Entity types are at the core of knowledge organization, since they provide a structure for our understanding of the world.

And because entity types play a central role in our quest for information, we will often return to these notions, and even debate their definitions. For example, is *cell phone* an entity type? Not in the same way as COMPOSER is, yet we can talk about cell phones in general, and individual phones do exist under the broader umbrella of CELLPHONE. Although in our quest for information, we would rarely be interested in the specific phone Mr. X owns, but we might be interested in a particular Samsung or Nokia phone, just being put on the market. My purpose here is not to enter in a philosophical debate about ontological commitment or separation of classes and individuals. I simply want to bring awareness to the impact the difference between searching for entity types versus individuals can have on searching strategies and search results.

Compared to the previous chapter, in which we discussed generic and specific entities, notice how the current chapter introduces a different terminology, more commonly used in NLP and in the Semantic Web, of individuals and entity types. In the previous chapter, we used the term **specific entity** to refer to an individual and **generic entity** to refer to an entity type.

Interest in individuals and entity types is pervasive in the Semantic Web and NLP communities. The term **Named Entity Recognition**, abbreviated **NER**, refers to an important field of research within NLP aiming at recognizing named entities in corpus. We yet introduce another term: **named entity** which sense is closest to what we had called specific entity. In a strict sense, a named entity is an instance of an entity class, uniquely identified via a name. In this same strict sense, named entities are unique individuals. People, organizations, locations, and dates are all examples of things that are unique in our world. But a NER search might be interested in detecting other *important information* in a text, such as amounts of money or quantities. This extends the definition of named entity toward a less strict sense including individuals as well as other precise and important information.

As the reader, you might find this confusing to be introduced to many similar terms having partially overlapping meaning. It is confusing, but it is important to know about all these terms, since you are likely to encounter them in different books and research articles written over many years. The effort to define types of named entities and recognize them in text goes back twenty years to *The Sixth Message Understanding Conference* during which an NER task was introduced. At that time, the named entities to be recognized were given one of three possible labels:

- ENAMEX: PERSON, ORGANIZATION, LOCATION
- TIMEX: DATE, TIME
- NUMEX: MONEY, PERCENTAGE, QUANTITY

Later, efforts were made to define more fine-grained lists of entity types, some examples being:

- PERSON: ACTOR, ARCHITECT, DOCTOR, POLITICIAN
- ORGANIZATION: AIRLINE, SPORTS_LEAGUE, GOVERNMENT_AGENCY, NEWS_AGENCY
- LOCATION: CITY, COUNTRY, ROAD, PARK
- PRODUCT: CAR, CAMERA, COMPUTER, GAME
- ART: FILM, PLAY, NEWSPAPER, MUSIC
- EVENT: ATTACK, ELECTION, SPORTS_EVENT, NATURAL_DISASTER
- BUILDING: AIRPORT, HOSPITAL, HOTEL, RESTAURANT
- OTHER: TIME, COLOR, EDUCATIONAL_DEGREE, BODY_PART, TV_CHANNEL, RELIGION, LANGUAGE, CURRENCY

Beyond these more generic entity type lists, efforts have also been made in individual domains to define entity types specific to them (e.g., GENE and PROTEIN in biology).

Once entity types are defined, how would we devise a text mining process to identify in a corpus sentences mentioning these types. A first strategy is to use lists of individuals belonging to these types, as we see next.

3.2 Gazetteers

One approach to finding named entities in text is to have lists of the individuals, often referred to as **gazetteers**. On the Web (e.g., in Wikipedia), we can find lists of just about anything imaginable: varieties of rice, car brands, romantic symphonies, countries, and so on. Let us take art museums as an example. The following query submitted to DBpedia SPARQL endpoint would provide a long list of hundreds of museums:

```
PREFIX dbr: <http://dbpedia.org/resource/>
PREFIX rdf: <http://www.w3.org/1999/02/22-rdf-syntax-ns#>
select ?X where {
    ?X rdf:type dbr:Art_museum .
}
```

This list could easily become a gazetteer for an ArtMuseum entity type to be used for searches in text. Table 3.1 provides some examples. Each of the entities has a variety of surface forms, all of which could be used in a search.

Table 3.1 Gazetteer for ArtMuseum

No.	Museum label
1	Berkshire Museum
2	The Louvre
3	Museum of Modern Art, Antwerp
4	Hirshhorn Museum and Sculpture Garden
5	Museum of Fine Arts of Lyon
6	Kosova National Art Gallery
7	Art Gallery of Algoma
8	National Gallery of Canada
9	Museu Picasso

Similarly, using the following query into DBpedia SPARQL endpoint, we can find many composers classified under the *Viennese Composers* category in Yago.[1]

```
prefix rdf:  <http://www.w3.org/1999/02/22-rdf-syntax-ns\#>
prefix yago: <http://dbpedia.org/class/yago/>
select ?X where {
    ?X rdf:type yago:VienneseComposers
}
```

Results of the query can be used to generate a gazetteer for the VienneseComposer entity type, as in Table 3.2. This list would include many contemporaries of *Ludwig van Beethoven*, the individual of our earlier investigation.

Table 3.2 Gazetteer for VienneseComposer

No.	Composer label
1	Wolfgang Amadeus Mozart
2	Franz Schubert
3	Johann Strauss I
4	Franz Lehar
5	Ludwig van Beethoven
6	Johannes Brahms
7	Joseph Haydn
8	Anton Webern
9	Alban Berg
10	Arnold Schoenberg

[1]Yago is a large Semantic Web resource, described at http://www.mpi-inf.mpg.de/departments/databases-and-information-systems/research/yago-naga/yago/.

An unfortunate drawback to all lists is that they are likely to be incomplete and thus insufficient. Despite this, lists are important in the search for named entities, and are widely used, most often in combination with other strategies. In Chap. 13, as we revisit entity types as constraints for relation search, we will investigate voting strategies to combine gazetteers with other methods of entity type validation.

For now, let us explore a second strategy for finding mentions of an entity type in a corpus, using regular expressions.

3.3 Capturing Regularities in Named Entities: Regular Expressions

Certain entity types have fairly regular ways of expressing their individuals, which we can easily detect. The individuals for the entity type ART MUSEUM, as shown in Table 3.1, do include a few words that appear repeatedly (museum, fine art, art gallery), but still, we would have to consider more data to better convince ourselves of regularity within that class. What about an entity type SYMPHONY, to continue on our musical theme, would that contain regularities?

Table 3.3 Examples of instances of the SYMPHONY type

No.	Symphonies
1	Symphony no. 8
2	Beethoven's symphony no. 6
3	Symphony no.4, op. 47
4	Symphony no 5 in b flat
5	Symphony no. 1 in d minor
6	Schubert's Symphony no. 4
7	Symphony "pathetique"
8	Symphony no. 3 in b-flat minor
9	Abel's Symphony no. 5, op. 7

Consider a short list of individuals, belonging to the SYMPHONY type, as shown in Table 3.3. As you can see, there is still quite a lot of variation within these examples, but we can identify certain patterns emerging. In an attempt to concisely capture and represent the variations seen here, we turn to **regular expressions**.

Regular expressions provide a concise way of expressing particular sequences of text. Although they can seem intimidating at first, it is essential to master them for NLP, since they provide a very flexible and powerful tool for text search. Most programming languages define text search libraries allowing the use of regular expressions. The best way to become familiar with writing these expressions is simply to practice. The process is comparable to learning a new language, practice is key.[2]

Below are examples of what regular expressions can capture in text:

- single character disjunction: `[tT]able` → table, Table
- range: `[A-Z]x` → Ax, Bx, Cx, Dx, ... Zx
- explicit disjunction: `[a-z|A-Z]` → all letters
- negation: `[^Ss]` → everything except uppercase and lowercase 's'
- previous character optional: `favou?r` → favor, favour
- repetition of 0 or more times: `argh*` → arghhhhhhh, arghh, arg
- repetition of 1 or more times: `x+` → x, xx, xxx
- wildcard on a single character: `ax.s` → axis, axes
- specification of number of characters: `x{2,4}` → xx, xxx, xxxx
- escape for special characters: `\(a` → (a

As you can see, the language provided by regular expressions includes five important aspects: repetition, range, disjunction, optionality, and negation. As we can combine these aspects in various ways and apply them on either single characters or groups of characters, there is an infinite number of text segments which can be captured with regular expressions. That explains how regular expressions capture the representation of very long lists within a single expression.

Granted, for the SYMPHONY type, it may be possible to list all the existing symphonies, but what about entity types such as DATE, PHONENUMBER, or EMAILADDRESS? Regular expressions allow for the concise representation of variations within these non-enumerable entity types. Table 3.4 shows examples of different regular expressions to recognize particular entities.

---

[2]There are some online regular expression testers, such as *Regexpal*, available at http://regexpal. com/ which allow you to write regular expressions and use them to search in text. You can also use the regular expression matcher libraries within your favourite programming language to write and test the search capacity of regular expressions.

Table 3.4 Examples of regular expressions for specific entity types

RegEx	Examples
Abbreviated winter month, optional final period	
`(Jan|Feb|March).*`	Jan. / Feb
Any year between 1000 and 3000	
`[12][0-9]{3}`	1977 / 2015
Postal codes in Canada	
`[A-Z][0-9][A-Z][0-9][A-Z][0-9]`	H2X3W7 / Q1Z4W8
Avenue names	
`(1rst|2nd|3rd|[4-20]th) (Avenue|Ave.|Ave)`	3rd Avenue / 6th Ave.
Any street name	
`[A-Z][a-z|A-Z]* (Street|St.|St)`	Wrench St. / Lock Street
North American phone numbers	
`\([1-9]{3}\) [1-9]{3}(-*| )[0-9]{4}`	(456) 245–8877 / (123) 439 3398
Symphony name	
`[Ss]ymphony [Nn]o.* *[1-9]`	Symphony no.4 / symphony No 5

Notice how we require **repetition** for capturing sequences of 3 digits in a row for telephone numbers, **range** for capturing the notion of a digit (1–9), **disjunction** to provide alternatives for months, and **optionality** to allow street names to contain a period after St or not. Out of the five aspects of regular expressions, only **negation** is missing in Table 3.4.

Now, let us design an experiment to put regular expressions to the test and study their behavior in an entity type search.

3.4 Experiment — Finding Dᴀᴛᴇ Instances in a Corpus

Let us now tackle the problem of finding dates. Dates are important in Information Extraction, since we often want to know *when* things happen. Moreover, they represent a type of entity for which the enumeration of instances would be much too lengthy to be practical. Because of this, Dᴀᴛᴇ is an entity type where regular expressions should prove quite useful.

3.4.1 Gold Standard and Inter-Annotator Agreement

First, we need to establish a gold standard against which we can evaluate our algorithm through its phases of development. Table 3.5 provides such a possible gold standard.

Table 3.5 Examples of sentences containing (or not) a DATE

No.	Sentence	DATE instance?
1	He was born on the *8th of July 1987*.	Yes
2	Cancel the flight 2000 by Sept. 10th to avoid paying fees.	No
3	A date to remember is *August 10, 1999*.	Yes
4	I wrote "*10/04/1999*" on the form, next to my name.	Yes
5	Class 20–09, that was a nice course.	No
6	The wedding was in *2008, on April 20th* exactly.	Yes
7	Flight Air Canada 1987, is 6th in line to depart.	No
8	The expiration date is *15/01/12*.	Yes
9	Your appointment is on *October 31, 2012*.	Yes
10	It is Dec. 15 already, hard to believe that 2011 is almost over.	Yes
11	*November 1986, on the 7th day*, the train departed.	Yes
12	There was 5000 mm of rain in 7 days.	No
13	He was in his 7th year in 1987.	No
14	The product code is 7777–09.	No
15	He arrived 31st in rank at the 2005 and 2008 runs.	No
16	The event happens *March 10–12 2015*.	Yes
17	The big day is *November 20th, 2017*	Yes

When creating a gold standard, it is tempting to include only target sentences. In our case, this would mean exclusively including sentences that contain dates. The problem with this approach is that it would not allow us to evaluate the number of false positives produced by our algorithm. After all, if all the sentences qualify for our search, then we have not given the algorithm the chance to falsely identify one as qualifying when it does not. And, as we saw in Chap. 2, Sect. 2.2, identifying false positives is an important part of the evaluation of an algorithm's precision.

For this reason, we should intentionally include non-date sentences in our gold standard. To further ensure the precision of our algorithm, we should contrive these negative examples to differ only slightly from the positive ones. You can think of this as testing the algorithm's precision by including sentences that are almost, but not quite, what we are looking for, and seeing whether it 'takes the bait'.

In the last column of Table 3.5, you will notice that I have marked examples as either positive or negative. Do you agree with my decisions? We might agree on some, but probably not all examples. Since there are many possible interpretations of what qualifies as a positive or negative example of an entity, annotators (human judges) are rarely in full agreement until the task is very well defined. I will reiterate my classifications below (Judge 1) and invent another hypothetical set, which I will attribute to a fictive other judge (Judge 2).

Judge 1: {1, 3, 4, 6, 8, 9, 10, 11, 16, 17}
Judge 2: {1, 2, 3, 4, 6, 8, 9, 10, 11, 13, 15, 16, 17}

What we now have before us is a problem of **inter-annotator agreement**. Within NLP, we talk of inter-annotator agreement to represent the degree to which two human judges agree on a particular annotation task. In the current example, the annotation was to determine Yes/No for each sentence, as containing an instance of a DATE or not. Inter-annotator agreement is an important concept to understand, since it will come back again and again in the development of NLP evaluation sets.

Certain measures have been proposed for the specific purpose of determining levels of inter-annotator agreement. One such measure is **Cohen's Kappa**. This measure requires a matrix similar to the contingency table we used earlier (see Sect. 2.2) for comparing an algorithm to a gold standard. Table 3.6 shows where we (*Judge 1* and *Judge 2*) agreed and disagreed in our earlier classifications of date and non-date sentences.

Table 3.6 Judge comparison for DATE search example

		Judge 2	
		correct	incorrect
Judge 1	correct	10	0
	incorrect	3	4

The Kappa measure also requires that we account for agreement that could occur by chance alone. In other words, what is the probability $Pr(e)$ that closing our eyes and marking Yes/No beside the various sentences would result in agreement? Once we know the value of $Pr(e)$, we can compare our actual agreement $Pr(a)$ against it. Both $Pr(a)$ and $Pr(e)$ are part of the Kappa measure, as shown in Eq. 3.1.

$$\kappa = \frac{Pr(a) - Pr(e)}{1 - Pr(e)} \tag{3.1}$$

Since we only have two classes in this case (Yes/No), our probability $Pr(e)$ of agreement by chance is 50%. If there were ten different classes, the probability of two judges agreeing would be reduced to 10%. In cases of open set of annotations, when the number of classes is not set in advance, measuring such agreement becomes quite difficult.

Our actual agreement $Pr(a)$ is the number of times both judges said Yes (10 times) + the number of times both judges said No (4 times) divided by the total number of examples (17).

$$Pr(a) = \frac{(10 + 4)}{17} = 0.824$$

$$Pr(e) = 0.5$$

$$\kappa = \frac{(0.824 - 0.5)}{1 - 0.5} = 0.65$$

So, does a κ of 0.65 mean we agree? How should we interpret this result? Although there is no universal standard for interpreting Kappa scores, the scale below is often used.

$\kappa < 0$ would indicate no agreement
$0 > \kappa < 0.20$ slight agreement
$0.21 > \kappa < 0.40$ fair agreement
$0.41 > \kappa < 0.60$ moderate agreement
$0.61 > \kappa < 0.80$ substantial agreement
$0.81 > \kappa < 1.00$ almost perfect agreement

Based on this scale, we have attained substantial agreement. This is not a bad result, but we could do better. A less-than-perfect measure of inter-annotator agreement can be taken in two ways: either the task is not well defined or the task really is highly subjective. In our case, we could potentially reach a higher level of agreement if we refine the definition of our task. In order to accomplish this, we should ask ourselves certain questions: What does it mean to find dates? Are we only interested in finding full dates that we can map to a calendar day? Do we want year only mentions to be included? Do we want to include ranges of dates?

The answers to these questions will be determined by how we intend to apply our results. To clarify this intention, we should consider why we are extracting dates and what will we do with them once we have them. In our current experiment, we have not yet defined a particular application, but we can still try to be as specific as possible in defining our task. My criterion for answering Yes in Table 3.5 was that the sentence must contain a date specific enough that I can map it to a calendar day. Knowing this, do you now agree with my classifications? If so, what would our new Kappa be?

3.4.2 Baseline Algorithm: Simple DATE Regular Expression

For our first exploration, let us come up with two regular expression baselines, one generic (high recall) and one very specific (high precision), and define them. Although up to now we have mostly seen regular expressions written as one long string, when programming them we can take advantage of the fact that programming languages allow us to use variables to contain strings. This further allows us to define partial elements of the regular expressions and to later combine them in different ways. In the example below, I first define regular expressions for months, years, and days and then I show how to combine them using a string concatenation operator (+), to generate the two baselines:

```
Year     = [12][0-9]{3}
Month    = (January|February|March|April|May|June|July|
           August|September|October|November|December)
DayNum = ([1-9]|[1-2][0-9]|30|31)
Baseline 1 : Year
Baseline 2 : Month + " " + DayNum + ", " + Year
```

The regular expression for *Year* allows a range from year 1000 to 2999, forcing the first digit to be 1 or 2, and then requiring 3 consecutive digits, each in the range 0–9. The regular expression for *Month* is simply a list of possible month names. The regular expression for *DayNum* allows a range of 1 to 31, by combining 4 subranges: between 1 and 9, or between 10 and 29, or 30, or 31.

The baseline 1 for high recall only uses the regular expression for the *Year*. The baseline 2 for high precision requires a sequence of Month followed by a space, followed by a Day, a comma, another space, and a Year (e.g., January 5, 1999).

Table 3.7 displays the Yes/No results of these two baseline algorithms, in comparison with the gold standard defined by Judge 1 earlier. Table 3.8 shows the contingency tables for both algorithms.

Table 3.7 Results of two baseline algorithms for the extraction of DATE instances

No.	Sentence	Judge 1	Baseline 1	Baseline 2
1	He was born on the 8th of July 1987.	Yes	Yes	No
2	Cancel the flight 2000 by Sept. 10th to avoid paying fees.	No	Yes	No
3	A date to remember is August 10, 1999.	Yes	Yes	Yes
4	I wrote "10/04/1999" on the form, next to my name.	Yes	Yes	No
5	Class 20–09, that was a nice course.	No	No	No
6	The wedding was in 2008, on April 20th exactly.	Yes	Yes	No
7	Flight Air Canada 1987, is 6th in line to depart.	No	Yes	No
8	The expiration date is 15/01/12.	Yes	No	No
9	Your appointment is on October 31, 2012.	Yes	Yes	Yes
10	It is Dec. 15 already, hard to believe that 2011 is almost over.	Yes	Yes	No
11	November 1986, on the 7th day, the train departed.	Yes	Yes	No
12	There was 5000 mm of rain in 7 days.	No	No	No
13	He was in his 7th year in 1987.	No	Yes	No
14	The product code is 1111–09.	No	Yes	No
15	He arrived 31st in rank at the 2005 and 2008 runs.	No	Yes	No
16	The event happens March 10–12 2015.	Yes	Yes	No
17	The big day is November 20th, 2017	Yes	Yes	No

Table 3.8 Contingency table for baseline algorithms

		Judge 1 (Gold standard)	
		correct	incorrect
Baseline 1	correct	8	6
	incorrect	1	2
Baseline 2	correct	2	0
	incorrect	7	8

From Table 3.8, we can evaluate recall, precision, and F1 measures for both algorithms, as following:

Baseline 1—High recall   Baseline 2—High precision

$$Recall = \frac{8}{9} = 88.9\%$$ $$Recall = \frac{2}{9} = 22.2\%$$

$$Precision = \frac{8}{14} = 57.1\%$$ $$Precision = \frac{2}{2} = 100.0\%$$

$$F1 = 2 * \frac{88.9 * 57.1}{88.9 + 57.1} = 69.6\%$$ $$F1 = 2 * \frac{22.2 * 100}{22.2 + 100} = 36.4\%$$

As expected, the first baseline shows quite high recall, and the second baseline shows low recall but high precision. We now try to refine our regular expressions to maintain a high recall, but not at the expense of a low precision.

3.4.3 Refining the DATE Expressions

At this point, we will have to engage in what is essentially a process of trial and error, where we observe the data and try to find expressions that maximize both recall and precision. Both the individual elements defined earlier (the patterns for months, years, and days) and the patterns of combination can be refined to create different options. Here are some ideas:

```
Year        = [12][0-9]{3}
Month       = (January|February|March|April|May|June|July|
              August|September|October|November|December)
MonthShort  = (Jan|Feb|Mar|Apr|May|Jun|Jul|Aug|Sep|Oct|Nov|Dec).*
DayNum      = ([1-9]|[1-2][0-9]|30|31)
DayEnd      = (1rst|2nd|3rd|[4-9]th|1[0-9]th|21rst|22nd|
              23rd|2[4-9]th|30th|31rst)
RegExDate1  = "(" + Month + "|" + MonthShort + ")" + " " +
              "(" + DayNum + "|" + DayEnd + ")" + ", " + Year
RegExDate2  = DayNum + "/" + MonthNum + "/" + [0-9]{2}
```

How far did that refinement take us? Well, an extraction process relying on both *RegExDate*1 and *RegExDate*2 now finds *August 10, 1999, 10/04/19, 15/01/12,* and *October 31, 2012* and provides a recall of 33%. Although this is still not high, it is higher than baseline 2, which had recall of 20%. The precision is now at 75%, right between baselines 1 and 2. I will leave it as an exercise for the reader to verify the precision/recall of this extraction process, and more importantly, to continue the iterative cycle of development and evaluation, as to further refine the set of regular expressions used for extracting instances of DATE.

At the end of this **iterative refinement process**, the real test for our strategy would come from gathering a completely new and unseen set of sentences, generate a new gold standard by annotating the sentences as to their mention Yes/No of a DATE, perform the extraction process on that new set of sentences, and evaluate the results against the new gold standard. Since we used the set of sentences from Table 3.5 during the refinement cycle, we should refer to these sentences as our **development set**. It is too lenient to evaluate strategies on the development set, since that is the set on which we tried to optimize both precision and recall. The final evaluation of a strategy should be on a **test set**, never seen during the refinement cycle. It is important to understand the difference between the two sets and the variation on results which can occur, depending on which set we evaluate on. Being aware of this differentiation can help sometimes understand why results presented in research articles may vary widely, not just because of their variation in terms of strategies, but also in terms of their evaluation method.

When test sets are not available, an approximation of an algorithm's performance in test condition can be measured using a **cross-validation** approach. The idea in cross-validation is to separate the development set into N subsets, develop the rules based on $N - 1$ subsets, and test them on the Nth subset, repeating such process N times and averaging the results. Cross-validation is most often optimistic in its evaluation, as it is based on a somewhat artificial setting, which in theory is valid, but where in practice, "pretending" that we have not seen part of the data either for rule development or feature development (in machine learning approaches) is not realistic. Still, cross-validation is widely used as an evaluation approach for many different categorization tasks.

3.5 Language Dependency of Named Entity Expressions

In Chap. 2, Sect. 2.6, we discussed the fact that entities themselves are referred to differently in different languages. But what about entity classes? Well, if we were to try to find information about an entity class in a multilingual setting (e.g., COMPOSER), using gazetteers of entities (e.g., *L.V. Beethoven and W.A. Mozart*), we would find ourselves once again faced with the original problem, this time generalized to all entities of a class.

When it comes to classes that are better represented by regular expressions (e.g., non-enumerable entities), there is equal potential for linguistic and/or cultural variation. When searching in different languages and/or in text written in different countries, we should be aware that this variation affects even the simplest of writing practices. Dates, for example, can be represented in many different ways, and a mention like *11/12/2016* could refer to the 11th day of the 12th month, or to the 12th day of the 11th month, depending on the country.

Dates are just one example. The writing of numbers can vary as well, with some countries using a comma to represent decimals, and others using a period (e.g., 2.54 versus 2,54). Other examples include elements of daily life in text, such as phone numbers and zip/postal codes. These too have different formats depending on the country.

If we wish to define and test regular expressions for particular entity types, and if we aspire to have them work in a multilingual setting, it is essential that we create a gold standard that contains positive and negative sentences from the languages we intend to cover. This process might begin with writing regular expressions that are language independent, but they would eventually be refined to be language specific.

3.6 In Summary

- The term *named entity* can be interpreted in a strict sense to mean entities that can be uniquely identified, or in a looser sense to mean any identifiable information that would be of importance in text understanding.
- Different authors have proposed varying lists of named entity types, some more coarse-grained, others more fine-grained.
- Regular expressions serve as a good alternative (or complement) to lists/gazetteers, which themselves are never complete.
- Regular expressions provide a powerful way of expressing certain entity types, in order to search for them in text.
- An iterative refinement process can be used for the development of regular expressions, which aims at maximizing both recall and precision on a development dataset.
- When it comes to classification tasks, people are not always in agreement. *Cohen's Kappa* is useful for evaluating inter-annotator agreement.
- Low inter-annotator agreement can be interpreted in two ways: either the task is not well defined or the task is very subjective.
- In a multilingual context, entities are often expressed in slightly different ways. We should not assume that previously defined regular expressions are simply transferable from one language to another.

3.7 Further Reading

Entity types: Early definitions of named entities, in the Message Understanding Conference (MUC-6), are found in Sundheim (1995). An example of a fine-grained list, the *Extended Named Entity list*, is presented in Sekine et al. (2002) and further described at http://nlp.cs.nyu.edu/ene/version7_1_0Beng.html. Some examples of entity types presented in this chapter are taken from another fine-grained list used in Ling and Weld (2012).

Named Entity Recognition: A survey of NER is presented in Nadeau and Sekine (2007). In Ratinov and Roth (2009), the emphasis is on challenges and misconceptions in NER. In Tkachenko and Simanovsky (2012), the focus is rather on features important to the NER task. The references above will at one point mention the use of gazetteers as an important element in NER.

Inter-Annotator Agreement: Cohen's kappa is presented in the Wikipedia page http://en.wikipedia.org/wiki/Cohen's_kappa which also describes some variations. The Kappa interpretation scale presented in this chapter was proposed by Koch and Landis (1977).

3.8 Exercises

Exercise 3.1 (Entity types)

a. In Sect. 3.1, we presented a fine-grained list of entity types. For each entity type
in the list (e.g., ACTOR, AIRLINE, RELIGION, and RESTAURANT), determine which of the
two approaches, either gazetteers or regular expressions, would be the most appropriate
in an extraction process. Discuss your choices and provide examples to support them.

Exercise 3.2 (Regular expressions)

a. Go to the site http://regexpal.com/, which allows you to enter regular expressions
and test them on different texts. You can also use the regular expression matcher
libraries within your favourite programming language if you prefer. Make up
test sentences and try the regular expressions defined in Table 3.4 to extract various type of information. Try new expressions. Play around a little to familiarize
yourself with regular expressions.
b. Write a regular expression that would be able to detect URLs. Then, write another
one for emails and a third for phone numbers.
c. Find ways to make the regular expressions in Table 3.4 more general. How would
you go about this?
d. Go back to Table 3.3 and write regular expressions to cover all the variations
shown.

Exercise 3.3 (Gold standard development and inter-annotator agreement)

a. What would be the impact of choosing negative examples for the entity DATE that
do not contain any numbers? Discuss.
b. Assuming you have access to a large corpus, what could be a good way of gathering sentence candidates for positive and negative examples for the DATE entity
type?
c. In assessing the presence of dates in the examples of Table 3.5, assume a third
judge provided the following positives: {1, 3, 4, 5, 6, 8, 10, 11, 15, 16, 17}. What
would be her level of agreement with the other two judges?

Exercise 3.4 (Iterative development process)

a. Continue the development of regular expressions for finding dates in Table 3.5.
Try to achieve 100 % recall and 100 % precision on that development set. Then,
develop a new test set, including positive and negative examples, or better yet, to
be completely unbiased, ask one of your colleagues to build that test set for you.
Try the set of regular expressions you had developed. Do you still achieve good
recall and precision? How much does the performance drop? Discuss.
b. Assuming we want to extract a person's birthdate from the short abstract (in
DBpedia) describing that person's life. Write a set of regular expressions which
automatically extract the birth date from the abstracts for some well-known people. Develop the regular expressions in your program using a first development

set of 10 famous people and then perform a final test of your program using a new test set of 10 other famous people.

c. Choose 5 entity types from Exercise 3.1 for which you thought regular expressions would be appropriate. Gather examples for these types from DBpedia (or another resource). For each type, gather 10 examples for your development set, and 10 examples for your test set. Use your development set to create regular expressions. Then, test your regular expressions on the test set. Do results vary depending on the entity type? Discuss.

Chapter 4
Comparing Surface Forms

In our quest for information about *Ludwig van Beethoven* in Chap. 2, we started
with a Semantic Web entity provided by the URI dbr:Ludwig_van_Beethoven
and used its various surface forms to search for occurrences of the entity in text.
We saw that we could obtain a list of surface forms either through the predicate
dbo:wikiPageRedirects or through generative approaches (e.g., plural, capitalization, or abbreviation formation rules).

Using these two methods, we gathered a variety of surface forms including
Beethovens, Beetehoven, L.V. Beethoven, van Beethoven, and others. Even with all
these variations however, our search in the BEETHOVENCORPUS (see Sect. 2.3) obtained
a recall of 87.5 % or 7 out of 8 sentences. The missing sentence was the following:

> *Betthoven*, too, used this key extensively in his second piano concerto.

Why did we miss this one? The answer is simply that this particular variation
was not on our list of surface forms. The problem with using pre-compiled lists
of surface forms from resources is that it is virtually impossible to anticipate every
possible variation that could present itself. Beyond the example above, should our list
have included *Beathoven, Betovhen*, or even *Beetowen*? Even if we included every
possible variation we could think of, there would almost certainly be at least one we
neglected to consider.

In Chap. 3, we discussed how regular expressions could be used to detect particular
named entities in text. Perhaps we could use this same approach to capture the
variations of the name *Beethoven* then? A regular expression like the one shown
below would allow for many variations, including *Beeeethoven, Beetoven, bethovan*,
and *Beethovan*.

```
[Bb]e+th?ov(e|a)n
```

The expressiveness of regular expressions can be seen here as a single expression
explicitly captures typical orthographic variations such as the first 'e' repeated, a

© Springer International Publishing Switzerland 2016   39
C. Barrière, *Natural Language Understanding in a Semantic Web Context*,
DOI 10.1007/978-3-319-41337-2_4

possibly missing 'h' and a change of the last 'e' into an 'a'. Here again though, we are sure to overlook certain possibilities for variations when predefining these expressions.

An alternative approach, explored in this chapter, is to consider methods for comparing the surface forms found in text to a limited list previously gathered. This way, the task becomes one of matching the variations found in text to the known surface forms, as opposed to attempting to formulate (through regular expressions) or gather (through a pre-compiled list) an exhaustive list of all possible variations. This follows a normalization strategy, as opposed to a generative one.

We will explore two string comparison algorithms to try to match surface forms, one based on the written form, called **Edit Distance**, and one based on sound equivalence, called **Soundex**. We will devise an experiment in which Soundex and **Levenshtein Distance** (a popular variation on the Edit Distance) compete in the same entity search task. This comparative setting will highlight, as expected, that both of these algorithms have their own strengths and limitations.

4.1 Edit Distance — A Dynamic Programming Algorithm

Given the large number of variations of surface forms that humans generate, it is highly beneficial to be able to automate the process of finding words that are close variations of each other. One popular algorithm for doing exactly that is **Edit Distance**. In the context of this algorithm, distance between words is defined by the nature and number of missing letters (e.g., *driveway* versus *drivway*), or letters that have been interchanged (e.g., *driveway* versus *drivewya*).

When comparing words based on their written forms, we go through a process of comparing their characters one by one in order to determine whether and to what extent they are the same. Edit Distance allows us to characterize the number of editing steps required to transform the first string into the second (or vice versa) and thus determine their level of closeness or similarity.

The three operators used in Edit Distance are **insertion** (adding a letter), **deletion** (removing a letter), and **substitution** (interchanging two letters). Looking at two example strings, *table* and *tiles*, we could go from the first to the second by a substitution from 'a' in *table* to 'i', then a deletion of 'b', followed by an insertion of 's'. The word *table* would thus go though the following transformations:

table → tible → tile → tiles

As we required three steps in the transformation from *table* to *tiles*, the Edit Distance between the two words would be equal to 3, since standard Edit Distance attributes a cost of 1 to each step. In a variation on the Edit Distance, known as the **Levenshtein Distance**, the costs are slightly different. When comparing words, it seems appropriate to consider substitution at a higher cost than deletion or insertion. A substitution can be seen as a deletion followed by an insertion, justifying to bring the cost of a substitution to 2, as is done in the Levenshtein Distance. We use the following notation $L(Word_1, Word_2)$ to represent the Levenshtein Distance between $Word_1$ and $Word_2$. If we go back to our example of *table* versus *tiles*, we would obtain $L(table, tiles) = 4$.

How do we automatically discover which steps are needed for transforming $Word_1$ into $Word_2$. With our small example, it was easy to do it mentally, but what if the two words were *calendar* and *rollerblade*, or *dragonfly* and *raffle*? You might still be able to do it mentally, but already we see that the number of possibilities of operations is becoming quite large, in fact growing exponentially with the lengths of the words.

How can we explore such a large number of possibilities in an efficient way? Luckily, a very useful general class of algorithms called **dynamic programming** helps us do this. The main idea of dynamic programming is simple, but powerful. It suggests to first think of solving a complex problem by recursively solving its simpler subproblems, and then solving these subproblems by solving their simpler sub-subproblems, and then solving the sub-subproblems by solving their even simpler sub-sub-subproblems and so on, until we reach very small problems for which solutions are trivial. When we have reached that point, dynamic programming suggests to construct back the solution to the complex problem by combining all the small pieces of solution.

A dynamic programming approach requires three important building blocks:

1. A definition of what constitutes a subproblem.
2. One or more solutions to trivial problems.
3. A combination strategy for constructing the final solution from the partial solutions.

We adapt the dynamic programming building blocks for the Levenshtein Distance as follows:

1. A subproblem will rely on splitting a string into substrings.
2. The trivial problems for which we know solutions correspond to the three basic operations defined in Edit Distance: deletion, insertion, and substitution.
3. The combination strategy will consists in adding the distances calculated on the substrings.

Let us now go back to our example comparing *table* and *tiles* to illustrate the three building blocks:

1. Possible subproblems of $L(table, tiles)$, are $L(ta, tiles)$, or $L(tab, t)$, or $L(t, ti)$.
2. $L(xy, x) = 1, L(x, xy) = 1$ and $L(x, v) = 2$ are respectively examples of trivial cases of deletion, insertion, and substitution.
3. $L(table, tiles) = L(tab, til) + L(le, es)$ is one possible combination among many, another one being $L(table, tile) = L(ta, ti) + L(ble, les)$.

To be able to express the many substring decomposition possibilities in a concise manner, let us first introduce variables to represent possible letter positions of both words being compared. Let us use i to indicate a position in the first word, $Word_1$, and j to indicate a position in the second word, $Word_2$. Then, let's introduce the notation $D(i, j)$ to represent *the Levenshtein Distance between the substring from*

Word₁ ending at position i, *and the substring from Word₂ ending at position* j. Notice that only ending positions are required in defining $D(i, j)$, as we assume that all substrings start from the beginnings of the words.

Let us look at some examples of how $D(i, j)$ denotes the comparison of substrings of *table* and *tiles*, at various word positions i and j:

$$(i = 5, j = 5) \rightarrow D(5, 5) = L(table, tiles)$$
$$(i = 2, j = 4) \rightarrow D(2, 4) = L(ta, tile)$$
$$(i = 3, j = 1) \rightarrow D(3, 1) = L(tab, t)$$
$$(i = 0, j = 3) \rightarrow D(0, 3) = L(|, til)$$
$$(i = 4, j = 0) \rightarrow D(4, 0) = L(tabl, |)$$

Notice in the examples above how we use the position 0 to mean the empty string, represented as |. Now, let us see how we calculate the Levenshtein Distance between two words using the dynamic programming approach given above. To do so, we will use a matrix D to contain all the partial distances, meaning all the $D(i, j)$ for all possible i and all possible j. If we define the length of the first word as I, and the length of the second word as J, then we construct a $I \times J$ matrix, with $0 < i < I$ and $0 < j < J$.

Our first step is to initialize D, as shown in Table 4.1. See how on the first row of D, for example, $L(|, til)$ is equal to 3, as it requires three insertions to go from an empty string | to the substring *til*. Then in the first column of D, we have for example $L(tabl, |)$ equal to 4, as it takes four deletions to go from the substring *tabl* to the empty string |.

Table 4.1 Initializing Levenshtein matrix D for comparing *table* and *tiles*

	| (0)	t(1)	i(2)	l(3)	e(4)	s(5)
|(0)	$L(\|, \|) = 0$	$L(\|, t) = 1$	$L(\|, ti) = 2$	$L(\|, til) = 3$	$L(\|, tile) = 4$	$L(\|, tiles) = 5$
t(1)	$L(t, \|) = 1$	.	.	.	.	.
a(2)	$L(ta, \|) = 2$	.	.	.	.	.
b(3)	$L(tab, \|) = 3$	.	.	.	.	.
l(4)	$L(tabl, \|) = 4$	.	.	.	.	.
e(5)	$L(table, \|) = 5$	.	.	.	.	.

From this initialization, we build the rest of the matrix D using the dynamic programming algorithm presented in Algorithm 1 which assign to each cell of $D(i, j)$ the minimal Levenshtein Distance between the two substrings ending respectively at position i and j. For each $D(i, j)$, to decide on minimal distance, we must consider 3 possibilities corresponding to the three operations: insert, delete, substitute. This step is shown in Algorithm 1 as a selection of a minimum value between the three operations.

\\ *1. Define a matrix D of size I by J*
Define D[I,J] ;
\\ *2. Initialize the matrix D containing all partial distances*
for *each i=1..I* **do**
| $D(i, 0) = i$;
end
for *each j=1..J* **do**
| $D(0, j) = j$;
end
\\ *3. Calculate the minimal distance for each pair i, j.*
for *each i=1..I* **do**
  for *each j=1..J* **do**
    $D(i, j)$ = MINIMUM between the following:
      $D(i - 1, j) + 1$ *(deletion)*
      $D(i, j - 1) + 1$ *(insertion)*
      $D(i - 1, j - 1) + 2$ *(substitution, $Word_1(i) \neq Word_2(j)$)*
      $D(i - 1, j - 1) + 0$ *(equality, $Word_1(i) = Word_2(j)$)*
  end
end
$D(I, J)$ contains the minimal distance.

Algorithm 1: Levenshtein Distance Algorithm

At the end of the algorithm, $D(I, J)$ will contain the minimal distance between the two words. Table 4.2 provides an example of the matrix calculation for our earlier words *table* and *tiles*. The end result (last row, last column) shows that $L(table, tiles)$ equals 4.

Algorithm 1 produces a distance between two strings but it does not tell us whether these two strings actually refer to the same entity or not. This will require further empirical processing, as we will see next.

4.2 From Distance to Binary Classification — Finding Thresholds

Let us return to our trusty example of *Beethoven*. Let us assume that the surface form *Beethoven* is the correct one against which we compare possible variations found in text, using the Levenshtein Distance we just learned about. Table 4.3 provides examples of **misspellings** for the name *Beethoven*. Each variation X is given in the second column, along with its Levenshtein Distance to *Beethoven*, $L(X, Beethoven)$ in the third column.

Table 4.2 Constructing the Levenshtein matrix D for comparing *table* and *tiles*

	(0)	t(1)	i(2)	l(3)	e(4)	s(5)
l(0)	$L(|,|) = 0$	$L(|,t) = 1$	$L(|,ti) = 2$	$L(|,til) = 3$	$L(|,tile) = 4$	$L(|,tiles) = 5$
t(1)	$L(t,|) = 1$	$L(t,t) = 0$	$L(t,ti) = 1$	$L(t,til) = 2$	$L(t,tile) = 3$	$L(t,tiles) = 4$
a(2)	$L(ta,|) = 2$	$L(ta,t) = 1$	$L(ta,ti) = 2$	$L(ta,til) = 3$	$L(ta,tile) = 4$	$L(ta,tiles) = 5$
b(3)	$L(tab,|) = 3$	$L(tab,t) = 2$	$L(tab,ti) = 3$	$L(tab,til) = 4$	$L(tab,tile) = 5$	$L(tab,tiles) = 6$
l(4)	$L(tabl,|) = 4$	$L(tabl,t) = 3$	$L(tabl,ti) = 4$	$L(tabl,til) = 3$	$L(tabl,tile) = 4$	$L(tabl,tiles) = 5$
e(5)	$L(table,|) = 5$	$L(table,t) = 4$	$L(table,ti) = 5$	$L(table,til) = 4$	$L(table,tile) = 3$	$L(table,tiles) = 4$

Table 4.3 Levenshtein Distance for misspellings of *Beethoven*

No.	Misspelling (X)	$L(X, Beethoven)$
1	Beethoven	0
2	Beethovens	1
3	Baytoven	5
4	Beeethoven	1
5	Beetehoven	2
6	Betoven	2
7	Baethoven	2
8	Bethoven	1

A distance-based approach naturally leads to a ranking of alternatives. By looking at their Levenshtein Distance measures, we can quickly compare misspelling scores and determine which are closer and farther from the correct form. For example, we can say that *Beetovens*, given $L(Beetovens, Beethoven) = 1$, is closer to *Beethoven* than *Betoven* is, with $L(Betoven, Beethoven) = 2$.

Sometimes though, we will want the distance measures of variations to lead to a **binary decision**, that is, a Yes/No classification instead. For example, if I find *Baethoven* in a sentence, does this sentence refer to *Beethoven*, yes or no? Or more formally, given the value $L(X, Beethoven)$ for a particular variation X, can we say that a sentence containing X refers to *Beethoven*, yes or no? In an **Information Extraction pipeline**, this Yes/No answer will determine whether or not the sentence is sent on to the next process. This next process, for example, could be a relation extractor module trying to extract biographical facts from sentences.

One approach to transforming a measure into a binary decision is simply to insert a threshold in the measure. The yes's would fall on one side, and the no's on the other. For the Levenshtein Distance, given a threshold T, we define:

$$L(Word_1, Word_2) \leq T \Rightarrow Word_1 \equiv Word_2$$
$$L(Word_1, Word_2) > T \Rightarrow Word_1 \neq Word_2$$

(4.1)

And, in the specific case of categorizing a variation as being *Beethoven* or not, we would have the following rules, where X represents any variation:

$$L(X, Beethoven) \leq T \Rightarrow X \equiv Beethoven$$
$$\Rightarrow \text{interpret as Yes (positive)}$$
$$L(X, Beethoven) > T \Rightarrow X \neq Beethoven$$
$$\Rightarrow \text{interpret as No (negative)}$$

(4.2)

This leads to the question of what would be an appropriate threshold T for our Levenshtein Distance measure.

A general strategy for determining a good threshold T for an algorithm A, is to work with a development set[1] against which we try to optimize the performances of A. As A is dependent on T, varying T will make A's performance vary, and we will select T so as to maximize A's performances.

Let us explore this strategy for our *Beethoven* example. First, we gather a development set as shown in the first three columns of Table 4.4. The third column provides the binary classification, determining the equivalence between the variation X (second column) and *Beethoven*.

Table 4.4 Binary classification of name variations for *Beethoven*

No.	Variation (X)	Yes/No ($X \equiv Beethoven$?)	$L(X, Beethoven)$
1	Beethovens	Yes	1
2	Baytoven	Yes	5
3	Beeethoven	Yes	1
4	Beetehoven	Yes	2
5	Betoven	Yes	2
6	Baethoven	Yes	2
7	Bethoven	Yes	1
8	Aeethoben	No	4
9	Brativen	No	7
10	Brochowen	No	8
11	Beatolen	No	5
12	Bathavan	No	7
13	Topoven	No	8
14	Beetleman	No	6

Remember how, as we have discussed before, human judges often disagree on their evaluation of positive and negative examples? Perhaps you would like to classify the examples in Table 4.4 differently?

A reason for differences in classification, in the current case, is that I chose negative examples to be near-misses of the positive examples, making it harder for human judges to agree. For example, it would be easier to agree that *Rudolf* is not equivalent to *Beethoven* than it is to agree on the fact that *Beatolen* is not equivalent to *Beethoven*. It is important during development to put your algorithm in hard conditions, so as to aim toward boosting precision and recall through refinement of your algorithm.

It is even harder to agree given that the examples in Table 4.4 are taken out of context. It would be quite different if the variations were shown within their sentence of occurrence. I purposely did not do that, so as to focus the discussion on the

---

[1]See Sect. 3.4.3, where we introduced the idea of a development set for the refinement of regular expressions. Other concepts from Sect. 3.4 will be revisited in the current section, such as inter-annotator agreement (Sect. 3.4.1) and the importance of including near-misses negative examples in the development set (Sect. 3.4.3). I encourage the reader to go back to the experimental design in Sect. 3.4 for a review of these concepts.

misspellings themselves (and not on contextual cues) and to encourage the reader to challenge my annotations and reflect on the difficulty of establishing and agreeing on gold standards.

That said, let us continue on our threshold search and devise a method to find it. The idea is to simply iterate through various thresholds, and for each one, apply the categorization rules in Eq. 4.2 on the variations in the development set (column 2 in Table 4.4) to obtain classification results. Then compare these classification results against the required answer (column 3 in Table 4.4) to calculate the F1 measure.[2] At the end, we select the threshold, among all those tried, which maximizes F1.

Table 4.5 shows the recall, precision, and F1 scores for possible thresholds from 1 to 8. The numbers in the second column refer to the misspellings identifiers provided in the first column of Table 4.4. Notice that results for precision decline as those for recall increase, as is usually the case.

Table 4.5 Calculated F1 at different thresholds for accepted misspellings

Threshold	Accepted misspellings	Recall	Precision	F1
1	{1,3,7}	0.571	1.0	0.727
2	{1,3,4,5,6,7}	0.857	1.0	0.923
3	{1,3,4,5,6,7}	0.857	1.0	0.923
4	{1,3,4,5,6,7,8}	0.857	0.857	0.857
5	{1,2,3,4,5,6,7,8,11}	1.0	0.778	0.875
6	{1,2,3,4,5,6,7,8,11,14}	1.0	0.7	0.823
7	{1,2,3,4,5,6,7,8,9,11,12,14}	1.0	0.583	0.737
8	{1,2,3,4,5,6,7,8,9,10,11,12,13,14}	1.0	0.5	0.667

Being the highest (the closest to 1.0), the most favorable F1 for this dataset has a threshold of 2 (both 2 and 3 are in equality, at 0.923, so we arbitrarily choose 2).

Would this be a valid threshold for *all* applications? Certainly not, since we have only calculated it for this small made-up sample containing a single entity. Still, we will put our threshold to the test in Sect. 4.4, as we compare a binary classifier based on Levenshtein Distance, with a Soundex algorithm, on a name search comparison task. Now, let us introduce the Soundex algorithm, so as to understand both competing algorithms.

4.3 Soundex — A Phonetic Algorithm

Many mistakes in text stem from people having heard words before, but not necessarily having seen them in their written form. When searching for them in text, we make guesses at the written form of words we have never seen. As well, in the current world of text messages, writers (texters) often want to generate their message

---

[2]Notions of precision, recall and F1 measures were introduced in Sect. 2.2.

quickly, and therefore approximate the spelling of one word using a shorter, similar sounding word (e.g., *cuz* for *because*).

An algorithm called **Soundex**, patented as early as 1918, was developed for the purpose of matching similar sounding words in English. The idea is to perform **sound encoding** for words, transforming each one into a **Soundex Code**. The resulting codes can then be compared to each other, to determine whether they are similarly sounding words.

Before we go into the details of the algorithm, let us look at Table 4.6 to first experience examples of pairs of real words and made-up words with their Soundex codes.

Table 4.6 Comparing words through Soundex Codes

Word 1	Code 1	Word 2	Code 2
Robert	R163	Rupert	R163
Chardwddonnay	C635	Chardoney	C635
Although	A432	Alto	A430
Baken	B250	Bacon	B250
Cauliflower	C414	Califoler	C414
Bryce	B620	Price	P620
Testing	T235	Testify	T231
Archive	A621	Arkiv	A621
Bad	B300	Bat	B300
Prawn	P650	Drawn	D650
Bored	B630	Board	B630
Puffy	P100	Pop	P100

Some pairs, such as *(archive,arkiv), (baken,bacon)*, when pronounced out loud, do sound very similar, and their Soundex codes, unsurprisingly are the same. But Table 4.6 also shows some slightly different sounding words, such as the pairs *(Robert,Rupert), (Puffy,Pop)* which also map to a unique code. Let us look further into the Soundex algorithm to understand why that is.

The Soundex algorithm relies on the following rules and observations:

1. The first letter of a word is important.
2. Certain groups of letters sound the same or similar, and should be merged. For example {b,f,p,v} are similar, and so are {m,n}.
3. Double letters should be reduced to one.
4. Vowels are often confused with each other and can be removed.

The algorithm in its entirety is shown below (Algorithm 2). It is surprisingly simple, and essentially consists of a series of replacements. By generally keeping the first letter of words, allowing for similar sounding letters to be interchanged, allowing one letter to stand in for a double letter and removing vowels all together, the algorithm can reduce words to their fundamental sounds and in so doing develop a sound code for them.

Starting with a *word* of size N letters;
\\ *1. Remember the first letter of the word*
Set $FirstLetter$ to $word[1]$;
\\ *2. Build a first version of the code.*
Set $Code$ to $Word[2..N]$;
\\ *2a. Perform a series of consonant replacements.*
In $Code$, replace all (b,f,p,v) by '1' ;
In $Code$, replace all (c,g,j,k,q,s,x,z) by '2' ;
In $Code$, replace all (d,t) by '3' ;
In $Code$, replace all (l) by '4' ;
In $Code$, replace all (m,n) by '5' ;
In $Code$, replace all (r) by '6' ;
\\ *2b. Remove letters h,w.*
In $Code$, replace all (h,w) by '' ;
\\ *3. Refine code by removing adjacent doubles of '1' to '6'.*
for *char x = '1' to '6'* **do**
| In $Code$, replace all multiple consecutive occurrences of x by a single one;
end
\\ *4. Remove the vowels. We must wait till this step to remove them, as their presence is important in determining consecutive presence or not of codes in previous step.*
In $Code$, replace all (a,e,i,o,u,y) by '' ;
if *length of Code < 3* **then**
| Add paddings with '0' at the end;
end
else if *length of Code > 3* **then**
| Set $Code$ to the first 3 letter;
end
Set final $Code$ to be $FirstLetter$ kept earlier + $Code[1..3]$;
\\ *At the end, Code contains the Soundex code.*

Algorithm 2: Soundex Algorithm

Let us now put this Soundex algorithm to the test in a comparative experiment described in the next section.

4.4   Experiment — A Comparative Setting for Misspelling Detection

With two algorithms in our toolbox, we now have the interesting opportunity to compare their performances. To carry out our comparison, we will need to situate the two algorithms together in an experimental setting.

Our task of misspelling detection can be formally stated as the following. Given a gold standard of N entities, $e_1..e_N$, each one with a corresponding correct surface form $s_1..s_N$, we are presented, for each entity e_i, with a set of K_i possible misspellings, $e_i(1)..e_i(K_i)$. For each possible misspelling, $e_i(j)$ we must determine if it corresponds (Yes/No) to s_i.

Our comparative setup for our algorithms will be as follows:

1. The two algorithms to test are Soundex and Levenshtein Distance.
2. We will use these algorithms as binary classifiers in the misspelling detection task.
   - For Levenshtein Distance, the distances less than or equal to the previously determined threshold of 2 (see Sect. 4.2) will count as positives. All others will count as negatives.
   - For Soundex, only words having the same code will count as positive.[3]
3. We will measure the individual performance of each algorithm on the same pre-defined gold standard.
4. We will compare the results of the two algorithms.

Certainly, this setup may appear unnecessarily formal for such a small experiment. My main reason for insisting on the necessity of defining an experimental setting clearly is that uncertainty is inherent to NLP. Since we rarely have deterministic answers that are universally agreed upon, the notion that 'it depends...' is almost always lurking somewhere beneath the surface of our results. In the face of such uncertainty, it is good practice to err on the side of modesty when presenting results that are valid within a particular experimental setting, but not necessarily seen as the universal truth. It is therefore important to decide on a particular experimental setting and to understand its reach and limitations.

It is also important that the experimental setting be determined *before* performing an evaluation. If we had not specified ahead of time that we were to use a threshold of 2 for our evaluation of Levenshtein Distance for example, we could potentially be tempted to change the threshold when testing our algorithm. This would be less than honest, since we would effectively be further adapting our algorithm to our *test set*, when the threshold was defined on the development set (see Table 4.3). Even when there is room for improvement on an algorithm, it is important to 'freeze' it in particular incarnations, stand back, and measure its performance. In a way, this is similar to freezing code in software design, when we assign it version numbers (e.g., 1.1, 1.5 etc.) at certain stages of development, and then continue to improve on it. This process of freezing and measuring provides us with benchmarks along the road of development, which help us objectively evaluate our improvement over time.

4.4.1 Gold Standard

Let us pretend we are given Table 4.7 as gold standard, being told that lists found in the third column are all recognized misspellings $(e_i(1)..e_i(K_i))$ for the entity which normalized surface form (s_i) is found in the second column. Notice how the surface forms are given in a compressed way to make them compatible input for our two

---

[3]We have not discussed partial matching of Soundex codes. I leave it to be explored as an exercise (see Exercise 4.2).

algorithms. Eventually, the algorithms should be adapted to work with **compound nouns** as to make them more flexible (see Exercise 4.4).

Table 4.7 Gold standard for acceptable surface form variations

Num. (i)	Correct surface form (s_i)	Variations ($e_i(1)..e_i(K_i)$)
1	Chardonnay	Chardonnay, Chardenay, Chardenai, Chardenet, Chardennet, Chardonay, Chatenait, Chaudenet, Chaudent
2	CzechRepublic	CzechRepublic, CeskoRepublika, CheckRepublic, CeskaRepublika, CechRepublic, CzechiRepublika, CzechoRepublic, TjechRepublic, TscheRepublic, ChezRepublic
3	ElvisPresley	ElvisPresley, ElvisPresely, ElvisPressley, ElvisPressly, ElvisPrestly, ElvisPrestley
4	Hirshhorn	Hirshhorn, Hishorn, Hishon, Hichorn, Hirsshon, Ichon, Irshhorrn
5	Italy	Italy, Itàlia, Italia, Italie, Itali, Italië, Italija, Italio, Yitalia
6	KeithJarrett	KeithJarrett, KeteJarrett, KeithJaret, KeithJarret, KateJarrett, KeyJarrett
7	Mehldau	Mehldau, Meldau, Meldauh, Melhdau, Meldaugh
8	Mozart	Mozart, Moatzart, Mosart, Motzart, Mozzart
9	TheBeatles	TheBeatles, Beatle, Beetals, TheBeatals, TheBeetals, TheBeetles, TheBealtes, DieBeatles
10	VanGogh	VanGogh, VanGoh, VanGoth, VanGough, VanGo, VanGogh, VanGhoh, VanGooh

Having seen in the previous chapters the need for including both positive and negative examples in a gold standard, you should recognize that this is not a quality gold standard, since it only contains positive examples.

This gold standard will only allow for the measure of recall. Why? Remember that precision requires the number of false positive in its calculation (the number of 'no' falsely tagged as 'yes'), which cannot occur when we are only provided with positive examples in the first place.

If we had known that recall was the measure to be used for testing our algorithms, we would have optimized our threshold T (Sect. 4.2) for the Levenshtein Distance on recall instead of F1. But we did not know. I am presenting this hypothetical scenario to demonstrate the way things often unfold in the real world. I gathered this gold standard test set from the predicate `dbo:WikiPageRedirects`, which was the first source of surface forms we explored in Chap. 2. This predicate leads to positive examples of misspellings. Although less than ideal, a gold standard made up of solely positive examples is sometimes all there is available for an NLP task, and researchers then try to be creative in making up negative examples.

For our current experiment, let us only keep the positive examples provided, and compare our algorithms using the recall measure, as we see next.

4.4.2 Looking at Results

Table 4.8 shows the average recall obtained for each name by the Levenshtein and Soundex algorithms, as well as the difference between them.

Table 4.8 Recall results for both algorithms: Soundex and Levenshtein Distance

Num. (i)	Correct surface form (s_i)	Lev. Dist	Soundex	Difference
1	Chardonnay	0.22	0.67	0.45
2	CzechRepublic	0.3	0.3	0.0
3	ElvisPresley	1.0	1.0	0.0
4	Hirshhorn	0.286	0.143	−0.143
5	Italy	0.222	0.556	0.334
6	KeithJarrett	0.5	0.833	0.333
7	Mehldau	0.8	0.8	0
8	Mozart	1.0	0.6	−0.4
9	TheBeatles	0.5	0.5	0
10	VanGogh	1.0	0.375	−0.625
	Average	0.583	0.578	0.005

The average results, presented on the last row of the table, indicate the two algorithms arriving almost *ex aequo* at the finishing line. But looking at the individual results in Table 4.8, we observe that one algorithm performs better than the other in some cases and less well in others. For example, Soundex's performance was better for the name *Chardonnay*, but worse for *VanGogh*. This could be an indication that there is a complementary relationship of sorts between these algorithms, which could incite us to combine them in order to obtain a more global solution. In Chap. 13, Sect. 13.4.3, we will introduce the idea of voters and vote combination, which could very well apply in our present case, making Soundex and Levenshtein algorithms, both voters for the same task.

There are also possible variations on the Edit Distance, which will make the algorithm perform very similarly to the Soundex, as we discuss next within an analysis of the algorithms in a broader multilingual setting.

4.5 Soundex and Edit Distance in a Multilingual Setting

Our previous section defined a task of misspelling detection, which more accurately should have been called a task of *English* misspelling detection. Comparative results on a French, Spanish, or German misspelling task, with the same two algorithms would have led to quite different results. Changing to a language other than English would actually not be fair to Soundex, since it was specifically developed for the English language and the replacements it suggests are therefore based on groups of letters that sound similar in English. This may not be the case for other languages. For example, in French, a final 't' is often silent, meaning the words *Pinot* and *Pineau* would be pronounced in the same way, given also that an 'eau' sequence in French has an 'o' sound. Unfortunately, the Soundex algorithm would encode these words differently (P530 for *Pinot* and P500 for *Pineau*), in spite of the fact that from a French speaker standpoint, they sound virtually identical.

The Edit Distance algorithm, on the other hand, provides a language-independent approach, simply considering operators (insertion, deletion, substitution) on letters. But to actually make the Edit Distance perform better, we need to modify it a bit to not be so agnostic to the content of the words. Numerous variations to the algorithm have been suggested over the years, on the theme of **weighted Edit Distance** meaning that various weights can be assigned to the different operators and varied based on the letters on which the operators are applied. It might be more intuitive to think of a weight as a cost of an operation, since our final goal is to calculate a distance, and that distance will be the sum of the weight (or cost) or each operation.

Below are some examples of ways to vary the costs of operations in Edit Distance.

- **First letter**: Assign a higher cost to a change in the first letter of a word.
- **Vowels versus consonants**: A substitution involving two vowels could be assigned a lower cost than one involving a vowel and a consonant.
- **Letter matrix**: We could construct a full matrix to represent the cost of substitutions between any letter and any other letter. This would constitute a very fine-grained variation of the cost, possibly learned from typical writing mistakes in different languages.
- **Close keyboard keys**: Letter changes involving keys that sit close together on the keyboard could be assigned lower costs.
- **Close sounds**: Similar sounding letters (e.g., *b, p, v*) could be assigned lower costs.
- **Repeated letters**: Reduce or completely remove the cost of insertion when it involves the doubling of a letter.

Some variations are related to the application or type of text to be analyzed. If we hope to search for names in very informal blogs for example, we can expect many keyboard typing mistakes, and attempt a weighted Edit Distance adapted to take into account the close keyboard keys. But most variations, such as suggesting different costs for different letter pairs, address aspects intrinsic to the language, and would require adaptation to each language to perform adequately. Given that each language has its own writing rules, its own common and less common sounds, its own set of characters, it is certain that word comparison algorithms, whether phonetic or character-based, will not be language independent and will require language adaptation.

4.6   In Summary

- Edit Distance is a very useful algorithm for comparing strings. It relies on basic operators for insertion, deletion, and substitution of characters.
- The Levenshtein Distance is a commonly used variation on the Edit Distance, where the cost of an insertion or deletion is 1, and the cost of a substitution is 2.
- Soundex is a phonetic-based algorithm used for comparing strings, which works nicely for spelling errors involving variations of similar sounding letters and phonemes.
- The change from a distance measure to a Yes/No classification implies the use of thresholds. We can learn to establish appropriate thresholds by optimizing the threshold-dependent algorithm on recall, precision, or F1 using a development set.
- When comparing algorithms, we should look beyond average results, at the individual results, which might hint at their complementarity.
- There are many possible variations of the Edit Distance algorithm. Most would consist in changing the weights (costs) of different operators, and adapting these weights to particular letters, letter pairs or the position of letters in words.
- When used in a multilingual context, string comparison algorithms should be adapted properly to the phonetic and orthographic particularities of each language.

4.7   Further Reading

Edit Distance and Soundex description and variations: The best starting point for further exploration of the Edit Distance is simply its own Wikipedia page, whereas for Soundex it is better to start from the higher level description of phonetic algorithms, at https://en.wikipedia.org/wiki/Phonetic_algorithm which will also point to more recent phonetic algorithms such as the NYSIIS, the Metaphone and Double Metaphone.

Competitive trend in NLP: The emphasis on experimental setup in this chapter can be related to the competition-oriented trend increasingly present in NLP over the past 15 years. As one example, the National Institute of Standards and Technology (NIST) regularly hosts a TAC (Text Analysis Conference) in which various competing tracks are suggested (http://www.nist.gov/tac/2016/KBP/index.html) covering topics from sentiment analysis to Entity Linking and knowledge base population.

4.8   Exercises

Exercises 4.1   (Levenshtein Distance)

a. Program the Levenshtein Distance algorithm, shown in Algorithm 1. Make sure your program is correct by testing it on the different variations in Table 4.4.

b. Gather possible surface forms of five entities of your choice in DBpedia, using the predicate dbo:WikiPageRedirects. Discuss how appropriate the Levenshtein Distance is for expressing the closeness of these forms to the one found through the rdfs:label. To help your discussion, go back to Chap. 2, Sect. 2.10, to Exercise 2.2, and go through the surface form variation categories you had defined. Is the Levenshtein Distance more appropriate for some categories than others? Use examples from your five chosen entities to illustrate your point.

Exercises 4.2 (Soundex)

a. Program the Soundex encoding algorithm, shown in Algorithm 2. Make sure your program is correct by testing it on the different variations in Table 4.6.
b. Try your Soundex program on the variations of *Beethoven* in Table 4.4. Do they all lead to the same Soundex Code? If not, which ones are different?
c. Modify your program above to work with noun compounds. If you look at the noun compounds in Table 4.7, do the results change between applying the original algorithm on the condensed versions (e.g., ElvisPresley) or your new version on the real name (e.g., Elvis Presley)?
d. Our approach to the use of Soundex in this chapter has been very strict: either the codes match or they do not. You probably noticed a similarity between the codes of similar words. Think of how to express code similarity using Soundex. Discuss.

Exercises 4.3 (Threshold search and Edit Distance variations)

a. Program the threshold search algorithm, discussed in Sect. 4.2. Test it using the data in Table 4.4 to make sure it works correctly.
b. Modify the Levenshtein Distance algorithm to (a) increase the penalty for operations on the first letter, (b) only penalize changes in vowels by 1, and (c) have no penalty for the insertion of a letter that results in a double letter (e.g., inserting a k after another k). Redo the threshold search, programmed above, using the new Levenshtein Distance algorithm to optimize the threshold. Is the result very different?

Exercises 4.4 (Experimental Setting)

a. Be critical of the experimental setup we described in Sect. 4.4. What do you think of the names chosen in the gold standard? Do you think they will bias the results toward Soundex or Levenshtein? Is 10 examples enough? Do you agree that all variations provided are possible variations of the entity's correct name? Why is only measuring recall problematic?

Part II
Working with Corpora

Given the preponderance of **statistical problem-solving approaches** in current NLP research, as fostered by the online availability of large corpora, it is important, for our exploration of NLP and more specifically of Information Extraction (IE), to spend a bit of time exploring what corpora have to offer and how we can devise even simple statistical methods to extract information from them. This is our goal in this Part II of the book, *Working with Corpora*.

We will first spend time in *Chap. 5, Exploring Corpora*, to discuss different types of corpora and to get a sense of how words behave in them. We will look at **quantitative approaches**, relying on measures inspired from the field of information theory and **qualitative approaches** through the use of a concordancer, allowing to view words in their immediate contextual environment, within a corpus.

We will then look at words in corpus as they form predictable sequences. These sequences are at the core of **statistical language models**, so useful in NLP for various tasks from Machine Translation to error correction. *Chapter 6, Words in Sequence*, will provide a brief introduction to probabilistic modelling of word sequences and will use the models in a misspelling correction task.

We then venture into a bilingual comparative setting in *Chap. 7, Bilingual Corpora*. We will look at bilingual term extraction, using the methods from *Chap. 5*, inspired from information theory, to find **term equivalents** in bilingual corpora. We will also show how the language models from *Chap. 6* can be applied for **automatic language detection**.

Chapter 5
Exploring Corpora

In previous chapters, we have worked with very small corpora. Some were even constructed manually to specifically illustrate a particular point, and they have generally contained ten to twenty sentences each. These have been sufficient for our purposes of familiarizing ourselves with the learning material (e.g., variations in surface forms, the use of regular expressions to find entity types, measuring Levenshtein Distance between surface forms), but much larger corpora are available in the real world, and it is important for us to explore the behavior of surface forms in this broader context as well.

We will start this chapter by providing alternate definitions for the word **corpus** and then further characterizing the documents which can be included in a corpus, through different criteria such as genre and domain.

We then provide a brief overview of various **corpora resources**, so as to show the availability and the diversity of corpora, and incite readers to further look for resources corresponding to their needs. The reader can find references to all resources and software tools mentioned in this chapter in Sect. 5.10, as part of the *Further Reading* material.

We then investigate two different ways of exploring the content of corpora: **quantitative exploration** and **qualitative exploration**.

For our quantitative exploration, we will look at measures of **word frequency**, as well as measures provided by the field of information theory, such as **Information Content** and **Mutual Information**, which respectively help to determine which words or combinations of words are more informative than others in a corpus.

For our qualitative exploration, we will build a **concordancer**, which is a tool designed to provide a concise view of corpus words within their immediate contextual environment.

© Springer International Publishing Switzerland 2016
C. Barrière, *Natural Language Understanding in a Semantic Web Context*,
DOI 10.1007/978-3-319-41337-2_5

5.1 Defining Corpora

The word **corpus**, or its plural form **corpora**, has become such an integral part of NLP today that its definition is rarely explicit within research articles describing corpus-based experiments. But really, what is intended by the word *corpus* might vary from one article to the other, a variation that is likely influenced by the publication year and the subdiscipline (e.g., NLP in medicine, NLP in humanities) of the article.

To discuss these variations, let me make up a few definitions, which could correspond to various implicit definitions of the term *corpus* as used in research articles.

(a) A corpus is a set of electronic documents.
(b) A corpus is a large number of documents.
(c) A corpus is a set of documents freely available online.
(d) A corpus is a set of annotated documents.
(e) A corpus is a set of documents selected based on particular criteria.

Definition (a) is probably the one most often assumed by current NLP research. We often think of a corpus as being, quite simply, a set of electronic documents. However, the criterion of availability in **electronic form** is not essential for a set of documents to be called a corpus. Corpora existed before the electronic age, and a set of paper documents can still be a corpus. Unfortunately, such a corpus is not directly accessible as input for NLP study, unless it is processed through an OCR (optical character recognition) program, which depending on its quality, would result in more or less recognizable and therefore analyzable text. OCR is a field of study in itself, playing an important role in the conservation and study of historical texts.

The criterion of **size**, as emphasized in definition (b), is also not essential for a set of documents to be called a corpus. That being said, we would probably not refer to a group of only two documents as a corpus, but rather assume it consists of at least a few. Working with very large corpora is a common trend in current NLP research, going hand in hand with the trend of using statistical approaches which require large amount of text to generate realistic probabilistic models.

The criterion of **free access**, as emphasized in definition (c), is not essential either. There are plenty of corpora that are made available by different organizations at varying costs through varying licensing agreements. However, free access is often a factor in the popularity of a corpus since researchers will generally tend to choose corpora which are free of cost. This is such a pervasive phenomenon that it has created a bias in research over the years, since researchers have focused more on free availability than anything else in their choice of corpora. This has meant that certain corpora are used extensively simply because they are free and not because they are particularly well constructed or well suited to specific tasks.

Definition (d) serves to highlight the difference between raw and annotated texts. **Raw text** refers to text in its original, untouched form. **Annotated text**, on the other hand, here refers to text into which humans have manually inserted information such as part-of-speech tags (e.g., noun, verb, adjective) or sense numbers taken from a dictionary. Examples of annotated text are the Penn Treebank corpus for part-of-speech tagging (discussed in Chap. 8) and the SemCor corpus, which is annotated with WordNet senses (discussed in Chap. 9). Annotated texts are costly, since they required many human annotation hours to be generated. They are commonly used in NLP for the development of supervised machine learning models which require annotated data for their model learning.

My reason for including the final definition (e) was to focus our attention on the fact that a corpus is not necessarily just a random selection of texts, but that selection can be based on **document characterization** criteria. In earlier work on corpus linguistics, selection criteria were always stated and explicit, since the very idea of a corpus was dependent on these criteria. An unqualified group of documents would, at one time, not have been considered a corpus. Let us further explore, in the next section, the different ways in which documents can be characterized.

5.2 Characterizing Documents

There are multiple ways of characterizing a document. Language, country of origin, domain, text genre, medium, language level, and purpose are all examples of characteristics reflecting variations in the form and content of a document. Below is a list of these seven characteristics which provides more information about each one, along with examples.

- Any text is written in a particular **language**, whether it is English, French, Spanish, Mandarin, or any other language of the world. In multilingual studies, we are interested in looking at corresponding texts in different languages.
- Beyond the actual language, the **country of origin** of the writer can affect the resulting corpus as well, in terms of its style, its cultural references (which are ever present in text), or the choice of vocabulary.
- The **domain** of a text refers to its subject matter or its central topic. There are texts belonging to countless domains, including medicine, computers, gardening, food, and automobiles.
- The **text genre**, also referred to as the **text type**, characterizes the intent and the formatting of the text, rather than the topic. Examples of genres would be technical reports, blogs, recipe books, scientific articles, and news articles. Each text genre implies a particular style of writing, a factor which will influence the approach we take for extracting information from it.
- The **medium** of a text refers to how the text came about, whether through speech or writing. Spoken corpora are made up of transcriptions of speech. Most often consisting of dialogues, these require particular methods of analysis and entail many speech-specific elements of language, including pauses, repetitions, and false starts. We will deal exclusively with written corpora in this book.
- The **language level** of a text is often directly related to its genre. For example, familiar, colloquial language is characteristic of a blog, but we would expect to find more formal language in a scientific article.

- The **purpose** of a text refers to the intention behind its being written in the first place and its intended audience. For example, the purpose of a news story is to inform, whereas the purpose of a textbook is to teach, and the purpose of publicity text is to sell.

There is so much to say about each of the aspects of text described above that each one could become the subject of an entire book. The purpose of this brief overview is simply to familiarize the reader with some of the terms that are used when describing corpora. It will also contribute to building an awareness of the variability of corpora. This awareness will serve us well when it comes to deciding where to search for information, as well as how to adapt our Information Extraction tools for searches on different types of corpora.

5.3   Corpora Resources

There are many corpora available to us for download and exploration. The most important element of working with a corpus, however, is knowing whether it is appropriate for the task at hand. To discover the extent of the variability in corpora in terms of not only size, but domain, language, and more, I encourage the reader to look into corpora repositories such as the **Linguistic Data Consortium (LDC)**. Another good place to look for corpora is among the list of resources provided by the **Stanford NLP group**, as well as the **Corpora4Learning** site which provides links to various corpora and the tools needed to explore them.

Below is a tiny sample of currently available corpora, of interest from an NLP point of view. The sample aims to provide an eclectic survey of corpora and illustrate the degree to which one can differ from the next. The best way to familiarize yourself with these corpora is to explore them yourself both qualitatively and qualitatively, with the tools we will develop in the further sections. Through the presentation of the corpora, I sometimes mention research topics related to these corpora, even if they are outside the scope of this book. So as not to divert the reader too much toward further explanations of these topics, I preferred to include definitions for them in the *Glossary*, at the end of this book.

British National Corpus (BNC): The BNC was one of the first widely used corpora in NLP and is still used today. It is a collection of samples of spoken and written language texts, totaling 100 million words. It can be downloaded in full for your own research and exploration with a license agreement, or it can be searched directly online through their Web search tool. Table 5.1 shows the usage of the surface form *mobile phone*, our example from Chap. 2. The codes in the first column represent specific documents from specific sources within the BNC. The purpose in showing this table is to heighten the reader's awareness toward the eclectic content of sentences found in **general language corpus**, containing day-to-day language of a narrative nature, as opposed to an **encyclopedic corpus**, containing formal and definitional sentences, such as Wikipedia.

Table 5.1 Examples from BNC for *mobile phone*

```
AJ6/275   Close behind his PA, the formidable Helen Liddell, kept her mobile
          phone clamped to her ear and an anxious eye on her watch.
BM5/287   Some mobile phone retailers are now supplying the once popular car
          phone free, bar an installation charge, and rely on bill-related
          bonuses to make up the entire profit.
CB8/1590  Answer our survey and you could receive a free mobile phone on the
          Cellnet Lifetime service.
CBC/8249  It used to be only the City yuppie, but now most people can afford
          a mobile phone.
CBG/4873  But I've got the mobile phone, the furry coat and the big cigar.
CEK/6346  When she discovered that he had called her repeatedly on a mobile
          phone she flew into a rage.
CH6/8859  Di has frequently told friends she fears that her conversations were
          bugged and uses a mobile phone more and more.
CRC/2981  For surveyors and civil engineers, relief workers and war
          correspondents, the ultimate mobile phone looks like a bargain.
HGJ/274   He picks up his mobile phone, dials his stockbroker in Tokyo.
K1H/889   A federation representative is on call 24 hours a day by mobile phone.
```

Wikipedia archive: The Wikipedia archive is more commonly referred to as the **Wikipedia dumps**, so as to express the fact that on a regular basis, a few times per year, all the contents of all the pages of Wikipedia are "dumped" into large files, freely available for download. Wikipedia dumps are probably the most widely used corpora in current NLP research. An easy explanation for this is that Wikipedia dumps are both free and of significant size (gigabytes of text), two favorable criteria for corpus selection as we have discussed in the previous section. We follow the trend in this book by selecting multiple illustrating examples from Wikipedia. Although easy to access, Wikipedia dumps are not trivial to store and process locally (on your own computer) because of their large size. Wikipedia dumps are better explored locally if stored within an **information retrieval system**, such as made possible by the popular freely available indexing software *Lucene*, commonly used in NLP.

Reuters: Automatically determining the central topic of a text is an important task in NLP, known as **text categorization**. A useful corpus for testing approaches to categorization is the Reuters-90 categories corpus, which contains close to 13,000 documents, split into 90 classes, or domains. The domains include fuel, corn, cocoa, lumber, and oat. In this chapter, you will make use of the Reuters corpus to perform comparative studies of domain-specific corpus word frequencies (see Exercise 5.2).

Gutemberg project: The Gutemberg project contains a large set of freely available e-books. Although the Gutemberg project is better known in the digital humanities for language studies than in NLP, I believe it is an important repository to know about, and it can be a useful place to acquire knowledge and information about particular subjects, if performing domain-specific Information Extraction. For an **ontology expansion** task in the domain of gardening for example, one of the Gutemberg project e-books, the *A-B-C of Gardening*, would be a good source of information.

Google Books n-grams: This is an example of a preprocessed resource based on a very large corpus. The resource contains n-gram probabilities as precalculated on the Google Books. These n-grams are either available for download or for online consultation through the Google Books n-gram viewer. An **n-gram** is a text segment made of n consecutive words. For example, *a large cat* is a trigram (three words), whereas *large cat* is a bigram (two words). An interesting part of Google Books n-grams is that they allow for **diachronic studies,** as they provide the n-grams for particular years. This means that they gathered, for each year, all books published in that year, and then extracted the n-grams for that year-specific corpus.

Let us continue, in the next section, with the Google Books n-gram viewer to perform a first comparative quantitative analysis of surface forms in corpus.

5.4 Surface Form Frequencies in Corpus

For our first quantitative exploration, let us revisit our example of *mobile phones* from Chap. 2. Remember that there were various surface forms for the entity dbr:Mobile_phone. When searching for different surface forms in a corpus, we cannot expect to find them all with equal frequency, since some are bound to be more popular than others.

Let us investigate the popularity of individual forms. A useful tool to help in this endeavor, as introduced in the last section, is the Google Books n-gram viewer.

Table 5.2 shows a list of surface forms for *mobile phone*, in decreasing order of probability, for the year 2008.[1]

Table 5.2 Google Books frequencies for various surface forms of *mobile phone*

Surface form	Google Books percentage
cell phone	0.0005950%
mobile phone	0.0001922%
cellular phone	0.0000335%
cell-phone	0.0000142%
cellular telephone	0.0000128%
cell telephone	0.0000003%
celluar phone	N/A

The numbers, in the second column of Table 5.2, must be interpreted as the percentage of all possible bigrams found in the Google Books, which explains why they are all quite small. Clearly, *cell telephone* is much less common than *cell phone*. But in theory, if *phone* and *telephone* are synonyms, why wouldn't it be as likely to find

---

[1] The year 2008 is the latest year indexed in the Google Books n-gram viewer at the time of writing.

cell phone and *cell telephone* in corpora? A quantitative view of this corpus reveals that although certain variations are equally possible from a compositional point of view, they differ in terms of actual usage. The further study of why certain surface forms prevail over others in communication within a society is one of the topics of interest in the field of **terminology**.

As we saw earlier, corpora vary widely along various axes (genre, domain, purpose, etc.). When studying surface forms in a corpus, it is important to understand the nature of the corpus itself. In the case of Google Books n-gram viewer, the corpus is comprised of books indexed by Google. It comes at no surprise then that searching for the typographic error *celluar phone* yields no result, as shown in Table 5.2.

This does not mean the error never occurs, but simply reflects the fact that books are edited to eliminate such errors before being published. The situation is radically different on the Web. A search for the correct form *cellular phone* on the Google search engine returns over nine million hits, but a search for the typographic error *celluar phone* still returns over four million hits (see Table 5.3). In the scheme of things, this is not such a large difference. It goes to show that the **Web-as-corpus** is a much noisier place than Google Books, and each of these corpora provides evidence for different linguistic phenomena.

Table 5.3 also shows that single words (e.g., *cell*) are orders of magnitude more frequent than multi-words (e.g., *cell phone*). From this, we can extrapolate that due to this high frequency, single-word synonyms are likely to be very polysemous, as they can take on many different senses by being part of other multi-words (e.g., *cell prison*, *battery cell*, *body cell*). Although high frequency is not necessarily synonymous with polysemy, the two are often correlated. By likely being polysemous, single words will introduce noise if they are used as surface forms for an entity search in text.

Table 5.3 Google hit counts for different synonyms of *mobile phone*

Surface form	Google hit counts
mobile	5.9 billions
phone	4.4 billions
cell	1 billion
mobile phone	252 millions
cellular telephone	12 millions
cell phone	219 millions
cellular phone	9 millions
celluar phone	4 millions

It is interesting to explore the relative frequencies of different surface forms within a corpus, and it can be equally interesting to explore them *between* corpora. We can compare corpora along any of the axes mentioned earlier (domain, language level, purpose, etc.) and thus obtain relative frequencies. I chose country of origin as the criterion for comparison in the example below. Even within a single language, there can exist variations from country to country. Table 5.4 contrasts the use of *cell phone* and *mobile phone* in the USA, the UK, and Australia as obtained by specifying a country of origin in the Google search engine.

Table 5.4 Google hit counts for country preferences for synonyms of *mobile phone*

Label	USA	UK	Australia
cell phone	186 millions	2.7 millions	27 millions
mobile phone	116 millions	44 millions	557 thousands

We can observe that *mobile phone* is a much more popular form than *cell phone* in the UK, which seems to be the opposite in Australia. The numbers are not completely obvious to compare since they are not normalized. A normalized measure would take into account the total number of words in each corpus (or country for our example). The Information Content, which we explore next, is a normalized measure which will allow for more direct comparison between corpora.

5.5 Information Content

An important measure that can be derived from corpus frequency (or estimated based on it) is a word's self-information, or **Information Content**. The Information Content of a word, $IC(w)$, refers to the level of surprise that its presence in text offers, based on its probability of occurrence. Take the words *the*, *large*, *bird*, and *chiropteran* as examples. Intuitively, since it is the least common of the four, we can say that *chiropteran* is the word we would be most surprised to find in text. In contrast, finding the word *the* in a text does not bring with it any level of surprise. *The* is a word that is likely to occur in the vast majority of texts, and thus, each of its occurrence in text carries little Information Content.

Equation 5.1 shows the definition of $IC(w)$, in which $P(w)$ refers to the probability of a word w to occur in text.

$$IC(w) = \log \frac{1}{P(w)} = -\log P(w) \tag{5.1}$$

Unfortunately, we cannot estimate a real $P(w)$ which would refer to the overall probability of w to occur in any possible text available in the world. We instead approximate the probability of occurrence of a word through its observation in a specific corpus. This approximation, called $\hat{P}(w)$, will always be affiliated with the corpus within which it was observed.

Equation 5.2 shows how to calculate this approximate probability of word occurrence, where *freq(w)* represents the number of occurrences of a word *w* in a given corpus and *N* represents the total number of words in that corpus.

$$\hat{P}(w) = \frac{freq(w)}{N} \tag{5.2}$$

In the early days of corpus linguistics in the 1990s, the **Brown Corpus** was often used to perform frequency counts. It contained 1 million words from 500 texts, each limited to 2000 words. Although this seemed large at the time, frequency evaluations today are performed on much larger corpora. Let us continue with our four earlier example words (*the*, *large*, *bird*, and *chiropteran*), to understand why small corpora can be problematic for probability estimations.

Table 5.5 Examples of word frequency and Information Content in the Brown Corpus

word (*w*)	*freq(w)*	$\hat{P}(w)$	*IC(w)*
the	69967	0.069967	2.66
large	359	0.000359	7.93
bird	32	0.000034	10.35
chiropteran	0	∞	N/A

Table 5.5 shows their frequencies in the Brown Corpus, as well as their Information Content (*IC*), as calculated using Eq. 5.1 based on the approximate word probabilities calculated using Eq. 5.2. Notice how the rare word *chiropteran* is absent from the corpus, and therefore, no probability and no *IC* can be estimated on it. This is referred to as the **sparse data problem**. Sparse data are issues for single-word frequencies, but become even more problematic for n-gram estimations, as we will discuss in Chap. 6.

Let us now perform a comparative study of the Information Content of words using two domain-specific corpora. We will see how the top words in each corpus, ranked according to their *IC*, can actually tell us about the nature of the corpora.

5.6   Experiment — Comparing Domain-Specific Corpora

In Part I of this book, *Searching for entities in text*, our experiments focused on finding information about particular entities or entity types in text. Our current experiment will approach things from another angle and assume that corpora contain information of their own that we want to discover. We will use frequency analysis and Information Content as our tools for this endeavor.

Let us establish a comparative setting, so as to explore word frequencies and *IC* for two domain-specific corpora. We will keep this process quite exploratory and not restrict ourselves by setting it in the context of a particular evaluation task. This will be our first experiment following a **knowledge discovery** approach.

Let us divide our experiment into the following four steps:

1. Build domain-specific corpora.
2. Tokenize the text.
3. Calculate the frequency and *IC* for each token.
4. Observe and compare the results.

5.6.1 Building Domain-Specific Corpora

Thus far, we have had access to word frequencies through online viewers into already-built corpora. It will be important to perform a quantitative analysis of our own corpus as well, but first we must build one. Although we could simply download a corpus from one of the sites listed in Sect. 5.3, we really should learn how to build our own. Doing so will have the added benefit of affording us more control over the choice of our raw material. Remember that Information Extraction starts with a corpus. Having control over the nature of that corpus will affect later tool development and therefore our results.

For our current comparative study, *domain* is our criterion of interest. We will need two corpora, each within a different domain. In keeping with our examples of *Ludwig van Beethoven* and *mobile phone* from Chap. 2, let us use *classical music composers* and *mobile telecommunications* as the respective domains for our two corpora. These domains are far enough apart that they should provide an interesting comparative setting.

One way of developing a domain-specific corpus is to make use of the **Wikipedia categories**. In Wikipedia, most pages are assigned one or more categories, representing their content. Specificity of categories varies widely, such as illustrated by the following list, sampled from the categories assigned to *Ludwig van Beethoven*: *1770 births, 1827 deaths, 18th-century classical composers, 18th-century German people, Burials at the Zentralfriedhof, Composers for piano,* and *Deaf classical musicians*.

In DBpedia, the predicate `foaf:primaryTopicOf` links individual entities to their corresponding Wikipedia page titles, and the predicate `dct:subject` links them to their list of Wikipedia categories. We can therefore use the SPARQL query below, as performed at the DBpedia SPARQL endpoint,[2] to retrieve all the page titles for the category *Classical-period_composers*. You could adapt this query to fit the category of your choice.

```
PREFIX dbr:   <http://dbpedia.org/resource/>
PREFIX dct:   <http://purl.org/dc/terms/>
PREFIX foaf:  <http://xmlns.com/foaf/0.1/>
select distinct ?Y where {
```

---

[2]Information about SPARQL and the DBpedia endpoint can be found in Appendix A.

```
    ?X dct:subject dbr:Category:Classical-period_composers .
    ?X foaf:isPrimaryTopicOf ?Y .
}
```

The query above results in a list of Wikipedia page titles. From there, you can use your preferred programming language to write a program which will download and clean the content of each page in the list. For the download step, most programming languages contain libraries which allow us to easily connect to a URL and download its content. Note that this approach of page-by-page download should be used with caution and ONLY be attempted for short lists of pages, less than a few hundreds, since it puts much burden on the Wikipedia server. The pages should be downloaded once and stored to be used locally. For building larger corpora, as we will do in Chap. 6, we must make use of the Wikipedia dumps, earlier described in Sect. 5.3.

As for the cleaning step, commonly called **boiler plate removal** when it comes to Web pages, this step can be difficult, depending on how noisy the downloaded Web pages are. Many programming languages offer open source libraries for boiler plate removal, which should remove all html tags and metadata and provide readable text. This removal process is not trivial, and we should not expect the results to be perfect. The outputted text will be somewhat "clean" as it would mainly be made of uninterrupted paragraphs of texts, but it might still contain some metadata and html tags. The process might also have removed parts of the text that should have been kept. When building corpora, we often underestimate the time needed for this cleaning step, or the negative impact on the results if we neglect it, especially if we wish to further use linguistic tools on the resulting text (see NLP pipeline in Chap. 8). Linguistic tools usually require cleaned text data to achieve good performances.

The domain-specific corpora would be the result of a concatenation (merging) of all downloaded and cleaned pages. Let us refer to them as CLASSICALCOMPOSER and MOBILETEL corpora. Table 5.6 shows the number of Wikipedia pages falling under each of our two chosen domains and provides examples of Wikipedia page titles for each (excerpts of the resulting corpora can be found in Tables 5.10 and 5.11, in Sect. 5.8).

Table 5.6 Domain-specific corpora corresponding to Wikipedia categories

Category	Nb Pages	Nb Tokens	Examples of pages
Classical Period Composers	310	420,468	Domenico Alberti, Muzio Clementi, Franz Lauska, Wolfgang Amadeus Mozart
Mobile Telecommunications	180	247,213	Mobile translation, Bulk messaging, Transcoder free operation, 4G, Microcell

Table 5.6 also includes the total number of tokens found in each corpus. Notice how I say tokens and not words. That is because corpora are made of words, but also punctuation marks, symbols, and numbers. Let us investigate this word versus token issue a bit further, in the next section.

5.6.2 Tokenizing the Corpora

When we set our experiment in the context of knowledge discovery, as we are doing now, a new and significant challenge emerges: determining **word boundaries** in a corpus. This challenge stems from the fact that we no longer have a specific surface form that we are searching for in a corpus. Let me elaborate a bit on this **search versus discovery** issue as it is important both for the development of NLP methods and for their evaluation.

In **search**, we know ahead of time what we are looking for. For example, we look for *cell phone*, *cellular phone*, and *mobile phone* as possible surface forms for the URI dbr:Mobile_phone. A programming language would store these surface forms in a *string* data structure. The corpus in which we search would also be stored as a long string. The programming language will further provide a very useful substring match operator. Using this operator, we can relatively easily determine at which positions in the corpus would each surface form be matched.

In **discovery**, on the other hand, we do not know ahead of time what we are looking for. We wish to discover in the corpus some *interesting* information. An example of "interesting" information could be additional surface forms for *mobile phone*. These cannot be found with any substring match operator, as there is nothing to match. We want these forms to emerge from the corpus. The only knowledge that the programming language has is that the corpus is a long string. It does not know about words. Much of NLP work is trying to make the corpus reveal information, using various strategies inspired by linguistic and statistical studies of language. Most strategies minimally assume that the long string which represents the corpus can be broken up in smaller pieces, each one more easily analyzable. That is the purpose of a tokenizer.

A **tokenizer** splits a string into substrings (tokens), using a specified list of **separators**. The choice of separators will therefore have a major impact on the resulting list of tokens. Table 5.7 illustrates this point, by presenting two possible lists of tokens derived from the same original sentence, but which were obtained using different separators.

John listened to Beethoven's Symphony No.2 over the week-end.

There is much more to tokenizing than what we have seen here, but we will save the more detailed discussion for Chap. 8, which deals with ***Linguistic Roles**. For now,

Table 5.7 Different separators for tokenizing

Separator	NbTokens	Resulting tokens
space only	9	John, listened, to, Beethoven's, Symphony, No.2, over, the, week-end
apostrophe, punctuations, dash	12	John, listened, to, Beethoven, s, Symphony, No, 2, over, the, week, end

let us assume that we have a basic tokenizer, using spaces, apostrophes, punctuations, and dashes as separators, as shown in Table 5.7 and move on to finding frequencies for the resulting tokens in our domain-specific corpora.

5.6.3 Calculating Frequencies and IC

Once we have our list of tokens, we can calculate their frequency and Information Content (*IC*). We do this by going through the text and gathering occurrence counts for each token, as shown in Algorithm 3.

\\ *1. Initialise total count of tokens to 0;*
TotalCount = 0 ;
\\ *2. Keep a table of token counts*
Initialise *TableTokenFreq* ;
\\ *3. Go through the text to capture the occurrences of all tokens.*
for *each token in the text* **do**
    Increment *TotalCount* ;
    if *TableTokenFreq contains token* **then**
        Add 1 to its count in *TableTokenFreq* ;
    end
    else
        Insert new token in *TableTokenFreq* and set its count to 1 ;
    end
end
\\ *4. Calculate the IC for each token.*
for *each token in TableTokenFreq* **do**
    Calculate its *IC* with $-log(\frac{TableTokenFreq}{TotalCount})$;
end

Algorithm 3: Evaluating frequency and *IC* for corpus tokens.

As you can see, the algorithm goes through all the tokens, incrementing the frequency count for each one as it encounters it. It also keeps track of a total count of tokens, so as to use it, at the end, to evaluate the *IC* for each token (see Eqs. 5.1 and 5.2).

Even without any further NLP processing, the resulting list of frequencies and *IC* will provide insight into the content of a corpus, as we will see in the coming section.

5.6.4 Observing and Comparing Results

Having built our two domain-specific corpora, CLASSICALCOMPOSER and MOBILETEL, and ran Algorithm 3 on them, the final result would be a list of tokens with their frequencies and *ICs*. Table 5.8 shows the top twenty highest frequency tokens for each corpus.

The total number of tokens for each corpus was previously mentioned in Table 5.6, showing 420,468 for the CLASSICALCOMPOSER and 247,213 for the MOBILETEL. These numbers help explain the differences in frequencies in Table 5.8. With the total number of tokens for the MOBILETEL corpus being significantly smaller, it follows that frequencies of individual words are also lower.

Table 5.8 Top 20 tokens in CLASSICALCOMPOSER and MOBILETEL

CLASSICALCOMPOSER			MOBILETEL		
Token	Frequency	IC	Token	Frequency	IC
the	16356	3.25	the	9549	3.25
in	11804	3.57	and	5309	3.84
of	11068	3.64	of	5111	3.88
and	8807	3.87	to	4577	3.99
to	5831	4.28	in	3997	4.12
wikipedia	4507	4.54	mobile	3155	4.36
his	4456	4.55	is	2162	4.74
was	4174	4.61	for	1943	4.85
for	3800	4.71	on	1629	5.02
with	3619	4.76	with	1468	5.13
he	3600	4.76	by	1455	5.14
by	3286	4.85	as	1435	5.15
major	3037	4.93	phone	1385	5.18
at	2442	5.15	from	1254	5.28
from	2405	5.16	this	1232	5.30
as	2390	5.17	retrieved	1220	5.31
articles	2187	5.26	wikipedia	1176	5.35
music	2088	5.31	that	1104	5.41
this	2001	5.35	or	1075	5.44
on	1976	5.36	are	986	5.52
is	1953	5.37	at	934	5.58
composers	1775	5.47	network	927	5.59
page	1755	5.48	be	894	5.62
identifiers	1628	5.55	use	783	5.75
that	1308	5.77	page	780	5.76
no	1253	5.82	lte	739	5.81
classical	1246	5.82	phones	706	5.86
works	1141	5.91	may	661	5.92
op	1127	5.92	it	651	5.94
composer	1103	5.94	was	648	5.94

Word *ICs* on the other hand, which in their calculation imply a normalization respective to the total token frequencies of each corpus, are directly comparable between corpora. For example, we see that the word *the* is equally unsurprising (low *IC*) in both corpora. Let us categorize the different unsurprising words which made it to the top 20 of both corpora as shown in Table 5.8.

Stop words: This small experiment highlights the fact that the most common words in language, including but not limited to determiners (e.g., *a, the*), conjunctions (e.g., *with, or*), and prepositions (e.g., *on, at, of*), are also the most frequently used tokens in a corpus, regardless of the domain. As a group, these common words are most often referred to as **stop words**. Stop words are in opposition to **content words** (e.g., nouns, verbs, adjectives).

Source-specific words: Certain tokens simply identify sources of information. For example, the tokens *Wikipedia* and *page* were specific to our earlier corpus building strategy, made entirely of Wikipedia pages. When building a corpus, there will generally be a number of tokens that appear on every page (e.g., copyright information, resource provider) and therefore end up on the list of high-frequency tokens. Another example would be a corpus of patents, for legal information search. In such corpus, chances are that among the top tokens would appear the words *invention, disclosed,* and *claims*, all being part of the patent description terminology.

Common verbs, auxiliaries, and pronouns: Auxiliary verbs (e.g., *may, can*) and common verbs (e.g., *be, have*) are likely to have high frequencies and may even be included on some lists of stop words. As much as they could appear to carry little valuable information, we should be wary of dispensing with them all together. For example, a higher occurrence of *was* over *is* might indicate that the domain is more relevant to the past (CLASSICALCOMPOSER) than the present (MOBILETEL). This example may seem simple, but it is designed to illustrate the point that we never know when and in what way certain tokens may become useful. We should therefore not assume, as a rule, that stop words and common verbs will prove to be unhelpful for all tasks.

Now, let us focus on the tokens which made it to the top of the lists but which are different from one corpus to the other. For our comparative setting of domain-specific corpora, those are the tokens of interest since they usually reveal the domain of the corpus. In CLASSICALCOMPOSER, the tokens *composers, classical, works,* and *composer* emerge, and in MOBILETEL, the tokens *mobile, phone, network,* and *phones* emerge. We call those **domain words** or **single-word terms**.

We see how a comparative frequency analysis could become a baseline algorithm for an application of **term extraction**, which aims at discovering domain terms in specialized corpora.

Let us continue and add yet another tool to our toolbox for quantitative corpus exploration. In the next section, we will investigate how to go about measuring the likelihood that certain words, or tokens, will be found together in text.

5.7 Mutual Information and Collocations

In corpus exploration, beyond discovering individual token frequencies, it can be interesting to also discover how and when certain tokens appear together. Groups of words that consistently appear together are called **collocations**. Collocations can reveal multi-word expressions or multi-word terms. The term **multi-word expression** is more encompassing than the term **multi-word term**, as the latter would refer to domain-related terms made of more than one word (e.g., *laser printer, mobile telecommunication network*), but the former would also include any expression in text, such as fixed expressions (e.g., *brake a leg*, meaning *good luck*) or verb-particle compounds (e.g., *moving on, lie down*). Although collocations can contain any number of words, we will limit our exploration to groups of two words.

Collocations would further reveal habitual combinations of words, which seem to be favored by native speakers for no other reason than just common usage. For example, do we say *rapid car* or *fast car*? Do we refer to yeast as being *fast rise* or *quick rise*? Because they are synonyms, *fast, quick,* and *rapid* are theoretically interchangeable in relation to *rise* or *car*. But corpus exploration would show that some combinations are more likely to occur than others. This is reminiscent of our earlier discussion in Sect. 5.4, when we observed that although *cell phone* and *cell telephone* are equally possible from a compositional point of view, their usages are quite different.

One fairly often used measure of collocation strength is called **Mutual Information (MI)** and is derived from words' joint probability. We earlier saw how to estimate a word's probability $\hat{P}(w)$ through its frequency (see Eq. 5.2). Similarly, the joint probability of two words w_1 and w_2 can be estimated by observing their joint frequency, and the Mutual Information of two words is defined by the following equation:

$$MI(w_1, w_2) = log_2(\frac{P(w_1, w_2)}{P(w_1) * P(w_2)})$$
$$= log_2(\frac{\hat{P}(w_1, w_2)}{\hat{P}(w_1) * \hat{P}(w_2)}) \qquad (5.3)$$

The quantity resulting from Eq. 5.3 is more accurately called **Point-wise Mutual Information (PMI)** since it only considers joint occurrences ($P(w_1, w_2)$). The more general Mutual Information formula also requires to find out the probability of two words not occurring together ($P(\neg w_1, \neg w_2)$).

Let us continue exploring our examples of *car* and *rise* and calculate the Mutual Information between all possible combinations with *fast, quick,* and *rapid* to determine if any combination will be put to the forefront. To perform these measures, we need to decide on the corpus on which we will calculate word and word pairs' frequencies.

Let us go for the largest there is, this time, and use the **Web-as-corpus**. Our access to this gigantic corpus will be rather indirect, possible through search engines, such as Google, Yahoo, or Bing. These search engines only provide us with **hit counts**, meaning the number of pages containing a word or expression. Still, hit counts can serve as an approximation of frequencies (see Exercise 5.1).

The second column of Table 5.9 shows Google hit counts for the words taken individually and in combination.[3] We need one last number to be able to estimate word and word pair probabilities, and that is the total numbers of words (or in this case Web pages) in the corpus. Again, unfortunately, we have no direct access to this number, and instead, we will use the Google hit counts for the common words *a*, *the*, or *of* as an approximation of the total number of pages on the Web, following the assumption that these common words would be present in all pages. The hit counts for these common words is given as the first line of Table 5.9.

Table 5.9 Collocation strength evaluation using Mutual Information based on hit counts

w_1 or (w_1, w_2)	Google hit counts	$\hat{P}(w_1)$ or $\hat{P}(w_1, w_2)$	$PMI(w_1, w_2)$
the, a, of	25,270,000,000	1	
car	3,410,000,000	0.1394	
fast	2,880,000,000	0.1140	
quick	2,040,000,000	0.0807	
rise	746,000,000	0.0295	
rapid	467,000,000	0.0185	
fast car	7,640,000	0.0003	**0.0196**
rapid car	351,000	0.000014	0.0056
quick car	428,000	0.0000017	0.0016
fast rise	404,000	0.0000016	0.0047
rapid rise	2,570,000	0.0001	**0.1864**
quick rise	348,000	0.0000013	0.0058

The results in the rightmost column of the table show that *rapid rise* has a higher *PMI* than its competitors, *fast rise* and *quick rise*. This means that *rapid rise* is a more likely collocation than either of the other two options. Likewise, the *PMI* of *fast car* is high in comparison with the alternatives *rapid car* and *quick car*. Collocations are interesting from the point of view of language acquisition, since while the appropriate form would be obvious to a native speaker, it is likely to appear completely arbitrary to a non-native speaker.

[3]Numbers were obtained by performing a Google search on the individual words and combinations, March 2015.

The Point-wise Mutual Information is not the only measure of collocation strength. Several other measures are commonly found in the NLP literature, and three of them are shown hereafter: **dice coefficient** $(Dice(w_1, w_2))$, χ^2-**test** $(\chi^2(w_1, w_2))$, and **log-likelihood ratio** $(LLR(w_1, w_2))$.

$$E(w_1, w_2) = \frac{f(w_1) * f(w_2)}{N}$$

$$Dice(w_1, w_2) = \frac{2 * f(w_1, w_2)}{f(w_1) + f(w_2)}$$

(5.4)

$$\chi^2(w_1, w_2) = \frac{f(w_1, w_2) - E(w_1, w_2)^2}{E(w_1, w_2)}$$

$$LLR(w_1, w_2) = 2 * \frac{log_2(f(w_1, w_2)^2)}{E(w_1, w_2)}$$

Notice that all of the measures above use the same basic information of individual word frequencies, $f(w_1)$ and $f(w_2)$, as well as the joint frequency $f(w_1, w_2)$. The first equation $E(w_1, w_2)$ is called the **expected value**, $E(w_1, w_2)$, and is used in both χ^2-test and log-likelihood ratio.

I leave experimentation with these new measures as an exercise for the reader (see Exercise 5.3), as we now continue toward a different kind of exploration of corpora: qualitative exploration. We will see that by observing words in their context, we will also learn about probable collocations.

5.8   Viewing Candidate Collocations through a Concordancer

Now that we have learned how to gather statistics about word occurrences and measure strengths of collocations, the time has come to dig a little deeper into the corpus itself and observe words in use.

A **concordancer** is a very helpful tool for exploring a corpus, used for viewing words, terms, and even semantic relations (as we will explore in Part IV of this book). A concordancer also has the benefit of being simple and easy to program. What exactly *is* a concordancer? It is a tool that allows for a combined view of the multiple occurrences of a particular term of interest in a corpus, with the term becoming the center of attention.

Table 5.10 shows the typical output of a concordancer, this one resulting from a search for the term *mobile phone* within the MOBILETEL corpus built in Sect. 5.6.1.

Table 5.10 Example of the output of a concordancer, showing *mobile phone* in MOBILETEL

```
study to access their NHS and mobile phone records. Participants are cont
ctive. Australia introduced a mobile phone recycling scheme.[63] Conflic
 provocation of subjects with mobile phone related symptoms". Bioelectro
h.[60] Environmental impact A mobile phone repair kiosk in Hong Kong This
s 15 and 24 participated in a mobile phone research study; 387 males, 557
 2013) A display of bars on a mobile phone screen A mobile phone signal (
ting that bundling iPhone and mobile phone service could be violating the
 to offer, free or subsidized mobile phone service in exchange for subscr
nes  ^ "Emirates offers first mobile phone service onboard A380 Aircraft"
n the high levels of societal mobile phone service penetration, it is a k
 are much more expensive than mobile phone services and provide slow data
f ring tones, games and other mobile phone services. Such services are us
ges, contacts and more. Basic mobile phone services to allow users to mak
arah (10 November 2009). "NFC mobile phone set to explode". connectedplan
"Are some people sensitive to mobile phone signals? Within participants d
.[26][27] This designation of mobile phone signals as "possibly carcinoge
? ????????? ^ "BBC News - Jam mobile phone signals in prisons, says inspe
e Sure Signal - boosting your mobile phone signal". Vodafone.ie. Retrieve
 User Identity Module Typical mobile phone SIM card GSM feature phones re
(May 2010) A roaming SIM is a mobile phone SIM card that operates on more
ient one-charger-fits-all new mobile phone solution."[34] The ITU publish
group to improve the CDMA2000 mobile phone standard for next generation a
pers Mobile viewComparison of mobile phone standards - Wikipedia, the fre
(August 2007) A comparison of mobile phone standards can be done in many
in each country Comparison of mobile phone standards Equipment: Cellular
```

As you can see, the concordancer has simply gathered all occurrences of the term of interest in the center of a fixed-size **context window**. A context window is a designation of how much information on either side of the term of interest is to be considered relevant for context. The limits of the window are defined by how far the context extends, in terms of numbers of characters, to the right and left of the term.

In Table 5.10, the context window was defined as spanning thirty characters to the left and right of the relevant term *mobile phone*. Keeping the context window to a consistent size, regardless of the boundaries of sentences, allows us to focus on the term in the center of the window and observe how other words vary around it. A concordancer is said to display a **KWIC**, or a **keyword in context**, and is an important tool for corpus exploration among translators, terminologists, and language teachers. By displaying words in their contextual surroundings, concordancers can also help reveal a word's possible collocations, as we touched on in the previous section.

So, how would we go about programming such a tool? Think back to our discussion of regular expressions in Chap. 3. A regular expression can be used to define the limits of context around a word, which is the first step in programming a concordancer.

Below is an example of a regular expression, to center the term *mobile phone* within a 30-character context window.

```
.{30} mobile phone .{30}
```

Remember that in regular expressions, '.' refers to any character, and the number in the curly brackets indicates the number of repetitions. So, the regular expression above represents any character ('.'), repeated thirty times (30), followed by a space, followed by the term *mobile phone*, and followed by another space and again by any character repeated thirty times.

Applying this regular expression to our MOBILETEL corpus yields the context window results shown in Table 5.10.

A closer look at Table 5.10 may lead to the observation that the words on the right of *mobile phone* have been sorted alphabetically. A concordancer typically allows for either a **right context sort** or a **left context sort**, to give us a better grasp of what tends to come before and after our term of interest. Sorting emphasizes repetition in the surrounding context, since the same words preceding or following end up grouped together. For example, in Table 5.10, sorting has highlighted the fact that *mobile phone services*, *mobile phone signals*, and *mobile phone standards* are all quite common and are likely to be three-word terms. *Mobile phone SIM card* could even be a four-word term, in the domain of mobile telecommunication.

The specifications for sorting are essential and must be included in the programming of a concordancer (see Exercise 5.4).

Table 5.11 shows the results of a left context sort which happens to be centered around the word *works*. To provide some variation on possible collocations, I have only included examples in the table of collocations that repeat at least three times. My motivation for investigating the word *works* stemmed from our quantitative exploration. If you look back to Table 5.8, which displays the most frequent units within the CLASSICALCOMPOSER corpus, you may see how this list can be a source of ideas for further exploration. Among all the words on the list, I was most curious about *works*, which seemed somehow out of place alongside other, seemingly much more fitting words, such as *composer* and *music*. However, our search using the concordancer has confirmed that *works* is indeed at the center of the classical music domain, and furthermore, that it has multiple collocations.

Table 5.11 Example of the output of a concordancer, searching for *works* in CLASSICALCOMPOSER

```
o the study of Rousseau's life and works Works by Jean-Jacques Rousseau at
 with notes on Steibelt's life and works"(diss.Eastman School of Music,1975
ter Park (1760{1813): the life and works of an unknown female composer, wit
oard sonatas, and numerous chamber works, including string quartets, piano
alia found that Schubert's chamber works dominated the field, with the Trou
masses and operas, several chamber works, and a vast quantity of miscellane
ificant number of vocal and choral works, particularly in the last few year
ondos and dances, cantatas, choral works, and airs. He died in Schwerin, ag
is often recognized for his choral works, such as Go Congregation Go! and S
ing project to record his complete works, led by Miklós Spányi?(de) on the
ical catalog of Michael's complete works using a single continuous range of
ed a 26-CD box set of the complete works for solo piano on the German recor
46, borrowed much from his earlier works, a method that was to re-occur thr
utilized by Rossini in his earlier works, and marks a transitional stage in
ivals and revisions of his earlier works. But then in 1772 came Antigona|an
edited and sometimes conducted his works. Lambert had already launched the
y foremost rank. He considered his works excellent as studies for practice,
upils { they continued copying his works. The St. Cecilia Mass (CPM 113) wa
y melodic style differentiates his works from those of his family. He compo
 of performances of his orchestral works can be found on 18th-century progr
ated by two large-scale orchestral works, although he continued to produce
and continuo in F major Orchestral works BR C1 \ Symphony in C major (F 63)
```

The concordancer points to what I would call *candidate* collocations, in the sense that their joint occurrence is highlighted but not their collocation strength yet, for which we need measures, such as *PMI*, presented earlier. For *chamber works* may be a candidate which turns out to have a strong collocation strength, telling us it might even be an important term within the classical music domain. But *his works* might be a candidate highlighted by the concordancer just because *his* is a common high-frequency word, and its connection to *works* is not necessarily any stronger than it is to any other word.

Notice that we have come full circle with this last example of *works*. First, using quantitative exploration, we discovered that it is a frequently recurring token in the CLASSICALCOMPOSER corpus. Then, using qualitative exploration, we observed its candidate collocations using a concordancer. Finally, we circled back to quantitative exploration, pointing out that we could measure the strength of these candidate collocations using *PMI* or other measures.

Quantitative and qualitative corpus explorations should be used in tandem. Each has its own value and contributes in its own way to our understanding of language.

5.9 In Summary

- A corpus can be characterized in terms of its domain, language level, purpose, medium, and genre.

- Many corpora are available online at various research center or university Web sites, as well as in large corpus repositories where we can search for those that correspond specifically to our needs.
- We can perform a simple and useful quantitative exploration of a corpus through the use of token frequency and Information Content.
- Not all surface forms for a particular entity are equally common, as observed through corpus frequency.
- Information Content expresses the level of surprise brought on by a particular surface form in a particular context.
- Performing search in a corpus assumes we have defined ahead of time what we are looking for. This is in contrast to being in discovery mode, where we instead explore a corpus with tools to help us get insight as to its content.
- One approach to building a domain-specific corpus is to take advantage of the existing system of categorization in Wikipedia and gather pages belonging to a certain category.
- Tokenizing may seem simple at first glance, but it can be approached in many ways. The choice of separators will have an impact on the resulting tokens.
- Mutual Information is a measure of collocation strength, commonly used in NLP.
- Other measures of collocation strength are the log-likelihood ratio, the dice coefficient, and the χ^2-test.
- Using a concordancer to explore a corpus is a good way to discover candidate collocations and also to study words behavior.
- A concordancer is the tool of choice for exploration of language in use and is widely used by terminologists, translators, and language teachers.

5.10 Further Reading

Web genre: The study of Web genre covers multiple dimensions of characterization of text which we covered in this chapter. For an early exploration on Web genre, with a categorization of various genres (e.g., concert review, product information, demographic data), see Crowston and Williams (1997). For a more recent collection of papers on the subject, see the book *Genres on the Web* (Mehler et al. 2010).

Corpora repositories:

- Linguistic Data Consortium (LDC) is available at https://www.ldc.upenn.edu/.
- At http://www-nlp.stanford.edu/links/statnlp.html, we find the list of resources gathered by The Stanford NLP group.
- The site http://corpora4learning.net/resources/materials.html proposes a list of corpora and corpus exploration tools.

Annotated corpora:

- Penn Treebank corpus, a series of part-of-speech annotated texts, is available at https://catalog.ldc.upenn.edu/LDC95T7 for a substantial amount.

- The SemCor corpus, available at https://web.eecs.umich.edu/~mihalcea/downloads. html, is a corpus semantically annotated with WordNet senses. SemCor is one of the resources made available on this site by researcher Rada Mihalcea, from University of Michigan, very active in the area of computational semantics.

Early general language corpora:

- Word frequency lists extracted from the Brown Corpus (Francis and Kucera 1982) can directly be downloaded from http://www.lextutor.ca/freq/lists_download/.
- The British National Corpus is available at http://www.natcorp.ox.ac.uk/index. xml and is free for research purposes.
- The American National Corpus (ANC) was the American counterpart to the BNC and originally also contained 10 million words. A newer version (second release) is available at LDC https://catalog.ldc.upenn.edu/LDC2005T35 for a small cost.

Eclectic list of corpora:

- Wikipedia dumps are available at http://dumps.wikimedia.org/. They are updated regularly.
- The Reuters-90 categories corpus (referenced as reuters21578) is available at http://kdd.ics.uci.edu/databases/ among many other corpora used for categorization tasks, not necessarily based on text data.
- The Gutemberg project is found at http://www.gutenberg.org/.
- Google Books n-grams are available at https://books.google.com/ngrams (follow the raw data download link), and the Google Web 1T n-grams is available at LDC https://catalog.ldc.upenn.edu/LDC2006T13.

Indexing tools: I highly recommend to readers interested in working with large corpora to become familiar with Apache Lucene (https://lucene.apache.org/), which is an extremely useful and freely available indexing tool. As we hope to work with larger portions or even the totality of Wikipedia in future chapters, Lucene can be used to efficiently index all its pages locally.

Collocations and term extraction: Early work on collocations using *PMI* is found in Church and Hanks (1990). Another pioneer work on collocation search is found in Smadja (1993). Various measures, such as dice coefficient, χ^2-test, and log-likelihood ratio, are largely used in research on term extraction. Term extraction is an area of study in itself aiming at discovering important terms within a domain-specific corpus. See Kageura and Umino (1996) for an early survey on term extraction and Drouin (2003) for term extraction using a corpus comparison approach. This research field having started in the years 1990s, it is valuable to go back to the early papers before exploring current methods, which will likely be sophisticated variations inspired from the earlier methods.

Google Books n-gram Viewer: Being a very useful corpus exploration tool, I encourage readers to explore the multiple search options it offers as explained at https:// books.google.com/ngrams/info.

Web-as-corpus: We do not have access to the full set of documents on the Web, and the closest is probably the resource called Common Crawl (http://commoncrawl. org/). I would suggest to wait until you are very familiar with NLP and are comfortable with large datasets before venturing into this extremely large dataset. For example, the ClueWeb12 Dataset (http://lemurproject.org/clueweb12/) is available for a medium cost and covers over 700 million Web page crawled. Then, if you simply wish to get a sense of word and collocation frequencies through hit counts, you can use commercial search engines, such as Google (http://google.com/) or Bing (http:// bing.com/).

Concordancer: If you are not writing your own concordancer, you can still explore some of the corpora mentioned in this chapter (e.g., Brown, BNC) through the use of an online concordancer available at http://www.lextutor.ca/conc/, as part of a set of tools for corpus analysis.

5.11 Exercises

Exercise 5.1 (**Word frequencies and hit counts**)

a. Go to the Google Books n-gram viewer, and experiment with a few alternate synonyms for different entities of your choice. Choose your entities (use URIs on DBpedia), find their various possible surface forms (using the predicate `dbo:WikiPageRedirects`, and then search for them within the n-gram viewer. Explore differences when using capitalization, flexible endings, and other variations the viewer allows to search for.

b. Are the synonyms *laptop computer* and *portable computer* used in equal proportion in Canada, the USA, England and Australia? Use the country restriction in the commercial Google search engine to find out.

c. Download the book *A-B-C of Gardening*, or any other book of your choice from the Gutemberg Project site. Write your own tokenizer using space and punctuations as separators. Tokenize the text, and perform a frequency and *IC* analysis on it. What kind of tokens do you find at the top of your list (most frequent)? Experiment using different separators for your tokenization. Do they change your results?

d. It was mentioned in Sect. 5.7 that word frequency can be approximated by a Web hit count. Discuss why the hit count is an approximation and not an exact word frequency.

e. Take a subset of 20 words found in exercise (c) through your frequency analysis. Choose words at different frequency ranks (e.g., 1, 2, 5, 10, 20, 50). Search for each word's hit count through a search engine and rank the hit counts by decreasing frequency. Compare the ranking obtained to the one you started with as calculated on your local corpus. Discuss.

Exercise 5.2 (Comparative study of corpora)

a. Build the two corpora for classical music composers (CLASSICALCOMPOSER) and mobile telecommunications (MOBILETEL) discussed in Sect. 5.6.1. Make sure to store the corpora locally as to limit querying the Wikipedia server for your downloads.

- Clean the corpora using open source boiler-plate removal software available in the programming language of your choice.
- Perform a frequency analysis on both corpora to obtain their respective lists of token frequencies.
- Write an algorithm to automatically gather a list of stop words from the two individual token frequency lists.
- Using your newly built list of stop words, filter the individual lists to remove the stop words from them. Do you find that more domain terms become part of the top 20 highest frequency words? Discuss.

b. Try building a new domain-specific corpus, for a domain totally unrelated to those we explored in this chapter. Examples of domains could be berries (Category:Berries) or cars (Category:List_of_car_brands). Perform frequency counts on your new corpus. Do your highest frequency tokens resemble those from CLASSICALCOMPOSER and MOBILETEL corpora? Are the results significantly different if you filter your results with your list of stop words previously built in exercise (a)?

c. Download the Reuters-90 corpus for a term extraction experiment. First, build a domain-specific corpus from the files in each category. Then, using the methods you have developed in (a) for removing stop words, extract the domain-specific terms for each category. Do they correspond to the domain-related words as suggested by category names, such as *oil*, *cocoa*, *corn*, and *lumber*?

Exercise 5.3 (Mutual Information)

a. Program the *PMI*, Eq. 5.3, and the other collocation measures: *dice*, χ^2, and *LLR*, Eq. 5.4. Use the raw frequencies in the second column in Table 5.9 to test your measures. Do the measures yield comparable results?

b. Be critical of the results in Table 5.9. Are we sure *rapid rise* has more collocation strength than the two others? (hint: rise is ambiguous). Suggest how to adapt the Web search to obtain hit counts that provide better estimates.

c. Using the CLASSICALCOMPOSER corpus, measure the strength of the possible collocations highlighted by the concordancer in Table 5.11 (e.g., *chamber works*, *orchestral works*, *life and works*, *his works*, *complete works*, and *earlier works*). Use the various measures you programmed in (a). Discuss your results.

Exercise 5.4 (Concordancer)

a. Write your own concordancer. Start by including a regular expression allowing to obtain a list of context windows surrounding a word of interest. Then, program the right context sort. Next, work on the more complicated task of sorting the left side of the context window. Hint: You will need to first tokenize the left context and then build a temporary list of strings containing the words in reverse order, so that you can sort on that list rather than the original string.

b. Start from the list of high-frequency tokens derived from the book you downloaded in Exercise 5.1 (c). Search for domain-specific words and use them as input for your concordancer. Do you see any candidate collocations emerge? If so, validate and compare their collocation strength using the various measures you programmed in Exercise 5.3.

Chapter 6
Words in Sequence

We saw in the previous chapter that certain words are more likely to be found in combination than others. For example, we established that *fast car* is a more likely combination than *rapid car*. This finding was based on the mutual attraction of the two words. In this chapter, our focus shifts to **word sequences** as we explore the predictability of certain words following others.

There is great interest in the predictability of word sequences in NLP. After all, text does not only involve words in isolation or randomly dispersed in corpora, but it involves sequences of words that, when strung together in a particular order, form sentences. Sentences are of course more than sequences, in that they must obey certain grammatical constraints and in doing so display a particular **syntactic structure**. We will study syntactic structures in Chap. 8, but for now, we will consider sentences in terms of sequences of words, not relying on grammar rules. Through **probabilistic language models**, we will be able to determine the likelihood of certain word sequences based on probabilities. Although these models have their limitations, by solely looking at words, they bring with them an element of simplicity and have the advantage of being **language independent**, meaning we can apply them to any language.

The hypothesis behind the use of language models is that sequences repeat within a language, enough that we can determine the word that is most likely to occur after a particular sequence of words. For example, various possibilities might spring to mind for a word to follow the sequence *he was late for....* Examples might be *work*, *school*, and *lunch*. The probabilities of these words completing the given sequence are most likely to be fairly high. The probability of certain other words, however, such as *apple*, finishing the same sequence would be close to zero. On the other hand, *apple* would be a good contestant for completing the sequence *I ate an...*, whereas the earlier words *work* and *school* fare much less well in this case.

In this chapter, we will discover just how useful the predictability of words can be. After presenting the idea itself, and the equations associated with probabilistic language models, we will demonstrate the usefulness of this predictability,

© Springer International Publishing Switzerland 2016
C. Barrière, *Natural Language Understanding in a Semantic Web Context*,
DOI 10.1007/978-3-319-41337-2_6

in conjunction with the Edit Distance measure (see Chap. 4), in the context of spelling correction.

6.1 Introduction to Language Modeling

Let us define a sequence S as being made up of n words, themselves referred to as w_1, w_2, w_3, all the way to w_n. In a **language model**, we are interested in the probability of certain words occurring one after the other, in a particular order. One way of building a model is to assume that we will go through the entire sequence, from the first word to the last. This means that the probability of a word occurring in position i (the probability of w_i) will depend on the probability of the entire sequence up to the word occurring right before it, at position $i - 1$, that is $w_1..w_{i-1}$. The equations below show this process, starting from a sequence of two words, building to three, four, and all the way to n words.

$$P(w_1, w_2) = P(w_2|w_1) * P(w_1)$$
$$P(w_1, w_2, w_3) = P(w_3|w1, w2) * P(w2|w1) * P(w1)$$
$$P(w_1, w_2, w_3, w_4) = P(w_4|w_1, w_2, w_3) * P(w_3|w1, w2) * P(w2|w1) * P(w1)$$

$$\dots$$

$$P(w_1, w_2, ...w_n) = \prod_i P(w_i|w_1, ..., w_{i-1}) \tag{6.1}$$

As stated earlier, these equations assume that a word's probability is conditional on the entirety of the sequence up to that point. Is this really necessary though? Perhaps, for practicality's sake, we could calculate our probability more efficiently.

Returning to our earlier example *he was late for...*, the full sentence might have been *Every day, John sets his alarm for 8:00am, but he has a hard time waking up, and as usual this morning he was late for...* Does having this additional information make predicting the last word any easier? It could be said to benefit us by eliminating certain possibilities such as *lunch*, but this benefit is slight, and the fact is that taking this whole sentence into account would be unrealistic from a computational point of view.

Let us try to understand why. One may think that, containing a total of 25 words, our example sentence is unusually long. Not quite so, since sentences are often this long or longer. Assuming a vocabulary V of English words containing 100,000 words ($|V| = 100,000$), the number of possible sequences of 25 words would be a staggering $100,000^{25}$. This would be an impossibly large number for a computational model to handle.

For this reason, conditioning the probability of w_i on all preceding words, as is done in Eq. 6.1, is unrealistic. A better approach is to limit the size of the conditioning sequence. In this vein, researchers often work with *bigram*, *trigram*, or *4-gram* models, which use one, two, and three previous words, respectively, for predicting an upcoming word. Reducing too far can result in the loss of information, however, as is shown below. Notice what happens when we move from a 5-gram to a unigram (no previous word) model on our example.

5-gram → *he was late for w_i*
4-gram → *was late for w_i*
3-gram → *late for w_i*
2-gram → *for w_i*
1-gram → *w_i*

In general, models like these are called *n-gram models*, where *n* varies and we use the synonyms *unigrams*, *bigrams*, and *trigrams* to indicate 1-gram, 2-grams, and 3-grams, respectively. In our discussion and model presentation, the number before *gram* refers to the number of previous words in the sequence being considered plus the word that is being predicted. The numbering might be used differently by other authors, so it is worth noting.

A **unigram model** corresponds to the probability of a word w_i, $\hat{P}(w_i)$, as we estimated in the previous chapter through its corpus frequency ($freq(w_i)$), divided by the total number of words in the corpus (N). A **bigram model** is likely to be highly ambiguous, since the first word (*for*, in our example) could lead to many different possibilities. With such little context, the possibilities for sequences are much more open ended. A **trigram model** already provides significantly more context, and we start to see a significant reduction in the set of possible words to follow.

Returning now to our estimation of the probability of a sequence, Eq. 6.2 represents a trigram model, since it considers two previous words for predicting the third.

$$P(w_1, w_2, ...w_n) = \prod_{i=1}^{n} P(w_i | w_{i-1}, w_{i-2}) \tag{6.2}$$

This trigram model, as opposed to a full sentence model (Eq. 6.1), largely reduces the number of possibilities to calculate. Assuming our earlier vocabulary V of 100,000 words, we would now have to keep track of $100,000^3$ possibilities. Although this is still a very large number, it is orders of magnitude smaller than our previous $100,000^{25}$. Throughout this chapter, we will see that most of these theoretically possible sequences do not in fact exist.

6.2 Estimating Sequence Probabilities

In order to calculate a sequence's probability, we have to access the n-gram estimations for its subsequences. We will go through the process of calculating these estimations ourselves in the next section, but for now, let us use Google Books n-gram viewer, which we introduced in the previous chapter (Sect. 5.3).

Assume our example sentence is *the student is late for school*. Let us consult the Google Books n-grams to estimate the probability of this sequence, using both a bigram and a trigram model. In Table 6.1, the leftmost column shows the actual bigram (e.g., *the student*), the second column shows the bigram's coverage percentage provided by the viewer.[1] The third and fourth columns show the conditioning unigram (e.g., *the*) and its coverage percentage, and the final column shows the results of the conditional probability, $P(w_i|w_{i-1})$, as obtained from $\frac{P(w_{i-1},w_i)}{P(w_{i-1})}$ (e.g., $\frac{0.001643}{4.63}$ for $P(student|the)$).

Table 6.1 Subsequences in a bigram model for *the student is late for school*

Bigram w_{i-1}, w_i	Bigram prob $P(w_{i-1}, w_i)*100$	Unigram w_{i-1}	Unigram prob $P(w_{i-1})*100$	Conditional prob $P(w_i|w_{i-1})$
the student	0.001643	the	4.63	$P(student|the) =$ 0.0003548
student is	0.0001737	student	0.008573	$P(is|student) =$ 0.020261
is late	0.0000543	is	0.8236	$P(late|is) =$ 0.00000659
late for	0.000250	late	0.01360	$P(for|late) =$ 0.01838
for school	0.0002399	for	0.6541	$P(school|for) =$ 0.0003667

Table 6.2 contains the same information as Table 6.1, for a trigram model.

Table 6.2 Subsequences in a trigram model for *the student is late for school*

Trigram w_{i-2}, w_{i-1}, w_i	Trigram prob $P(w_{i-2}, w_{i-1}, w_i)*100$	Bigram w_{i-1}, w_i	Bigram prob $P(w_{i-1}, w_i)*100$	Conditional prob $P(w_i|w_{i-1}, w_{i-2})$
the student is	0.00007346	the student	0.001643	$P(is|the, student)$ = 0.04471
student is late	0.0000001253	student is	0.0001737	$P(late|student, is)$ = 0.000721
is late for	0.000003210	is late	0.0000543	$P(for|is, late)$ = 0.05911
late for school	0.000007316	late for	0.000250	$P(school|late, for)$ = 0.02926

---

[1]Remember that the Google Books n-gram viewer does not give raw frequencies for words, but rather percentages of the total number of either unigram, bigram, or trigram, depending on which applies.

Given the results of either model, the next step is to multiply the conditional probabilities in the final column to obtain the sequence probabilities, as shown in Eq. 6.3.

$$
\begin{aligned}
P_{bigram}(w_1, w_2, ...w_n) &= P(the) * P(student|the) * P(is|student) * P(late|is) \\
&\quad * P(school|for) \\
&= 0.0463 * 0.0003548 * 0.020261 * 0.00000659 * 0.01838 \\
&\quad * 0.0003667 \\
&= 1.479E - 017 \\
P_{trigram}(w_1, w_2, ...w_n) &= P(the) * P(student|the) * P(is|the, student) \\
&\quad * P(late|student, is) * P(for|is, late) * P(school|late, for) \\
&= 0.0463 * 0.0003548 * 0.04471 * 0.000721 * 0.05911 \\
&\quad * 0.02926 \\
&= 9.158E - 013 \quad\quad\quad\quad\quad\quad\quad\quad\quad (6.3)
\end{aligned}
$$

What does this tell us? Is the bigram model a good model for sequence probability estimation? Is the trigram model better? Well, absolute values are often not that meaningful in and of themselves, but they become much more informative when placed in a comparative setting. For example, we should test our bigram and trigram models by comparing their probability estimates of our sequence *the student is late for school* to their probability estimates of a sequence such as *the student school for late is*, which includes the same words in a random order. The **better model**, meaning the model with more accurate **predicting capability**, should provide greater differentiation between the random sequence and the actual sequence (see Exercise 6.1).

One thing the absolute values of Tables 6.1 and 6.2 *do* show is how small the sequence probabilities become when we start multiplying small numbers by other small numbers. It follows then, that the longer the sequence, the smaller the probability. This can be problematic, likely leading to **computer underflow**. Computer underflow occurs when a number that is being manipulated by a computer becomes so small that it is beyond the level of precision that the program allows, and thus is considered as zero. To counter this problem, we can opt to work in a different mathematical space, the **log-space** instead of the linear space. In log-space, a number is replaced by its logarithm. For example, in log-space using a base 10, the very small number 0.0000001 can be replaced by its $log_{10}(0.00000001) = -8.0$, and a slightly larger but still very small number 0.00000005 can be replaced by its $log_{10}(0.00000005) = -7.3$. The resulting numbers (-8.0 and -7.3) will be easier for the computer program to manipulate.

The reason we can perform such transformation with no impact on our sequence probability result analysis is that in probability estimation, as we mentioned before, we are interested in relative probabilities. We analyze various sequence probabilities by comparing their values and not by looking at their absolute values. In that sense, the numbers in the log-space (-8.0 versus -7.3) keep the same relation to each other (the second one being larger than the first one) as in the linear space (0.00000001 versus 0.00000005).

For our earlier trigram model, for example, we would modify the earlier Eq. 6.2 to work with the logarithm of the sequence probability, as shown in Eq. 6.4 (line 2). Then, we can perform a further mathematical transformation, as shown in the third line of Eq. 6.4, changing the log of the product ($\log \prod_{i=1}^{n}$) of individual probabilities into the sum of the logarithms ($\sum_{i=1}^{n} \log$) of the individual probabilities.

$$P(w_1, w_2, ...w_n) = \prod_{i=1}^{n} P(w_i|w_{i-1}, w_{i-2})$$

$$log(P(w_1, w_2, ...w_n)) = \log \prod_{i=1}^{n} P(w_i|w_{i-1}, w_{i-2}) \qquad (6.4)$$

$$= \sum_{i=1}^{n} \log P(w_i|w_{i-1}, w_{i-2})$$

Working in this log-space would lead to the results, shown in Eq. 6.5 below, for the bigram and trigram model probability estimation of the sentence *the student is late for school*. Again, these numbers do not carry much meaning in isolation. To get a better sense for them, they should be compared to the probability of either another sentence or the same set of words in a random order.

$$
\begin{aligned}
log(P_{bigram}(w_1, w_2, ...w_n)) &= log(P(the)) + log(P(student|the)) \\
&+ log(P(is|student)) + log(P(late|is)) \\
&+ log(P(school|late)) \\
&= (-1.33) + (-3.45) + (-1.69) + (-5.18) \\
&+ (-1.74) + (-3.43) \\
&= -16.83 \\
log(P_{trigram}(w_1, w_2, ...w_n)) &= log(P(the)) + log(P(student|the)) \\
&+ log(P(is|the, student)) + log(P(late|student, is)) \\
&+ log(P(for|is, late)) + log(P(school|late, for)) \\
&= (-1.33) + (-3.45) + (-1.35) + (-3.14) \\
&+ (-1.23) + (-1.53) \\
&= -12.04 \qquad (6.5)
\end{aligned}
$$

Let us now move on to experiment with what we have learned and also explore how we can obtain bigram and trigram estimations from our own data, rather than relying on those provided by the Google Books n-gram viewer.

6.3 Gathering N-Gram Probabilities from Corpora

At this point, we will begin to explore how we can obtain our own n-gram estimates, using our own corpus, to later build a probabilistic sequence model relying on those estimates. First, we must create a corpus by gathering a collection of texts. Second, we must tokenize the corpus and go through it, gathering the frequency of occurrence of all combinations of two or three consecutive tokens, so as to have bigram or trigram estimates. As we analyze our resulting estimates, we will notice various issues which will be discussed at the end of the section.

6.3.1 Building a Domain-Independent Corpus

In Chap. 5 (see Sect. 5.6), we built two domain-specific corpora: one on classical music composers and the other on mobile telecommunications. We did this for the purposes of comparing their word frequencies. This time around, we will assume that we do not have a particular domain in mind, but instead wish to cover various domains within a single **domain-independent corpus**. One approach to building such a corpus is to return to Wikipedia, but gather pages randomly rather than focusing on certain ones that relate to a particular category.

Building a domain-independent corpus is in many ways simpler than building a domain-specific one. This is because it is enough to blindly take the first N pages from the vast archives of Wikipedia or decide to go through the archives selecting every X page until we have gathered the desired number of pages. Having said that, since we will require a large number of pages here, we should not attempt to perform a URL transfer for each page as we did for our earlier domain-specific corpora, which were very small. We should instead use the Wikipedia article large XML dump file and extract the pages directly from it.[2]

For the n-gram modeling results presented in the next section, we will use a corpus of 10,000 randomly selected Wikipedia pages, totaling 125 MB. We will call this CORPUSR. Note that all the numbers that will be presented, as results of statistical analysis of the corpus, will be drawn from that one version of CORPUSR. The numbers you would obtain on your own version of CORPUSR would certainly be different since your program's random selection of 10,000 pages would lead to different pages than mine.

---

[2]All dumps are available at https://dumps.wikimedia.org/, and various software packages are available in different programming languages to parse through the large files. The English version of Wikipedia used at the time of this writing is *enwiki-20150515-pages-articles.xml* and contains all English Wikipedia pages.

6.3.2 Calculating N-Gram Probabilities

The algorithm for gathering n-gram frequencies is very similar to the algorithm we used in the previous chapter (see Sect. 5.6.3) for calculating token frequencies. That earlier algorithm simply needs to be extended, from unigrams (tokens) to bigrams, trigrams, and so on, as shown in Algorithm 4.

\\ *1. Determine the size of n-gram to gather;*
Ngram Size = 3;
\\ *2. Initialize a table to contain n-gram counts*
Initialise *TableNgramFreq*;
\\ *3. Tokenize the text.*
Tokenize the text to obtain a set of tokens;
Set *TotalNb* to the total number of tokens in the text;
\\ *4. Go through the text to capture the occurrences of all the different n-grams.*
for *tokenPosition = 1 to TotalNb-NgramSize* **do**
    \\ *4.1. Combine groups of N tokens into a n-gram, separated by spaces*
    for *i = 0 to NgramSize-1* **do**
        ngram += token at position(tokenPosition + i) + " ";
    end
    \\ *4.2. Update the n-gram frequency count*
    if *TableNgramFreq contains n-gram* **then**
        Add 1 to its count in *TableNgramFreq*;
    end
    else
        Insert new ngram in *TableNgramFreq* and set its count to 1;
    end
end

Algorithm 4: Gathering n-gram frequencies from a corpus.

Table 6.3 shows the total numbers of observed unigrams, bigrams, trigrams, and 4-grams for CORPUSR, resulting from applying Algorithm 4 on it to gather the various n-grams.

Table 6.3 Number of n-grams, per size, in CORPUSR

n-gram size	Number of different n-grams
unigram	295,062
bigrams	4,158,144
trigrams	9,943,984
4-grams	12,844,945

The total number of tokens in CORPUSR is just over 16.5 million (16,594,400). Meanwhile, the total number of *different* tokens is indicated in Table 6.3 by the number of unigrams (295,062). This seems like a large number, doesn't it? Indeed, it is, but it is not surprising. We should, however, acknowledge that this total includes many tokens other than words we would normally find in a dictionary (e.g., numbers, serial numbers, misspellings, proper names, and abbreviations). Also, notice that the numbers of observed n-grams in Table 6.3 are much smaller than the maximum possible numbers, based on a vocabulary size of 295,062. For example, the total number of possible trigrams would be $295,062^3$, which far exceeds the 9.9 million we observed.

Now, let us further look at individual n-gram estimates resulting from applying Algorithm 4 on CORPUSR for the particular example sentence below in order to highlight both the interesting facts that emerge and the potential problems of these models.

He walked on the beach for a long time.

Let us start with the unigram (1-gram) frequencies calculated on CORPUSR which are part of our example sentence above. Table 6.4 shows each unigram (column 1) with its raw frequency (column 2) and its probability (column 3) which results from dividing its raw frequency by the total number of tokens (16,594,400) found in CORPUSR.

Looking at the numbers, we can make similar observations to those we made in Chap. 5. Common words such as determiners (e.g., *a, the*) are the most frequent, followed closely by prepositions (e.g., *on, for*) and commonly used content words (e.g., *long, time*).

I have presented both the raw frequencies and probabilities in Table 6.4 to reinforce the previously highlighted fact that probabilities are very small numbers. The next tables will only contain frequencies, which are sufficient for our discussion.

Table 6.4 Unigrams from CORPUSR for sentence *He walked on the beach for a long time*

Unigram w_i	Raw frequency $freq(w_i)$	Probability $P(w_i)$
he	51,342	0.00309
walked	147	0.00000885
on	105,593	0.00636
the	1,179,406	0.0711
beach	702	0.0000523
for	137,183	0.00827
a	343,659	0.0207
long	5,853	0.000353
time	19,056	0.00115

Let us now move from unigrams to bigrams. Consider the data in Table 6.5. What do you notice? Combinations of stop words, such as *on the* are fairly frequent, but other combinations, such as *beach for*, show a dramatic drop in frequency.

Table 6.5 Bigrams from CORPUSR for sentence *He walked on the beach for a long time*

Bigram w_{i-1}, w_i	Frequency $freq(w_{i-1}, w_i)$	Reversed bigram w_i, w_{i-1}	Frequency $freq(w_i, w_{i-1})$
he walked	12	walked he	0
walked on	14	on walked	0
on the	33,392	the on	170
the beach	188	beach the	15
beach for	2	for beach	1
for a	8,097	a for	145
a long	1,060	long a	32
long time	182	time long	3

We earlier discussed how absolute frequencies or probabilities in sequence modeling are difficult to interpret, and that we require a comparative setting for interpreting results. The third and fourth columns of Table 6.5 are included for a comparative setting, showing frequencies of the reversed bigrams pertaining to our example sentence. Notice how different the probabilities would have been if we had searched for bigrams on the same sentence written in reverse.

Moving on, let us look at trigrams (data shown in Table 6.6). When we consider both these data and our previous data for bigrams together, we can observe that there must be many possibilities for words that follow certain common combinations such as *on the*, since as a bigram its frequency was 33,392, but the more specific trigram *on the beach* has a frequency of only 30. We can assume that all the other 33,362 occurrences of *on the* in CORPUSR lead to a quite varied list of words, each one with a small probability. I am pointing this out to illustrate how even trigram models, which in our early investigation seemed to have a good predicting capability, should best be characterized as having a variable predicting capability dependent on the actual words. For example, *late for* has a much higher predicting capability than *on the*.

Also, notice that a search for trigrams on the sentence in reverse leads to an empty table, as shown by the zeros in the second column.

Table 6.6 Trigrams from CORPUSR for sentence *He walked on the beach for a long time*

Trigram w_{i-2}, w_{i-1}, w_i	Frequency $freq(w_{i-2}, w_{i-1}, w_i)$	Reverse trigram w_i, w_{i-1}, w_{i-2}	Frequency $freq(w_i, w_{i-1}, w_{i-2})$
he walked on	1	on walked he	0
walked on the	9	the on walked	0
on the beach	30	beach the on	0
the beach for	1	for beach the	0
beach for a	1	a for beach	0
for a long	142	long a for	0
a long time	143	time long a	0

Finally, Table 6.7 presents data for the 4-gram model on our example sentence. Here, even sequences we may have thought would be fairly common, such as *he walked on the*, do not occur in our corpus even once. This is evidence of *sparse data estimation*, one of four common problems that arise in language modeling, as we will discuss in the next section.

Now that we have learned how to gather n-gram frequencies from a corpus and have looked a bit at various 1-gram to 4-gram results, let us summarize the issues which could impact our further use of these n-gram estimates in probabilistic sequence modeling.

Table 6.7 4-grams from CORPUSR for sentence *He walked on the beach for a long time*

4-gram $w_{i-3}, w_{i-2}, w_{i-1}, w_i$	Frequency $freq(w_{i-3}, w_{i-2}, w_{i-1}, w_i)$
he walked on the	0
walked on the beach	0
on the beach for	0
the beach for a	1
beach for a long	0
for a long time	103

6.3.3   Issues in N-Gram Estimation

Probabilistic sequence modeling is widely used in NLP, thanks to its strong predictive power. This power was illustrated in the previous section, when we observed the drastic difference between n-gram corpus frequencies for bigrams and trigrams in the proper order and the same sequence in reverse. Like any other method, however, probabilistic sequence modeling has its benefits and drawbacks.

We will now explore four of these potential drawbacks: out-of-vocabulary tokens, sparse data estimation, corpus influence, and lack of modeling power for long-distance dependencies.

Out-of-vocabulary words: In general, word frequency distributions are **long-tail distributions** meaning that there are only a few frequent words, and a very large number (the long tail) of **hapax** (words with a single occurrence), that number often accounting for up to 50 % of possible word occurrences.

Let us see whether our current CORPUSR follows the same kind of distribution. In Table 6.3, we saw that there are 295,062 possible unigrams in CORPUSR. For the purposes of this discussion, I went ahead and removed all the unigrams that occurred only once, and the number of remaining unigrams dropped to 148,408. This tells us that, as would be predicted by the long-tail distribution, almost *half* of the words encountered in our corpus occur only once. These hapax can take many forms. They could be rare words, names of places, foreign words borrowed from another language, or even misspelled words. Below is a sample of hapax taken from CORPUSR.

applewood, calnexin, amiri, asunder, genschers, cenomani, massenpunktes, oomycete, kinzua, biconditionals, amini, lavolta, klaatu, folland

We can extrapolate from this and conceive of how, given that so many words are rare enough to occur only once in 10,000 pages, a different corpus we intend to analyze is also likely to contain at least one word that is not found in the original corpus used to build the probabilistic model. Remember that we build the model using a corpus, but that corpus does not include the sentence we intend to analyze. The equations described earlier in Sect. 6.1 will fall short for words that were not part of the corpus used to build the model, since their frequencies, and therefore their probabilities, will be zero.

The words we are talking about, those that are unobserved in the original corpus, are known as **out-of-vocabulary** words, or **OOV**'s. Encountering OOV's is related to the more general sparse data problem, discussed next.

Sparse data estimation: In Table 6.3, we saw that the number of trigrams in CORPUSR is close to 9.9 million, and the vocabulary consists of 295,062 tokens. We also discussed the fact that if we were to observe all combinations of three tokens, we would end up with the much greater total of $295,062^3$. At only 10,000 pages, CORPUSR could be considered relatively small for building a language model. That said, even in the case of an extremely large corpus, it is unlikely that we will obtain probabilities for all possible trigrams, or even bigrams.

To convince ourselves, let us return to the Google Books viewer to demonstrate this phenomenon. Despite the fact that an extremely large corpus has been indexed in this case (all of the Google books), it still does not contain all possible trigrams. If we try searching a selection of trigram variations inspired from our sequence *the student is late for school*, we will see that certain simple variations are not present, as shown in Table 6.8.

Table 6.8 Google n-gram viewer results, highlighting sparse data problem

n-gram	Google n-gram relative frequency
student is late	0.0000000825
student is tall	N/A
student is never	0.0000002292
student is writing	0.0000003483
student is funny	N/A

One problem with sparse data is that the nature of the missing information cannot be determined. As we have just seen, legitimate data of plausible sequences will be missing, but so will nonsensical, arbitrary sequences such as *wall horse* or *cat schoolbag*. Although these two kinds of missing data are missing for entirely different reasons, they both fall under the category of missing data, and as such become lumped together.

Missing data are also problematic from the point of view of probability estimation, since an n-gram that is not in the corpus used to build the model will show a probability of zero, which will immediately set the probability of the entire sequence at zero. This is due to the mathematical fact that anything multiplied by zero equals zero. Since our probability calculations consist of chains of multiplied numbers, if one of those numbers is zero, the final product will be zero as well.

Probabilities of zero will also cause a problem when working in the log-space (see Sect. 6.1), since the log of 0 does not exist. One possible approach to counter this problem, unavoidable in virtually all language modeling, relies on the idea of smoothing. In **smoothing**, we modify the probability estimates in order to redistribute some of the **probability mass** to unobserved data (OOV's). In a technique called **Add-1 smoothing** (also known as **Laplace smoothing**), a count of 1 is added to all possible n-grams, both observed and unobserved. It is important to remember that in doing this, the total number of n-grams will increase by the vocabulary size $|V|$, since all $|V|$ word counts will be increased by one. The new probability of a word, when smoothed using Laplace smoothing, is given in Eq. 6.6.

$$P_{add-1}(w_i|w_{i-1}) = \frac{freq(w_{i-1}, w_i) + 1}{freq(w_{i-1}) + |V|} \tag{6.6}$$

If the vocabulary is quite large, you can imagine that this approach would lead to significant changes in the probabilities, to the point of altering too much the original probabilities. This is not desirable, since the results become less and less representative of the true picture of probabilities. For this reason, researchers have suggested redistributing a smaller proportion of the probability mass, instead adding a count of δ to all n-grams, and thus augmenting the total number of n-grams by the smaller value of $\delta * |V|$. This δ can be seen as a **smoothing redistribution parameter** to be adjusted.

Choice of corpus: I cannot emphasize enough the fact that probabilistic models, as well as the information theory models presented in the last chapter, are corpus dependent. The choice of corpus inevitably has an influence on the resulting model.

A first approach to countering this corpus dependency is to use a very large amount of data. By building a model on a corpus that is very large, we have a better chance of accounting for all domains, genres, language levels, and so on. Another approach is to acknowledge the problem and work with it, rather than trying to overcome it. That is, instead of trying to build a large, neutral, all-encompassing corpus, we can build a corpus that is tailored to be specifically representative of our pending task. Remember that building a model is not an end in itself, but a means to an end. For example, if we require predictive language models to analyze medical texts, certainly the best idea is to build a large medical corpus to learn a model on it.

In our case, we used *he walked on the beach for a long time* as our test example (see Sect. 6.3.2). Thinking critically, one could posit that using a random selection of Wikipedia pages was not the best choice for building our model in the purpose of analyzing such sentence. Perhaps using tourism books or blogs would have been more appropriate. This may be, but it is difficult to decide on the best corpus based on a single sentence. These decisions are usually made at the application stage and not on a per sentence basis.

Long-distance dependencies: The last drawback to probabilistic sequence models that we will discuss is the fact that they do not capture long-distance dependencies, meaning dependencies between words that do not appear near each other in a sentence. I will illustrate this with an example. Consider the following four sentences:

Sam walked on the beach.
Sam walked on SandBanks beach.
Sam walked on this beautiful beach.
Sam walked with his dog on this beautiful beach.

The relationship between the words *walked* and *beach* is the same in all of these sentences. Regardless of which beach Sam walked on, or with whom, and regardless of how beautiful it was, the beach remains the location where the walking happened. The sentences all express the same dependency between *beach* and *walked*. However, as you can see, the word *beach* in the example sentences gets progressively farther away from the word *walked*.

As much as n-gram models capture sequences of words, they do not account for any other type of dependency than a sequential dependency. But sentences, constructed using grammatical rules (see Chap. 8), allow the expression of syntactic dependencies, such as subject, object, modifier, and these do not necessarily correspond to a sequential dependency, as we illustrated above. In our case, *beach* is a locative modifier for *walked*, one among the many possible grammatical dependencies which are brought forward by dependency grammars, as we will explore in Chap. 12.

At this point, it is time to move on to spelling correction, an application that makes use of the predictive power of probabilistic sequence models.

6.4 Application: Spelling Correction

In this section, we will look at one possible application of probabilistic sequence models, **spelling correction**, in which we try to correct a surface form containing an orthographic error (e.g., *choroegraphy*) to a proper surface form (e.g., *choreography*).

Think back to our comparison of the Levenshtein Distance and Soundex algorithms in Chap. 4 and the related discussion of finding close matches for misspelled words. In that earlier experiment, we tried to match erroneous surface forms (e.g., *Chardenay, Chardenai, Chardenet*) to a correct surface form (e.g., *Chardonnay*), associated with a particular entity (e.g., dbr:Chardonnay).

When working with long surface forms (e.g., *Hirshorn Museum*), even if two errors occur (e.g., *Hirshirn Muuseum*), the correct entity will definitely be the closest one in surface form, as estimated through Levenshtein Distance.

However, shorter surface forms can be problematic in this regard. For example, the misspelled word *raie* is equally close to *rate, rage, rare, raid, rail*, and more. It is in this kind of a situation that we turn to our sequence modeling approach. The model can help choose the best fit from a list of candidates, based on the probabilities of sequences, as conditioned by the previous words.

Table 6.9 shows examples of bigram estimates taken from CORPUSR, which we built earlier. To show interesting bigram examples, I have intentionally excluded bigrams with common preceding words such as *on* and *the*. Even a bigram model can help in deciding among a list of word candidates, for example, by choosing the more probable *rail* over *rate* when the preceding word is *commuter*, but choosing *rate* over *rail* when the preceding word is *growth*.

Let us work through a pair of examples from start to finish. First, returning to our example sequence *he walked on the beach for a long time*, let us assume the word *beach* has been misspelled as *beich*. We will then compare two existing words, *bench* and *beach*, both of which are one letter away from *beich*, meaning they would

Table 6.9 Examples of CORPUSR bigrams for candidate corrections for misspelled *raie*

Word	Bigram examples
rate	growth rate (140), fertility rate (120), birth rate (116), unemployment rate (111), mortality rate (111), exchange rate (102)
rage	single rage (3), jealous rage (3), drunken rage (2), namely rage (2)
rare	very rare (83), extremely rare (42), relatively rare (29)
raid	air raid (25), bombing raid (7), gunmen raid (5), police raid (4)
rail	commuter rail (65), light rail (56), british rail (44), national rail (18), passenger rail (14)

be equally possible from an Edit Distance point of view. Next, let us assume the sentence *He lost track of time.* follows the first sentence, and that *lost* has been misspelled as *lsst*. In this case, our Levenshtein algorithm would provide multiple candidates, among which we would find these three: *list, last,* and *lost*. With this, the two sentences for which we will calculate alternative sequence probabilities are presented below.

He walked on the (bench, beach) for a long time.
He (last, list, lost) track of time.

To estimate the probability of each sentence, we will use the n-gram models we built earlier on CORPUSR. In addition to the model, we will need a smoothing approach to address sparse data estimations, since we cannot guarantee that our model contains all the bigrams and trigrams found in the sentences above. Let us experiment using the Laplace smoothing we introduced in Sect. 6.3.3.

Earlier, we discussed the fact that assuming an extra count of 1 for all unseen n-grams can have a disruptive effect on the estimates, especially in small corpora. Given that CORPUSR is a small corpus, we will therefore set that count to 0.001 to all unseen n-grams, rather than 1. I have chosen this number arbitrarily for learning purposes, but I could just as easily have chosen another value. I encourage the reader to experiment with this process using alternative numbers. The chosen count 0.001 is included in Eq. 6.7, showing the smoothed probability estimation equation.

$$P_{add-1}(w_i|w_{i-1}) = \frac{freq(w_{i-1}, w_i) + 0.001}{freq(w_{i-1}) + 0.001|V|} \tag{6.7}$$

Let us now slightly increase the complexity of our modeling strategy, by using an **interpolation model**. We have not yet discussed this idea in this chapter, but as it is commonly used in language modeling, it is worth introducing here.

An interpolation model is a way to combine the estimates from the individual unigram, bigram, and trigram models in order to obtain an overall sequence probability. A simple interpolation model linearly combines the individual models, by summing their weighted results. Each model is assigned a weight ensuring that the sum of the weights is equal to 1.

Equation 6.8 below is the general equation for the linear combination, with weights of $\lambda_{trigram}$, λ_{bigram}, and $\lambda_{unigram}$ assigned to the trigram, bigram, and unigram models, respectively.

$$\log(P(w_1, w_2, ...w_n)) = \lambda_{trigram} \sum_{i=1}^{n} \log P(w_i|(w_{i-1}, w_{i-2})) +$$

$$\lambda_{bigram} \sum_{i=1}^{n} \log P(w_i|w_{i-1}) + \tag{6.8}$$

$$\lambda_{unigram} \sum_{i=1}^{n} \log P(w_i)$$

In Eq. 6.9, we have the same linear combination model, this time with weights set to 0.7 for the trigram model, 0.25 for the bigram model, and 0.05 for the unigram model. These weights have been chosen to reflect the fact that the degree of importance afforded to the models decreases along with their complexity (e.g., the more complex trigram model is assigned a higher weighting than the simpler unigram model). Again, these weights have been chosen arbitrarily for the purposes of the example, and I encourage the reader to experiment with different weights and measure the impact.

$$\log(P(w_1, w_2, ...w_n)) = 0.7 * \sum_{i=1}^{n} \log P(w_i|(w_{i-1}, w_{i-2})) +$$

$$0.25 * \sum_{i=1}^{n} \log P(w_i|w_{i-1}) + \tag{6.9}$$

$$0.05 * \sum_{i=1}^{n} \log P(w_i)$$

As we will combine the three models, we require unigram, bigram, and trigram estimates. For example, if we use the second sentence *he (list,lost,last) track of time*, we need frequency estimates from CORPUSR for the following n-grams:

unigrams : *he, list, last, lost, track, of, time*

bigrams : *he list, he lost, he last, list track, lost track, last track, track of, of time*

trigrams : *he list track, he lost track, he last track, list track of, last track of, lost track of, track of time*

Normalizing the frequency estimates by the total number of either unigrams, bigrams, or trigrams in CORPUSR, we obtain probabilities to be used in Eq. 6.9. This leads to the results presented in Table 6.10.

When working in log-space, we can interpret a difference of 2 (e.g., between -154 and -156) as a difference of 10^2 in base 10 or 100. It follows then, that these results generally show the correct sentences as being 100 times more probable than the incorrect sentences.

Admittedly, our corpus was small for calculating this kind of estimate. Nevertheless, we obtained some interesting results and were able to see a full application of two methods we have learned so far in this book: the Edit Distance method from

Table 6.10 Comparing sequence probabilities

Sentence $w_1...w_n$	log-space probability $\log(P(w_1..w_n))$
he walked on the beach for a long time	**-154.73**
he walked on the bench for a long time	-156.43
he lost track of time	**-73.35**
he last track of time	-75.62
he list track of time	-76.26

Chap. 4 and the language modeling approach from this chapter. Spelling correction is only one of many applications of language models. The upcoming chapter will explore yet another one of language detection in a multi-lingual context.

6.5   In Summary

- Words are not randomly dispersed in corpora, but occur in predictable sequences.
- Estimating n-gram models requires a large corpus, in order to avoid data sparseness as much as possible.

- When choosing a corpus for n-gram estimation, we should take into account the anticipated applications of the resulting model.
- Although n-gram lists are available online, we can also build our own, using our own corpora.
- Various problems can arise in language modeling, including data sparseness (n-grams not found in the corpus) and OOV's (words not found in the corpus).
- Since data sparseness is virtually unavoidable, it is necessary to have a smoothing approach in place.
- More complex models (e.g., 4-gram and 5-gram models) are more sparse in their estimates than less complex ones (e.g., unigrams, bigrams), since the number of possible combinations of words grows exponentially as n increases.
- Probabilistic sequence models cannot account for long-distance grammatical dependencies.
- Language models can aid in spelling correction by determining the most probable candidates among the ones detected by algorithms such as the Levenshtein Distance.

6.6 Further Reading

Language models: Language models are so important in fields such as speech recognition and Machine Translation that there is a whole community of researchers working with these models. One of the NLP most recognized reference books, Speech and Language Processing (Jurafsky and Martin 2007), has a full chapter on n-grams in which they discuss various smoothing techniques (Good–Turing, Kneser–Ney, Witten–Bell, etc.). The reader can consult this same reference to learn more about interpolation models, and even automatic estimation of weights in these models. Studies in language modeling date quite a while back. There is an early survey (Chen and Goodman 1999) which already refers to multiple smoothing techniques and compares them in an empirical setting.

Spelling correction: Spelling correction is quite a popular application, included in most commercial search engines. This topic is covered in the book mentioned above (Jurafsky and Martin 2007), as well as in a book chapter looking at *Natural Language Corpus Data* (Norvig 2009).

6.7 Exercises

Exercises 6.1 (**Language modeling**)

a. Revisit the example from Sect. 6.3, *the student is late for school*. Compare the bigram and trigram sequence probabilities provided for this example with the probabilities you obtain for a random sequence made up of the same words (*e.g., the student late for is school*). To obtain the estimates for the random sequence, use the Google Books n-gram viewer, which was also used to generate the data in Tables 6.1 and 6.2. Which of the two models (bigram or trigram) result in a larger gap between the random and the correct sentences?

b. Come up with a set of 20 short sentences (10 words maximum). Use this set of sentences to compare the performances of a bigram and trigram models. A good model should differentiate between a correct sentence and a random or reversed sentence. Determine which is the model that does the best job of differentiating, on average. To obtain the bigram and trigram estimates for your models, build a corpus of 10,000 Wikipedia pages, your version of CORPUSR, using the strategy described in Sect. 6.3.1, and then use the Algorithm 4 shown in Sect. 6.3.2.

c. Repeat the experiment in (b), but obtain bigram and trigram estimates on the two corpora, CLASSICALCOMPOSER and MOBILETEL, which you built in the previous chapter. How are these models behaving on your 20 sentences? Analyze and discuss.

Exercises 6.2 (Mispelling correction)

a. Imagine we had found the misspelled word *beich* in the following sentence:

> *I love sitting on the (bench/beach) and looking at the ocean.*

From a sequence modeling point of view, why is this sentence more challenging than the examples we used in Sect. 6.4? By challenging, I refer to the capability of the sequence model to actually choose between *bench* and *beach* as a proper correction for *beich*. Discuss.

b. Table 6.10 only provides final results for the sequence probabilities. For example, -73.35, for *he lost track of time*. Details of the calculations were not given. Perform the calculations yourself, using n-gram estimates from your own CORPUSR you built in Exercise 6.1 (b). Given that your corpus will be different than the one used to obtain the results of Table 6.10, for sure your results will be different, but would you say they are comparable? Discuss.

c. In Sect. 6.4, we used the arbitrary value of $\delta_{smoothing} = 0.001$ for smoothing, to redistribute the probability mass to the n-grams that were unobserved in the corpus. You can use the set of sentences you developed in Exercise 6.1 (b), as a development set, to decide on a better value of $\delta_{smoothing}$. To do so, calculate the average probability of all sentences using the interpolated model (trigram/bigram/unigram) presented in Sect. 6.4, varying the value of $\delta_{smoothing}$ $\{0.000001, 0.00001, 0.0001, 0.001, 0.01, 0.1, 1\}$. Which smoothing redistribution parameter $\delta_{smoothing}$ provides more differentiation between correct and random sentences?

d. In the previous exercise, we varied $\delta_{smoothing}$. Another possibility is to vary the interpolation weights assigned to the three models. Those were also set arbitrarily in Sect. 6.4 to ($\lambda_{unigram} = 0.05$, $\lambda_{bigram} = 0.25$, $\lambda_{trigram} = 0.7$). Set up an experiment for determining "good" weights and discuss your results.

Chapter 7
Bilingual Corpora

So far, we have used English as the language for all our examples, and our explorations of the behavior of various algorithms have likewise been performed on written text in English. In this chapter, we will attempt to find relations between texts written in different languages. **Multilingual corpora** are useful resources for comparing languages. These can range from **bilingual corpora**, made up of documents written in two different languages, to corpora containing three or more languages. Since our current exploration will be limited to a comparison of two languages, a bilingual corpus will suffice. We will start by presenting two common types of bilingual corpora in NLP, namely **parallel corpora** and **comparable corpora**.

Next, we will return to the statistical models we have seen in preceding chapters, namely the information theory inspired model of **Mutual Information** (Chap. 5) and the probability inspired sequential **language model** (Chap. 6). These are two important models in NLP having a number of different applications. In this chapter, we will zero in on how they are used in a bilingual context. To do this, we will first explore the task of **language identification** using a probabilistic sequence model and later look at finding **term equivalents** using Mutual Information. Term equivalents are simply terms in different languages that refer to the same entity.

7.1 Types of Bilingual Corpora

Many researchers in NLP are interested in bilingual corpora, whether it be for developing Machine Translation models, performing bilingual keyphrase extraction, bilingual text summarization, or the many other potential applications. The most common type of corpus for performing these tasks is a **parallel corpus**. When parallel corpora are not available for a particular language pair or domain however, we turn to **comparable corpora**. Let us investigate what distinguishes one type of corpus from the other and in what ways their usages differ.

© Springer International Publishing Switzerland 2016   105
C. Barrière, *Natural Language Understanding in a Semantic Web Context*,
DOI 10.1007/978-3-319-41337-2_7

Parallel corpora: A parallel corpus contains documents that are translations of each other. These corpora are commonly used by governments of bilingual (or multilingual) countries or organizations. The bilingual (English and French) transcription of all parliamentary debates within the Canadian government is a good example of this. The resulting parallel corpus, called **Canadian Hansards**, was at the center of development of early statistical Machine Translation models. Another example is the **EuroParl corpus**, a collection of European parliament proceedings in 21 different languages.

An initial task that researchers have worked on using parallel corpora is that of performing automatic **sentence alignment**, which means to explicitly establish links between corresponding sentences (translation of each other) within the parallel corpus. A parallel corpus on which sentences have been aligned results in what is called a **sentence-aligned parallel corpus**. Table 7.1 is an example of an automatically generated sentence-aligned English–French parallel corpus. The corpus, called the **Giga-FrEn corpus**, was initially compiled for a shared task on Machine Translation,[1] but is now widely used within the NLP research community. It contains 2.8 gigabytes of information, which is more than adequate for performing experiments.

Table 7.1 Example sentences as found in a parallel corpus

No.	English	French
1	Software for hearing aid fitting	Un logiciel d'ajustement des aides auditives
2	The laptop computer had gone missing one year before.	L'ordinateur portatif avait disparu un an plus tôt.
3	Did the student receive a medical diagnosis?	L'élève at-il été évalué par un spécialiste?
4	LEO/GEO merge allows event location with as few as two LEO location points.	La fusion des systèmes LEO/GEO permet de déduire l'emplacement d'un incident à partir de seulement deux points de positionnement LEO.
5	Use your own re-usable coffee cup, rather than a disposable cup.	Prenez votre café dans une tasse réutilisable plutôt que dans un gobelet jetable.

Comparable corpora: A comparable corpus contains documents that concern the same subject matter, in two or more languages. Because these documents are not translations of each other however, they are likely to contain different information. Besides being on the same subject matter, we can further impose that the documents in each corpus match a set of criteria to further increase their level of comparability. By criteria, I refer to genre, language level, medium, or other document characterizing criteria described in Chap. 5 (see Sect. 5.2). For example, we could have a comparable corpus of *spoken* English and Spanish documents on the topic of *fuel cells*. The fact that the documents share a common topic (*fuel cells*) is the minimum requirement

---

[1]A *shared task* is a type of competition, open to all researchers, for which a particular corpus is provided, as well as a well-defined task that is to be performed on it. Participating research teams compete to obtain the best results on the task. As another example, SemEval is a shared task related to semantic analysis presented in Chap. 9, Sect. 9.1.

for qualifying as a comparable corpus. The fact that they both use the same medium (*spoken*) would be an additional restriction making their content further comparable.

Wikipedia is the most widely used comparable corpus in NLP today. To contrast the information from a parallel corpus shown in Table 7.1, let us consider short excerpts of the Wikipedia pages for *cell phone* in English and French.[2] Table 7.2 shows the excerpts, consisting of the first few lines of the history section from the relevant pages.

Table 7.2 Example of information found in a comparable corpora

A hand-held mobile radiotelephone is an old dream of radio engineering. In 1917, Finnish inventor Eric Tigerstedt filed a patent for what he described as a "pocket-size folding telephone with a very thin carbon microphone". Among other early descriptions is one found in the 1948 science fiction novel Space Cadet by Robert Heinlein. The protagonist, who has just traveled to Colorado from his home in Iowa, receives a call from his father on a telephone in his pocket. Before leaving for earth orbit, he decides to ship the telephone home "since it was limited by its short range to the neighborhood of an earth-side [i.e. terrestrial] relay office."

Le téléphone mobile est le résultat de différentes technologies qui existaient déjà, pour la plupart, dans les années 1940. Son invention est attribuée au docteur Martin Cooper, directeur de la recherche et du développement chez Motorola qui en a fait la démonstration dans les rues de New-York le 3 avril 19734. Le premier téléphone mobile commercial est lancé le 6 mars 1983 par Motorola, avec le Motorola DynaTac 80005. Ces premiers appareils analogiques à la norme AMPS ont ensuite été remplacés par des appareils utilisant les normes numériques américaines D-AMPS et CDMA et les normes d'origine européenne GSM, UMTS puis LTE.

Despite the fact that these excerpts are written in the same encyclopedic style and concern the same subject matter, the information they provide is quite different. For example, the English version credits the Finnish inventor Eric Tigerstedt with the invention of the cell phone, whereas the French version credits Dr. Martin Cooper. Since the information contained within them differs, their sentences cannot be aligned. When using comparable corpora, we must first search for sentences that appear to have similar content and attempt to further extract the information from there. Although it is much more difficult to use comparable corpora for NLP, researchers have not given up trying. This continued effort is due to the persuasive argument for using them, which is that parallel corpora are often hard to come by, especially when it comes to less common languages and rare topics. In this chapter, for a first introduction into bilingual corpora, we will limit our focus to parallel corpora.

7.2 Exploring Noise in Bilingual Corpora

There is a tendency in NLP research today to gather corpora from the Web, given that it is a gigantic source of information. But the Web is a noisy place in which not all sources are trusted. By source, I refer to a person or an organization publishing

---

[2]Excerpts were taken in August 2015 and may have changed if searched at a later time.

Web pages for people to consult. For example, a **reliable source** would be an official government site in which we are sure to find well-written documents.

But corpora are sometimes generated automatically through **Web crawling**, which involves a robot navigating the Web and automatically downloading Web pages from different Web sites. If the Web sites are selected randomly, the crawled Web pages are bound to contain noise. Although noise can be due to encoding or formatting, in this section, since we are interested in bilingual corpora, we will focus solely on noise related to the bilingual content.

Table 7.3 provides examples of noisy sentences taken from the parallel corpus *Giga-FrEn* (introduced earlier), which is itself derived from a Web crawl. The table includes sentences exemplifying different types of noise, which we now take a moment to characterize.

Table 7.3 Noisy examples from *Giga-FrEn* corpus

No.	English	French
1	The persistence of these archaic attitudes and patterns of behaviour contradicts reality and the present day image of the woman liberating herself and claiming full equality.	French: III.
2	Finnish women were the first in the world to be granted both the right to vote and the eligibility for office.	Lors des premières élections générales de 1907, 10 % environ des élu(e)s étaient des femmes.
3	Le numéro du premier trimestre de 2008 de la publication Statistiques laitières, vol.	Ce rapport est publié conjointement par Statistique Canada et Transports Canada.
4	In addition, the other ILECs were directed to show cause why the same regime applied to Bell Canada should not apply in their respective territories.	In addition, the other ILECs were directed to show cause why the same regime applied to Bell Canada should not apply in their respective territories.
5	Steps to achieving viable operators Alison Gillwald 2002-02 Open file	Steps to achieving viable operators Alison Gillwald 2002-02 ouvrir le fichier
6	Ontario Ann Montgomery is an associate midwife and preceptor with the Midwifery Collective of Ottawa.	Ontario Ann Montgomery est sage-femme associée et préceptrice au Midwifery Collective of Ottawa.

Sentence alignment: Examples 1 and 2 show problems with sentence alignment. This either means that the original corpora contain errors (some of their documents are not exact translations of each other), or that the sentence alignment algorithm applied on the parallel corpora generated errors. In Example 1, even someone who does not speak French can suspect that the alignment is off, simply by noticing the dramatic difference in sentence length between the English and French sentences. In Exercise 7.3, you will be asked to develop a corpus filter based on differences in sentence length. A filter of this kind is an efficient tool for removing many errors of sentence alignment from parallel corpora. Example 2 is harder to identify (for both human and an automatic system) as a sentence alignment problem since not only are the sentence lengths comparable, but the topics are similar (e.g., women and elections).

Wrong language: In Example 3, the English side is actually not in English at all, but in French, and in Example 4, the French side is actually in English. This problem is common enough to motivate the development of a language identification filter. We will do exactly this in the coming section, basing our procedure on the probabilistic sequence modeling ideas we explored in Chap. 6.

Untranslated links and proper names: Many sentences taken from Web pages will contain not only flowing text (e.g., paragraphs), but also menu items, most likely hyperlinks that lead to other Web pages. As in Example 5, these menu items often go untranslated, most likely because the document they are linked to *is* in the original language (English, in this case) and remains itself untranslated. Example 6 shows another situation, where the names of people and organizations are not translated, perhaps by mistake, or perhaps by conscious choice.

Automatic translation: These days it is becoming less and less of a reliable assumption that Web pages are written, or translated, by humans. Sentence 6 is a good example of a sentence that is likely to have been automatically translated, since *est sage-femme* is not correct French (a francophone would know to say *est une sage-femme*). The prevalence of this type of noise has increased in recent years, as it has become common practice to use statistical Machine Translation software to generate Web content in different languages. This type of noise can be quite hard to detect for an automatic system, since the sentences are often almost correct but not quite perfect.

Unfortunately, we do not have the time or space to explore solutions to all of the problems listed above in this book. We will instead zero in on one particular strategy, **automatic language identification**, which could help preprocess a parallel corpus in identifying sentences written in the wrong language so as to remove them before further processing.

7.3 Language Identification

In order to further process bilingual corpora, a situation may arise where we want to automatically validate that the texts we are investigating are written in the languages that we think they are. For example, we may ask ourselves if a given text that is supposed to be written in Spanish is, in fact, in Spanish. This involves a process known as **language identification**, in which, as the name suggests, we automatically identify the language of a given text.

For our language identification algorithm, we will rely on the principles of probabilistic modeling of words in sequence, seen in Chap. 6, now adapted to letters in sequence.

7.3.1 Estimating Letter Trigram Probabilities

One approach to language identification is to start by building a **probabilistic language model** for each language of interest, which captures the particularities of that language. So, if we have L different languages, we build L models $M_1..M_L$ using L monolingual corpora, one for each language.

How can we capture the particularities of a language? Well, something as simple as sequences of letters can accomplish this. Table 7.4 shows the top 20 most probable letter trigrams for English, French, and Spanish, as estimated based on three different corpora, one for each language. Letter trigrams are very good indicators of a language, since certain sequences of letters are permissible in, or characteristic of, certain languages, while being less likely or even forbidden in others.

Table 7.4 Most common trigrams for different languages

English	Prob	French	Prob	Spanish	Prob
' th'	0.0091	' de'	0.0112	' de'	0.0155
'the'	0.0082	'es '	0.0111	'de '	0.0123
'he '	0.0072	'de '	0.0093	'os '	0.0065
'ed '	0.0048	'e d'	0.0061	' la'	0.0065
'ion'	0.0044	'le '	0.0058	'la '	0.0056
' in'	0.0042	' le'	0.0057	' en'	0.0056
' of'	0.0040	'ion'	0.0055	'el '	0.0055
'and'	0.0040	'er '	0.0054	'es '	0.0055
'on '	0.0039	' co'	0.0052	' co'	0.0054
'of '	0.0038	'on '	0.0051	'as '	0.0052
' an'	0.0037	'ent'	0.0044	'en '	0.0045
'nd '	0.0035	'tio'	0.0042	'ent'	0.0041
'tio'	0.0035	'nt '	0.0039	' el'	0.0040
' co'	0.0035	' la'	0.0038	'ión'	0.0038
'er '	0.0034	're '	0.0038	' es'	0.0037
'es '	0.0034	'e c'	0.0038	'e l'	0.0036
'in '	0.0033	's d'	0.0037	'o d'	0.0036
'ing'	0.0032	'les'	0.0037	'ón '	0.0034
' re'	0.0031	'e l'	0.0035	'aci'	0.0034
' to'	0.0029	'ati'	0.0034	'a d'	0.0033

Let us investigate how these numbers were obtained. Thinking back to the previous chapter, we saw that the first step to building a probabilistic model is to obtain a corpus. In Sect. 6.3.1, we learned how to automatically build a random corpus from Wikipedia, simply by choosing N pages at random from the overall set of pages. This approach to building a corpus is not restricted to English, but can also be used for French, Spanish, and virtually all languages covered in Wikipedia. Wikipedia dumps are available in all languages, allowing us to build corpora for most any one.

So, using three monolingual corpora (let us call them CORPUSENGLISH, CORPUS-FRENCH, and CORPUSSPANISH), each built from 1000 randomly chosen Wikipedia pages for its respective language, we can obtain the numbers seen in Table 7.4. To do this, we would go through the corpus for each language and cumulate the frequencies for each possible trigram. The algorithm ultimately transforms the frequencies into probabilities, by dividing each trigram frequency by the total number of trigrams in the corpus.

Such algorithm is very similar to Algorithm 4 from Chap. 6, used for gathering word trigrams from text (see Exercise 7.1 for adapting the algorithm). When NLP researchers speak of trigrams, or any n-gram for that matter, they are most likely speaking of sequences of words. However, we can also speak of n-grams of letters, which are particularly useful for tasks such as language identification. All of the methods seen in Chap. 6 for working with word n-grams can be adapted to work with letter n-grams.

Notice that, simply by looking at the top 20 trigrams for each of the three languages in Table 7.4, we can see that French and Spanish are more similar to each other in this respect than either one is to English. English does share certain common trigrams with the other two languages (e.g., ' es'), but Spanish and French share a greater number (e.g., ' de', ' la', ' co'). It is also worth noting that spaces are included as valid characters in the trigrams. Doing so allows a differentiation between letters occurring at the beginning of a word (usually preceded by a space) from the ones occurring at the end of a word (followed by a space). A differentiation means that they will be assigned different probabilities, providing a further refinement that will be taken into account by the probabilistic model.

At this point, it is an arbitrary decision to include the space in the trigrams. We could also include (or not) punctuation marks or even differentiation between lower case and upper case letters. Decision on which trigram probabilities to calculate should be based on the impact of that decision on the language identification capability of the probabilistic model which will rely on these estimates. Let us look at how to build such trigram probabilistic model in the next section.

7.3.2 Testing a Letter Trigram Model for Language Identification

Now that we have gathered the trigram probabilities for different languages, we can use them to estimate the probability of a sentence emerging from one of those languages. We wish to build three language models $M_{Spanish}$, $M_{English}$, and M_{French}. To do so, we will adapt Eq. 6.4 from the previous chapter to take characters at different positions in a sequence and calculate the overall probability of a sentence based on the probabilities of the trigrams it contains. The adapted equation is shown in Eq. 7.1.

$$\log(P_m(c_1, c_2, ...c_n)) = \sum_{i=1}^{n} \log P_m(c_i|c_{i-1}, c_{i-2}) \qquad (7.1)$$

Notice that we have also added an index m to represent the language used in the estimate $P_m(c_1...c_n)$. For our three languages, we will have $P_{Spanish}(c_1..c_n)$, $P_{English}(c_1..c_n)$, and $P_{French}(c_1..c_n)$, corresponding to our three language models $M_{Spanish}$, $M_{English}$, and M_{French}. Each one provides the language-specific probability of the sentence containing the characters $c_1..c_n$.

Now let us see how well our models are able to predict the language of a sentence. As a small example experiment, we will consider the three sentences shown in Table 7.5.

Table 7.5 Example of three parallel sentences from three languages

Language	Sentence
$S_{English}$	The project was labeled as a historic and important step in reducing carbon pollution from power plants.
S_{French}	Le projet a été étiqueté comme un événement historique et important pour la réduction de la pollution au carbone dans les centrales électriques.
$S_{Spanish}$	El proyecto fue etiquetado como un paso histórico e importante en la reducción de la contaminación de carbono de las centrales eléctricas.

Table 7.6 shows the probability of each sentence, as estimated by each of the three language models. For each sentence, the correct language is estimated as the most probable by the corresponding model for that language, indicating that our models successfully detected the language of the sentences. The highest probability for each sentence is indicated in bold in the table.

Table 7.6 Results of a small language identification experiment

Sentence	$\log(P_{English}(c_1..c_n))$	$\log(P_{French}(c_1..c_n))$	$\log(P_{Spanish}(c_1..c_n))$
$S_{English}$	**−753.79**	−825.41	−833.08
S_{French}	−938.11	**−824.28**	−927.49
$S_{Spanish}$	−983.78	−932.91	**−853.48**

At this point, we have seen a very basic implementation of language identification, through an experiment involving only one sentence in each of the three languages. A reliable evaluation will require multiple sentences in each language, as suggested to perform in Exercise 7.1.

Nevertheless, applying a language identification algorithm like the one presented above can serve as a preprocessing step to the use of bilingual corpora.

7.3.3 Language Identification as Preprocessing Step

Using a language identification as a preprocessing step will help remove from the parallel corpus sentences which are not in the correct language. This will provide a *cleaner* corpus, to be used in a subsequent task, such as finding term equivalents, as we will describe in Sect. 7.4.

Algorithm 5 presents the steps required in corpus filtering. The algorithm removes all sentences for which the language detector evaluates the wrong (opposite) language as being the most likely (e.g., French for English, or English for French).

Initialize *ListPairs* to contain all pairs of sentences in Giga-FrEn;
Initialize *FilteredListPairs* to contain the pairs which are in correct languages ;
\\ *Go through all sentences in the target language to gather possible equivalents.*
for *each sentence pair S in ListPairs* **do**

    Assign $S_{English}$ to the English side of S;
    Assign S_{French} to the French side of S;
    \\ *Test both models on the two sides.*
    Apply English language model on $S_{English}$ to obtain $P_{English}(S_{English})$;
    Apply French language model on $S_{English}$ to obtain $P_{French}(S_{English})$;
    Apply English language model on S_{French} to obtain $P_{English}(S_{French})$;
    Apply French language model on S_{French} to obtain $P_{French}(S_{French})$;
    if $P_{English}(S_{English}) > P_{French}(S_{English})$ *AND* $P_{English}(S_{French}) < P_{French}(S_{French})$
    then
        Add S to *FilteredListPairs*;
    end

end

Algorithm 5: Bilingual corpus filtering with language identification

---

Table 7.7 shows the impact on corpus size of applying the language identification filter. We can calculate the reduction in corpus size by dividing the total number of filtered pairs (e.g., pairs tagged as being in the opposite language, totaling 1,215,168) by the total number of pairs before filtering (22,520,400). In this case, the result is 0.054, meaning that filtering based on language identification reduced the size of our corpus by 5.4 %.

Table 7.7 Impact of language identification filtering on number of sentence pairs in the corpus

Pair description	Nb Pairs
Total before filtering	22,520,400
Where English side is tagged as "French"	473,574
Where French side tagged as "English"	741,594
Where either French or English side tagged as opposite language	1,215,168
Remaining after filtering	21,305,232

Note that we are not actually evaluating the language identification algorithm by showing the reduction impact. We are simply noting that the preprocessing step does find about 5 % of the sentences that it thinks are not in the correct language. To properly evaluate what is in these 5 % of sentences, we would require a proper sampling of these pairs to get a sense of what is actually filtered (See Exercise 7.3).

Let us move on to the next task of term equivalent search, assuming our preprocessing step has helped in leaving us with a cleaner corpus.

7.4 Searching for Term Equivalents in Parallel Corpora

A typical task performed using parallel sentence-aligned corpora is the development of translation models for use in **Statistical Machine Translation (SMT)**. SMT is an important field in NLP (see references in Sect. 7.7), to which many research groups devote the entirety of their efforts. We make a very small incursion into the field through our exploration of **term equivalents** in a parallel corpus. Term equivalents are terms in different languages that refer to the same entity.

As an example, if we do not know the different surface forms corresponding to the term *cell phone* in French, we could attempt to find them using a parallel corpus. Let us see whether Table 7.8 which provides a small sample of English/French sentence pairs could help us. Restricting the set of English-side sentences to the ones containing the term *cell phone* allows us to observe variations for that term on the French side.

Table 7.8 Examples from *Giga-FrEn* corpus for the term *cell phone*

No.	English	French
1	Cell phone number	Numéro de téléphone cellulaire
2	Cell Phone Replacement Batteries	Piles de remplacement des téléphones portables
3	Keep a cell phone for emergencies.	Gardez votre cellulaire pour les urgences.
4	Cancellation of account (after Cell phone)	Tous les dossiers sont restitués
5	Identification requirements for cell phone services	Exigences relatives à l'identification pour obtenir des services de téléphone cellulaire
6	Cell phone use is, however, not entirely risk-free.	Toutefois, le cellulaire n'est pas tout à fait sans risque.
7	SAR alerting by cell phone (9-1-1):	Appels de détresse SAR par téléphone cellulaire (9-1-1)
8	Outside the capital, cell phone coverage is often unavailable.	Les réseaux de téléphonie cellulaire sont souvent inaccessibles en dehors de la capitale.
9	Cell phone reception outside of townsites is unreliable.	Les téléphones cellulaires ne fonctionnent pas bien à l'extérieur des agglomérations.
10	Also, cell phone carriers and mp3 carriers are popular.	Une tuque est une bonne idée en raison de la prochaine saison.
11	Cell phone use is prohibited in the research centre.	L'utilisation du téléphone cellulaire est interdite au centre de recherche.
12	For safety's sake, don't use your cell phone while driving.	Pour un maximum de sécurité, n'utilisez pas votre téléphone cellulaire lorsque vous conduisez.

An ideal situation for quickly finding the French equivalent to *cell phone* would be that all target side (French side) sentences would contain a single repeated term, *téléphone cellulaire*, which would for sure be the answer we are looking for. An algorithm searching for a repeated string on the French side would find it. Unfortunately, this ideal situation would imply that language is normalized, which would mean that a single term in French is allowed for a particular entity. But French is no different than English in that matter; French does contain multiple surface forms for each entity. Let us further use the examples in Table 7.8 to discuss how the lack of normalization in language is likely to cause much interference to a redundancy-based equivalent search algorithm.

Synonymy: Interestingly, we have come back to our discussion from Chap. 2 about the existence of various surface forms for a particular entity, only this time in a bilingual context. We saw at that time that the entity (URI) *mobile_phone* has multiple synonyms in English (*cell phone* being among them), and now we see that there are likewise multiple synonyms in French, such as *téléphone cellulaire* (Sentences 1, 7, 9, 11 and 12), *téléphone portable* (Sentence 3), and *cellulaire* (Sentence 6).

Compositionality: Due to the compositional nature of terms, *cell phone* may appear in certain sentences as a component of a longer term. For example, Sentence 1 refers to a *cell phone number*, which translates to the French term *numéro de téléphone cellulaire*. In this example, all the English components are directly translated to produce the French equivalent (*number/numéro*, *cell/cellulaire*, and *phone/téléphone*). Sentence 5 is similar, with all the components of *cell phone services*, being translated to produce *services de téléphone cellulaire*. Neither of these examples is problematic, since each English component corresponds neatly to its French equivalent. However, a term such as *cell phone coverage* (Sentence 8) becomes *réseaux de téléphonie cellulaire* in French, which is not quite as direct a translation since it includes a shift in emphasis from one language to the other (the English sentence emphasizes *coverage*, while the French sentence emphasizes the underlying phone networking, *réseaux de téléphonie*). Such variation in the components of compositional terms will generate noise for our equivalent search algorithm. Without knowledge of these larger terms, in a case like this, the algorithm would embark on the fruitless search for an equivalent for *cell phone* in the French sentence.

Implicit/explicit information: Although not necessarily a problematic phenomenon, it is worth mentioning that the amount of explicit information is not always the same from one language to another. Sentence 6 is a good example of this. The English version of this sentence mentions *cell phone use*, emphasizing the *use* of the phone as potentially risky, whereas the French version assumes that the *usage* is implied and simply states that the cell phone is not entirely without risk.

Degree of nominalization: In writing, people may choose to convey certain information in noun form or instead decide that the same information is best expressed using a verb. When comparing two languages, there are bound to be times when a noun was chosen by the source language writer, but a verb was used by the translator (or vice versa). The process of changing a verb into its noun form is called **nominalization**. Sentence 9 provides an example of this, when the English writer uses a nominalization, *cell phone reception*, but the French translator opts for a verb to convey the same notion. Technically speaking, if we were to translate directly, the French verb should have been *reçoivent*, but the more general verb *fonctionnent* was chosen, which literally means *works* or *functions*. As a second example, the English word *use* appears in its noun form in Sentence 11, but in its verb form in Sentence 12. In this case, the French side is the same, showing *utilisation* (a noun) in Sentence 11 and *utilisez* (a verb) in Sentence 12.

Beyond these variations in surface forms, there can also be much noise in the data (see Sect. 7.2) such as noise generated by the sentence alignment process. Sentence 10 is an extreme example of this, with the English and French sentences being completely unrelated (the word-for-word translation of what appears on the French side would be *A hat is a good idea because of the upcoming season*).

Yet, even with the surface form variations and possible sources of noise we have seen so far, it is still evident that the word *cellulaire* appears in several of the French sentences in Table 7.8. This repetition of a particular string in the target language is still something we can try to exploit to make some candidate terms emerge. Since we do not have much more than this redundancy to go with, we can hope that if the corpus is large enough, repetition of correct term equivalents will occur.

Let us devise a term equivalent search which will require two steps:

1. Index a sentence-aligned parallel corpus.
2. Adapt the Point-wise Mutual Information algorithm (Chap. 5) to work on bilingual corpora.

7.4.1   Obtaining and Indexing a Parallel Corpus

Since it is freely available and large enough to provide us with interesting results, we will use the Giga-FrEn corpus as the parallel corpus for our example. We will further refer to this corpus as GIGACORPUS. Its size warrants the use of indexing software, such as Lucene[3] to allow for quick searches in it. We could also build our own index, by going through the corpus and keeping track of where (e.g., in which sentences) we find each word or bigram of interest.

Regardless of whether we use open-source indexing software or choose to build our own index, we will require an index table such as the one shown in Table 7.9. This index table should include the language (column 1), all n-grams of interest (column 2), and for each n-gram, a list of sentence IDs in which it occurs (column 3).

An indexed corpus will be necessary to run the algorithm described next, which searches for term equivalents.

Table 7.9 Sentence indexed corpus GIGACORPUS

Language	word / n-gram	Sentence IDs
English	cell	8, 12, 40, 127, 256
English	cell phone	12, 256, 386
English	genome	677, 800, 1240, 1241
French	cellulaire	12, 127, 256, 350, 425
French	genome	800, 1241, 1300

---

[3]Lucene is available at http://www.lucene.apache.org.

7.4.2 Adapting PMI for Term Equivalent Search

The Point-wise Mutual Information (PMI) measure was presented in Chap. 5 as a means of finding collocations in a monolingual corpus. Collocations are words which tend to occur together frequently. We will now transpose this idea to a bilingual context and attempt to find English and French words (or n-grams) which are similar (or share Mutual Information) in the sense that they tend to occur in sentences with similar meanings.

A parallel sentence-aligned corpus is essential for putting this idea into practice, since the sentences within it comprise the units in which we will look for these similar words. The underlying assumption here is that both sentences of every English/French pair carry the same meaning, by virtue of being translations of each other. If the meaning of the parallel sentences is the same, then the words they consist of must have something in common or share Mutual Information.

For example, in Table 7.9, the words *cell* and *cellulaire* share sentences 12, 127, and 256. Identifying the sentences that certain words have in common is a key element in the calculation of the Mutual Information of those words.

Equation 7.2 represents the Point-wise Mutual Information (PMI) between two words of different languages. Rather than specifying the language in the equation (English/French), the equation has been made more general by introducing the notion of a word appearing in a source language w_S or a target language w_T. A **source language** is the original language, the language from which we translate, and the **target language** is the language to which we translate. So, if we start with an English sentence and translate it to French, English is the source language and French is the target language.

In Eq. 7.2, $SentProb(w_S, w_T)$ refers to the number of sentence pairs in which w_S and w_T co-occur, divided by the total number of sentences in the corpus. Similarly, $SentProb(w_S)$ refers to the number of sentence pairs in which w_S occurs, divided by the total number of sentences in the corpus. $SentProb(w_T)$ is calculated in the same way as $SentProb(w_S)$, but for w_T. Here, as we have seen in previous chapters, we are working in logarithm space to avoid dealing with very small numbers.

$$PMI(w_S, w_T) = \log(\frac{SentProb(w_S, w_T)}{SentProb(w_S) * SentProb(w_T)}) \qquad (7.2)$$

This equation is central to Algorithm 6 which searches for the term equivalent of a particular source word, or n-gram.

```
\\ Use the sentence pair index;
Assign IndexPairs to link to the index of GIGACORPUS;
Assign TotalSent to be the size of the number of pairs in GIGACORPUS;
\\ Decide on an English word to test;
SourceWord = "cell phone" ;
\\ Retrieve sentence pairs from the index.
Assign ListPairs to gather pairs from IndexPairs containing SourceWord;
\\ Set a list to gather all possible source language ngrams.
Initialize NgramList;
\\ Set a limit to the size of candidates being explored.
Initialize MaxNgramSize to 3;
\\ Set a minimum to the number of occurrences of a candidate within ListPairs.
Initialize MinSentCount to 0.1 * size of ListPairs;
\\ Go through all sentences in the target language to gather possible equivalents.
for each target sentence S in ListPairs do
   │  for each group of consecutive tokens of size 1 to MaxNgramSize do
   │  │  if NgramList does not contain the ngram then
   │  │  │  Include the ngram in NgramList;
   │  │  end
   │  end
end
\\ Assign a list to contain the candidates and their PMI.
Initialize CandidateNgramList;
\\ Find the frequency of each candidate in the whole corpus
for each ngram in NgramList do
   │  Assign FreqXY = number of pairs in ListPairs containing this ngram;
   │  if FreqXY > MinSentCount then
   │  │  Assign FreqX to be the number of pairs it is part of on the target side using
   │  │  IndexPairs ;
```

$$Assign\ PMI = \frac{log((FreqXY/TotalSent)}{((FreqX/TotalSent)*(FreqY/TotalSent)))}\ ;$$

```
   │  │  Put the ngram with its PMI in CandidateNgramList
   │  end
end
Sort CandidateNgramList in decreasing order of PMI.
```

Algorithm 6: Term equivalent search on a parallel corpus.

You will notice two arbitrary parameters in the algorithm: $MaxNgramSize$ (maximum n-gram size) and $MinSentCount$ (minimum sentence count). The purpose of the first parameter, $MaxNgramSize$, is to determine the maximum size of candidate terms on the target side, with size referring to the number of words contained in the term. In the algorithm, the $MaxNgramSize$ has been set to 3, which means we will search for terms comprised of a maximum of three words. The second parameter, $MinSentCount$, limits the search time, by stipulating that only candidates on the target side that occur a minimum number of times with the source word will be investigated. In the algorithm, that $MinSentCount$ is set to 10 %, meaning that candidates must appear with the source word in a minimum of 10 % of the sentences in order to qualify. These filters can be changed and experimenting with them will demonstrate their impact on the results. Now, let us see, through an experiment, how well the algorithm can actually do.

7.5 Experiment — Term Equivalent Search

Even if we are not expecting perfect results, given all the possible types of corpus noise (Sect. 7.2) and target language variations in surface forms possibly hindering our Algorithm 6, we still put it to the test in this section.

The corpus used for our experiment is the GIGACORPUS which we assume would be indexed such as described in Sect. 7.4.1.

We will go through the following steps:

1. Decide on a dataset to use for testing, run the algorithm, and perform an a posteriori evaluation.
2. Challenge the evaluation through a discussion on inter-annotator agreement.
3. Assess our term equivalent search algorithm.

7.5.1 Dataset and a posteriori Evaluation

Since this will be our first experiment using our new technique, and since our main goal is to determine where it succeeds and where it fails, let us start by simply coming up with a list of English words to test. Our list will be composed of single- and multi-word terms ranging from common to specific, including nouns, verbs, people's names, and even conjunctions. Covering a wide range of words with different natures and corpus frequencies will help stimulate discussion. The list of words appears in the first column of Table 7.10.

Ideally, we would develop a gold standard containing the French equivalent terms for our list of English words. This is not an easy task however, since it would be a challenge to come up with all possible candidates ahead of time. As we have just discussed in the previous section, there are likely multiple surface forms in French, or in any other language for that matter, to refer to entities. Even if we were to include *téléphone cellulaire* as a known equivalent for *cell phone*, it is quite possible, maybe even likely, that we would overlook other valid equivalents, such as *téléphone portable* in this case. If that were to happen, and if we were to go on to evaluate our algorithm with traditional precision/recall measures, the algorithm would pay the price. It would be penalized for finding candidates that may actually be correct, simply due to their not appearing in the gold standard.

When searching for information in text, we are often uncertain of being able to provide an exhaustive list of correct answers in the gold standard. In such cases, we can opt for an a posteriori evaluation. In an **a posteriori evaluation**, the evaluation is performed *after* the system has generated its results. First we obtain the results and then we manually assess them to determine which are right and which are wrong.

Let us consult Table 7.10 for the results of an a posteriori evaluation that I performed on our dataset, consisting of the list of words in column 1. The second column of the table shows the number of sentence pairs in GIGACORPUS that contain the English term in the English sentence. The third column shows the top 5 results obtained using Algorithm 6 on the GIGACORPUS. Because we set the maximum n-gram size to 3, for each English term our search allows for unigrams, bigrams, and trigrams on the French side. The candidates I deemed as being correct are indicated in bold in the table.

7.5.2 Inter-Annotator Agreement

Let us challenge my a posteriori evaluation, of results in Table 7.10. It is debatable whether or not my assignments would be accepted by other judges. We discussed this notion of inter-annotator agreement (IIA) in Chap. 3, as well as the *kappa* measure that is used for determining levels of agreement.

Our current example typifies an evaluation that would benefit from discussion between judges. In a case like this, it would be important to have several judges perform their own a posteriori evaluation and to make note of their level of agreement or disagreement using the *kappa* measure. This is especially important when running a larger experiment, since low IIA might be an indicator of the judges having different interpretations of the task.

The problem of **boundary detection** can be seen in the results of Table 7.10, as evidenced by the fact that some candidates vary by a single determiner, such as in *le diagnostic médical*, *un diagnostic médical*, and *diagnostic médical*. This problem also extends to other NLP tasks, such as Named Entity Recognition (see Chap. 3) in which we look for named entities, and we must determine in the text, where they begin and end.

Here, the question becomes, where does the term equivalent start and end? For example, is *un téléphone cellulaire* correct or not (e.g., is it a valid equivalent for *cell phone*)? The literal translation would be *a cellular phone*, due to the inclusion of the determiner *un*. *Le, la, un,* and *une* are all determiners in French. Given how often they appear in the table, the decision of how to evaluate the candidates that include them (e.g., correct or incorrect) will significantly change the results. That said, there is no right answer, since the decision may be contextual, based on the intended use of the equivalent search module.

Assuming my evaluation is accepted (although I do encourage the reader to consider and criticize it) and that all candidates indicated in bold in Table 7.10 are in fact correct answers, we can now perform result analysis, as we see next.

Table 7.10 Results for French equivalents using PMI

English term	Nb Sent	French equivalent candidates
jaywalking	2	passages réservés ou (-0.69) peines sévères relativement (-0.69) cracher de fumer (-0.69) **traversée illégale** de (-0.69) hors des passages (-0.69)
italian restaurant	16	carmello (-1.79) carmello ottawa total (-2.08) italian restaurant (-2.77) quartier animé du (-2.77) un **restaurant italien** (-2.77)
coffee cup	26	servie ou achètent (-3.26) est servie ou (-3.26) achètent une tasse (-3.26) café en carton (-3.48) coffee cup (-3.55)
parental guidance	38	milieu familial et (-7.34) milieu familial (-9.11) familial et (-9.41) parental (-10.05) des parents (-11.12)
critical condition	109	terminale ou dans (-4.90) phase terminale ou (-5.43) terminale ou (-5.78) un **état critique** (-6.84) **état critique** (-6.93)
chamber music	273	chamber music society (-5.64) chamber music (-5.71) **musique de chambre** (-6.06) music society (-6.93) de musique de (-7.72)
medical diagnosis	285	le **diagnostic médical** (-6.20) un **diagnostic médical** (-6.26) **diagnostic médical** (-6.56) un diagnostic (-9.30) diagnostics (-10.14)
flashlight	321	une lampe de (-6.26) **lampe de poche** (-6.30) lampe de (-6.43) une lampe (-7.16) lampe (-7.59)
hearing aid	449	**prothèse auditive** (-6.55) une prothèse (-7.31) **prothèses auditives** (-7.39) prothèse (-7.70) auditives (-8.44)
cell phone	910	**téléphone cellulaire** (-8.21) **cellulaires** (-9.49) **cellulaire** (-10.04) téléphones (-10.34) **cellulaires** (-10.88)
laptop	913	un **ordinateur portatif** (-7.25) **ordinateur portatif** (-7.40) **ordinateurs portatifs** (-8.32) portatif (-9.21) **portable** (-9.63)
merge	1301	**fusionner** (-8.42) de **fusionner** (-8.44) **fusion** (-11.69) deux (-15.41) se (-15.97)
cup	4263	**coupe** du (-8.95) **tasse** (-9.10) la **coupe** (-9.38) **coupe** (-10.12) du monde (-12.55)
coffee	6033	**café** et (-8.95) de **café** (-9.00) **café** (-9.37) thé (-10.33) produits (-15.29)
wrong	9374	pas (-15.68) ne (-15.75) fait (-15.80) si (-15.80) il (-16.04)
reside	5326	**résider** (-9.86) **résident** (-12.15) dans (-16.37) sont (-16.42) ou (-16.70)
parental	12070	congé *parental* (-9.82) **parental** (-10.01) **parentales** (-10.05) **parentale** (-10.11) de maternité (-10.80)
james	20085	**james** (-10.35) et (-18.25) la (-18.35) de (-1000.00)
india	25174	**inde** (-11.05) en (-17.21) le (-17.63) la (-17.68) et (-17.74)
nevertheless	25333	**néanmoins** (-11.41) **toutefois** (-14.35) il (-16.19) pas (-16.33) que (-16.68)
guidance	60074	document (-14.62) sur (-16.76) aux (-17.01) des (-17.02) pour (-17.08)
table	182917	**table** (-12.43) **table** des (-12.54) **tableau** (-12.83) des (-17.25) le (-17.77)

7.5.3   Result Analysis

To continue emphasizing variability in evaluation, let us look at four slightly different
ways of obtaining results which lead to quite different numbers.

The first one, shown in the second column of the Table 7.11, only considers the top
1 candidate, meaning the candidate with the highest *PMI* score. For 13 words of the
22 found in the dataset, the algorithm does find a correct candidate at the top of the
list, for a 59.1 % precision (Precision A). If we give further chance to the algorithm,
and let it look in the top 5 of the list, results go up, as shown in the third column of
Table 7.11 with 18 English terms for which there is a correct French terms among
the top 5, giving a precision of 81.8 % (Precision B).

Now, let us further look at the top 5 candidates. We can also try to see how many
correct candidates there are among them. The fourth column shows that among a total
of 110 candidates (22 terms * 5 candidates each), only 42 of them are correct answers,
providing a precision of 38.2 % (Precision C). And finally, let us be even more critical
of the discovery capability of our algorithm and look at how many different term
equivalent it provided. There are only 25 different French term equivalents among
the 110 possibilities. The numbers are in the fifth column with a precision of 22.7 %.

Table 7.11   Different precision results for French equivalent search using PMI

	Precision A	Precision B	Precision C	Precision D
Absolute numbers	13/22	18/22	42/110	25/110
Percentage	59.1 %	81.8 %	38.2 %	22.7 %

Which of Precision A, B, C, or D is the actual precision of the algorithm? They
all are. We can say that Precision B is an **optimistic evaluation**, in the sense that it
allows the algorithm place for errors (considering the top 5 results instead of the top
1 as in Precision A). On the other hand, we can say that Precision D is an **pessimistic
evaluation**, in the sense that it assumes that there should be 5 different various French
surface forms for each English term, which might not be the case.

The quantitative evaluation we have just performed certainly gives us the sense
that our algorithm is accomplishing valuable work, but it can often be difficult to
interpret the resulting precisions.

Still, our optimistic precision is quite high for such a simple term equivalent search
performed using the *PMI* measure. Knowledge about this approach can prove useful
for discovering surface forms in different languages, which could be included within
a multilingual dictionary or even knowledge base. When working with an approach
that is not 100 % certain however, as for most tasks in NLP, we can always turn to
human validation post-processing. Although this may seem like a bothersome extra
step, going this route is still quite efficient, since choosing among the term equivalent
candidates suggested by an algorithm will always be easier for a human than to come
up with the correct term equivalents from scratch.

7.6   In Summary

- A parallel corpus contains documents which are translations of each other.
- A comparable corpus contains documents in different languages relating to the same subject matter. These documents are not translations of each other, but are assumed to appear in their original language.
- For a bilingual corpus to be considered comparable, we can add further restrictions on the documents, such as all being of the same genre, or language level.
- There are many potential types of noise in a corpus compiled from unknown Web sources. One that is important to consider when dealing with multilingual corpora is the presence of sentences not written in the language they are supposed to be in.
- A language identification model can be built as a character sequence model. To build the model, we can use a relatively large monolingual corpus and find the probability of each n-gram of characters within it.
- To perform language identification of a sentence, we can measure the probability of that sentence according to different language models built for various languages and then choose the most probable one.
- Language identification can be performed as a preprocessing step prior to the use of a bilingual corpus.
- An interesting and useful use of parallel corpora is in the search of term equivalents. Term equivalents are terms which have the same meaning in both source and target languages.
- We can use Mutual Information to capture term equivalents in a sentence-aligned bilingual corpus.
- A search for term equivalents will generally be more successful for terms that occur a minimum number of times in a corpus. Measures of detection, including *PMI* and others, are probabilistic and will not work well for rare words.
- A single polysemous term on the source language side (e.g., English *cup* referring to *coffee cup* or *soccer cup*) can become two different terms on the target language side (e.g., French *tasse* and *coupe*), corresponding to two different meanings.
- Variability in the surface forms of a term in both the source and target languages will make it difficult for a statistical approach to correctly identify term equivalents.

7.7   Further Reading

Parallel corpora: The Canadian Hansards is available at http://www.isi.edu/natural-language/download/hansard/. The site http://www.statmt.org/europarl/ gives access to the EuroParl corpus (1996-2011). The *Giga-FrEn* corpus was used in a machine translation shared task, described at http://www.statmt.org/wmt09/translation-task. html. The corpus can be downloaded from that site.

Statistical Machine Translation Rather than suggesting a particular article, I refer the reader to the site http://www.statmt.org/ providing a set of tutorials, software, and available corpora.

Sentence alignment: One of the first sentence alignment algorithms, still in use today, is described in Gale and Church (1993). As sentence alignment in parallel corpora is almost considered a solved task, some recent work focuses rather on searching for parallel sentences but within comparable corpora Smith et al. (2010).

Comparable corpora: The workshop BUCC, Building and Using Comparable Corpora, is collocated, every year with major conferences in Natural Language Processing, and it is a good place to look for recent research. See the 2016 edition for example at https://comparable.limsi.fr/bucc2016/.

Term equivalent search: In this chapter, we assumed that the English lexicon was available and we were looking for French equivalents. Some research rather assumes that neither lexicon exists and from a bilingual corpus tries to build a bilingual lexicon. Early work on bilingual lexicon extraction task using parallel corpora can be found in Dagan and Church (1994), and work using both parallel and comparable corpora, can be found in Fung (1998). More recent work in bilingual terminology mining using comparable corpora can be found in Bouamor et al. (2013).

7.8   Exercises

Exercise 7.1 (Language identification).

a. Adapt Algorithm 4 from Chap. 6 (Sect. 6.3.2), originally written to gather word trigrams, to gather letter trigrams instead. Run your algorithm to build language models for 3 languages of your choice (e.g., English, French, and Spanish). As language-specific corpora for gathering letter trigrams, you will require 3 monolingual corpora, one for each language. To build these corpora, use Wikipedia pages from each language, building a corpus with a random selection of 1000 pages. You had already performed this process in Exercise 6.1, in Chap. 6, to build a small English corpus. You can adapt your code to work with the Wikipedia dumps provided for the other two languages.
b. First, program the language identification strategy described in Sect. 7.3. Then, devise an experimental setup to test the language identification strategy, using 20 sentences for the 3 languages that you have trigram models for. Again a good place to find sentences of each language is in Wikipedia pages. Gather 20 sentences of different lengths from these pages to form your test set. Make sure any sentence in the test set is not included in the corpus used to build the language model. Perform your tests. Discuss results.
c. Vary the information in your trigrams, including or excluding punctuation, including or excluding spaces, considering upper case letters or not. Do these variations impact the results of the previous experiment?

d. How does the trigram model compare to a 4-gram model? Expand your code from exercises (a) to be able to build a 4-gram model and use it in language identification. Compare the results using the experimental setup you defined in exercise (b). Do the results improve?

Exercise 7.2 (Finding term equivalents).

a. Program the algorithm given in Sect. 7.4.2 to be able to perform your own term equivalent searches.
b. Adapt the measures Dice, χ^2-test, and likelihood ratio, from Sect. 5.7 in Chap. 5 to be used for finding term equivalents. Provide them as alternatives in your program.
c. Using the measures above, perform comparative tests using the dataset from Sect. 7.5.1. Since you might not be familiar with French, use the answers marked as correct in Table 7.10 as your gold standard. Using this gold standard will be different than the a posteriori evaluation we performed in Sect. 7.5.1. Discuss this.
d. As an alternative dataset, start with the correct French terms shown in Table 7.10. This means you need to perform your equivalent search using French as source language and English as target language. Adapt your code to do so. Evaluate your results.

Exercise 7.3 (Corpus filtering).

a. Write a sentence length matching filter for the Giga-FrEn corpus which will be able to remove sentence pairs in which the English and French sentences differ in their length by more than a standard deviation away from their average length difference. To do so, perform the following steps:

1. Calculate the average sentence length difference between English and French sentences for all pairs.
2. Calculate the standard deviation of the differences.
3. Go through each sentence pair, test the length difference, and only keep the pairs which vary in length less than the average plus or minus the standard deviation.

Did that filter many sentences? If you manually sample through 20 removed pairs, are they all alignment problems? What if you change the threshold to be less than two standard deviations away, does that provide better or worst results?

Part III
Semantic Grounding and Relatedness

In Part I, as we searched for entities in text, we explored different surface forms for entities, and how they can be found in text. In Part II, as we looked at corpora, we further examined the behavior of entity's surface forms in text, by themselves, in conjunction with others, and in different languages.

In Part III, *Semantic Grounding and Relatedness*, let us try to link back the surface forms found in text to the actual entities which they represent. Our main obstacle will be that not only do entities have multiple surface forms, but many of these surface forms are polysemous, meaning they could link to various entities. This part of the book looks more closely at this major challenge of **polysemy**.

Chapter 8, *Linguistic Roles*, introduces the NLP processes of **tokenization, sentence splitting, lemmatization, part-of-speech tagging**, and **parsing**. This pipeline of processes forms what is sometimes referred to as the **NLP stack** or **NLP pipeline**. This will give us insights into the linguistic nature of words as well as the rules guiding the organization of words into sentences. We will see that analyzing surface forms linguistic nature can be a first step into disambiguation. We will look at the contrast between *to cook* and *a cook* as an example to illustrate this point.

Chapter 9, *Definition-Based Grounding*, looks at **word sense disambiguation** and **Entity Linking**, meaning determining a surface form semantic nature through its contextual surrounding so as to link it to a particular entity. For example, take the word *Paris*, as it is found in different sentences in Wikipedia:

The group consisted of lead singer Priscilla *Paris*.
Ohio *Paris* is an unincorporated community in Northwestern *Paris* Township, Ohio.
He visited *Paris* and London.
Paris metro line 7 is one of sixteen lines of the *Paris* metro system.
Paris Hilton endorses the clothing line.

The different occurrences of the surface form *Paris* in text do not refer to a single entity but to multiple possible entities. Chapter 9 explores text comparison methods to determine which entity is the most likely one.

Chapter 10, *Relatedness*, looks at how we can automatically extract related terms from corpora. The chapter provides a first incursion into the popular NLP field of **distributional semantics**, as we use statistical measures of word co-occurrences in corpora to infer their relatedness. We will explore one possible use of word relatedness, slightly modifying the definition-based grounding algorithm defined in the previous chapter to obtain better performances.

Chapter 8
Linguistic Roles

In Chap. 2, we saw that entities can be expressed in many different ways. A *mobile phone* can be referred to as a *cell phone*, a *cellular phone*, or even simply as a *cell*. This last surface form is quite problematic, since it is highly ambiguous. Just think of the many possible meanings of *cell*: a *battery cell*, a *skin cell*, a *prison cell*, just to name a few. This phenomenon of a single surface form referring to many meanings is known as **polysemy**.

This chapter will focus on one particular type of polysemy, when surface forms take on several linguistic roles (e.g., verb, noun, adjective). For example, the word *cook* can be used as a verb, as in *My friend likes to cook*, or as a noun, as in *The restaurant hired a great cook*. We can refer to these linguistic roles as **parts of speech** (POS). And as you can see, the single surface form *cook* has taken on two different parts of speech.

So, how would we go about searching for a particular word with a specific part of speech in text? How can I find sentences in which *cook* is used as a verb? Unfortunately, sentences do not explicitly provide the part of speech for the words they contain. This means that some kind of processing must be applied to the text before we can perform any direct search for verb occurrences of *cook*. This is where Natural Language Processing (NLP) comes in, to render the content of sentences explicit from a linguistic point of view.

This chapter will introduce five main NLP processes which make up for a typical **NLP stack** or **NLP pipeline**: **tokenization**, **sentence splitting**, **lemmatization**, **part-of-speech tagging** and **parsing**. Our purpose will be to explore these processes at a high level of understanding and develop the analytical skills needed to consider results generated by current NLP software.

Continuing the experimental path taken in this book, we will define a linguistic-based disambiguation task relying on the output of a POS tagger. This will allow us to discuss two important types of evaluations in NLP: intrinsic evaluation and extrinsic evaluation. In the **intrinsic evaluation**, we will measure the performance of the POS tagger for its own purpose, that of performing part-of-speech tagging,

© Springer International Publishing Switzerland 2016
C. Barrière, *Natural Language Understanding in a Semantic Web Context*,
DOI 10.1007/978-3-319-41337-2_8

where as in the **extrinsic evaluation**, we will measure the performance of the POS tagger indirectly through its impact on the performance of another task relying on it. That other task, in our case, will be a linguistic-based disambiguation task.

8.1 Tokenization

The first NLP process to look into is **tokenization**. We have already explored tokenization in Chap. 5, more specifically in Sect. 5.6.2, when we discussed performing word frequency analysis as to get insight into the content of a corpus. It would have been hard to get this far into a Natural Language Understanding book without introducing tokenization, since it is one important process that triggers our thinking of the difference between strings (surface forms) and lexical units (words or groups of words with a particular meaning).

We would hope for tokenization to split a text into a list of lexical units, but not quite so. Tokenization is the first major challenge in analyzing text, since lexical unit boundaries are not that easy to find. For example, in the sentence below, *week-end* is a lexical unit, so is *U.S.*, and so is *Las Vegas*, but their boundaries are not explicit (one contains a dash, another contains periods, and the third includes a space between its two parts).

> During his last trip to the U.S., Lucy's father spent two week-ends in Las Vegas.

From the point of view of text processing, this sentence is no more than a continuation of characters, just one long string. The most common approach to processing such sentence is to first split the series of characters into **tokens**, which can sometimes be words, but can also be digits, punctuation marks, or other symbols. Next, we attempt to reconstruct lexical units using these tokens.

Tokenization refers to the process of finding tokens. A **tokenizer** takes a longer string and splits it into substrings (tokens), using a specified list of **separators**. A separator is an actual character within the string where the split should happen. The list of separators is a very important element in the process, since it acts to produce the tokens which become the building blocks for later steps in text processing. The space is the basic separator, but there are many others, including punctuation marks (period, comma, colon, semicolon, etc.), quotation marks, apostrophes, and dashes. To understand the impact of the various separators within the tokenization process, Table 8.1 shows the lists of tokens that result from three possible sets of separators.

What at first glance seems to be a simple process has suddenly become quite complicated. The main issue is the variability in the ways in which lexical units are written, and the fact that specific variants conflict with what we might call "typical" boundaries of lexical units. All separators are only *possible* separators, not definite ones. Let us briefly explore the variations highlighted in the example above.

Noun compounds: These are lexical units made up of multiple words. Named entities, such as people's names and city names, are often noun compounds. For example,

Table 8.1 Impact of different separators on tokenizing results

Separator	Resulting tokens
Space only	during, his, last, trip, to, the, U.S., Lucy's, father, spent, two, week-ends, in, Las, Vegas
Punctuations	during, his, last, trip, to, the, U, S, Lucy's, father, spent, two, week-ends, in, Las, Vegas
Apostrophe, dash, punctuations	during, his, last, trip, to, the, U, S, Lucy, 's, spent, two, week, ends, in, Las, Vegas

Los Angeles, *Las Vegas*, and *New York* are all city names which are also noun compounds. Noun compounds, or more generally multiword lexical units, are so complex that a significant amount of research in NLP is devoted specifically to them. We touch on them regularly throughout this book, especially in connection to their compositionality. The notion of compositional meaning was introduced in Chap. 2 with the example of *mobile phone* being a compositional noun compound.

Possessive and contraction marker: In English text, possession is often expressed through the apostrophe, such as *John's hat*, or *Lucy's father*. The apostrophe also serves as a contraction marker, such as *we're*, *let's* or *hasn't*. These phenomena are less problematic than noun compounds, however, since there is more regularity in their usage.

Abbreviations: Abbreviations are very common in text, since communication is made more efficient through the use of short forms. Rather than continually repeating long forms of expressions in text, it is very common for authors to suggest an abbreviation that they will proceed to use in the remainder of their text. This is known as *explicit* abbreviation, since the long form of the expression is first stated and only later abbreviated. Another way in which abbreviations are used is when a long form refers to a concept that is assumed to be known by the reader (e.g., United States). In these cases, authors will not hesitate to simply use an abbreviation (e.g., U.S.) from the beginning, without defining it. This is known as *implicit* abbreviation, since the long form is not necessarily stated. Abbreviation expansion is a topic that is studied by many researchers in NLP, and the two forms just mentioned (explicit and implicit) lead to the development of different algorithms for understanding them.

Orthographic variations: We have already seen these variations in Chap. 2, in the context of lexical units having various equivalent forms. These forms include a one-word form, a dash-separated form, and a space-separated form (e.g., weekend, weekend, week end). We even went as far as discussing rules for automatically generating such variations. It is important to be aware of whether or not the tokenizer being used separates on the dash (-), so as to correctly perform a subsequent text search.

The task of tokenizing can become quite difficult with the many variations and inconsistencies in language. A particular list of token separators might work well in one application but not in another. The space is an essential separator, but can also be quite problematic. It is the default separator, but it is also found in many multiword lexical units, especially proper nouns (city names, country names, company names, etc.). Then, the period (.) is also a problematic separator. It should not be considered as a separator when occurring within abbreviations, but it should be considered a separator when indicating the end of a sentence.

There are several open source tokenizers for different languages (e.g., English, Spanish), in various programming environments (e.g., python, java, scala). In our current exploration, we will neither favor one tool over another, nor seek to demonstrate the particular strength or weakness of any given tool. For the purposes of discussion and reflection, I have chosen to carry out our exploration in the context of a well-known software platform, but I strongly encourage readers to explore other tools, in the programming language of their choice. In this book, we will work with the **Stanford CoreNLP software**, which has been developed over many years and is widely used within the world of NLP, thanks to its implementation of state-of-the-art approaches.

Table 8.2 shows the results of applying the Stanford CoreNLP tokenizer to the sentence from our earlier discussion of tokenization, repeated below.

During his last trip to the U.S., Lucy's father spent two week-ends in Las Vegas.

Table 8.2 Tokenizing with Stanford CoreNLP tokenizer

Position	Token	Lemma	POS
1	During	during	IN
2	his	he	PRP
3	last	last	JJ
4	trip	trip	NN
5	to	to	TO
6	the	the	DT
7	U.S.	U.S.	NNP
8	,	,	,
9	Lucy	Lucy	NNP
10	's	's	POS
11	father	father	NN
12	spent	spend	VBD
13	two	two	CD
14	week-ends	week-end	NNS
15	in	in	IN
16	Las	Las	NNP
17	Vegas	Vegas	NNP
18	.	.	.

After observing the resulting tokens (column 2) in Table 8.2, we can see that this tokenizer did use the space as a separator, but seemingly did not use the period. This would explain why *U.S.* stayed as one unit whereas *Las* and Vegas were separated.

Also, the *'s* was separated from *Lucy*, meaning that the possessive marker was recognized, but *week-end* remained one piece, indicating that the dash was not used as a separator. Notice that we are hypothesizing about the nature of the algorithm based on its results, while not knowing for sure.

Even if for most NLP task we would not write our own tokenizer, but simply use one provided by open source software, I encourage the reader to do so (see Exercise 8.1) for two reasons. The first reason is simply for learning purposes, to get a better sense of token variations caused by different separators. The second reason is to acknowledge that sometimes special situations do require to go outside of what is provided by open source software. An example of a special situation is the analysis of unusual types of text containing many abbreviations, or uncommon combinations of characters (e.g., "00-X1.08"). In this case, typical separators would probably be insufficient, and open source software might not perform well. A second example is when working on less common languages for which NLP tools do not already exist. In such case, we actually have no other choice than to write our own tokenizer.

Now, going back to Table 8.2, we see that it also provides the results of lemmatization (column 3) and part-of-speech tagging (column 4). These tasks will be the topics of further sections, as we continue our journey through the NLP pipeline. But first, let us see how tokenization is an important step for the task of sentence splitting.

8.2 Sentence Splitting

Sentence splitting is perhaps the best NLP task to become aware that a trivial human process becomes quite complex to capture within an algorithm. Our first intuition to segment sentences is simply to use *end-of-sentence* punctuation marks as separators, such as interrogation point (?), exclamation point (!), and period (.). But similarly to lexical unit boundaries being hard to find, sentence boundaries are also hard to find, due to the fact that end-of-sentence markers are also used for other purposes.

Let us go back to *Lucy's father* example, and expand a bit on it.

During his last trip to the U.S., Lucy's father, spent two week-ends in Las Vegas. That was a welcome change from his usual days in his office A.405, next to his loud neighbour, Mr. A.K. Dorr.

Now, it is probably trivial to a human to determine that the example above contains two sentences, but a naive sentence splitter based on the period as a separator will actually generate 8 sentences, as seen below.

S1. During his last trip to the U
S2. S
S3. , Lucy's father, spent two week-ends in Las Vegas
S4. That was a welcome change from his usual days in his office A
S5. 405, next to his loud neighbour, Mr.
S6. A
S7. K
S8. Dorr

This is an unacceptable result, caused by the polysemous nature of the period ('.'). Further examining the context surrounding a possible sentence boundary will help determine if it really is indicative of a sentence boundary or not. For example, assume a period found at position p_i in a sentence, some factors that we can consider are as follows:

- Is the word following p_i capitalized?
- Is there a space after p_i?
- Is there another '.' within X characters before/after p_i?
- Is the word following p_i part of a dictionary of known words?
- Assuming the period at p_i were a real sentence splitter, would the resulting sentence (before p_i) be of a normal length (within a standard deviation of normal sentence size)?
- Is there a digit before/after p_i?
- Is p_i within a known abbreviation, as found in a gazetteer?

These factors can be seen as heuristics to be combined in a **rule-based system** (see Exercise 8.2). Some of them could be written as a set of regular expressions. These factors could also become features within a **supervised learning approach**. A learning approach, based on annotated data, would learn how to combine and weigh each factor. Annotated data for this task, contrarily to many NLP tasks, are not too hard to obtain, as although it can be time-consuming to identify each period in a text as end-of-sentence or not, it is at least a task for which the inter-annotator agreement is very high.

Both approaches (rule-based and supervised learning) are used in different open source software performing sentence splitting. Researchers rarely rewrite their own sentence splitter unless they work on nonstandard texts (e.g., product descriptions, patents) for which open source software would not perform well.

Let us move on to the next step, lemmatization, which takes us within the realm of linguistic analysis.

8.3 Lemmatization

In the following examples, a tokenizer, such as the Stanford NLP tokenizer previously used, would identify the tokens *cooking* and *cooks*. Despite the fact that both refer to the same concept of *cook* as a verb (an action), they are still alternate surface forms. We have to *lemmatize* the sentences in order to obtain the base form of the verb *cook*.

Cooking pasta is easy.
The chef at this restaurant *cooks* pasta al dente.

Lemmatization is a standard task in the NLP pipeline. From the point of view of processing, its aim is to find a base or canonical form of words encountered in text. This base form is the one found in dictionaries. Two common variations of words are derivations and inflections. **Inflection** refers to transformation within the same part of speech, such as different forms of a verb (e.g., arrive, arrived). **Derivation** refers to transformation *between* parts of speech, such as between a noun and adjective or past participle (e.g., hospital, hospitalized).

Lemmatization is used for inflections and therefore does not change the part of speech of a word. Lemmatization rules are both part-of-speech specific and **language specific**. For example, verb variations in French are much more extensive than in English, with the conjugated verb forms varying for each person. Table 8.3 contrasts the variations for the verb *cook* in French and English.

Table 8.3 Verb variations in French and English

Person	French (cuisiner)	English (to cook)
First singular	je cuisine	I cook
Second singular	tu cuisines	you cook
Third singular	il cuisine	he cooks
First plural	nous cuisinons	we cook
Second plural	vous cuisinez	you cook
Third plural	ils cuisinent	they cook

In the case of nouns, English lemmatization rules would transform plural forms into singular forms (e.g., symphonies/symphony). As for other parts of speech, although English may not have any variations on them, other languages do. In French for example, there are different modifications of adjectives, depending on the context. The phrase *a nice woman* would be written with the feminine version of the adjective (*une femme gentille*), whereas the phrase *a nice man* would take on the masculine version of the adjective (*un homme gentil*).

Table 8.2, introduced earlier, contains the results of applying the Stanford CoreNLP lemmatizer to our earlier example about *Lucy's father* (column 2). We can see the past tense *spent* lemmatized to *spend*, and the plural *week-ends* lemmatized to the base form *week-end*.

Writing a lemmatizer would require profound knowledge of the language rules for conjugating verbs, as well as those for transforming nouns and adjectives from their plural to their singular forms. This would be further complicated by the fact that certain languages explicitly mark variations based on the role of a particular word in a sentence. For example, in some languages, a word ending would be different depending on whether the word is the subject or the object of the verb. Notice that talking of verb objects and subjects moves us into the realm of *parsing*, which involves the consideration of words in relation to each other. A word can be a noun and a subject, or a noun and an object. We will cover the concept of parsing in a later section, but for now let us focus on the last column of Table 8.2, the **POS tag**, which goes hand in hand with the **lemma**.

8.4 POS Tagging

POS tagging is the process of assigning a part-of-speech tag to each token in a sentence. Various sets of tags have been suggested over the years and several different ones are used today. A tag set can be coarse grained, or more fine grained. Grouping all adjectives together would be an action of a coarse-grained tag set, whereas a more fine-grained set would make more distinctions, between comparative, superlative, and numeric adjectives for example. A popular tag set today is the Penn Treebank. This set is used in the Stanford NLP Core and is shown in Table 8.4, with examples to illustrate each tag.

POS taggers can be thought of as classifiers, since they take each word and classify it within a set of categories. There are 36 categories in the Penn Treebank (see Table 8.4), which can be characterized as fairly fine grained, since it differentiates between different types of nouns (e.g., proper, plural) and verbs (e.g., base, past, gerund).

Since most words can be assigned different tags depending on context, POS taggers will take context into consideration. For example, a **rule-based tagger** is often performed in a two-pass process. In a first pass through the text, default tags associated with particular words are assigned. For example, the default tag for *cook* could be VB (verb). Then, in a second pass through the text, the tags can be changed based on the word's context. The tagged context for *cook* after the first pass can be {*night/NN, the/DT, cook/VB, improvises/VB, new/JJ*}. An example of a rule to change a tag in the second pass would be to look in the tagged context and realize that there is a determinant (DT) before a verb (VB), which is not possible, and then change the verb into a noun, generating this new tagged segment: {*night/NN, the/DT, cook/NN, improvises/VB, new/JJ*}.

Rules and changes of this kind are manually built into the tagger. Throughout the development process of a rule-based tagger, the rules are continually refined and applied against a gold standard to evaluate their performance. In rule-based tagging, the assumption is that the most likely tag is the correct one 90 % of the time. Correction rules can then be defined to apply in particular situations. These situations are most often ones where we find other particular tags within a window of plus or minus N words from the word being tagged. The central problem with rule-based taggers is that they are a challenge to develop, especially as the number of rules grows and the amount of interference between them increases. Other POS tagging approaches are supervised learning approaches requiring annotated data and using machine learning to learn a classification model.

POS tagging is a fairly low-level NLP process, likely to be used in many different applications. That said, it is not trivial to carry out, and even state-of-the-art open source software is likely to make errors, especially when working with sentences that contain multiple ambiguous words. We will see this through examples in our experiment in Sect. 8.6. For now, let us study one more module in the NLP pipeline, the parser.

Table 8.4 Penn Treebank list of POS tags

Num	POS Tag	Description	Example
1	CC	coordinating conjunction	or, and
2	CD	cardinal number	5, 12
3	DT	determiner	a, the
4	EX	existential there	there is
5	FW	foreign word	coeur
6	IN	preposition/subordinating conjunction	in, for, of
7	JJ	adjective	large, simple
8	JJR	comparative adjective	larger, simpler
9	JJS	superlative adjective	largest, simplest
10	LS	list marker	1) 2.
11	MD	modal	would, should
12	NN	noun, singular or mass	key, piano
13	NNS	noun plural	keys, pianos
14	NNP	proper noun, singular	Denise, Karima
15	NNPS	proper noun, plural	Canadians, Germans
16	PDT	predeterminer	both the boys
17	POS	possessive ending	cat's, body's
18	PRP	personal pronoun	she, you, they
19	PRP$	possessive pronoun	his, her
20	RB	adverb	simply, here, slowly
21	RBR	comparative adverb	slower
22	RBS	superlative adverb	slowest
23	RP	particle	come in, lift up
24	SYM	symbol	+, &
25	TO	to	to do, to bake
26	UH	interjection	ahhhhhh, ohhh
27	VB	verb, base form	go, eat, look
28	VBD	verb, past tense	went, ate, looked
29	VBG	verb, gerund/present participle	going, eating, looking
30	VBN	verb, past participle	gone, eaten, looked
31	VBP	verb, sing. present, non-3d	go, eat, look
32	VBZ	verb, third person sing. present	goes, eats, looks
33	WDT	wh-determiner	what, where, why
34	WP	wh-pronoun	whom, which
35	WP$	possessive wh-pronoun	whose
36	WRB	wh-abverb	where, when

8.5 Constituency Parsing

In parsing, part-of-speech tags become the building blocks in structuring rules, which dictate how correct sentences should be organized. These **grammar rules** are language dependent and vary widely in their complexity. We will use a few examples to explore grammar rules and the syntactic processing which uses these rules to generate a **phrase-structure tree**, or as we call it in NLP, a **parse tree**. This example-based approach has for goal to make us become familiar with parsing but not go as far as unraveling the details of how parsing is performed.

A basic principle of language is that grammar rules allow constituents to be combined to form larger constituents, in a bottom-up manner, eventually forming the ultimate constituent that is a sentence. In NLP, **parsing** a sentence refers to recovering the set of rules which lead us from a sequence of words to a sentence (S). The result of this process can be represented in a tree, where (S) is the root, the phrase constituents (noun phrase, verb phrase, prepositional phrase, etc.) are the intermediate nodes, and the words, together with their POS tags, are the leaves.

```
The cook supervises all kitchen staff.
S --> NP --> (DT The)
       --> (NN cook)
  --> VP --> (VBZ supervises)
       --> NP --> (DT all)
              --> (NN kitchen)
              --> (NN staff)
```

The parse tree shown above was generated by the Stanford CoreNLP Parser. It exemplifies four grammar rules, which I have listed below, along with their interpretations.

(1) S → NP, VP
A sentence (S) consists of a noun phrase (NP) followed by a verb phrase (VP).
(2) NP → DT, NN
A noun phrase (NP) consists of a determiner (DT) followed by a noun (NN).
(3) VP → VBZ, NP
A verb phrase (VP) consists of a conjugated verb (VBZ) followed by a noun phrase (NP).
(4) NP → DT, NN, NN
A noun phrase (NP) consists of a determinant (DT) followed by two nouns (NN).

The English grammar within the parser contains many rules such as these. This would be true for French, Spanish, or any language which requires encoding language-specific grammars. Furthermore, most parsers today are probabilistic parsers, meaning that they use annotated data[1] to learn the contextual cues for assigning appropriate weightings on the rules, then allowing their decisions to vary according to context. By context, we mean the lexical items (the choice of words) used in the sentence.

Our purpose here is not to learn the entire set of rules in the Stanford CoreNLP parser, but to familiarize ourselves with the notion of grammar rules more generally, as well as the ambiguity that is possible in sentences, which can complicate the

---

[1] See Chap. 5, Sect. 5.1, for a brief introduction to annotated corpora.

use of these rules. Certainly, two main causes of ambiguity are **conjunctional and prepositional attachment**, as we look at below.

Conjunctional attachment problem: One important type of ambiguity, in parsing, is conjunctional attachment. The problem arises, for example, when words can be interpreted as nouns or verbs, and then can be in coordination with other nouns or verbs in the sentence. As shown in the parse tree below, the word *cooks* is interpreted as a plural noun (NNS), leading to the somewhat odd semantic interpretation that both cooks and pottery can be created. The noun phrase (NP) *pottery and cooks* is the result of the conjunction between *pottery* (NN) and *cooks* (NNS) as allowed by a grammatical rule *NP → NN, CC, NNS*.

```
She continues to write, and also creates pottery and cooks.
S --> NP --> (PRP She)
  --> VP --> VP --> (VBD continues)
                --> S --> VP --> (TO to)
                              --> (VB write)
          --> ,
          --> (CC and)
          --> VP --> ADVP --> (RB also)
                  --> (VBZ creates)
                  --> NP --> (NN pottery)
                         --> (CC and)
                         --> (NNS cooks)
```

Contextual variability of the parser, as mentioned above for probabilistic parsers, can be tested by making small lexical changes and observing variations in the resulting parse tree. For example, substituting *cooks* for *bakes*, we can elicit an interpretation, shown in the parse tree below, which favors the conjunction *she creates pottery* and *she bakes*, which is semantically more likely.

```
She continues to write, and also creates pottery and bakes.
S --> NP --> (PRP She)
  --> VP --> VP --> (VBD continues)
                --> S --> VP --> (TO to)
                              --> (VB write)
          --> ,
          --> (CC and)
          --> VP --> ADVP --> (RB also)
                  --> VP --> (VBZ creates)
                         --> NP --> (NN pottery)
                  --> (CC and)
                  --> VP --> (VBZ bakes)
```

Prepositional attachment problem: A second important type of ambiguity, in parsing, is prepositional attachment. Ambiguity with prepositions is created by the fact that they can attach to verbs or nouns to form verb phrases (VP) or noun phrases (NP). To illustrate this point, let us look at Sentence 12 from the CookCorpus (see the corpus in Table 8.5 used in the experiment of Sect. 8.6).

```
They're cooking it for us.
S --> NP --> (PRP They)
  --> VP --> (VBP 're)
        --> VP --> (VBG cooking)
              --> NP --> (PRP it)
              --> PP --> (IN for)
                    --> NP --> (PRP us)
```

In the interpretation above, provided by the parser, the prepositional phrase (PP) *for us* is attached to the verb *cooking* through the use of the rule (a) *VP → VBG NP PP*. Another possible interpretation is shown below, where the prepositional phrase is moved inside the noun phrase *it for us*:

```
They're cooking it for us. (alternate interpretation)
S --> NP --> (PRP They)
  --> VP --> (VBP 're)
        --> VP --> (VBG cooking)
              --> NP --> NP --> (PRP it)
                    --> PP --> (IN for)
                          --> NP --> (PRP us)
```

In the latter case, the rule (b) *NP → NP PP* was used. Notice how the two rules, (a) and (b), allow the inclusion of the PP to form larger VP or NP. These two possible attachments for PP are the source of prepositional attachment ambiguity. This ambiguity, in most probabilistic parsers today, is resolved based on probabilistic evidence gathered from annotated training data. In the case above, we can deduct that the training data provided more evidence for attaching *for us* to *it*, than attaching *for us* to *cooking*. This shows how, when using an off-the-shelf probabilistic parser, we should inquire about the corpora which was used for its training.

In this most recent example, the semantics of both possible parse trees are very close. Either the *cooking* is *for us*, or the result of cooking, *it*, is *for us*.

There are cases where this kind of variation in prepositional attachment has a much larger semantic impact, as in the following variation on the classic NLP textbook example *The fruit flies like yellow bananas.*

```
The fruit flies like yellow bananas. (1)
S --> NP --> (DT The)
        --> (NN fruit)
        --> (NNS flies)
  --> VP --> (VBP like)
        --> NP --> (JJ yellow)
              --> (NNS bananas)

The fruit flies like yellow bananas. (2)
S --> NP --> (DT The)
        --> (NN fruit)
  --> VP --> (VBZ flies)
        --> PP --> (IN like)
              --> NP --> (JJ yellow)
                    --> (NNS bananas)
```

The semantics of interpretation (1) have fruit flies enjoying bananas. Notice how *the fruit flies* is held together as one unit in the NP of this interpretation. Interpretation (2), however, has a particular fruit flying like bananas do. Notice that the NP here is only made up of *the fruit*, and the verb has changed from *like* to *flies*. The second interpretation clearly requires a lot of imagination, and its semantics are far fetched, but from a grammatical standpoint, both interpretations lead to valid (syntactically correct) sentences. This situation stems from the fact that the word *flies* can be a noun or a verb, and at the same time the word *like* can be a verb or a preposition, allowing for both sentence interpretations.

This example illustrates the important difference between syntax and semantics. **Syntax** concerns the building of correct sentences with respect to specific grammar rules for combining words. These rules are arbitrary and are defined for each particular language. The syntactic rules for French, for example, are not the same as those for English. Syntax is about form, not content. **Semantics**, on the other hand, is concerned with the actual meaning of the sentence. Semantics are linked to our individual and collective knowledge of the world, which allows us to determine what makes sense and what does not. If we have never encountered flying fruits, we are likely to decide that interpretation (2) is not semantically viable.

Admittedly, this brief introduction to parsing does not provide us with enough knowledge to write our own parser. We have learned however, that parsers are a series of grammar rules applied to construct a tree-like structure and that ambiguity in the language allows multiple possible constructions from a single sentence. Many sentences can be correct from a syntactic point of view, even if their semantic interpretations are not all equally probable.

The trees shown in this section have two main names, either **phrase-structure trees**, or **constituency trees** and they are the result of **phrase-structure parsers** or **constituency parsers**.

We now have a full NLP pipeline in our NLP toolbox: the tokenizer, the sentence splitter, the lemmatizer, the POS tagger and the constituency parser. Going forward, we should bear in mind that these modules are imperfect, since they will influence our later results. This knowledge will not prevent us from continuing our exploration though, or in this case, from going back to our original quest of searching for sentences containing the word *cook* in a particular linguistic role. We will return to this original quest in the next section.

8.6   Experiment — Classifying Groups of Entities

We now turn our sights back to our original goal and to our working example of the word *cook*. Let us set up a proper experiment, defining our experiment steps, and then going through them, one by one.

1. Define our goal.
2. Define our gold standard and evaluation method.
3. Define and test our approach.
4. Evaluate our results.
5. Analyze and discuss.

8.6.1 Goal of the Experiment

The overall purpose of our task is to link occurrences of surface forms found in text toward the proper underlying entities which they represent. The small CookCorpus, shown in Table 8.5, contains occurrences of a polysemous word *cook* which would link to different entities. Some sentences in the corpus have been used in the previous section to illustrate parsing ambiguity.

Table 8.5 Dataset CookCorpus

No.	Sentence
1	The *cook* supervises all kitchen staff.
2	*Cook* joined the expedition here.
3	Dumplings are *cooked* balls of dough.
4	Stir well and *cook* for some time.
5	Chicago is also part of *Cook* County.
6	A lawsuit ensued, which *Cook* ultimately won.
7	*Cook* rice by steaming it.
8	It is written in *Cook*'s book.
9	She continues to write, and also creates pottery and *cooks*.
10	The two *cooks* reflected and found a way out.
11	A grill pan *cooks* food with radiant heat.
12	They're *cooking* it for us.
13	*Cooking* outside in the summer helps keeping the house cool.

Let us now state an assumption which will result into a subgoal that we will work toward. The assumption is that a linguistic-based coarse-grained disambiguation is a first step toward a more fine-grained entity disambiguation. This means that before we even try to differentiate between two senses of *cooking* (e.g., a *grill pan cooking* (ex. 11) versus *them cooking* (ex. 12)), or between two senses of a person named *Cook* (e.g., *James Cook* (ex. 2) or *another Mr. or Mrs. Cook* (ex. 6)), we should first perform a coarse-grained split of the senses based on their linguistic roles. Our three coarse-grained categories will correspond the following:

Definitions:
(C1) name Cook : a person or location (a named entity) named Cook
(C2) cooking   : the action of cooking
(C3) a cook   : a person who is a chef, or who is simply creating a meal

The new subgoal then can be restated as a **categorization task**, one that must distinguish between the 3 categories above.

8.6.2 Gold Standard and Evaluation Method

Now that we have defined our goal as a categorization task, we can classify, by hand, the examples of Table 8.5, to obtain our gold standard. We manually assign the 13 sentences into the three categories, as shown below.

Gold Standard:
(C1) name Cook : Sentences 2, 5, 6, 8
(C2) cooking   : Sentences 3, 4, 7, 9, 11, 12, 13
(C3) a cook   : Sentences 1, 10

How will we evaluate an algorithm's output in comparison with these category assignments? We will make use of **overall precision**, since we can count the number of sentences properly classified over the total number of sentences. It might be interesting to further evaluate if the algorithms are particularly good or bad for certain categories, then evaluating its **per-class precision**.

8.6.3 Our Method: Classification through POS Tagging

Let us define our method in 4 steps:

1. Establish a correspondence between POS tags from the Penn Treebank and each category we wish to identify.
2. Use a POS tagger to tag each sentence.
3. Retrieve the POS tag assigned to each occurrence of *cook*.
4. Classify the sentence in the category corresponding to the POS tag found.

For the first step, let us establish the following correspondences:

POS tags:
(C1) name Cook : NNP (proper noun, singular), NNPS (proper noun, plural)
(C2) cooking :   VB (verb, base form), VBD (verb, past tense),
                       VBG (verb, gerund/present part.),
                       VBN (verb, past part.), VBP (verb, sing. present, non-3d),
                       VBZ (verb, third.p.s. present)
(C3) a cook :   NN (noun, singular or mass), NNS (noun plural)

For the second step, let us use the Stanford POS tagger. Table 8.6 shows the results of applying the tagger onto the CookCorpus sentences.

Table 8.6 CookCorpus tagged using the Stanford POS tagger

No.	Sentence
1	The/DT cook/NN supervises/VBZ all/DT kitchen/NN staff/NN.
2	Cook/VB joined/VBD the/DT expedition/NN here/RB.
3	Dumplings/NNS are/VBP cooked/VBN balls/NNS of/IN dough/NN.
4	Stir/VB well/RB and/CC cook/VB for/IN some/DT time/NN.
5	Chicago/NNP is/VBZ also/RB part/NN of/IN Cook/NNP County/NNP.
6	A/DT lawsuit/NN ensued/VBN ,/, which/WDT Cook/VBP ultimately/RB won/VBN.
7	Cook/VB rice/NN by/IN steaming/VBG it/PRP.
8	It/PRP is/VBZ written/VBN in/IN Cook/NNP 's/POS book/NN.
9	She/PRP continues/VBZ to/TO write/VB ,/, and/CC also/RB creates/VBZ pottery/NN and/CC cooks/NNS.
10	The/DT two/CD cooks/NNS reflected/VBD and/CC found/VBD a/DT way/NN out/RP.
11	A/DT grill/NN pan/NN cooks/NNS food/NN with/IN radiant/JJ heat/NN.
12	They/PRP 're/VBP cooking/VBG it/PRP for/IN us/PRP.
13	Cooking/NN outside/IN in/IN the/DT summer/NN helps/VBZ keeping/VBG the/DT house/NN cool/NN.

From these results, we can perform the third and fourth steps, resulting in the following categorization.

Results:
(C1) name Cook : 5, 8
(C2) cooking   : 2, 3, 4, 6, 7, 12
(C3) a cook   : 1, 9, 10, 11, 13

8.6.4   Performance Evaluation

As we saw in Chap. 2, it is important to evaluate even the simplest algorithms in order to establish a baseline for comparison with later (and likely improved) algorithms.

Table 8.7 shows the results of the classification, using individual sentence numbers. The columns correspond to the gold standard categories, and the rows show the algorithm's results. The two are not always in agreement, as we can see if we take a closer look at Sentence 2, for example. According to the gold standard, it belongs to C1 (Cook), but the algorithm assigned it C2 (cooking).

Table 8.7 Classification results for using POS to differentiate senses of *cook*

		Gold Standard		
		C1 (Cook)	C2 (cooking)	C3 (a cook)
	C1 (Cook)	[5, 8]		
Algorithm	C2 (cooking)	[2, 6]	[3, 4, 7, 12]	
	C3 (a cook)		[9, 11, 13]	[1, 10]

The results shown in Table 8.7 are summarized in Table 8.8. Summarizing the information allows us to easily see the number of sentences in each category and makes for easy comparison between the gold standard and the results of the algorithm.

Table 8.8 Classification per-class and overall precisions

Class	Assigned	Total in GS	Precision
C1 (Cook)	2	4	0.500
C2 (cooking)	4	7	0.571
C3 (a cook)	2	2	1.0
Overall	8	13	0.615

The bottom row of Table 8.8 provides the overall precision, whereas the previous three rows provide the per-class precision. These would be of interest if we are looking for high performance on a particular class, but if we are more interested in the overall performance of the method, the overall precision score is a more relevant measure. We obtained 8 correct classifications among 13 possibilities, which translates to an overall precision score of 8/13, or 61.5 %. This seems quite low, especially when compared to the typical POS tagging performance of NLP software, which is often advertised as falling in the 90 % range. We will investigate the reason for this discrepancy in the following section.

8.6.5 Result Analysis — Intrinsic versus Extrinsic Evaluation

The evaluation we performed in the previous section is not a typical POS tagger evaluation. What we have just done would be known as an **extrinsic evaluation**, since we applied the results of the tagging process to a subsequent task (e.g., sense classification), and based our evaluation on that data. In contrast to this, the typical POS tagger evaluation is more likely to be an **intrinsic evaluation**, meaning that it would measure the performance of the tagger itself.

It is important to bear in mind the distinction between intrinsic and extrinsic evaluations, both as a user of NLP and as a potential future developer of NLP tools. There are times where much effort can be spent refining algorithms for performance gains on intrinsic evaluations, only to later realize that this has no effect on extrinsic evaluations.

So, how would we go about performing an intrinsic evaluation of the POS tagger? As usual, the first step is to build a gold standard, this time for the tagging task itself. In this case, this would mean manually assigning a part of speech to each word in all sentences of the CookCorpus. This seems like a difficult task, doesn't it? It would certainly be time-consuming, considering that tagging using the Penn Treebank tag set is not something we practice everyday, and so we are probably ill-prepared for such a task. We would first have to refer back to Table 8.4, master the 36 tags, and then call upon the English grammar rules we learned in school to encode the sentences with permitted sequences of tags. This would all be feasible, but certainly not trivial.

One approach that helps human annotators perform tasks like these more efficiently is to perform output correction, as opposed to full tagging (these are also known as **corrective annotation** and **full annotation**, respectively). In other words, we begin with an imperfect set of results which we then scan for errors and correct (output correction), as opposed to attempting to generate the results ourselves, from scratch (full tagging).

For example, to generate the gold standard in Table 8.9, we would start with the automatically tagged corpus (Table 8.6) and correct it. The trade-off between full annotation and corrective annotation depends on the performance level of the algorithm. Although it is true that corrective annotation is often more efficient, in cases where a large percentage of the tags generated by the algorithm needs correction, the burden on us as the user can end up being heavier than if we had generated the results ourselves. This is not the case in our current situation though, since less than 10 % of the results of the Stanford CoreNLP tagger need correcting. Table 8.10 shows the changes to each sentence that would be necessary to bring the algorithm's results into line with the gold standard.

The last line of Table 8.10 shows that overall 88 out of a total of 95 words were tagged correctly. This translates to an overall precision score of 92.6 %, which is quite high, and much more in line with what we would expect for NLP tagging software.

The difference between the extrinsic and intrinsic evaluations here is striking. Remember, our extrinsic evaluation yielded a precision of only 61.5 %, whereas we have just calculated 92.6 % precision for our intrinsic evaluation. Why the big gap? It is possible that the data we used for our extrinsic evaluation was simply anomalous,

Table 8.9 COOKCORPUS: manually annotated POS information

No.	Sentence
1	The/DT cook/NN supervises/VBZ all/DT kitchen/NN staff/NN.
2	Cook/NNP joined/VBD the/DT expedition/NN here/RB.
3	Dumplings/NNS are/VBP cooked/JJ balls/NNS of/IN dough/NN.
4	Stir/VB well/RB and/CC cook/VB for/IN some/DT time/NN.
5	Chicago/NNP is/VBZ also/RB part/NN of/IN Cook/NNP County/NNP.
6	A/DT lawsuit/NN ensued/VBN ,/, which/WDT Cook/NNP ultimately/RB won/VBN.
7	Cook/VB rice/NN by/IN steaming/VBG it/PRP.
8	It/PRP is/VBZ written/VBN in/IN Cook/NNP 's/POS book/NN.
9	She/PRP continues/VBZ to/TO write/VB ,/, and/CC also/RB creates/VBZ pottery/NN and/CC cooks/VBZ.
10	The/DT two/CD cooks/NNS reflected/VBD and/CC found/VBD a/DT way/NN out/RP.
11	A/DT grill/NN pan/NN cooks/VBZ food/NN with/IN radiant/JJ heat/NN.
12	They/PRP 're/VBP cooking/VBG it/PRP for/IN us/PRP.
13	Cooking/VBG outside/IN in/IN the/DT summer/NN helps/VBZ keeping/VBG the/DT house/NN cool/JJ.

Table 8.10 COOKCORPUS POS tagging intrinsic evaluation

No.	Correct tags	Nb tags	Required changes
1	6	6	–
2	4	5	cook: VB → NNP
3	5	6	cooked: VBN → JJ
4	7	7	–
5	7	7	–
6	7	8	Cook: VBP → NNP
7	5	5	–
8	7	7	–
9	10	11	cooks: NNS → VBZ
10	9	9	–
11	7	8	cooks: NNS → VBZ
12	6	6	–
13	8	10	cooking: NN → VBQ, cool: NN → JJ
Total	88	95	

and we can therefore chalk it up to bad luck. Or perhaps we performed our extrinsic evaluation on a task that did not make proper use of the highly accurate results of tagging, and so the results do not depict the strength of the tagger. In this case, we may have simply run into bad luck. The word *cook* may be particularly difficult to tag. After all, out of the 7 tagging errors made by the tagger, 6 were on the word *cook* and its variations.

So, what can we learn from this experiment? Well, one thing we have seen is that a randomly selected example (*cook*) can lead to bad luck and misleading results. Secondly, we should now understand that we cannot fairly evaluate an algorithm based on a single example. We should also be cautioned against assuming that the results of an intrinsic evaluation will transfer directly onto a subsequent task.

8.7   In Summary

- Although tokenization is simple in theory, it leads to significant questioning about what exactly defines lexical units, and how to determine lexical unit boundaries in sentences.
- Sentence splitting is a seemingly simple task, which turns out to be complex due the polysemous roles of end-of-sentence markers, mainly periods.
- Lemmatization transforms an inflected form of a word into its base form. It is a language-dependent process that requires knowledge of the various word inflections, based on an understanding of part-of-speech and grammar rules of each language.

- POS tagging refers to the process of assigning a POS tag to each word in a sentence. A popular tag set is the Penn Treebank tag set.
- Manually performing POS tagging on sentences is time-consuming and far from trivial. This contributes to the scarcity of available POS-annotated data.
- In phrase-structure grammars, the grammar rules are constituent combination rules. They outline how to combine constituents, in a bottom-up manner, starting from words, and culminating in a sentence.
- Conjunctions and prepositions are two main causes for ambiguity in parsing. The prepositional attachment problem is a long known problem in NLP, and it is still not resolved today.
- Most parsers today are probabilistic parsers, meaning that they learn from tagged data different probabilities for ambiguous attachments depending on their context of occurrence.
- Open source NLP pipelines that include tokenizers, sentence splitter, lemmatizers, POS taggers, and parsers are available for public use. The best way to evaluate their usefulness for specific applications is to test them on various sentences and to understand where they succeed, and where they fail.
- Evaluation of NLP modules can be intrinsic or extrinsic. An intrinsic evaluation is performed on the module itself (e.g., on the POS tagger), whereas an extrinsic evaluation is performed on the results of a task that depends on the module (e.g., classification using the results from the POS tagger).
- POS tagging can be used for coarse-grained disambiguation of words, as it differentiates verb forms from noun forms (e.g., *to cook, a cook*).

8.8 Further Reading

Annotated corpora: Manually generated a POS-tagged corpus is costly, as it requires many work hours by skilled annotators. Some annotated corpora, such as the popular Penn Treebank, are available through the Linguistic Data Consortium, https://catalog.ldc.upenn.edu/, at a cost.

NLP stack: The best way to understand in more details each process in the NLP stack is to actually experiment with various open source software which offer all or part of the pipeline.

- Stanford CoreNLP: The Stanford CoreNLP software, containing multiple modules, from tokenizer to parser, is available at http://nlp.stanford.edu/software/corenlp.shtml.
- Open NLP: a machine learning based toolkit for text processing, available at https://opennlp.apache.org/.
- LingPipe: A toolkit for text processing, available at http://alias-i.com/lingpipe/.

NIF: There is an ongoing effort for the development of a standard, called NIF (Natural Language Processing Interchange Format), to allow interoperability of NLP processing tools, resources and annotations (see http://persistence.uni-leipzig.org/nlp2rdf/). In this book, I explain ideas and methods without reference to particular formalisms, but it is important to acknowledge large community efforts devoted to developing such standards which will benefit both the NLP community and the Semantic Web community (see Hellmann et al. 2013).

8.9 Exercises

Table 8.11 Small HURTCORPUS

No.	Sentence
1	No one was hurt.
2	The noise starts hurting.
3	My knees still hurt.
4	Rejected and hurt, John leaves.
5	Sure, this will hurt William, but he will recover.
6	Mississipi John Hurt was also an influence.
7	Hurt was born in Darley Dale.
8	The Hurt Locker was a good movie.
9	The Great Depression hurt O'Neill's fortune.
10	William Hurt won the Academy Award for Best Actor.
11	Hurt, Rachel begins to defy Frank's painstaking security measure.
12	Wesley apologizes for getting her hurt, but she blames herself.
13	Even if nobody was hurt, John's restaurant fire caused a lot of stress.

Exercise 8.1 (Tokenization).

a. Try writing your own tokenizer, programming the different variations for separators shown in Table 8.1. Test your variations on a corpus, such as the COOKCORPUS (Table 8.5), or the new HURTCORPUS (Table 8.11).

b. Using the same corpora suggested in (a), try out a few open source tokenizers, such as the ones included in NLP stack software mentioned in Sect. 8.8.

Exercise 8.2 (Sentence splitting).

a. Go back to the example "*During his last trip to the U.S., Lucy's father, spent two week-ends in Las Vegas. That was a welcome change from his usual days in his office A.405, next to his loud neighbour, Mr. A.K. Dorr.*" and try a few open source sentence splitters on this short text, such as the ones included in NLP stack software mentioned in Sect. 8.8. Are there any differences between them?

b. Gather short paragraphs (containing at least a few sentences) from different text sources, which would represent various text types (news stories, Wikipedia pages, medical blogs, patents) and test the sentence splitters you used in (a). What do you notice about performance in relation to text type? Discuss.

c. Program your own sentence splitter, by developing an algorithm (a rule or a regular expression) for each of the seven questions put forward in Sect. 8.2. Compare your sentence splitter to the open source ones, using the paragraphs from the previous exercise for evaluation. Remember that to be fair, if you have actually used the sentences from (b) as your development set to program your sentence splitter, you should find new paragraphs (from the same sources of text) to generate a test set on which you will test your sentence splitter.

Exercise 8.3 (Lemmatization).

a. To better understand lemmatization, program a lemmatizer for plurals in English. Take into account the following transformations: remove 's' ending, change 'ies' ending to 'y', change 'ves' ending to 'f', and change 'men' ending to 'man.' Try your lemmatizer on different words, such as *car*, *woman*, *child*, *lamp*, *baby*, *news*, *story*, *storey*, *glossary*, *gloss*, and *currency*. Are the transformations encoded able to generate the singular form of all these words? If not, add the necessary rules.
b. Test the combination of your tokenizer from Exercise 8.1 and your lemmatizer from (a) on the HURTCORPUS. Discuss how it compares to an open source tokenizer and lemmatizer.

Exercise 8.4 (Part-of-speech tagging).

a. Go through Table 8.4, and familiarize yourself with the various tags by providing one additional example for each one.
b. To test the Stanford NLP POS tagger we used in Sect. 8.4, try variations for the *fruit fly* example we presented. The original sentence was *The fruit flies like yellow bananas*. Try changing *flies* to *insects* or *bugs*, and change *like* to *taste* or *eat*. You can also remove the determiner at the beginning of the sentence and try the singular form *fruit fly likes*. What do you notice? How do the changes impact the POS tagger?

Exercise 8.5 (Parsing).

a. To test the Stanford CoreNLP parser we used in Sect. 8.5, use the variations you generated in Exercise 8.4(b), as different example sentences to test the parser. What do you notice? How do the changes impact the parser?

Exercise 8.6 (Entity search).

a. Redo all the steps of the experiment we performed in Sect. 8.6, replacing the COOKCORPUS dataset with the HURTCORPUS dataset built in Table 8.11. We would like POS tagging to allow the differentiation between the verb *to hurt* and the proper noun *Hurt*. What are the disambiguation performances obtained? Is there still a large gap between the intrinsic and the extrinsic evaluations, as we had found in the original experiment?

Chapter 9
Definition-Based Grounding

In Chap. 8, more specifically in the experiment of Sect. 8.6, we started our grounding quest. We used linguistic processing, particularly part-of-speech tagging, to identify three categories of senses for the word *cook*, senses related to the verb *to cook*, the noun *cook*, and the proper noun *Cook*. But linguistic processing can only highlight distinctions in meaning which are captured by variations in parts of speech. There are many more distinctions to uncover. For example, the name *Cook* is a popular surname, and there are ample different people with that same name. In the current chapter, we will aim at identifying which *Mrs. Cook* or *Mr. Cook* is referred to in a text. We refer to this process as **grounding**, since we will try to connect textual mentions to actual entities found in resources.

This grounding of textual surface forms to actual concepts is a complex semantic process. It can be referred to as **Entity Linking**, in the context of searching for named entities, or as **Word Sense Disambiguation**, in the context of searching for common words. The two processes will be individually presented at the beginning of this chapter. The term *grounding*, or more precisely **semantic grounding**, was not in common usage ten years ago, although it is becoming more and more popular in today's world of NLP. The term encompasses both Entity Linking and Word Sense Disambiguation, irrespective of the actual task at hand.

The task of grounding would be simple, were it not for **polysemy**. Without the complications of polysemy, there would be only one concept for each surface form. Unfortunately, this is not the case. In this chapter, we will expand our understanding of polysemy and look into disambiguation strategies which make use of the context of occurrence of mentions in text.

I will introduce a **definition-based grounding** approach, which requires that concepts be explicitly defined in a resource. Various resources do provide explicit concept definitions, and we refer to them as possible **grounding spaces** for our disambiguation process. In this chapter, we will look into WordNet and Wikipedia as possible grounding spaces.

© Springer International Publishing Switzerland 2016
C. Barrière, *Natural Language Understanding in a Semantic Web Context*,
DOI 10.1007/978-3-319-41337-2_9

Our definition-based grounding approach also requires that concept definitions, as well as the context of the ambiguous surface form, are to be transformed into **bag-of-words representations** or simply **BOWs** for short. The resulting BOWs are then fed as input into an algorithm we call **BOW-Match** which will decide on a specific word sense or entity to be assigned to the surface form.

In this chapter, we will describe the steps performed by this BOW-Match algorithm and test its performances in an **Entity Linking experiment**, using Wikipedia as a grounding space.

9.1 Word Sense Disambiguation

Word Sense Disambiguation is the ability to computationally determine which sense of a word is activated by its use in a particular context. (Navigli (2009))

The classic example of **Word Sense Disambiguation**, found in most NLP text-books, is the word *bank*.

(a) He went to the *bank* to get 900 dollars to pay his rent.
(b) Charlie sat on the *bank*, refusing to go in the water.

The two senses of *bank* implied by the sentences above are quite different. In Word Sense Disambiguation, or commonly **WSD**, we wish to automatically find which sense is appropriate for each sentence. A possible source of senses, commonly used in NLP, is WordNet. Here are some definitions sampled from the WordNet noun entry for *bank*.[1]

WordNet senses:
1. sloping land (especially the slope beside a body of water)
2. a financial institution that accepts deposits and channels the money into lending activities
3. a long ridge or pile
4. an arrangement of similar objects in a row or in tiers
5. a supply or stock held in reserve for future use (especially in emergencies)
6. the funds held by a gambling house or the dealer in some gambling games
7. a container (usually with a slot in the top) for keeping money at home
8. a building in which the business of banking transacted

The WSD task can be seen as a **classification task**. In the case of *bank*, each example sentence must be classified into one of the possible 8 senses (classes).

Let us try to perform this classification manually. Looking through the eight possible meanings of *bank* above, it seems straightforward to associate the example (b) to definition (1), but what about example (a)? Does it correspond to definition (2) or definition (8)?

This small example illustrates how far from trivial, even for human judges, this WSD would be. There will likely be disagreement between human judges. This

---

[1]The definitions are found in Version 3.1. of WordNet.

notion of agreement/disagreement between human judges is formalized in a measure of what we call **inter-annotator agreement**.[2] Prior to performing any task using an algorithm, it is important to consider the difficulty the same task would pose for human beings, and the subjectivity involved. Doing so helps us to maintain realistic expectations of our algorithms.

Awareness of WSD's difficulty and subjectivity has sparked efforts within the NLP community to establish common datasets and evaluation processes. In an effort to provide a focus to the field, an important Word Sense Disambiguation competition was started in 1998, under the original name *SenseEval*. The competition is now called **SemEval**, as it has evolved to include other challenging semantic processing tasks.

The value of the competition does not necessarily lie in finding unequivocal answers to questions, or in resolving issues for good. Instead, it lies in bringing together an entire research community, whose members can then compare systems, discuss algorithmic problems, and reflect on the underlying difficulties associated with certain task requirements. At SenseEval-2, competing teams did not achieve very high results, either in the lexical sample tasks (finding a sense for a few selected words) or in the all-word tasks (disambiguating all words in a sentence). Nonetheless, this led to important discussions about the appropriateness of WordNet as a *grounding space* for a WSD task.

The resource used in a disambiguation task can be thought as a **grounding space**, as being metaphorically related to the real world. In psychology, grounding refers to the process whereby a reader or hearer maps a word onto a particular object, either within the real world or a constructed mental world. This object could be something in the hearer's surrounding environment or something referred to by the speaker. In terms of human development, grounding occurs first for physical objects, people, and locations, and later for more abstract ideas.

Such real world does not exist for computer programs, and we must simulate it through resources containing knowledge about the world, as well as knowledge about the words used to describe that world. **WordNet** has been such a lexical-semantic resource of choice, used as a grounding space for Word Sense Disambiguation for many years. WordNet's popularity is due to its ease of use and availability, as well as its knowledge organization through synsets and semantic links. As a grounding space, WordNet poses one difficulty, which is due to the fine granularity used in its sense divisions. We touched on this **sense division granularity** issue earlier, mentioning the fineness of the line separating senses 2 and 8 for the word *bank*. Researchers have come up with many ways of dealing with this issue over the years. Adaptations have been made on the resource side, by explicitly providing coarse-grained senses (grouping some subsets of definitions) or providing domain tags (e.g., Medical, Art, and Computer) to definitions, but also in WSD evaluation process, by allowing algorithms to group or rank senses assigned to a surface form, instead of choosing a single one.

---

[2] See Chap. 3, Sect. 3.4.1, for an introduction to inter-annotator agreement and its related κ measure.

WSD is a fascinating and active field of research, and I encourage the reader to further read surveys and articles mentioned in Sect. 9.9. In this chapter, we will limit ourselves to the investigation of simple approaches, ones that will provide us with a window into the underlying issues and help reveal why researchers continue to struggle with WSD, even after 30 years of work on the task.

Now, we look at Entity Linking, a task very similar to WSD. Later, we will suggest an algorithm that can be used for both WSD and Entity Linking, which we refer together as **semantic grounding tasks**.

9.2 Entity Linking

The difference between **Entity Linking** and Word Sense Disambiguation lies more in their respective choice of grounding space than in their intent. In Entity Linking, similarly to WSD, the intent is to disambiguate a surface form by automatically choosing its contextually most appropriate sense among a set of possible senses provided by a grounding space. As to the content of that grounding space, in Entity Linking, we do assume that it will include descriptions of named entities, rather than solely common words, as expected in WSD.

As opposed to the earlier WSD examples of *bank* referring to its meanings of (a) banking institution or (b) river bank, the example sentences to be included in an Entity Linking task are intended to contain named entities referred to as *bank*, such as:

(c) Eva works at the gallery on Bank, near Somerset.
(d) Charlie Chaplin starred in the movie The *Bank*.
(e) Many artists from *BANK* presented their work at galleries in London.

An appropriate grounding space for these examples is **Wikipedia**. A sample of six of its entries related to *bank* are shown below.

- LOCATION

    1. Bank Street (Ottawa, Ontario)
    2. Bank, Iran, city in Bushehr Province, Iran.

- ORGANIZATION

    3. BANK (art collective), a 1990 London art collective
    4. Bank Street College of Education, a private graduate school for Early Childhood Education, in New York, NY, U.S

- FILM

    5. The Bank (1915 film) The Bank was Charlie Chaplin's tenth film for Essanay Films.
    6. The Bank is an 2001 Australian thriller/drama film starring David Wenham and Anthony LaPaglia.

Notice how the entities are grouped by entity types: Location, Organization, and Film.[3] This grouping does offer a coarse-grained classification of senses. A **Named Entity Recognition** system, or **NER**, would try to recognize these types.[4] An accurate NER output for the example sentences would assign example (c) as a Location, example (d) as a Film, and example (e) as an Organization.

The task of Entity Linking would further disambiguate which of the possible location, film, or organization is meant in each example. An accurate assignment would find example (c) as sense (1), example (d) as sense (5), and example (e) as sense (3).

Before the term Entity Linking came about, a more commonly used term was **Named Entity Disambiguation** or **NED**. The term implicitly implies a focus on named entities for the disambiguating process. Although today, the term **Entity Linking** seems more appropriate given that Wikipedia is commonly chosen as the grounding space for the disambiguation process, and that Wikipedia's content has expanded toward covering not only named entities, but also common words, as well as domain-specific terms. For example, below is a sample of additional definitions for *bank*, grouped under particular domains (instead of entity types).

- Biology and medicine

    7. blood bank: A blood bank is a cache or bank of blood or blood components, gathered as a result of blood donation or collection, stored and preserved for later use in blood transfusion.
    8. gene bank: Gene banks are a type of biorepository which preserve genetic material.

- Sports

    9. Bank shot, a type of shot in basketball

- Transportation engineering, and aviation

    10. Bank or roll, in aircraft flight dynamics, a rotation of the vehicle about its longitudinal axis

- Other uses

    11. Bank (surname)
    12. Data bank, a storage area for information in telecommunications
    13. Memory bank, a logical unit of storage
    14. Piggy bank, a device for money saving

It is interesting to note that Wikipedia is becoming so common as a grounding space, that it has triggered changes in the definition of some NLP disambiguation tasks. Wikipedia is not the only resource expanding its coverage. As much as Wikipedia is venturing into providing definitions for common words, WordNet is venturing into defining a few named entities. There is currently much interest in both NLP and Semantic Web communities to find correspondence between resources,

---

[3] Wikipedia does not actually provide a strict organization by entity types, but rather groups entries under particular headings. I have associated some headings with possible types for the sake of our discussion.

[4] We explored the use of regular expressions in Chap. 3 to find named entities, and we will further look at NER systems in Chap. 13.

so as to benefit from their complementary information. For example, the **Babel-Net** project suggests multilingual mappings between Wikipedia and WordNet (see Sect. 9.9).

From our perspective of performing Entity Linking using Wikipedia as a grounding space, we face a large number of senses, either corresponding to named entities, to specific-domain terms or to common words. All these senses become a large set of possible classes into which the Entity Linking task is supposed to categorize a particular instance. Entity Linking is quite a difficult task, and over time, researchers have developed more refined algorithms and have also adapted their algorithms to the structure of the grounding space and the type of information it contains. In this chapter, we are only touching the surface of the Entity Linking problem. We will attempt a first algorithm, one which is not dependent on any grounding space's particular structure.

Our algorithm does require the presence within the grounding space of definitions of the entities. These definitions will further be transformed into a commonly used NLP structure call bag-of-words, which we look at next.

9.3 Bag-of-Words Representation

The **bag-of-words representation**, or **BOW**, is very common in NLP, as it offers a simple representation of a text. Full documents, paragraphs, sentences, and virtually any segment of text can be transformed into a BOW. A BOW is *simply* the set of *tokens* found in a segment of text. As we know, nothing is ever *simple* in NLP, and this section will show how a single sentence can be transformed into very different BOWs, depending on the choice of text processes to include in the transformation.

As a first hint into the complexity underneath BOW generation, notice how I used the word *token* earlier to refer to the content of the BOW, instead of using the word *word*, reminding us of the discussion we had in Chap. 8 about the difficulty of even such a simple task as **tokenizing**. Since a tokenizer is one important text process involved in the creation of a BOW, all the issues related to tokenizing will also apply here.[5]

Let us revisit the five example sentences introduced in the two previous sections, to concretely explore the impact of various text processing choices[6] on resulting BOWs.

(a) He went to the bank to get 900 dollars to pay his rent.
(b) Charlie sat on the bank, refusing to go in the water.
(c) Eva works at the gallery on Bank, near Somerset.
(d) Charlie Chaplin starred in the movie The Bank.
(e) Many artists from BANK presented their work at galleries in London.

---

[5]For an introduction to tokenization and the impact of separators, see Chap. 8, Sect. 8.1.

[6]Text processing will be performed with the Stanford CoreNLP platform. An introduction to the different text processes used in this section was presented in Chap. 8.

Let us call a baseline BOW, one resulting from doing nothing else than tokenizing using the space as separator. Baseline BOWs for our example sentences are as follows:

Baseline BOW_s, with all tokens:
BOW_a = [bank, dollars, get, his, He, pay, rent, to, the, went, 900]
BOW_b = [bank, Charlie, go, in, on, refusing, sat, the, to, water, ',']
BOW_c = [at, Bank, Eva, gallery, on, near, Somerset, the, works, ',']
BOW_d = [Bank, Chaplin, Charlie, in, movie, starred, the, The]
BOW_e = [artists, at, BANK, from, galleries, in, london, many, presented, their, work]

I purposely show the content of the BOWs in alphabetical order to highlight one major drawback of the BOW representation: All sequential information is lost. To create a BOW from a sentence, we lump all the words together into a set (a "bag") and therefore do not retain any information about the order in which the words appeared in the original sentence.

Let us now go through possible variations in the creations of BOWs. In general, a variation will either increase the variety of tokens toward a more **fine-grained representation**, or on the contrary, it will decrease the variety of tokens, merging some of them together toward a more **coarse-grained representation**. We will consider that a variation has a *positive effect* on the BOW when it allows to better differentiate tokens which have similar surface forms but different meanings, as well as when it groups together tokens which have different surface forms but the same meaning. On the other hand, we will consider that a variation has a *negative effect* on the BOWs when it groups surface forms which should be kept separate given that they refer to different meanings, as well as when it separates surface forms which in fact do have the same meaning.

Case sensitivity: A first variation is to make BOWs case insensitive. This can be done by simply putting all the tokens in lowercase. A case-insensitive BOW is a more coarse-grained representation of a sentence than the baseline BOW, since tokens starting with an uppercase letter, and tokens written in all uppercase, will all become indistinguishable from the lowercase form of the token. In our examples, we can see that *The*, from *The Bank* (ex. (d)) becomes the same *the* used in other contexts in other sentences. Furthermore, the words *bank, Bank, BANK* from the different sentences now all contain the same token *bank*.

BOW with case-insensitive tokens:
BOW_a = [bank, dollars, get, his, he, pay, rent, to, the, went, 900]
BOW_b = [bank, charlie, go, in, on, refusing, sat, the, to, water, ',']
BOW_c = [at, bank, eva, gallery, near, on, store, somerset, the, works, ',']
BOW_d = [bank, chaplin, charlie, in, movie, starred, the]
BOW_e = [artists, at, bank, from, galleries, in, london, many, presented, their, work]

Negative effect: Proper nouns (Bank street, BANK art collective) and common nouns (river bank) become indistinguishable.

Positive effect: Case mistakes on words (e.g., *bank* written as *bAnk*), and words in sentence starting positions (which have a capitalized first letter) are now correctly grouped together under the same form.

Lemmatization: Instead of containing words in their original forms, BOWs content could rely on lemmas. Lemmatization does result in many changes in the tokens, which we can see if we compare the new BOWs with the baseline BOWs. For example, we see that *starred* is lemmatized to *star* (ex. (d)), or that *refusing* is lemmatized to *refuse* (ex. (b)).

BOW with lemmas:
BOW_a = [bank, dollar, get, go, he, pay, rent, to, the, 900]
BOW_b = [bank, Charlie, go, in, on, refuse, sit, the, to, water, ',']
BOW_c = [at, bank, Eva, gallery, near, on, Somerset, the, work, ',']
BOW_d = [Bank, Chaplin, Charlie, in, movie, star, the]
BOW_e = [artist, at, BANK, from, gallery, many, present, they, work]

Negative effect: Using lemmas will render *works* (ex. (c)) indistinguishable from *work* (ex. (e)) which actually refer to quite different meanings, and even to two different linguistic roles (verb in example (c), and noun in example (e)).

Positive effect: Lemmas are very good at gathering nominal and verbal word forms which were derived from the same word, and refer to the same meaning. For example, now *went* (ex. (a)) is transformed into *go*, making it equivalent to *go* in example (b), which has the same meaning. The same for *galleries* (ex. (e)) lemmatized into *gallery*, making it the same as *gallery* in example (c), both having the same meaning.

POS filtering: The BOWs so far contained all words found in the sentences, as we have not filtered out any words. A possibility is to reduce the BOW to contain only words of certain parts of speech. As a possibility, we can focus on nouns and verbs, and filter all other words (e.g., prepositions, conjunctions, and numbers). We see in the resulting BOWs below how much the size has reduced.

BOW with lemmas of Noun/Verb only:
$\overline{BOW_a}$ = [bank, dollar, get, go, pay, rent]
BOW_b = [bank, Charlie, go, refuse, sit, water]
BOW_c = [bank, Eva, gallery, Somerset, work]
BOW_d = [Bank, Chaplin, Charlie, movie, star]
BOW_e = [artist, BANK, gallery, present, work]

Negative effect: In few cases, removing prepositions or determiners might remove hints as to the sense of a word. For example, *The Bank* (ex. (d)), being the movie title, does rely on the presence of *The*. Or a different example, not included above, is the word *A*, which most often is a determiner, and therefore would be removed if only nouns and verbs are kept, but in compounds such as *Vitamin A*, it is important.

Positive effect: POS filtering on nouns and verbs greatly reduces the number of words and focuses the BOW's content on semantically significant words. This can help when comparing BOWs (see next section), since, for example, a word *the* shared by two BOWs should not be as indicative of their resemblance as a word *gallery*. Removing determiners and other function words from BOWs will prevent possible matches on less significant words.

Explicit POS tags: Now that we have reduced the content of the BOW, we might wish to reinject differentiating information, such as explicitly tagging the words with their POS tags. In the examples below, I have used a format *lemma/POS* to represent the tokens. Given this format, identical lemmas with different POS become different tokens. For example, *work/VBZ* and *work/NN* are two different tokens.

BOW with lemma/POS combinations of content words only:

BOW_a = [bank/NN, dollar/NNS, get/VB, go/VBD, pay/VB, rent/NN]
BOW_b = [bank/NN, Charlie/NNP, go/VB, refuse/VBG, sit/VBD, water/NN]
BOW_c = [bank/NNP, Eva/NNP, gallery/NN, Somerset/NNP, work/VBZ]
BOW_d = [Bank/NNP, Chaplin/NNP, Charlie/NNP, movie/NN, star/VBD]
BOW_e = [artist/NNS, BANK/NNP, gallery/NNS, present/VBD, work/NN]

Negative effect: There are cases where a word may appear in different linguistic roles, but have meanings that are similar nonetheless (e.g., *work* and *go for a work*). The new lemma/POS differentiation would not allow to identify their common meaning.

Positive effect: The two meanings of *work* as *work/VBZ* (ex. (c)) and *work/NN* (ex. (e)) are now distinguished as they should be.

This last variation shows that a same process can simultaneously result in positive and negative effects for very similar reasons (various linguistic roles of *work* possibly leading or not to various meanings). When two linguistic roles (POS) lead to different meanings, we wish for the BOW's content to differentiate them, but when they lead to a very similar meaning, we wish for the BOW's content to merge them into a single token. But this is unknown information at the time the BOW is being constructed. What we really want the BOW to be is a "Bag-of-Senses," but since we are constructing BOWs from text, all we have are words, and the resulting BOWs are bound to be ambiguous.

We construct BOWs hoping for them to be useful representations of sentences for later tasks, which, in our case, is Entity Linking. To perform Entity Linking, we want to compare BOWs representing the particular text mentions of an ambiguous surface forms, such as *bank* to the BOWs representing the possible meanings of *bank*. We will see in Sect. 9.5 how to compare two BOWs to establish their similarity, but one important question remains, how can we make these BOWs as content-rich as possible so that matching has a chance to succeed? We reflect on this question in the next section.

9.4 Bag-of-Words Content — Looking at Text Cohesion

In the previous section, we assumed mentions of the word *bank* were in isolated sentences, and we focused on all the processing steps that will impact the result of the BOW. But what about neighboring sentences, if they exist, would they be useful as well?

As seems to often be the case in NLP, the answer is: *It depends*. It depends on **text cohesion**, meaning the extent to which the preceding and following sentences discuss the same subject matter as the current sentence. For example, assume one of our previous example sentences is part of the following paragraph.

It is the same story every month, Eric Brass wakes up one morning to realize he's late in paying his rent. So this morning, he went to the bank to get 900 dollars to pay his rent. But of course, banks are closed on Sunday. Business hours are Monday to Friday only. But Eric works during those days and he must then run from work at lunch time to finally get the money from the bank. Why this young man doesn't use a cash machine like everyone else is a good question.

This is a very cohesive paragraph since it is on the same subject matter, just telling different succeeding events in a story related to *Eric Brass*. Automatic evaluation of text cohesion is a very complex topic in itself. One possible form of detection of cohesion is through coreference chains. **Coreferences** are various mentions in a text relating to the same entity, and **coreference chains** are ordered sets of such coreferences found in a text segment.

In general, coreferences come in different flavors, as we illustrate using the preceding paragraph.

- repetitions of the exact same surface form (e.g., *the bank*, *the bank*)
- pronouns (e.g., *Eric*, *he*) (see Sect. 2.7 on anaphora resolution)
- shortened forms (e.g., *Eric Brass*, *Eric*)
- hypernyms, entity types or simple descriptions (e.g., *Eric*, *this young man*)
- sets (e.g., *Monday to Friday*, *those days*)
- generalizations (e.g., *the bank*, *banks*)
- implicit (e.g., *Bank's business hours*, *business hours*)

Although some open source software do offer coreference chains detection capabilities, the quality of results is nowhere near that of other processes such as POS tagging or even parsing. Coreference analysis is very much an NLP research topic today, and pointers to current research are given in Sect. 9.9.

Finding coreference chains is not the only approach to establish text cohesion. Finding related vocabulary words in subsequent sentences would be another indicator. We will explore word relatedness in Chap. 10 in hope of establishing that words such as *money*, *bank*, *dollars*, and *cash machine* are highly related and therefore certainly indicative of cohesion in the text.

Most often, we see NLP processes use arbitrary segmentation of text into paragraphs or fixed-sized windows as an alternative to trying to establish text cohesion. Granted it is not a very satisfactory approach, but it is often a good approximation for a more complex, time-consuming, and still uncertain approach. Choosing the paragraph as a good cohesive unit is not totally arbitrary either, as language writing rules dictate that one should write each paragraph with a single message to convey.

Sometimes, the nature of the text itself reflects on its level of cohesion. In Sect. 9.7, for example, we will simply assume that Wikipedia pages are cohesive as they discuss a single topic and therefore build BOWs from full paragraphs without further validation of cohesion. We will compare such paragraph content to more restricted content, allowing further discussion on this question of what to actually put in the BOW.

Let us move to the last missing piece of our process, the actual method to compare BOWs once we have decided on the extent of their content (e.g., sentence, paragraph, or full document) and the type of preprocessing we will do (e.g., removing stop words and lemmatizing).

9.5 Bag-of-Words Comparison

We wish to compare two BOWs, BOW_1 and BOW_2, and provide a measure representative of the similarity of their content. Let us define a word w_i as any word contained in BOW_1. The *Overlap* measure goes through all w_i in BOW_1 and adds 1 each time w_i is also contained in BOW_2. Equation 9.1 shows this idea more formally.

$$Overlap(BOW_1, BOW_2) = \sum_{w_i \in BOW_1} \begin{cases} 1, & \text{if } w_i \in BOW_2 \\ 0, & \text{otherwise} \end{cases} \tag{9.1}$$

Notice how the choices for BOW representation discussed in the previous section will have direct impact on the result of this overlap measure. A coarse-grained representation, one which merges multiple forms together, will increase the chance of overlap between two BOWs, which might be desirable in some cases, or undesirable in others.

One variation we can do on the basic overlap equation is to include a notion of word significance, a word's **Information Content** (IC).[7] Measuring a word's IC requires an external corpus. We previously learned how to gather a corpus and measure IC for the various words it contains, in Chap. 5. To include the IC in our overlap equation, we can simply modify the constant "1" being added for each overlapping word to a varying increment given by $IC(w_i)$. Equation 9.2 shows the new overlap measure.

$$OverlapIC(BOW_1, BOW_2) = \sum_{w_i \in BOW_1} \begin{cases} IC(w_i), & \text{if } w_i \in BOW_2 \\ 0, & \text{otherwise} \end{cases} \tag{9.2}$$

Beyond its word content, the size of each BOW will also influence the overlap result. Larger BOWs might have more chance of having words in common. Assuming $N1$ is the number of words in BOW_1 and N_2 is the number of words in BOW_2, we can normalize the overlap measure by dividing its result by the minimum of the two BOW sizes (minimum of $N1$ and $N2$), as shown in Eq. 9.3.

$$OverlapICNorm(BOW_1, BOW_2) = \frac{OverlapIC(BOW_1, BOW_2)}{\min(N1, N2)} \tag{9.3}$$

---

[7]Information Content was introduced in Chap. 5, see Sect. 5.5.

We could go on to present many other BOW comparison measures and variations. But we will stop here, as this brief introduction is sufficient to understand the basic idea of comparing BOWs. We now have all the elements we need to attempt Entity Linking, using the BOW-Match algorithm we describe next.

9.6 Grounding Algorithm: BOW-Match

I now introduce our disambiguation algorithm: a **bag-of-words matching algorithm** (abbreviated to *BOW-Match*).

The purpose of the algorithm is to disambiguate a surface form of interest, called W, occurring within a context C, by grounding W toward one of the N senses of W, referred to as S_1 to S_N. As mentioned in Sect. 9.4, the context C could be a sentence, a text segment of arbitrarily length, or a cohesive text segment.

The algorithm builds on the ideas of BOW representation, content, and comparison introduced in the previous sections. As a first step, the context of occurrence C should be transformed into a BOW, called BOW_C. As a second step, each definition of senses S_1 to S_N should be transformed into BOWs, called $BOW_{S_1} ... BOW_{S_N}$.

As a third step, the disambiguation is performed by finding which of all possible BOWs, BOW_{S_1} to BOW_{S_N}, have the maximum overlap with BOW_C. The overlap can be measured in different ways, as shown in Sect. 9.5. The sense with the maximum overlap is considered the most likely sense of W within the context C.

The various steps of the **BOW-Match** algorithm are summarized in Algorithm 7.

Build a bag-of-words BOW_C to contain the words in the context of occurrence of the ambiguous word. ;
for *each possible sense s=1..S* **do**
　　Build a bag-of-words BOW_s to contain the words in the definition of sense s.
end
Assign MaxOverlap to 0; Assign BestSense to null;
for *each possible sense s=1..S* **do**
　　Measure *overlap* = Overlap(BOW_C,BOW_s) ;
　　if *overlap > MaxOverlap* **then**
　　　　MaxOverlap = overlap; BestSense = S;
　　end
end

Algorithm 7: BOW-Match algorithm

This BOW-Match algorithm compares a word's context of occurrence and its possible definitions. This type of algorithm is often referred to as a *Lesk-like* algorithm, although the original Lesk seminal paper addressed the idea of mutual disambiguation of two words, and finding the overlap between their respective definitions.

Let us take a small example to illustrate the algorithm. Assuming the following example sentence is C, and *bank* is the word to be disambiguated, W.

Charlie sat on the *bank*, refusing to go in the water.

First, we must construct a BOW for this sentence, deciding on text processing choices. Assuming we use the "BOW with lemmas of Noun/Verb only" (see Sect. 9.3), which results from tokenizing, lemmatizing, and filtering POS to only keep nouns and verbs, we would have the following:

BOW_C = [bank, Charlie, go, refuse, sit, water]

Then, let us assume there are only 2 senses of W, called S_1 and S_2, and provided by WordNet, our grounding space.

S_1 : sloping land (especially the slope beside a body of water)
S_2 : a financial institution that accepts deposits and channels the money into lending activities

From these definitions, we generate the corresponding BOWs, using the same text processing steps as for BOW_C.

BOW_{S_1} = [slope, land, body, water]
BOW_{S_2} = [institution, accept, deposit, channel, money, lending, activity]

Then, we perform the overlap, using Eq. 9.1.

$Overlap(BOW_C, BOW_{S_1}) = 1$ (the word *water* is shared)
$Overlap(BOW_C, BOW_{S_2}) = 0$ no words are shared.

This results in S_1 being the chosen sense given it has the maximum overlap with C. Let us put this algorithm to the test, in the Entity Linking experiment, performed next.

9.7 Experiment — Disambiguating *Beethoven*

Now that we have defined a baseline definition-based grounding algorithm for Word Sense Disambiguation and Entity Linking, we set up an experiment in which we will test this algorithm. Let us go through our steps.

1. Define a grounding space, a gold standard and evaluation approach.
2. Define the method to be tested.
3. Evaluate the performance of the algorithm.
4. Analyze the results and discuss.

9.7.1 Grounding Space, Gold Standard, and Evaluation Method

For our **test dataset**, we revisit the BEETHOVENCORPUS from Chap. 2, but modify it slightly for our current disambiguation testing purposes. Table 9.1 presents a modified version, called BEETHOVENCORPUSM, in which each longer surface form (e.g., *Ludwig van Beethoven*) has been reduced to the shorter, more ambiguous form *Beethoven*. This was done for the purposes of further testing our disambiguation algorithm. Also, in order to limit the grounding problem to two possible entities (*composer* or *film*), I have only kept the sentences that relate to either one of these entities. The sentence numbers are kept from the original BEETHOVENCORPUS, simply for reference purposes.

Table 9.1 BEETHOVENCORPUSM — modified for Entity Linking

No	Sentence
1	The andante favori is a work for piano solo by *Beethoven*.
2	The other great passion of the young Mirabehn was the music of *Beethoven*.
3	*Beethoven* spent the better part of his life in Vienna.
4	Charles Munch conducted the symphony no. 9 of *Beethoven* in 1962.
5	Among the few composers writing for the orphica was *Beethoven*.
6	*Beethoven*, too, used this key extensively in his second piano concerto.
7	Naue went to Vienna to study briefly with *Beethoven*.
8	Bonn is the birthplace of *Beethoven* (born 1770).
11	*Beethoven*, meanwhile, runs after a loose hot dog cart, and ends up on a merry-go-round.
12	*Beethoven* hit theaters in april 1992.

As for our **grounding space**, we use Wikipedia. It has two entries, one for each sense.

Composer: https://en.wikipedia.org/wiki/Ludwig_van_Beethoven
Film : https://en.wikipedia.org/wiki/Beethoven_(film)

We build our gold standard by manually assigning each sentence in our dataset to the entity it corresponds to.

Composer: Sentences 1, 2, 3, 4, 5, 6, 7, 8
Film : Sentences 11, 12

Now as to our evaluation method, we will use precision, recall, and F1 measures, as we often do.

9.7.2 Testing our BOW-Match Algorithm

Our method to be tested is the BOW-Match algorithm, shown in Algorithm 7 (see Sect. 9.6).

The algorithm relies on BOW representations of sentences and entities. Since we will be comparing BOWs to each other, it is important that we use the same processing when creating them. With that in mind, Table 9.2 shows the BOWs obtained for the various sentences in the BEETHOVENCORPUSM, as constructed using the following steps:

1. Tokenize the sentences.
2. Lemmatize in order to obtain base forms of words.
3. Filter using the POS tagger, keeping only nouns and verbs.

These steps correspond to the variation "BOW with lemmas of Noun/Verb only", from Sect. 9.3. It was chosen since it provides a good compromise between coarse-grained and fine-grained representations. However, I encourage the reader to test other variations as well.

Table 9.2 BEETHOVENCORPUSM — BOW representation

Sentence	Bag-Of-Words (BOW)
BOW_1	[andante, favorus, work, piano, solo, beethoven]
BOW_2	[passion, young, mirabehn, music, beethoven]
BOW_3	[beethoven, spend, life, vienna]
BOW_4	[charle, munch, conduct, symphony, beethoven]
BOW_5	[composer, write, orphica, beethoven]
BOW_6	[beethoven, key, piano, concerto]
BOW_7	[naue, vienna, study, briefly, beethoven]
BOW_8	[bonn, birthplace, beethoven, bear]
BOW_{11}	[beethoven, run, loose, hot, dog, cart, merry-go-round]
BOW_{12}	[beethoven, hit, theater, april]

As for representing the entities, we require defining contexts to be transformed into BOWs. Although the grounding space was decided as being Wikipedia, we did not specify what part of each entity's Wikipedia page would be considered as the defining context of the entity. In Wikipedia, we can assume that all the text contained in a single page does show cohesion, as it discusses the same topic (see discussion on text cohesion in Sect. 9.4). Let us try two possibilities.

Small Context: Use the first two lines of the Wikipedia page.
Large Context: Use the first paragraph of the page.

The larger context should lead to having more words in our "bag", meaning not only more chances for matches, but also more opportunity for noise.

The resulting small and large BOWs are shown in Table 9.3.[8]

---

[8]They were built from the first paragraph found in Wikipedia, as of spring 2015.

Table 9.3 Beethoven, Wikipedia, BOW representation

Entity	Variation	Bag-Of-Words (BOW)
Composer	Small	[ludwig, van, beethoven, baptise, december, march, german, composer, pianist, crucial, figure, transition, classical, romantic, era, western, art, music, remain, famous, influential]
	Large	[ludwig, van, beethoven, baptise, december, march, german, composer, pianist, crucial, figure, transition, classical, romantic, era, western, art, music, remain, famous, influential, composers, his, best-known, composition, include, symphony, concerto, piano, violin, sonata, string, quartet, compose, chamber, choral, work, celebrated, missa, solemni, song]
Film	Small	[beethoven, family, comedy, film, direct, brian, levant, star, charle, grodin, george, newton, bonnie, hunt, alice, series]
	Large	[beethoven, family, comedy, film, direct, brian, levant, star, charle, grodin, george, newton, bonnie, hunt, alice, series, it, write, john, hughe, pseudonym, edmond, dants, amy, holden, jone, story, center, st., bernard, dog, name, composer, ludwig, van, nicholle, tom, ryce, christopher, castile, ted, sarah, rise, karr, emily, stanley, tuccus, vernon, oliver, platt, harvey, dean, dr., herman, varnick, joseph, gordon-levitt, debut, student]

The core of the BOW-Match algorithm is to find overlaps between BOWs. In Table 9.4, we show, for each sentence to be tested, the result of the overlap process between each sentence from BEETHOVENCORPUSM and both $BOW_{Composer}$ and BOW_{Film} using the small contexts. The last column shows when a decision can be made toward either the *Composer* or the *Film*, depending on which overlap is largest.

Table 9.4 Overlap between BOWs of example sentences and Wikipedia small descriptions

Example	$BOW_{Composer}$	BOW_{Film}	Max Overlap
BOW_1	(beethoven)	(beethoven)	—
BOW_2	(beethoven, music)	(beethoven)	Composer
BOW_3	(beethoven)	(beethoven)	—
BOW_4	(beethoven)	(beethoven, charle)	Film
BOW_5	(beethoven, composer)	(beethoven)	Composer
BOW_6	(beethoven)	(beethoven)	—
BOW_7	(beethoven)	(beethoven)	—
BOW_8	(beethoven)	(beethoven)	—
BOW_{11}	(beethoven)	(beethoven)	—
BOW_{12}	(beethoven)	(beethoven)	—

The algorithm results in only 2 examples out of 10 being correctly disambiguated (e.g., 20%). In only two cases was the overlap with the correct sense larger than the overlap with the alternative sense, and in most cases, there is no overlap at all.

Let us look at matching results for the larger contexts, in Table 9.5:

Table 9.5 Overlap between BOWs of example sentences and Wikipedia large descriptions

Example	$BOW_{Composer}$	BOW_{Film}	Max Overlap
BOW_1	(beethoven, work, piano)	(beethoven)	Composer
BOW_2	(beethoven, music)	(beethoven)	Composer
BOW_3	(beethoven)	(beethoven)	—
BOW_4	(beethoven,symphony)	(beethoven, charle)	—
BOW_5	(beethoven, composer)	(beethoven, composer, write)	Film
BOW_6	(beethoven,piano, concerto)	(beethoven)	Composer
BOW_7	(beethoven)	(beethoven)	—
BOW_8	(beethoven)	(beethoven)	—
BOW_{11}	(beethoven)	(beethoven, dog)	Film
BOW_{12}	(beethoven)	(beethoven)	—

In Table 9.6, we put side by side the sense chosen for each example, given the small or large description being used. From this table, we derive Table 9.7 containing the overall precision and recall of the algorithm using two sizes of entity definitions.

The overall results are quite deceiving providing F1 measures of 31% (small context) and 53% (large context). Let us further discuss these results in the next section.

Table 9.6 Comparing Entity Linking results (small versus large definitions) on individual sentences

Example	Gold	Small descriptions	Large descriptions
1	Composer	—	Composer
2	Composer	Composer	Composer
3	Composer	—	—
4	Composer	Film	—
5	Composer	Composer	Film
6	Composer	—	Composer
7	Composer	—	—
8	Composer	—	—
11	Film	—	Film
12	Film	—	—

Table 9.7 Comparative Entity Linking results for small versus large definitions

Measure	Small descriptions	Large descriptions
Overall Precision	66.7% (2/3)	80% (4/5)
Overall Recall	20% (2/10)	40% (4/10)
Overall F1	31%	53%

9.7.3 Result Analysis

If we look at Table 9.6, we can see that example 2 remains a true positive, between small description and large description, but that example 5 has become a false negative. An additional 3 examples have become true positives (sentences 1, 6, 11) by using larger descriptions. Among the positive examples, there is at least one that surely resulted from chance. Example 11 shows a match between *dog* (Table 9.5), from *hot dog*, with the actual word *dog*. Interestingly in this case, an earlier error in tokenizing (we should have kept *hot dog* as one lexical entry) has proven helpful in a later process.

The grounding score is low for both definition sizes, but still using larger-size BOWs increases the F1 from 31% to 53%. The F1 measure is quite appropriate here, as it combines the somewhat high precision (0.8 for larger context) with quite low recall (0.4) providing balanced view. Definition size is not the only factor we could have varied. We have explored many BOW representation variations in Sect. 9.3 which can have an impact on the results, as well as further BOW comparison variations in Sect. 9.5 which can also have an impact.

But overall, the results are quite deceiving, but they certainly demonstrate yet again what we have talked about from the outset of this book, that surface forms vary widely, expressing synonymous or at least similar concepts. The exact string match, used to establish the overlap between BOWs, fails to capture such variations. Manually looking at the BEETHOVENCORPUSM bag-of-words in comparison with those of the two senses, we can see many word matching opportunities, by which I mean words that are not exact matches but that are related and which would be good to take into account as we measure the overlap.

Some examples of these matching opportunities are the word pairs: *piano/pianist, symphony/music, conduct/music, write/compose, compose/composer, orphica/piano, piano/pianist, concerto/music, Bonn/Germany, Germany/German, theater/film*. As human readers, we can recognize these pairs as **related words**. Our Entity Linking algorithm, however, does not yet have this knowledge about related words. Our next chapter is entirely devoted to the search of related words in corpus, which we will use to revisit the current Entity Linking task, hopefully, improving our results.

9.8 In Summary

- Word Sense Disambiguation is the commonly used term for linking surface forms of words to dictionary senses.
- Entity Linking is the commonly used term for linking surface forms of named entities to their unique description, but the term is sometimes relaxed to mean linking toward any entity described in a resource.
- Grounding, as used in this book, refers to the general process of linking surface forms in text to their underlying meaning described in a particular grounding space.
- The choice of grounding space (e.g., WordNet and Wikipedia) will have an impact on the results of the disambiguation algorithm.
- The granularity of sense division within the grounding space will also affect the results of the disambiguation process.
- Text cohesion is a difficult concept to define and to measure. Finding coreference chains in a text is one way to establish text cohesion.
- To best represent the context of occurrence of a word w, a bag-of-words (BOW) could be made from the cohesive segment of text surrounding w. Given the difficulty of finding this cohesive segment, we often use windows of arbitrary sizes around w as the context of w, calling it a context window.
- A BOW representation that is generated from a sentence depends largely on the preprocessing performed: tokenization, lemmatization, and POS filtering.
- Comparing BOWs can be done with an overlap approach, which can be further refined by using the IC of words, and normalizing with BOW sizes.
- BOW-Match is a grounding algorithm, which uses a BOW representation for the context of occurrence of words (BOW_C) as well as for the different senses of words, choosing the sense with the maximal overlap to BOW_C.
- BOW-Match provides baseline results, but further algorithms are needed, since the strictness of exact matching does not allow for all the lexical and semantic variations within definitions.

9.9 Further Reading

SemEval: Originally started as Senseval (Kilgarriff and Rosenzweig 2000), the name has since been changed to *SemEval*, and the event has expanded beyond Word Sense Disambiguation, into various other semantic shared tasks that slightly change from year to year. To get a sense of the importance of this competition to the world of NLP, and its broad coverage of semantic processing, I encourage the reader to look at past years' competitions, linked from SemEval Wikipedia page http://en.wikipedia.org/wiki/SemEval.

Word Sense Disambiguation and Entity Linking: A good place to start for WSD is a wide-coverage survey by Navigli (2009). For a nice overview of the design challenges in Entity Linking, as well as a comparative study on multiple datasets, see Ling et al. (2015). For a brief survey of techniques in Entity Linking, and application to a domain-specific task of linking gene mentions, see Dai et al. (2012). For a joint view of both WSD and Entity Linking tasks, see Moro et al. (2014).

Grounding spaces:

- WordNet: Most early papers on WSD will actually use WordNet as a grounding space. In Banerjee and Pedersen (2002), an adapted Lesk algorithm was used, comparing words in context and words in definition. Many variations on Lesk are presented in Vasilescu et al. (2004). I encourage the reader to go back to the original Lesk paper (Lesk 1986) targeting mutual disambiguation.
- Wikipedia: For WSD using Wikipedia, we can see Mihalcea (2007).
- Semantic Web resources: For two examples of recent work on performing Entity Linking toward DBpedia, Yago, or other Semantic Web resources, see Usbeck et al. (2014) and Pereira (2014). Many open source systems and public datasets are mentioned in these papers.
- BabelNet: BabelNet is an initiative merging WordNet and Wikipedia, which also could be used as grounding space (Navigli et al. 2010).
- UBY: An initiative to build a large Unified Lexical-Semantic Resource, which could be used as grounding space (Gurevych et al. 2012).

Text cohesion and coreference: We use the term coreference chains in this chapter as a general term including lexical chains (Silber and McCoy (2002)) and anaphoric references (see Poesio et al. (2010)). Many authors talk of coreference resolution (see a survey by Elango (2006)) to mean both finding elements in a coreference chain as well as solving to which entity the chain refers to. As mentioned, coreference is very much a research topic, and the Stanford multi-pass coreference system was presented at a shared task (Lee et al. 2011) on coreference resolution.

9.10 Exercises

Exercises 9.1 (Grounding space)

a. Look up the word *run*, in WordNet. There are multiple senses for the noun. What do you think about the granularity of sense division for this word? How well do you anticipate humans to be able to ground to the proper sense, provided a context of occurrence? Illustrate your answer with example sentences, either made-up or found in a corpus.
b. For the *Beethoven* example in this chapter, we used Wikipedia as our grounding space. Could we have used WordNet? Discuss.
c. Try using another resource, such as Wiktionary. How does it describe the word *bank*? Would this be an interesting grounding space to explore for Entity Linking and/or Word Sense Disambiguation? Discuss.

Exercises 9.2 (BOW-Match algorithm)

a. Program a BOW-Match algorithm to compare the two example sentences containing *bank* and the list of WordNet definitions provided (Sect. 9.1). Does your algorithm find the correct sense?

b. Modify your algorithm from (a) to include the WordNet examples in the BOW. You can find one or two examples for each sense, by searching the entry for *bank* through the WordNet online access. Does this change your results?

c. Go through the experimental setup described in Sect. 9.7 and play around with different variations of BOW construction (see Sect. 9.3). You have acquired sufficient knowledge in the previous chapters, mostly Chap. 8, to implement any of them, except the segmentation into lexical entries. How do the results vary?

d. Explore the different BOW overlap measures (see Sect. 9.5) for the experiment in Sect. 9.7. For the measures requiring *IC*, you can calculate the *IC* using a corpus you previously made, for example, the random corpus from Exercise 6.1, in Chap. 6. Is there any impact on results from changing the overlap measure?

e. A variation found in the literature for the BOW-Match algorithm is to extend the BOW of each word sense by using definitions of the words found in the original definition. For example, starting with the original BOW for the composer sense of *Beethoven* (German, composer, pianist, crucial, figure, ...), all words in the BOW would be searched in the grounding space (WordNet or Wikipedia), and the words found in their definitions would be added to the BOW to make a larger BOW. What do you think of this idea? What difficulties could arise in implementing it? What do you see as the pros and cons?

Chapter 10
Relatedness

When we think of relations, we usually think of specific semantic or world-knowledge relations such as `capitalOf(France, Paris)` or `ingredientOf(cake,flour)`. Such relations have names and are referred to as predicates within the Semantic Web. These relations are valuable, informative, and essential for knowledge structuring, as they provide explicit links between entities. The idea of **relatedness**, on the other hand, is more vague in its definition. Relatedness refers to some connection between words, which can be named or unnamed, which can also be weak or strong.

For example, let us say we have a group of words: *pool, goggles, summer, water*. The type of relations underlying each possible pair of words is quite different. Some of them are easy to name, such as `contain(pool,water)`, but others are harder to name such as between *pool* and *goggles*, or even *water* and *summer*. Relatedness should capture word connections which are hard to name.

Relatedness, in NLP, is often explored using corpora and is then referred to as **distributional similarity**. The idea goes back to Firth (1957) who said that "you know a word by the company it keeps." In this chapter, we will see how to extract a word's company, by looking at its co-occurring words in corpus. We refer to a word's company as its **co-occurrence vector**. For example, *eat, bake, cake, peel* could be the co-occurrence vector for the word *apple*, if we often find these words co-occurring with *apple* in corpus.

But the citation to Firth goes back to around sixty years ago, so why are so many researchers still working on distributional similarity today? First, defining a word's company is not as easy as it seems. We will understand why when we explore all the parameters that can contribute to variations in the co-occurrence vectors. This will not come as a surprise to the reader, given that we have already covered many variations in building Bag-Of-Word representation of contexts in Chap. 9, Sect. 9.3, in efforts of word disambiguation through contextual indicators.

Second, even once we have defined a word's co-occurrence vector, there are many possibilities on how to use it for measuring relatedness. For example, if the word

© Springer International Publishing Switzerland 2016

C. Barrière, *Natural Language Understanding in a Semantic Web Context*,

DOI 10.1007/978-3-319-41337-2_10

peach has a co-occurrence vector *eat, tree, pie, yellow*, how do we put that vector in relation to the one for *apple* to find relatedness between *peach* and *apple*? There are no single answer to that, and there has been a multitude of **relatedness measures** defined by researchers. But, since many of these relatedness measures are based on similar principles, we will try to understand their underlying principles to provide the reader with the insights necessary to pursue within that research field, if desired.

Continuing the experimental emphasis of this book, we will explore different approaches to measure relatedness and then perform both intrinsic and extrinsic evaluations. The **semantic similarity intrinsic evaluation** will use a similarity dataset to compare measures, and for the **extrinsic evaluation**, we will go back to the **Entity Linking task** from the last chapter and see if relatedness can help improve results for that grounding task.

10.1   Building a Co-occurrence Vector

The first step in distributional relatedness is to obtain a word's company from a corpus. Let us restate that first step as wanting to build a word's **co-occurrence vector** by exploring a word's neighbors in a corpus. How can we do that? Imagine a window moving over the text in the corpus, which only allows to see a few words at a time. For example, Table 10.1 shows a window moving over the following sentence:

A bat approaching a moth will sound louder and louder.

Table 10.1 Moving window on example sentence

w_{n-2}	w_{n-1}	w_n	w_{n_1}	w_{n+2}
—	—	*a*	bat	approaching
—	a	*bat*	approaching	a
a	bat	*approaching*	a	moth
bat	approaching	*a*	moth	will
approaching	a	*moth*	will	sound
a	moth	*will*	sound	louder
moth	will	*sound*	louder	and
will	sound	*louder*	and	louder
sound	louder	*and*	louder	—
louder	and	*louder*	—	—

Notice how each word of the sentence becomes, one at a time, the center of the moving window, most often called **context window**. We define that center position as n and the word at that position as w_n. Then, each column of Table 10.1 represents word positions from $n-2$ to $n+2$ and the words at those positions, as n varies. The window used in Table 10.1 is a symmetric window of size 2, meaning that it limits our view to two words on each side of the center word w_n.

From all the context windows observed, then we can build a **co-occurrence vector** for each word in the sentence. The co-occurrence vector of a word w, let us call it $Cooc(w)$, is built from counting the number of times that other words co-occur with w, when w is at the center. In Table 10.2, we show $Cooc(w)$ for the different words in the example sentence. The number besides each word from $Cooc(w)$ indicates the frequency of occurrence of that word.

Table 10.2 Resulting co-occurrence counts from the moving window on example sentence

w	$Cooc(w)$
a	bat 2, approaching 2, moth 1, will 1
bat	a 2, approaching 1, moth 1
approaching	a 2, bat 1, moth 1
moth	a 1, approaching 1, will 1, sound 1
will	a 1 moth 1, sound 1, louder 1
sound	moth 1, will 1, louder 1, and 1
and	sound 1, louder 2
louder	will 1, sound 1, and 2, louder 2

You might wonder why I chose a window of two words. That is an arbitrary decision. The window could be two, five, or fifteen words. Furthermore, in the current example, the window is symmetric, being on both sides of w. That, too, is an arbitrary decision, as nothing prevents the window from being asymmetric, only considering words on a single side, either before or after w. These decisions although arbitrary, are not without consequences, as we will see later. But, regardless of window size and position, the basic co-occurrence gathering algorithm remains the same.

Algorithm 8 shows the steps for counting co-occurrences of a single chosen word (e.g., *apple*). The reader can adapt this algorithm to gather the co-occurrences of multiple words simultaneously. A common approach is to start from a particular vocabulary of interest, for example, all the words in WordNet, and then gather all co-occurrence statistics for those words.

```
\\ 1. Determine word of interest
Set SearchedWord = 'apple';
\\ 2. Establish a window size
WindowSize = 3
\\ 3. Establish a window position: left, right, or both
WindowPos = 'both'
\\ 4. Initialise a frequency table to contain the cumulated word frequencies
Initialise FreqTable
\\ 5. Go through the text to capture the occurrences of all the different tokens.
Tokenize the text to obtain a set of tokens;
for each token position pos in the text do
    if token[pos] is SearchedWord then
        \\ 5a. Establish the boundaries of the window
        if WindowPos is 'both' then
            Set start = pos - WindowSize;
            Set end = pos + WindowSize;
        end
        else if WindowPos is left then
            Set start = pos - WindowSize;
            Set end = pos;
        end
        else
            Set start = pos;
            Set end = pos + WindowSize;
        end
        \\ 5b. Look at words in window
        for each token position p going start to end do
            if p not equal to pos then
                if word[p] qualifies... then
                    if FreqTable contains word[p] then
                        Add 1 to its count in FreqTable;
                    end
                    else
                        Insert new word in TableNgramFreq with a frequency of 1;
                    end
                end
            end
        end
    end
end
```

Algorithm 8: Building co-occurrence vectors

As Algorithm 8 shows, the basic idea of a word's distributional representation through its co-occurrence vector is relatively simple to implement, as we linearly go through a corpus and gather co-occurrence statistics. The complexity rather comes from all the possible parameters which we can adjust while compiling co-occurrences. Notice the line (*If word[p] qualifies...*) in Algorithm 8 to be replaced by different types of filtering based on those parameters. Not that it will necessarily be difficult to add the parameter variations to the basic algorithm, but the interpretation of the multiple resulting co-occurrence vectors can become quite overwhelming. Remember that we try to produce these co-occurrence vectors to serve as a *representation* of a word, and therefore, a word's co-occurrence vector should be informative of its semantic or syntactic nature.

To investigate different parameters, we will perform comparative experiments, in which we vary one parameter at a time. The purpose of doing so is to qualitatively evaluate the impact on the resulting co-occurrence vectors. To do our experiments, we will use three word pairs *car/automobile, coast/shore, furnace/stove* considered by humans to be somewhat high in their relatedness. These pairs actually come from a dataset, produced in an early work in psychology, by Miller and Charles (1991), and often used in relatedness evaluations in NLP. We later use this dataset in Sect. 10.4 for the intrinsic quantitative evaluation of different relatedness measures.

The parameters we will investigate are **corpus size**, **linguistic and statistical filtering**, **window size**, and **window position**.

10.1.1 Corpus Size

The raw material for gathering co-occurrences is a corpus. Therefore, the choice of our corpus is probably the most important factor influencing the resulting co-occurrence vectors. Choosing a corpus could mean deciding on the genre, topic, language level, or other characterizing criteria for its documents. Although important, we will not focus on these criteria in this section, but rather look at one single criteria, corpus size. Corpus size is an important criteria since distributional similarity relies on word statistics, and those statistics will only be significant if the corpus is large enough to observe word behavior.

We know how to build a corpus, as we have built domain-specific corpora in Chap. 5 and a domain-independent corpus in Chap. 6, all from Wikipedia. For our current investigation, to observe the impact of corpus size, we will randomly choose pages from Wikipedia, building a small corpus of 10,000 pages (SMALLCORPUS hereafter), or a larger corpus of a million pages (MILLIONCORPUS hereafter).

From these two corpora, we build co-occurrence vectors using our moving window algorithm, presented in Algorithm 8. We use a symmetric window of 3 words (meaning 3 words on each side) and do not perform any other filtering except for removing punctuations. To illustrate the impact of the corpus size parameter, we look at the resulting co-occurrence vectors for our first word pair, *car/automobile*. Table 10.3 shows the top 15 co-occurring words for *car/automobile*, as sorted in decreasing order of frequency. The table also shows, in the third column, the number of occurrences of the words *car* and *automobile*, to provide a reference for interpreting the co-occurrence numbers.

What are the differences observed as to corpus size? We see, without surprise, that the raw frequencies are quite different, taking for example the word *in*, which is a companion word of *car* 320 times in SMALLCORPUS compared to 5,558 times in MILLIONCORPUS. In general, corpus frequency in the SMALLCORPUS are quite small, especially for the word *automobile* which only has 392 occurrences even if it could be considered a quite common English word. Although there are no strict rules for

Table 10.3 Comparing co-occurrences between SMALLCORPUS and MILLIONCORPUS

Corpus	w	NbOcc	Cooc(w)
Small	car	3,266	the 755, a 367, in 320, of 256, electric 233, and 225, sales 163, to 130, retrieved 130, new 127, for 93, with 92, was 89, at 88, is 81
	automobile	392	the 58, in 33, of 32, manufacturers 23, and 23, a 21, an 17, by 13, retrieved 12, association 11, to 10, industry 9, is 7, from 7, propre 6
Million	car	36,929	the 11,922, a 9,056, in 5,558, and 4,757, of 3,559, to 3,343, was 2,023, his 1,924, by 1,680, with 1,541, for 1,432, is 1,410, on 1,308, as 1,068, from 1,032
	automobile	3,753	the 736, in 613, an 498, and 419, of 383, a 277, to 225, accident 189, for 147, was 138, by 128, is 110, first 93, with 92, as 88

deciding on corpus size, seeing such small numbers of co-occurrences for common words like *is* and *from* in relation to *automobile* (see second line in Table 10.3) is an indication that the corpus will lead to much sparseness in the statistical observations.

Sometimes, we do not have the luxury to choose the corpus size and rather use what is available. In our case, we are able to easily build a larger corpus, the MILLIONCORPUS, and we will continue with it for our exploration. You might wonder why we do not use all of Wikipedia then, to have an even larger corpus. Simply, in this book, for a compromise between processing time and corpus size, to allow the reader to work through examples without hours of delay in processing time.

Next, we will see if some kind of filter could bring more **content words** within the top words of the co-occurrence vectors. By content words, we mean nouns, verbs, adjectives which are usually what we look for when trying to understand the semantic nature of a word. Notice how in Table 10.3, especially for the MILLIONCORPUS, we do not know much about the semantic nature of *car* and *automobile* from co-occurring words such as *the, a, in, and, to*. These words are rather **function words** by which we mean determiners, prepositions, conjunctions, and pronouns. Function words, although essential for the proper syntactic structuring of sentences, are not informative as to the semantic nature of words they co-occur with.

10.1.2 Word Filtering — Linguistic versus Statistic

A first type of filtering we can perform relies on parts of speech. We have seen in Chap. 8 that part-of-speech (POS) taggers do perform quite well today, and we can apply such POS tagger on all the sentences from our corpus. Then, in Algorithm 8, as we build our co-occurrence vectors, we only keep the words which have been tagged of certain POS. If we wish to focus on content words, then we should keep words tagged as nouns, verbs, and adjectives.

Let us use our second word pair *coast/shore* to investigate the impact of applying a POS filtering to generate the co-occurrence vectors. In Table 10.4, the first set of co-occurrence counts is without any filtering on the MILLIONCORPUS, and then, the second set of co-occurrence counts uses a POS filter[1] on the same corpus. Notice how the sets before and after POS filtering are drastically different. Notice how content words reflecting a semantic of direction, such as *eastern, western, south, north*, are emerging in both *Cooc(shore)* and *Cooc(coast)*. Remember that we are building co-occurrence vectors to eventually establish word relatedness. Seeing similarity emerge in *Cooc(shore)* and *Cooc(coast)*, knowing that *shore* and *coast* are related, is encouraging.

Table 10.4 Comparing co-occurrences with different filtering strategies

Filter	w	Cooc(w)
None	coast	the 13,064, of 5,924, on 2,763, and 1,985, off 1,952, to 1,808, along 1,466, west 1,453, east 1,325, in 1,012, from 896, south 698, north 682, a 440, is 371
	shore	the 3,718, of 1,591, on 1,302, to 839, and 735, lake 473, from 355, along 309, a 291, north 254, in 220, at 187, elevation 182, volume 180, eastern 176
POS	coast	west 1,311, east 1,208, south 353, north 324, North 296, is 292, Atlantic 282, southern 277, California 265, Pacific 262, eastern 246, western 239, Sea 235, coast 235, northern 234
	shore	Lake 327, north 205, elevation 176, eastern 174, western 162, lake 147, southern 136, south 124, northern 123, bombardment 120, is 120, batteries 110, Bay 107, was 78, west 60
Stat	coast	off 1,952, along 1,466, east 1,325, near 352, island 339, southern 317, sea 314, western 295, coast 285, atlantic 277, pacific 273, california 273, eastern 272, northern 267, africa 208
	shore	lake 473, along 309, elevation 182, volume 180, eastern 176, western 166, near 156, off 140, southern 136, bay 129, northern 123, bombardment 120, batteries 110, close 92, sea 88

The co-occurrence vectors, although POS filtered, still contain two uninteresting words *is* and *was*, which are two conjugated forms of the verb *be*. These two words are kept by our content-word-only filter, since they are verbs. They are uninteresting because they are too common. Remember the notion of **Information Content**, *IC*, from Chap. 5 which was based on a word's probability? Information theory stipulates that very common words have low *IC*, since their commonality makes them non-surprising. Most function words have low *IC* but some common verbs or even common nouns have low *IC* as well. This brings us to a second type of filtering we can do, one based on word frequency (or *IC*) precalculated from a corpus. For example, here are the top 50 most frequent words in the MILLIONCORPUS:

---

[1]We use the Stanford CoreNLP POS tagger to perform the filtering.

the, of, and, in, to, a, is, for, on, was, as, that, with, by, it, this, be, at, from, an, not, he, i, are, his, or, has, have, page, which, new, but, you, center, were, name, also, no, article, its, one, first, may, they, their, been, date, should, discussion, had.

This list includes the conjugated and infinitive forms of *to be* since they are very frequent. We also notice some words, such as *page* and *article*, which seem to be making the top 50 because of the nature of the corpus (Wikipedia pages) and not because they would be that frequent normally in text. We see how the list is a mix of determiners, prepositions, common verbs, pronouns, etc. Such a list is often referred to as a **stopword list**, and it is very commonly used in NLP. There is no consensus as to the definition of a stopword, as some consider stopwords to be only function words, but others do consider stopwords as any frequent words. In any case, before using a stopword list, one should inquire how it was generated, and on which corpus.

For our purpose, we build a stopword list made of the top 200 most frequent words in MILLIONCORPUS. In our current task, we will use the stopword list as an exclusion list. In Algorithm 8, we only keep words that are not in the stopword list for the co-occurrence vectors. We will call this type of filtering a statistical filter, as opposed to the POS filter we described before.

The third set of co-occurrence counts in Table 10.4 shows *Cooc(coast)* and *Cooc(shore)* using the statistical filter. Notice how the results are slightly different than the ones resulting from the POS filter. In particular, notice how uncommon prepositions, such as *off* and *along*, are kept in the list, and common verbs *is* and *was* are removed. The directional words *western, southern*, discussed earlier, are still there.

One major advantage of a statistical filter is that it is language independent. When performing statistical filtering, there is no need for POS tagging, we only need to count, and that, we can do with the same algorithm, in any language. This is one reason it is often preferred within NLP tasks. Another reason is that not all words within the same part-of-speech categories behave the same way, and although it is true in general that function words are less informative, we did see for example that *along*, although it is a preposition, could be informative in defining *shore* and *coast*.

10.1.3   Window Dependency — Positioning

Let us now look at the actual moving window that we slide along the text to gather co-occurrences. In our experiments so far, we have used a symmetric window of 3 words, meaning that for any word w_n at position n, the window covers from w_{n-3} to w_{n+3}. Other windows could be asymmetric and cover only words to the left or to the right side. For this investigation, let us use our third word pair, *furnace/stove*. In Table 10.5, the first set of results is with a symmetric window ($w_{n-3}..w_{n+3}$), the second set is with words on the left (w_{n-3} to w_{n-1}), and the third set of results is with the words on the right (w_{n+1} to w_{n+3}). The difference between the resulting co-occurrence vectors is not that striking. There are a few words, such as *wood* and *gas*, occurring only on the left side of *stove*, indicative of the collocations *gas stove* and *wood stove*. But other words like *iron* do occur on both sides of *furnace*, perhaps coming from *iron furnace* and *furnace of iron*.

Table 10.5 Comparing co-occurrences with different window positions

Window	w	$Cooc(w)$
Symmetric	furnace	blast 93, iron 28, gas 19, electric 17, arc 15, built 13, fiery 12, hearth 11, puddling 11, room 10, boiler 9, vacuum 8, down 8, fire 8, large 8
	stove	pellet 21, gas 20, wood 13, cooking 13, fuel 12, kitchen 12, hot 12, coal 11, rocket 11, heat 10, tile 10, stove 10, cook 9, metal 8, camp 8
Left	furnace	blast 91, iron 21, electric 15, arc 13, fiery 12, gas 12, puddling 11, hearth 8, induction 8, vacuum 7, graphite 7, single 7, large 6, boiler 6, basement 5
	stove	pellet 19, gas 18, wood 12, kitchen 11, coal 10, tile 9, rocket 9, cooking 9, hot 8, cook 7, camp 7, pot 6, improved 6, heat 6, rococo 6
Right	furnace	room 10, built 10, iron 7, gas 7, fire 7, temperature 5, system 5, operated 5, forge 5, oil 5, chaldees 4, called 4, heated 4, combustion 4, water 4
	stove	fuel 9, stove 5, company 5, hot 4, designed 4, water 4, heat 4, cooking 4, parts 3, tablets 3, developed 3, works 3, metal 3, tells 3, oven 3

Varying window position generates co-occurrence vectors which differences are subtle and our current observation is not sufficient to anticipate possible impact for calculating word relatedness, or even for later tasks. Relatedness is rarely a goal in itself, and we might be interested in knowledge about similar words for tasks of grounding, of text summarization or even text translation. When insight is hard to gather with qualitative observation, then only quantitative evaluations on the particular tasks will reveal the possible differences, and such differences might vary depending on the task. For now, let us continue with symmetric windows, and rather look at the impact of varying window size.

10.1.4 Window Dependency — Size

Let us go back to our first word pair *car/automobile* to investigate the impact of varying window size on the resulting co-occurrence vectors. Results are presented in Table 10.6. The three sets show results for windows of size 1, 3, and 10.

In general, the resulting co-occurrence vectors are quite similar. One advantage of a larger window is that it can help counter the data sparseness problem. Notice in Table 10.6 how the same co-occurrences have larger frequencies as the window size augments. For example, the word *industry* co-occurs with *automobile* 72 times, 82 times, and 92 times for window sizes of 1, 3, and 10. Also, larger windows tend to

capture different surface forms (synonyms) of the same entity, and we find *car* in
Cooc(automobile) of size 10. The reason for finding synonyms in larger windows is
that although synonyms are rarely used just next to each other, they are often used
separated by a few words, to provide additional information about the same topic.

This is related to the notion of **text cohesion**, which we discussed in Chap. 9,
in Sect. 9.4. Remember how co-reference chains can be indicative of text cohesion.
When writing, as the author presents a particular story or subject, he/she tends to
repeat references to particular people or objects in the story. These repetitions, coreferents, are not necessarily provided in the exact same surface form, but there can be
synonyms or shorter forms used. A larger window would capture these coreferents.
But a too large window (beyond the paragraph level) risks enclosing words that are
unrelated to the window's center word, since cohesion beyond the paragraph level is
usually less strong.

Table 10.6 Comparing co-occurrences with different window sizes

Window	w	Cooc(w)
1 word	automobile	accident 189, industry 72, traffic 53, manufacturer 49, factory 38, manufacturers 35, manufacturing 30, company 28, production 28, racing 27, engine 23, insurance 21, british 19, engines 18, parts 18
	car	accident 957, park 929, sports 394, private 386, crash 383, racing 378, race 328, cable 254, stock 219, police 200, parking 187, touring 178, passenger 173, driver 157, bomb 149
3 words	automobile	accident 189, industry 82, manufacturer 60, traffic 57, company 51, factory 48, engine 47, killed 44, manufacturers 39, manufacturing 38, production 33, racing 31, died 28, produced 25, insurance 24
	car	park 991, accident 986, racing 473, race 453, crash 426, sports 421, private 404, car 385, driving 355, driver 310, drive 272, killed 270, police 262, cable 259, died 245
10 words	automobile	accident 197, company 111, manufacturer 108, engine 105, automobile 93, industry 92, car 79, production 76, traffic 74, killed 62, factory 53, motor 50, died 48, jpg 48, motors 48
	car	car 2,602, park 1,169, accident 1,108, race 850, racing 810, cars 726, get 666, driver 623, driving 621, road 559, crash 530, drive 519, killed 518, police 510, sports 504

At the opposite, a very small window of size one will be directly pointing to
collocations, and not only to companion words. Remember in Chap. 5, when we
looked at *rapid car*, versus *fast car* and *quick car*? Although *rapid*, *fast*, and *quick*
are synonyms, they are not interchangeable, and some of them, although semantically
correct, do "sound strange." In our current example, we have two synonyms, *car* and
automobile, and although these two synonyms seem interchangeable for *car accident*
versus *automobile accident*, only *car* seems acceptable in *car park* or *car crash*,
where as *automobile* is the more acceptable synonym in *automobile manufacturer*.

As for variations in window position, variations in window size do generate slightly different co-occurrence vectors, but it is not obvious through qualitative observation to anticipate an impact on a particular task, or even on relatedness itself, which is the topic of our next section.

10.2 Measuring Relatedness

In this section, we look at how to establish the **relatedness** between two words: w_1 and w_2. As mentioned at the beginning of this chapter, relatedness is not a named relation, it is more of a strength of association between two words. We will measure relatedness between two words using their distributed representation, as provided by their co-occurrence vectors which we learned how to build in the previous section.

10.2.1 First-Level Relatedness

A first method to measure word relatedness is to simply look within the co-occurrence vectors themselves. The hypothesis is that two words which tend to co-occur must be related. If a word w_2 is part of the co-occurrence vector of w_1 ($w_2 \in Cooc(w_1)$), then there is some relatedness between w_1 and w_2. For example, from Table 10.6, we would say that *accident, industry, traffic, manufacturer* are related to *automobile* because they co-occur with it. This is what we call a **first-level relatedness**, since we look directly within the word's co-occurrence vector.

But, for w_1 and w_2 to be related, we do not want w_2 to co-occur only a few times with w_1. We want to measure some sort of co-occurrence strength. To do so, let us go back again to information theory, and to the **Point-wise Mutual Information**, or *PMI*, measure. *PMI* previously helped us find collocations in Chap. 5 and then bilingual equivalents in Chap. 7. We use it again to measure relatedness.

Going from collocation strength to relatedness is an easy step since collocations are really like windows of only plus or minus one to each side of a word. The *PMI* equation, repeated below, is based on the number of times two words occur next to each other ($P(w_1, w_2)$), and the number of times each word occur in the corpus ($P(w_1)$ and $P(w_2)$). For relatedness, we relax the criteria of occurring next to each other, to occurring within the same window. Then, individual occurrences, for our example, would be the word frequencies in the corpus MILLIONCORPUS.

$$PMI(w_1, w_2) = log_2(\frac{P(w_1, w_2)}{P(w_1) * P(w_2)}) \tag{10.1}$$

Let us look in Table 10.7 at our three example pairs *automobile/car, coast/shore, furnace/stove*, and see the top ranking words, according to their *PMI*. We keep a symmetric window of size 3 and keep co-occurring words with a minimum frequency of 10. Remember how low-frequency words are problematic for *PMI* (see Chap. 5) as they can lead to very high *PMI* values that are not statistically relevant.

At first glance, the words in the lists of Table 10.7 seem to show some relatedness with the example words. Interestingly, as we mentioned earlier, the related words seem to be going in all directions and not just illustrate a single type of relation. Let us take the words related to *automobile* for example. A *dealership* sells automobiles, whereas *manufacturers* produce them. We can get into an *accident* in an automobile, and also be stuck in *traffic* in them. And typical parts of automobiles are *motors* and *tires*. We have a series of related words, all related to the word *automobile* in a different way.

Table 10.7 Applying PMI for our example pairs

Word	Top 15 *PMI*
automobile	dealership 7.61, accident 7.09, chrysler 6.57, manufacturer 6.34, manufacturers 6.30, tires 6.15, advent 5.90, automobile 5.68, manufacturing 5.67, defunct 5.66, factory 5.55, motors 5.47, repair 5.36, traffic 5.35, manufactured 5.29
car	jaunting 8.44, dealership 7.53, dealerships 7.40, parked 7.07, stereos 6.95, accident 6.46, rental 6.37, getaway 6.14, speeding 6.05, baggage 6.01, drove 6.00, oncoming 5.85, refrigerator 5.84, usac 5.83, pullman 5.78
coast	paralleled 6.55, adriatic 6.50, dalmatian 6.38, konkan 6.12, paralleling 5.81, cruised 5.73, brushed 5.52, ionian 5.49, malabar 5.44, jutland 5.43, patrolled 5.31, pembrokeshire 5.30, off 5.22, aegean 5.14, shipwreck 5.13
shore	bombardments 8.18, bombardment 7.27, batteries 7.06, bombarded 6.85, lough 6.60, caspian 6.25, installations 6.12, elevation 5.87, crab 5.75, loch 5.68, lake 5.56, washed 5.55, depth 5.27, battery 5.16, swim 5.12
furnace	puddling 10.70, hearth 9.03, blast 8.90, fiery 8.11, arc 6.74, iron 5.88, gas 5.52, electric 5.19, built 3.65, into 3.30, through 2.79, where 2.73, or 2.43, a 2.42, first 2.02
stove	pellet 10.32, cooking 7.39, kitchen 7.10, rocket 6.70, coal 6.26, gas 6.20, fuel 5.97, wood 5.77, hot 5.05, use 3.20, a 2.75, or 2.74, an 2.50, on 2.42, is 2.01

Of course, since the words in Table 10.7 are extracted automatically, noise might appear. We will evaluate how well the *PMI* measure behaves in a similarity test, in Sect. 10.4, as compared to second-level measures, which we now introduce.

10.2.2 Second-Level Relatedness

In **second-level relatedness**, the idea is that words are related, not because they directly co-occur, but because they co-occur with the same words. For example, *car* might be related to *accident*, at a first-level, if we often see *car* and *accident* together in sentences. But then, we can also establish that *automobile* is related to *car*, at a second-level, if both *car* and *automobile*, in their own sentences, tend to co-occur with *accident*.

The interest of this second-level relatedness is that we might have words that never co-occur, but are still related because of the co-occurrences they share. So, how do we measure such second-level relatedness? Actually, in so many different ways that semantic relatedness is itself a current research topic. Let me introduce only two measures: **Cosine Relatedness** and **Cosine of PMI Relatedness** as this will be sufficient to understand the fundamental idea of comparing co-occurrence vectors. References to other measures can be found in Sect. 10.7.

For describing these two measures, let us introduce the notion of a vocabulary V of size $|V|$. V is the set of all possible words that can co-occur with either w_1 or w_2. Let us call any word within V as w_i. We can then define $Freq(w_i, w_1)$ as the frequency of w_i within $Cooc(w_1)$ and $Freq(w_i, w_2)$ as the frequency of w_i in $Cooc(w_2)$. For example, if we go back to Table 10.6, let us assume we wish to measure relatedness between the pair *automobile/car*, so we have w_1 as *automobile* and w_2 as *car*. Then, the word *accident* is a possible w_i part of our vocabulary V. In the first set of results from the table, we have $Freq(accident, automobile)$ is 189 and $Freq(accident, car)$ is 2957.

The Cosine Relatedness measure ($CR(w_1, w_2)$) is given in Eq. 10.2, and the Cosine of PMI Relatedness measure ($CPMIR(w_1, w_2)$) is given in Eq. 10.3. Notice how the measures are quite similar, either using raw frequencies $Freq(w_i, w_1)$ in Cosine Relatedness as opposed to using $PMI(w_i, w_1)$ in Cosine of PMI Relatedness. Continuing our same example, $PMI(accident, automobile)$ is 7.09, and $PMI(accident, car)$ is 6.46, with numbers taken from Table 10.7.

$$CR(w_1, w_2) = \frac{\sum_{w_i \in V} Freq(w_i, w_1) Freq(w_i, w2)}{\sqrt{\sum_{w_i \in V} Freq(w_i, w_1)^2} \sqrt{\sum_{w_i \in V} Freq(w_i, w_2)^2}} \qquad (10.2)$$

$$CPMIR(w_1, w_2) = \frac{\sum_{w_i \in V} PMI(w_i, w_1) PMI(w_i, w2)}{\sqrt{\sum_{w_i \in V} PMI(w_i, w_1)^2} \sqrt{\sum_{w_i \in V} PMI(w_i, w_2)^2}} \qquad (10.3)$$

The word *accident* is just one example among all the words in the co-occurrence vectors which would be used in the second-level relatedness measure between *car* and *automobile*.

We now have a few relatedness measures, one for first-level relatedness and two for second-level relatedness. Before we move on to an intrinsic evaluation of these measures to compare their performances, let us yet introduce another word representation/similarity approach, that of using word embeddings.

10.3 Word Embeddings

It would be hard to present a chapter on word relatedness without mentioning **word embeddings**. Word embeddings is a distributed representation of words which has become so popular in the past few years that they are used in all sorts of applications.

Word embeddings are part of the revived enthusiasm for neural networks, now more commonly called **deep learning**. Without going into the details of how neural networks learn to classify and represent information, let us simply say that word embeddings are learned representations of words' ability at predicting their surrounding context words. So, comparing word embeddings will be similar in spirit to the second-level similarity presented in the previous section, since comparing word embeddings is somewhat similar to comparing cumulated contexts of these words. Imagine that the embedding of a word is some sort of summary of the cumulated contexts of occurrences of this word as gathered from a very large corpus.

What is interesting for the field of NLP is that even without being expert in deep learning, we do have access to word embeddings, since many researchers who build them, also make them publicly available. For example, researchers at Stanford University have released different datasets of embeddings called GloVe, *Global Vectors for Word Representation*. As any distributed representation, embeddings depend on the corpus on which they are learned. GloVe has some datasets trained on Wikipedia 2014 + Gigaword 5 (large news corpus) for a total of 6 billion tokens, covering a 400K vocabulary. It has other datasets based on an even larger corpus, the Common Crawl.

To get an idea of what word embeddings look like, we can see in Table 10.8, the first 5 dimensions and last 3 dimensions of embeddings of dimension 50. As examples of words, I chose words that will be part of the similarity dataset used in the next section.

Table 10.8 Example of GloVe of dimension 50

Word	D1	D2	D3	D4	D5	...	D48	D49	D50
food	−0.1648	0.91997	0.22737	−0.4903	−0.0018	...	−0.0679	1.50720	0.60889
car	−0.1684	−0.5382	0.31155	−0.5321	0.26678	...	0.39684	1.73400	−0.7078
coast	−0.7045	−0.1734	0.97958	−0.4942	−0.0683	...	0.41082	0.89916	−0.1065
brother	0.44172	−0.4223	0.16875	−0.7307	0.11421	...	−0.5258	−0.2190	−1.1951
hill	−0.2231	−0.0503	0.05087	0.21333	−0.2767	...	0.01969	0.89648	0.10250
boy	0.89461	0.37758	0.42067	−0.5133	−0.2829	...	−0.1366	0.04035	−0.8415

The dimensions in such vector representation are not directly interpretable, as they are in some sort, combined and reduced dimensions from the initial number of dimensions which corresponds to the size of the vocabulary. As part of GloVe, we can find embeddings in dimension 50, 100, 200, and 300, which is quite a reduction if compared to the 400K vocabulary size mentioned above.

I encourage the reader curious about this exciting field of deep learning and word embeddings to read through tutorials and also play with open source software mentioned in Sect. 10.7. If you learn how to build the embeddings yourself, you can then try the variations discussed in Sect. 10.1, since they will impact the resulting embeddings. Given that the embeddings are learned condensed representation of the context-predicting capability of a word, the type of context that was used during learning (window size, with or without stop words, lemmas or raw surface forms, etc) will impact the results.

Now, let us put our different representations and similarity measures to the test. For the word embeddings, since we are not constructing them ourselves, we will simply use the ones provided as GloVe.

10.4 Experiment 1 — Relatedness for Semantic Similarity

Now it is time to perform a quantitative evaluation on a **semantic similarity dataset** to witness measurable impact of the different variations in building co-occurrence vectors as well as impact of the different relatedness measures.

First, let us describe the dataset and the evaluation we can perform. Then, we will show results on a few experiments.

10.4.1 Dataset and Evaluation

Different similarity datasets have been developed over the years by different researchers and for different purposes. One such early proposal is a dataset by Miller and Charles (1991), the **MC dataset**, containing 30 noun pairs which have been evaluated by human judges as to their degree of similarity. The dataset of word pairs is shown in Table 10.9. Since we have already used three pairs from that dataset, *car/automobile*, *coast/shore*, and *furnace/stove* to explore different ideas in the preceding sections, we should remove these pairs from the dataset. When performing evaluation, it is good practice to use a test set which has not been previously investigated for the development and tuning of our algorithms.

The human judges were asked to provide for each noun pair a score between 0 and 4. The numbers in the third column of Table 10.9 are average scores over all human judges. If such human judgement is our gold standard, than we hope for an algorithm that will generate results comparable to the scores in Table 10.9. We hope for our algorithms to judge *noon/string* (last pair) with low relatedness and *gem/jewel* (first pair) with high relatedness.

Unfortunately, the similarity measures generated by our algorithms might not be numbers between 0 and 4, and therefore, comparing absolute scores between algorithms and human judges will not be possible. Instead, we will use a correlation measure, called **Spearman correlation** which works on **ranks**. That is why ranks are provided for the gold standard in the fourth column of Table 10.9. Notice how when two scores are equal, the ranks are adjusted accordingly.

Equation 10.4 shows the Spearman correlation ρ where N is the number of data points and d_i is the difference in rank between the algorithm tested and the gold standard for datapoint i.

$$\rho = 1 - \frac{6 * \sum_{i=1}^{N} d_i^2}{N * (N^2 - 1)} \tag{10.4}$$

For each experiment we will run, we will rank its results and then compare the ranked results with the ranked gold standard using the Spearman correlation. The highest the correlation, the better our algorithm is at evaluating relatedness. Between experiments, difference in correlation can vary widely. Statistical significance for the Spearman correlation is determined using Eq. 10.5[2] and we will refer to it in our comparisons. As we have 27 datapoints ($N = 27$) in our dataset of Table 10.9, any difference of 0.124 (as calculated with Eq. 10.5) between results of two experiments would be considered significant.

$$\sigma = \frac{0.6325}{\sqrt{N-1}} \qquad (10.5)$$

Table 10.9 The MC dataset

Word 1	Word 2	score	rank
car	automobile	3.92	–
gem	jewel	3.84	1.5
journey	voyage	3.84	1.5
boy	lad	3.76	3
coast	shore	3.70	–
asylum	madhouse	3.61	4
magician	wizard	3.50	5
midday	noon	3.42	6
furnace	stove	3.11	–
food	fruit	3.08	7
bird	cock	3.05	8
bird	crane	2.97	9
tool	implement	2.95	10
brother	monk	2.82	11
crane	implement	1.68	12
lad	brother	1.66	13
journey	car	1.16	14
monk	oracle	1.10	15
cemetery	woodland	0.95	16
food	rooster	0.89	17
coast	hill	0.87	18
forest	graveyard	0.84	19
shore	woodland	0.63	20
monk	slave	0.55	21
coast	forest	0.42	22.5
lad	wizard	0.42	22.5
chord	smile	0.13	24
glass	magician	0.11	25
rooster	voyage	0.08	26
noon	string	0.008	27

---

[2]The reference for this calculation is given in the Wikipedia page https://en.wikipedia.org/wiki/Spearman's_rank_correlation_coefficient.

10.4.2 Testing Relatedness Measures and Analyzing Results

We saw, in Sect. 10.1, that multiple parameters (e.g., corpus size, window size, window position, filtering) could be adjusted for building co-occurrence vectors, and furthermore, we saw in Sect. 10.2 that there were multiple possible relatedness measures.

First, let us only use the MILLIONCORPUS and then limit our window position to be symmetric. We will rather explore window size and statistical filtering, as well as the difference between first- and second-level relatedness. Not that other variations are not interesting to explore, but the purpose of the current section is rather to make the reader learn about experimentation and comparative result interpretation rather than provide exhaustive results on every possible parameter setting.

Table 10.10 Comparing similarity results: first-level scores, varying window size

Word pair		Window size = 3		Window size = 10	
Word 1	Word 2	PMI	Rank	PMI	Rank
gem	jewel	5.4939	2	6.1870	2
journey	voyage	3.0404	7	4.8322	6
boy	lad	3.8579	4	4.8387	5
asylum	madhouse	0.0000	19.5	0.0000	22.5
magician	wizard	0.0000	19.5	5.9743	4
midday	noon	7.3684	1	8.0615	1
food	fruit	2.7083	9	4.5977	8
bird	cock	4.2238	3	6.0155	3
bird	crane	2.7920	8	4.4014	10
tool	implement	3.8434	5	4.7597	7
brother	monk	2.0882	11	3.6463	12
crane	implement	0.0000	19.5	0.0000	22.5
lad	brother	0.0000	19.5	0.0000	22.5
journey	car	2.4825	10	3.3869	13
monk	oracle	0.0000	19.5	0.0000	22.5
cemetery	woodland	3.8404	6	4.1281	11
food	rooster	0.0000	19.5	3.3361	14
coast	hill	−1.0655	27	1.2858	17
forest	graveyard	0.0000	19.5	0.0000	22.5
shore	woodland	0.0000	19.5	4.5144	9
monk	slave	0.0000	19.5	0.0000	22.5
coast	forest	0.9392	12	2.1759	16
lad	wizard	0.0000	19.5	0.0000	22.5
chord	smile	0.0000	19.5	0.0000	22.5
glass	magician	0.0000	19.5	3.2786	15
rooster	voyage	0.0000	19.5	0.0000	22.5
noon	string	0.0000	19.5	0.0000	22.5
Spearman		−8.87		−7.85	

The first results we look at use first-level relatedness (*PMI*) with two different window sizes, a window of size 3 and a window of size 10, as shown in Table 10.10. We see both the *PMI* scores and the ranks for each pair in the dataset and for both possible window sizes. The last line of Table 10.10 shows the Spearman correlation between the experimental results and the gold standard (Table 10.9) calculated using Eq. 10.4.

The correlation results are not that different between the two window sizes, although beyond the significance threshold (more than 0.124). One corpus-related issue is emphasized by the comparison of the two window sizes and that is the issue of **data sparseness**. There are 14 pairs, for the window size of 3, which have a relatedness equal to zero, which means that the two words in these pairs never co-occur. Using a larger window brings this number of unseen co-occurrences to 10. In general, the fact that words do not co-occur is not a problem in itself and that should be true for most word pairs in the overall English language. But for a similarity dataset in which word pairs were specifically chosen to show various levels of similarity, that is problematic.

When looking at second-level similarity, data sparseness should be a bit less of an issue, since we are not observing direct co-occurrence but rather indirect similarity through co-occurring words, which we expect, there will be some. Still, let us keep the larger window for our exploration of second-level relatedness, and this time rather see the impact of applying a statistical filtering, using the Cosine Relatedness measure. Results are shown in Table 10.11.

Note first that although the Spearman correlation results in Table 10.11 are lower than for first-level relatedness (Table 10.10) that we do obtain relatedness measures for all 27 pairs, having a much larger coverage. Second, we note a large impact from filtering, which we expected based on our qualitative observation in Sect. 10.1.2. Remember that the statistical filter keeps significant words in the co-occurrence vectors, rather than common words. Since filtering with 200 words has such a large impact, we can further increase the filter to 500 or even 1000 words and measure the impact. We performed such experiments and show the results in Table 10.12. We see how filtering helps (up to 1000), but then too much filtering starts to remove important words and does not allow the Cosine to perform as well.

Table 10.12 also shows results using the other second-level relatedness measure, the *Cosine of PMI Relatedness*. Unfortunately *Cosine of PMI Relatedness* does not perform well, and the impact of statistical filtering on it is not statistically significant (see Exercise 10.2).

Now what about the word embeddings, the GloVe vectors we discussed in Sect. 10.3, how would they perform on this similarity task? Table 10.13 shows results of performing Cosine similarity between the embeddings of each word in the word pair, comparing the embeddings of dimension 100 and dimension 300. Interestingly, the embeddings have full coverage of the dataset as our second-level similarity did, but provide much better results.

So what can we conclude from these results? Certainly that different choices regarding how to measure relatedness will have an impact on the results. But with so many parameters, the number of experiments can grow exponentially, and running all of them blindly might not be the best way to go (unless we have infinite computer

Table 10.11 Comparing similarity results: second-level scores, varying statistical filtering

Word pairs		Cosine no filter		Cosine filter 200	
Word 1	Word 2	Score	Rank	Score	Rank
gem	jewel	0.0115	5	0.000127	7
journey	voyage	0.0086	11	0.000094	12
boy	lad	0.0082	14	0.000761	3
asylum	madhouse	0.0147	1	0.001044	1
magician	wizard	0.0107	8	0.000156	6
midday	noon	0.0082	13	0.000913	2
food	fruit	0.0049	27	0.000046	20
bird	cock	0.0107	7	0.000201	5
bird	crane	0.0078	17	0.000124	8
tool	implement	0.0056	26	0.000044	21
brother	monk	0.0059	25	0.000048	17
crane	implement	0.0077	19	0.000028	26
lad	brother	0.0061	24	0.000097	11
journey	car	0.0072	21	0.000034	25
monk	oracle	0.0090	10	0.000038	24
cemetery	woodland	0.0077	18	0.000081	13
food	rooster	0.0083	12	0.000047	18
coast	hill	0.0143	2	0.000107	9
forest	graveyard	0.0115	4	0.000063	15
shore	woodland	0.0082	15	0.000105	10
monk	slave	0.0079	16	0.000041	23
coast	forest	0.0113	6	0.000071	14
lad	wizard	0.0104	9	0.000286	4
chord	smile	0.0071	22	0.000048	16
glass	magician	0.0075	20	0.000020	27
rooster	voyage	0.0124	3	0.000047	19
noon	string	0.0064	23	0.000042	22
Spearman		−24.98		−13.29	

Table 10.12 Comparative similarity results for various relatedness measures and co-occurrence vector parameters

Experiment	Level	Window size	Measure	Filtering	Spearman (ρ)
1	First	3	PMI	N/A	−8.87
2	First	10	PMI	N/A	−7.85
3	Second	10	Cosine	0	−24.98
4	Second	10	Cosine	200	−13.29
5	Second	10	Cosine	500	−7.5
6	Second	10	Cosine	1000	−8.75
7	Second	10	Cosine	1500	−10.56
8	Second	10	CosinePMI	0	−23.73
9	Second	10	CosinePMI	500	−23.55

Table 10.13 Comparing similarity results: Embeddings GloVe 100 and 300

Word pairs		dimension = 100		dimension = 300	
Word 1	Word 2	Score	Rank	Score	Rank
gem	jewel	0.641545	4	0.482555	4
journey	voyage	0.768299	2	0.658506	2
boy	lad	0.395268	9	0.304399	8
asylum	madhouse	0.104345	21	0.013929	25
magician	wizard	0.661820	3	0.495469	3
midday	noon	0.785331	1	0.687142	1
food	fruit	0.573560	5	0.426590	5
bird	cock	0.275310	15	0.240727	12
bird	crane	0.337193	14	0.292822	9
tool	implement	0.389701	10	0.286681	11
brother	monk	0.427258	7	0.312645	6
crane	implement	0.024722	26	0.010687	26
lad	brother	0.229925	17	0.140602	16
journey	car	0.348662	12	0.184544	14
monk	oracle	0.059876	24	0.047226	22
cemetery	woodland	0.475344	6	0.307025	7
food	rooster	0.006616	27	0.039065	24
coast	hill	0.382474	11	0.165433	15
forest	graveyard	0.236179	16	0.111735	18
shore	woodland	0.227158	18	0.139701	17
monk	slave	0.220865	19	0.088553	20
coast	forest	0.410930	8	0.291576	10
lad	wizard	0.338028	13	0.202985	13
chord	smile	0.203811	20	0.100536	19
glass	magician	0.092205	22	0.059616	21
rooster	voyage	0.060487	23	0.039767	23
noon	string	0.037576	25	0.007039	27
Spearman		-10.59		-9.67	

processing time). It is best to perform qualitative evaluation, looking at the data, as we did in Sect. 10.1. Then, it is a good idea to work with a development set, on which we evaluate quantitatively the variations. This is what we are doing now, using the older Miller and Charles dataset, on which we try to discover good parameters. We have not tried so many parameters, but so far, our best results are with windows of 10, using either the first-level *PMI* or the second-level *Cosine*.

An important part of deciding on the best parameter setting for evaluating relatedness is by measuring their impact on the task for which we need such relatedness. Discovering relatedness is often not a goal in itself, but we hope for it to help in a later task, such as in grounding, as we investigate in the next section.

As for the word embeddings, they do provide a black box solution to word similarity, given that all the decisions (window size, lemmatization or not, etc) were made without our input at construction time. Yet, without any refinement, out of the box, they do work quite well for this intrinsic task. This makes them quite appealing. Although we will not carry along with the embeddings for the extrinsic evaluation, I encourage the reader to try (see Exercise 10.4) them.

10.5 Experiment 2 — Relatedness for Entity Linking

In the last chapter, we were trying to ground a surface form *Beethoven* occurring in different sentences, to one of two possible entities, the composer or the film (see Sect. 9.7). Unfortunately, but not surprisingly, we had relatively little success with our approach. The main problem is that the BOW-Match we developed (see Sect. 9.6) relies on exact string matching which is quite restrictive. Given the variations in language, exact matches are unlikely. But we did notice the following word pairs that should have contributed to our grounding decision, but were not exact matches: piano/pianist, symphony/music, conduct/music, write/compose, compose/composer, orphica/piano, concerto/music, Bonn/Germany, Germany/German, theater/film. These pairs show diverse relations, perhaps expressed by predicates such as *CapitalOf(Bonn, Germany)* or *TypicalObject(conduct,music)*.

We know that distributional relatedness cannot help us define the various nature of the relations in the above pairs, but it can minimally capture that some relation exists. If so, it should help the grounding process and improve the results of our experiment from the last chapter. Let us explore this idea.

10.5.1 Dataset and Evaluation

Table 10.14 shows $BOW_{Composer}$ and BOW_{Film} as constructed from the first lines of the corresponding Wikipedia pages. Wikipedia serves as the grounding space for this experiment.[3]

Table 10.15 shows the various BOWs extracted from the different test sentences, with the entity to which they should link.

The evaluation of our new algorithm can be performed through an overall F1 measure, which was highlighted as an appropriate measure for this experiment, in the previous chapter.

---

[3]The experiment using the baseline BOW-Match algorithm is presented in Chap. 9, and I strongly encourage the reader to revisit that experiment before continuing here.

Table 10.14 BOW representation of the first lines of *Beethoven* pages in Wikipedia

Entity	Bag-Of-Words (BOW)
$BOW_{Composer}$	[ludwig, van, beethoven, baptise, december, march, german, composer, pianist, crucial, figure, transition, classical, romantic, era, western, art, music, remain, famous, influential]
BOW_{Film}	[beethoven, family, comedy, film, direct, brian, levant, star, charle, grodin, george, newton, bonnie, hunt, alice, series]

Table 10.15 BEETHOVENCORPUSM—BOW representation

Sentence	Bag-Of-Words (BOW)	Link to
BOW_1	[andante, favorus, work, piano, solo, beethoven]	Composer
BOW_2	[passion, young, mirabehn, music, beethoven]	Composer
BOW_3	[beethoven, spend, life, vienna]	Composer
BOW_4	[charle, munch, conduct, symphony, beethoven]	Composer
BOW_5	[composer, write, orphica, beethoven]	Composer
BOW_6	[beethoven, key, piano, concerto]	Composer
BOW_7	[naue, vienna, study, briefly, beethoven]	Composer
BOW_8	[bonn, birthplace, beethoven, bear]	Composer
BOW_{11}	[beethoven, run, loose, hot, dog, cart, merry-go-round]	Film
BOW_{12}	[beethoven, hit, theater, april]	Film

10.5.2   Developing a BOW-Similarity Algorithm

Now, how can we modify the BOW-Match algorithm to include relatedness? Word relatedness inspires a different algorithm that of finding BOW-Similarity rather than BOW overlap. We develop a **BOW-Similarity algorithm**, as shown in Algorithm 9. Let us go through our example step by step, to understand the algorithm.

We wish to measure BOW-Similarity between BOW_C and $BOW_{Composer}$. To do so, we take each word w from BOW_C and measure its average similarity to all words in $BOW_{Composer}$. We repeat that for all words in BOW_C and sum all their similarities. For example, if we start with BOW_C containing the words *andante, favori, work, piano, solo* (Sentence 1 in Table 10.15), we can measure for each word its average similarity to all words in $BOW_{Composer}$ *(German, composer, pianist....)*. We start with the word *andante* and measure its individual similarity to *German*, and then *composer*, and then *pianist*, and so on. From all these individual similarities, we compute the average similarity of *andante* to the overall $BOW_{Composer}$ by summing all individual word similarities and dividing by the number of words in $BOW_{Composer}$. We then move to the second word in BOW_C, *favori*, and find its average similarity to $BOW_{Composer}$. We do the same for the remaining words in BOW_C: *work, piano,* and *solo*. Then, we can sum over the similarities found for all words in BOW_C, to obtain the similarity between BOW_C and $BOW_{Composer}$.

The same algorithm is used to calculate BOW-Similarity between BOW_C and BOW_{Film}. We will ground the surface form *Beethoven* to the entity which BOW generated the largest similarity.

Build a Bag-Of-Words BOW_C to contain the words in the context of occurrence of the ambiguous word. ;
for *each possible entity E=1..n* **do**
  | Build a Bag-Of-Words BOW_E to contain the words in the definition of the entity E.
end
Assign *MaxR* to 0 ;
Assign BestEntity to null; ;
for *each possible Entity E=1..n* **do**
  Assign *EntityR* to 0 ;
  for *each word w_S in BOW_S* **do**
    Assign *Total* to 0 ;
    for *each word w_E in BOW_E* **do**
      Measure $R = Relatedness(w_S, w_E)$;
      Add R to *Total* ;
    end
    Divide *Total* by the number of words in BOW_E ;
    Add *Total* to *EntityR* ;
  end
  if *EntityR > MaxR* **then**
    MaxR = EntityR ;
    BestEntity = E ;
  end
end

Algorithm 9: BOW similarity

Let us now apply our new BOW-Similarity algorithm on the Beethoven dataset, and evaluate its results as compared to our baseline BOW-Match algorithm.

10.5.3   Result Analysis

Table 10.16 shows the results from applying Algorithm 9 to the each test sentence from Table 9.2. The second column is the gold standard, showing the letter 'C', if the composer sense should be the most appropriate one, and the letter 'F' if the film sense is the most appropriate. Then, for two different measures, the first-level *PMI* and the second-level *CosineRelatedness*, we have three columns for each indicating first, the score obtained for the composer sense; second, the score obtained for the film sense; and third, a choice between 'C' or 'F' depending on the maximum relatedness found.

From this table, we calculate the precision, recall, and F1 measures for each measure (*PMI* and Cosine), as shown in Table 10.17. Notice that since the BOW-Similarity provides a similarity score for all examples, the recall will always be equal to the precision.

Table 10.16 Matching BOW representations of examples and Wikipedia descriptions (two sentences)

No.	Gold	PMI Composer	Film	C/F	Cosine (with 500 filter) Composer	Film	C/F
1	C	3.392	1.770	C	0.00031	0.00019	C
2	C	2.869	1.371	C	0.00021	0.00027	F
3	C	1.128	0.705	C	0.000114	0.000108	C
4	C	0.494	0.284	C	0.00013	0.00015	F
5	C	3.922	1.884	C	0.00020	0.00013	C
6	C	3.036	0.904	C	0.00048	0.00015	C
7	C	1.555	0.840	C	0.00009	0.00006	C
8	C	0.793	0.583	C	0.00035	0.00006	C
11	F	1.025	1.245	F	0.00017	0.00023	F
12	F	0.851	1.416	F	0.00014	0.00011	C

Table 10.17 Comparative Entity Linking results for small versus large definitions

Measure	PMI	Cosine
Overall precision	100 % (10/10)	70 % (7/10)
Overall recall	100 % (10/10)	70 % (7/10)
Overall F1	100 %	70 %

Grounding results, using the *PMI*, are beyond expectations. They provide a F1 of 100 %. The F1 for the Cosine measure is 70 %. Both are way beyond the 20 % obtained with the BOW-Match algorithm presented in the previous chapter, certainly demonstrating a potential impact of our relatedness measures. Obviously, we are only looking at a single example, which does not provide an adequate evaluation, but still, there is potential is using relatedness in grounding.

One variation we had tried in the previous chapter was to use larger BOWs for describing the entities, including in $BOW_{Composer}$ and BOW_{Film} words coming from the full first paragraph of their Wikipedia page, instead of the first 2 sentences only. We had done this hoping to augment our chances of finding overlapping words. Unfortunately, this same variation, using the BOW-Similarity algorithm, decreases the results of both measures, as shown in Table 10.18. Results are still better than the 40 % obtained in the previous chapter for these larger BOWs, but including more words in $BOW_{Composer}$ and BOW_{Film} did not help. A possible explanation is that we chose an averaging method in BOW-Similarity for establishing the similarity between a word W in BOW_C and all words from $BOW_{Composer}$ or BOW_{Film}. Perhaps, averaging is not adequate for larger BOWs which will tend to include more good words but also more noise. A different choice, instead of averaging, could be to find the maximum similarity, as suggested to experiment in Exercise 10.4.

Table 10.18 Matching BOW representations of examples and Wikipedia descriptions (first paragraph)

No.	Gold	PMI			Cosine (with 500 filter)		
		Composer	Film	C/F	Composer	Film	C/F
1	C	4.986	1.772	C	0.00112	0.00051	C
2	C	2.631	1.454	C	0.00019	0.00018	C
3	C	0.843	0.575	C	0.00012	0.00009	C
4	C	0.904	0.253	C	0.00028	0.00020	C
5	C	4.151	1.724	C	0.00019	0.00016	C
6	C	4.263	0.911	C	0.00133	0.00036	C
7	C	1.613	0.839	C	0.000087	0.000093	F
8	C	0.664	0.693	F	0.00026	0.00031	F
11	F	0.785	1.234	F	0.000213	0.000209	C
12	F	1.024	0.904	C	0.00016	0.00013	C
Precision				80%			60%

In conclusion, we see that relatedness provides a weighted strength of connection between words which can have a significant impact in a task, such as grounding. The number of parameters we can vary are enormous, from window size, to various types of filtering, to different relatedness formula. And that is only for the relatedness measures. We can also vary the size of Bag-Of-Words for the grounding. All these variations definitely bring us in a world of uncertainty and experimentation, and it is the world in which a lot of statistical NLP research lies today.

10.6 In Summary

- Word relatedness is defined as a weighted unnamed relation between words.
- An important building block for relatedness are the co-occurrence vectors, gathering information about co-occurrence of words in a corpus.
- To build a co-occurrence vector, we move a context window along a text and gather the number of times different words co-occur within the window.
- The choice of corpus used for building co-occurrence vectors will have a significant impact on their content. The corpus must be sufficiently large to provide word statistics that are significant.
- Although the basic algorithm for building a co-occurrence vector is simple, it can be modified in various ways, such as changing the window size, changing the window position (before, after, symmetric), performing POS filtering or statistical filtering through a stopword list.
- First-level relatedness directly computes the relatedness between two words based on their direct co-occurrences.
- A typical measure of first-level relatedness is the *PMI* between two words.

- Second-level relatedness computes the relatedness between two words based on the words they co-occur with.
- There exists multiple measures of second-level relatedness, and *Cosine Relatedness* and *Cosine of PMI Relatedness* are two examples.
- Word embeddings are part of the revived enthusiasm for neural networks, now more commonly called deep learning.
- Word embeddings can be viewed as learned representations of words' abilities at predicting their surrounding contexts.
- There exists different datasets to experiment with similarity measures, some older ones, such as the 30-word dataset of Miller and Charles, dating to psychological studies on relatedness.
- Word relatedness can be used to help other tasks, such as grounding, and the experimental design used in this chapter showed on a small example that relatedness could have a major impact.

10.7 Further Reading

Resource-based similarity measures: Although not covered in this book, it is interesting to compare distributional similarity to resource-based similarity, such as can be calculated on WordNet or Wikipedia in various ways. Such a comparison is shown in Agirre et al. (2009). In Budanitsky and Hirst (2006), we can find a comparative study of WordNet-based measures, and in Strube and Ponzetto (2006), semantic relatedness is measured on Wikipedia using its categories.

Distributional similarity measures: An early survey of methods is found in Dagan et al. (1999). In Bullinaria and Levy (2007), we find investigations into different aspects of the parameters described in this chapter, such as type of corpus and context window size. A nice tutorial on distributional similarity, given by Stefan Evert, is available at http://wordspace.collocations.de/doku.php/course:acl2010:schedule. A much cited paper, is the one from Lin (1998) which calculates similarity not with word co-occurrences but rather dependency co-occurrences. The reader could come back to this article after learning about dependencies in Chap. 12, Sect. 12.1.

Similarity of verbs: Relatedness research often focuses on similarity of nouns, but some research, see Resnik and Diab (2000) for example, has investigated the similarity of verbs both using resource-based measures and distributional measures.

Similarity datasets: Among the different datasets available today for word similarity are:

- WordSim-353 available at http://www.cs.technion.ac.il/~gabr/resources/data/wordsim353/
- MEN Test Collection, available at http://clic.cimec.unitn.it/~elia.bruni/MEN.html

- MTurk Dataset, available at http://tx.technion.ac.il/~kirar/Datasets.html

Word Embeddings: For the construction of the GloVe embeddings, see Pennington et al. (2014). They are available for download at http://nlp.stanford.edu/projects/glove/. Some of the GloVe embeddings have been learned on Wikipedia (free) and Gigaword corpus (available at https://catalog.ldc.upenn.edu/LDC2011T07 for a large fee), and others are learned from the Common Crawl (http://commoncrawl.org/). One of the first word embedding building approach to be explained, Word2Vec, is described in Mikolov et al. (2013), and available at https://code.google.com/archive/p/word2vec/. Different instantiations of word embeddings, trained on different corpora, can be downloaded in various places. Many deep learning open source software discuss them (e.g., TensorFlow https://www.tensorflow.org/versions/r0.7/ tutorials or Deep Learning for Java http://deeplearning4j.org/word2vec). Other popular open source deep learning software are Torch, Theano, and Caffe, and certainly more will be available in the future years.

10.8 Exercices

Exercises 10.1 (Building co-occurrence vectors)

a. Build your own version of the MILLIONCORPUS (see Sect. 10.1.1), gathering a random set of a million pages from the Wikipedia dump. To do so, simply adapt the corpus building code you wrote in Exercise 6.1 (b), from Chap. 6.
b. Implement Algorithm 8 from Sect. 10.1, for building co-occurrence vectors. Use your program to build co-occurrence vectors for the words *car, automobile, coast, shore, furnace, stove.* Allow for modifying the parameters (window size, window position, POS filtering) in your algorithm. Test various settings of these parameters using your version of MILLIONCORPUS (exercise (a)). Do you obtain results comparable to the ones shown in the different tables from Sect. 10.1. As your corpus will not be the same, we do not expect the results to be exactly the same, but discuss how comparable they are.
c. In Sect. 10.1.4, we experimented with three window sizes: 1, 3, and 10 words. Try even larger window size of 15 or 20 words. What do you notice on the resulting co-occurrence vectors for the example pairs (*automobile/car, coast/shore, furnace/stove*)? Try varying the window size, with and without the statistical filter. What do you notice then? The program you built in exercise (b) should allow you to do these tests.
d. An arbitrary number of 200 was used in the statistical filter described in Sect. 10.1.2. Try changing that number to 500, 1000, and 2000. What would be the impact on the resulting co-occurrence vectors for the example pairs (*automobile/car, coast/shore, furnace/stove*)? Again, the program you built in exercise (b) should allow you to do these tests.

Exercises 10.2 (Similarity datasets)

a. In Tables 10.10 and 10.11, we show the Spearman correlation with the Miller and Charles dataset for two similarity approaches (first-level, second-level), each with two different parameter settings. But as we saw in this chapter, there are many more parameter settings that could have been tried. Select two more settings for each approach and test them. Do they obtain better correlation measures with the gold standard? Discuss.

b. In Table 10.12, we see that statistical filtering does not have an impact when using Cosine of PMI Relatedness. Why is that?

c. Ask two friends to do the Miller and Charles similarity test. Show them the 30 pairs, in random order, and ask them to provide a score between 0 and 4 for each pair, with 4 being highly similar. If you rank their results and perform Spearman correlation between their result and the original Miller and Charles results, what do you obtain? Discuss the results.

d. In previous chapters, we have always worked with precision/recall, discuss why we cannot use these measures in Sect. 10.4?

e. Get the other datasets WordSim-353 and MEN and run the intrinsic evaluation on them (see the references in Sect. 10.7). Try a few different parameter settings. Discuss results within and between datasets.

Exercises 10.3 (Relatedness measures)

a. Implement Dice and Log-likelihood ratio Chap. 5 (see Eq. 5.4 from Sect. 5.7) as alternatives for the *PMI* for first-level relatedness. Test their result using the intrinsic evaluation (Miller and Charles) from this chapter. How do these measures perform?

b. Also try the measures (Dice, LLR) from exercise (a) on the dataset WordSim-353 and MEN. How do they perform?

c. Download the GloVe word embeddings (see the references in Sect. 10.7). Program a Cosine measure to be used between them to measure similarity. How do they perform on the WordSim-35 and MEN datasets in comparison with the other methods you implemented for first-level relatedness. Think of other measures for calculating the similarity between word embeddings and implement these measures. Do they perform better?

Exercises 10.4 (Relatedness for Entity Linking)

a. When we introduced grounding in Chap. 9, we looked at these two sentences containing the surface form *bank*:

   a. He went to the *bank* to get 900 dollars to pay his rent.
   b. Charlie sat on the *bank*, refusing to go in the water.

   Find definitions of two senses of bank (financial institution, river bank) in Wikipedia, and then try to ground the two example sentences using the original *BOW-Match* algorithm from Chap. 9 and the new BOW-Similarity approach, described in Algorithm 9. Which algorithm succeeds? Try a few different parameters for relatedness and discuss which ones help.

b. In the BOW-Similarity algorithm, we calculate for each w in BOW_C, its average similarity to all words in $BOW_{Composer}$ and BOW_{Film}. Instead of the average, modify the program to use the maximum similarity. Does that impact the grounding results for the Beethoven test sentences (Table 9.2)? What about the grounding of the word *bank* from the previous question, does average or maximum perform better?

c. How would the GloVe embeddings behave in the extrinsic evaluation performed in Sect. 10.5. Are they also making the BOW-Similarity algorithm work much better than the previous BOW-Match one? Show results on the Beethoven test (Table 9.2) and the bank example (exercise (a)).

Part IV
Knowledge Acquisition

In this Part IV, *Knowledge Acquisition*, we venture into the world of relations and the acquisition of these relations from corpora.

In Chap. 11, *Pattern-Based Relation Extraction*, we will investigate pattern-based approaches to relation extraction from text. Pattern-based approaches require **explicit mentions** of relations in text. For example, *was born in* is an explicit mention of the relation `birthdate` which we could find in text, in a sentence such as *Julie was born in 1995*. But similarly to entities, relations can be expressed through various surface forms, and each surface form likely leads to different relations. Language, at the level of both entities and relations, is bound to contain synonymy and polysemy, making the relation extraction task quite challenging. Still, we take on that challenge and spend a large part of the chapter revisiting **regular expressions** as possible implementations of patterns. Using regular expressions, we will build both **lexical and lexico-syntactic patterns**, which we will put to the test in an experiment for the acquisition of synonyms from Wikipedia pages.

In Chap. 12, *From Syntax to Semantics*, we will start on the syntactic side and introduce **dependency parsers**. We then jump to the semantic side and introduce **frames** as a knowledge representation formalism allowing for semantic interpretation of sentences. Frames are used to describe all kinds of events, some very concrete events such as *cooking* and *self-motion*, to other more abstract events such as *attempting something* or *opposing to something*. Each frame comes with a set of **frame elements** or **semantic roles** which are the important elements to take into consideration in describing the events. We will explore the resource **FrameNet**, containing the definition of many frames with their associated frame elements. The rest of the chapter will be spent on understanding the in-between steps necessary to go from a **syntactic interpretation** of a sentence, to a frame-based **semantic interpretation** of a sentence. At the end of the chapter, we show how searching for semantic roles in text is quite similar to the relation extraction task, presented in the previous chapter.

In Chap. 13, *Semantic Types*, we will discuss the importance of identifying semantic types in text, in order to largely constrain the semantic interpretation of sentences. For example, the sentence *Julie was born in Montreal.* takes on quite a different interpretation than the previous sentence *Julie was born in 1995.* Based on the semantic type of *Montreal* as a CITY rather than a DATE. For the identification of types such as PERSON, ORGANIZATION or LOCATION, we can turn toward **Named Entity Recogni-**

tion (NER) systems, particularly targeted for these types. We will revisit the task of NER, which we had touched on much earlier in Chap. 3, as we searched for DATE instances in text. For more specific semantic types, such as ARTMUSEUM, FOOD or even CONTAINER, we will investigate how different resources can provide **gazetteers** for these types, in particular looking at **WordNet** and **FrameNet**. This chapter will also explore how **textual resources** can themselves become sources of gazetteers, showing how to automatically construct a gazetteer from text. This allows us to come full circle within this part of the book as we go back to the lexico-syntactic pattern approach of Chap. 11 and the syntactic pattern approach introduced in Chap. 12, this time to search for explicit mentions of hypernymy.

Chapter 11
Pattern-Based Relation Extraction

A fundamental problem for Relation Extraction is that relations, being no different than entities in that matter, are expressed in text through various surface forms. For example, the relation `studyAt(Zoe,University_of_Ottawa)` is expressed in three different ways in the sentences below.

Zoe is a graduate student at University of Ottawa.
Zoe studies law at University of Ottawa.
Zoe goes to University of Ottawa for her studies.

These sentences further share the fact that they express **explicitly** the relation we are looking for. If we make use of variables S and U to replace *Zoe* and *University of Ottawa*, we have the following:

S is a graduate student at U.
S studies law at U.
S goes to U for her studies.

The remaining snippets of text can be seen as possible patterns that would be indicative of the `studyAt` relation. This is quite different from implicit relations, such as in a noun compound *wood table* which refers to a relation `made-of(table, wood)` but without explicit text to emphasize the relation. The current chapter discusses pattern-based Relation Extraction, and already, we can state that an important prerequisite for such approach is the explicitness of the relation. We start this chapter by discussing this notion of explicitness as it relates to various **types of relations** and also **types of texts**.

We then move on to the actual definition of patterns as ways of searching in text for instances of relations. There have been different names given to this idea of pattern search: **rote extractors**, **knowledge patterns**, and **knowledge probes**. The last one, knowledge probes, is less commonly use, but it does well express the fact that we are probing the text for information. The types of patterns we will look at in this chapter are **lexical patterns** and **lexico-syntactic patterns**. As our main probing approach,

© Springer International Publishing Switzerland 2016
C. Barrière, *Natural Language Understanding in a Semantic Web Context*,
DOI 10.1007/978-3-319-41337-2_11

we will revisit **regular expressions** first introduced in Chap. 3 to search for entity types. Regular expressions will provide the flexibility required to properly express both lexical and lexico-syntactic patterns, and the search capability required to look for instances of these patterns in text.

We then zoom in on one relation, **synonymy**, which is likely to be expressed explicitly in **informative texts**, such as Wikipedia. We will work on the development of lexical and lexico-syntactic patterns for this relation, and put our patterns to the test in a **synonym extraction experiment**, continuing on the experimental path put forward in this book.

Pattern development in this chapter is done manually, as a valuable way of understanding the richness and complexity of relations' surface forms. Yet, this manual exploration should inform our quest toward more automatic systems. That quest is the topic of the last section of this chapter.

11.1   Relation Types and Textual Resources

Many types of relations exist in order to represent various types of connections between entities. To get a sense of the variability of relations, I suggest looking at Appendix C, *Relation Lists*, which provides an overview of relations, grouped in nine categories, ranging from lexical relations to definitional relations, all the way to the infinite list of relations favoured in Open Information Extraction.

In this section, we look at a few types of relations: IS-A relations, world knowledge relations, common knowledge relations, lexico-semantic relations, categorized as such for the purpose of discussing the likelihood of discovering them in different types of textual resources through pattern-based approaches.

IS-A relations: The IS-A relation is central to knowledge representation and language understanding. In NLP, we often talk of the *IS-A relation* to mean either of two different relations within the Semantic Web, that of subclass and that of instantiation. The first relation would be used in ontologies to describe how a particular class of entities is contained within another class, and the second relation, that of instantiation, would rather be expressed by assigning a type to an individual.

In the Semantic Web, the `rdf:type` predicate is used between instances and classes, where as `rdfs:subClassOf`, is used between classes. For example:

(dbpedia:Romain_Gary, rdf:type, dbpedia-owl:Writer)
(dbpedia-owl:Writer, rdfs:subClassOf, dbpedia-owl:Artist)
(dbpedia-owl:Artist, rdfs:subClassOf, dbpedia-owl:Person)

In text, a *is-a* formulation can express both instantiation and subclass relations:

Romain Gary *is a* writer.
A writer *is an* artist.
An artist *is a* person.

Much of the early work on pattern-based Relation Extraction focused on the IS-A relation, suggesting just about any text would likely contain explicit patterns for this relation. Patterns such as *X1, X2, and other Y* or *Y such as X1, X2* would make it possible to extract instances of the relation from text. We will revisit the IS-A relation in Chap. 13 and even suggest a pattern-based Relation Extraction experiment for it (see Sect. 13.3).

Encyclopedic knowledge relations: Many relations found in the Semantic Web are of encyclopedic nature, meaning that they are used to describe entities in the world, such as cities, famous scientists, and famous artists. For example, the predicate `dbo:country(dbpedia:Bonn,dbpedia:Germany)` would be used to describe the city of *Bonn* as being part of *Germany*. This type of information is somewhat expected to be part of an encyclopedic text in a very explicit way *Bonn is a city in Germany*, but news stories, mentioning Bonn, would likely write *In Bonn, Germany, this incident...* Many other encyclopedic relations, describing city's populations, composer's date of birth, or organization's founding years, are likely to be present in encyclopedic text, but not necessarily in news stories. Encyclopedias, along with textbooks, would be considered **informative texts** specifically intended to explain information. **Narrative texts**, on the other hand, such as news articles, blogs, and novels, intend to tell stories.

Common knowledge relations: In contrast to the previous type of relations likely found in encyclopedia, there are relations linked to common knowledge that is quite likely not described anywhere explicitly in a generic way, but rather always seen through its instances. For example, we might be unlikely to see mentions of *films are played in theaters*, but likely to see *Starwars plays at Cinema 9*. Similarly, we are unlikely to see mentions of *a conductor conducts music*, but likely to see *Nagano conducted Bruch's Symphony*. If the Relation Extraction task is to extract instances, so as to **populate a knowledge base**, than it is likely to succeed, as there will be many mentions of such instances in appropriate texts (e.g., newspaper). On the other hand, if the Relation Extraction task is toward the **expansion of an ontology**, trying to automatically find possible relations between generic entities (e.g., films and theaters), then it is not obvious that this information would ever be written anywhere, as it is part of common knowledge which people have, but do not talk about.

Lexico-semantic relations: In English, there exists some regular lexical transformations that represent a regular shift in semantic, and these can be referred to as lexico-semantic relations. For example, for any musical instrument, there will be a player of that instrument, and that player's name can be derived from the instrument's name. We would have *piano/pianist, violin/violinist, harp/harpist*. And for countries, we usually assume that people will reside in it and have a name for the residents that can be derived from the country's name, *Germany/German, Canada/Canadian*, and *Japan/Japanese*. The construction rules, as we can see, are not as strict for country/resident as for instrument/player. These lexico-semantic relations are expressed through lexical changes and are not likely to be explicitly expressed in text, unless in children's school-related material, in definitional forms such as *A pianist is a person who plays the piano*.

At this point, we have awareness of how a type of relation might influence its chances of being found in different types of texts. We now move on to the actual definition of patterns and the variability of relations' surface forms.

11.2 Lexical Patterns

In this section, we explore a first type of pattern, the lexical pattern, made up solely of words in their various forms. In **lexical patterns**, linguistic information such as part of speech is not included. Pure **string patterns** would not even include any notion of words, but we will rather explore lexical patterns, in which notion of word boundaries will be useful.

Let us take a relation actor-in, as an example. Assume we especially like the Coen brothers movies and gather a small corpus, ActorCorpus, about who plays in their different movies. ActorCorpus is shown in Table 11.1.

Table 11.1 Small ActorCorpus

No.	Sentence
1	The film *Burn After Reading* stars *George Clooney*.
2	*The Big Lebowski* stars *John Turturro* in the main role.
3	The movie *Unbroken* revolves around the life of Louie, portrayed by *Jack O'Connell*.
4	*Fargo* also features *Frances McDormand*.
5	*True Grit* produced by the Coen brothers and starring *Jeff Bridges*, opened in 2010.
6	In *Inside Llewyn Davis*, Llewyn (*Oscar Isaac*) is a struggling folk singer.

As we did in the introduction of this chapter, let us first explore what remains of the sentences after we replace the participants in the relation by variables. We take each sentence of ActorCorpus and replace the film's title and the actor's names by variables F and A. This will give us a sense of the explicitness of the relation in text.

1. The film F stars A.
2. F stars A in the title role.
3. The movie F revolves around the life of Louie, portrayed by A.
4. F also features A.
5. F produced by the Coen brothers and starring A, opened in 2010.
6. In F, Llewyn (A) is a struggling folk singer.

These examples show a nice range of explicitness, as well as lexical variations. But should these snippets of text become the actual lexical patterns? They could, but they would certainly benefit from generalization to be more usable. What is at stake here is the precision/recall capability of a pattern.

As in any information retrieval and text mining task, ambiguous queries and patterns will lead to high recall but low precision, and very specific queries and patterns will have high precision but low recall. A *good pattern* would be general enough to have high recall, but be precise enough to have high precision. As we know, that is quite hard to achieve.

As a first generalization strategy, we could delimit our pattern to the segment of text contained in between the two entities (variables) of interest. The middle text is often sufficient as a pattern, but not always. For example, *F stars A* is a valid pattern, but the words *the film* on the left (Sentence 1) and *in the title role* on the right (Sentence 2) do provide additional restrictions, making the patterns more precise.

The single-word pattern *F stars A* will have very high recall, but for sure will bring a lot of noise. For example, the sentence *Some stars shine.* will lead to the instance `actor-in(shine, some)` which is totally possible from a lexical point of view. The word *star* is particularly polysemous, both at the linguistic level, e.g., *a star* and *to star*, as we explored in Chap. 8, and within the same part of speech, e.g., *a star* (astronomy) versus *a star* (popular person). Since patterns are based on words, they will inherit this polysemy, unless many other contextual cues become part of the pattern. This means that lexical patterns relying on very polysemous words, such as *stars*, will tend to be quite noisy and might benefit from the additional right or left contexts as part of the patterns.

On the other hand, some text between variables of interest is overly specific. What are the chances of finding *revolves around the life of Louie, portrayed by* in a corpus. This pattern might have very high precision, but very minimal recall. In this sentence, the film and actor entities are at a considerable distance from each other (8 words between them). We would like to introduce the notion of a multi-word wildcard (*) generalization in the pattern, resulting in something like *revolves around *, portrayed by* which has better chance at occurring more than once in text.

There are other sentences above containing parts that we can imagine to be optional at the word level. For example, *also* seems optional in *also features* (Sentence 4). Other parts seem like they would have valid alternatives, such as *the title role* being replaced by *the secondary role* (Sentence 2). We can further imagine optionality and alternatives at the character level, such as in *stars* versus *starred*.

Possibilities of generalization are endless, and as we develop our patterns, our goal will be to introduce generalizations which will capture positive instances of a relation, without introducing false positives. This will be quite a challenge.

As for the generalization mechanisms, notice how we have talked of optionality, alternatives, and replacement of groups of words which are all possible operators within regular expressions, making regular expressions, as we will see next, a natural choice for the representation of lexical patterns.

11.2.1 Regular Expressions for Lexical Patterns

In Chap. 3, we discussed **regular expressions**, or **regex** for short, as a powerful tool for finding entities or entity classes in text. Let us revisit regular expressions here; this time exploring how they can be used for searches of the lexical patterns discussed above.

First, we must have a way, in regular expressions, to capture the entities we are
looking for. Fortunately, regular expressions contain within their defining language
the idea of **capturing groups**. By explicitly grouping a subset of a regular expression
with parentheses, we can then retrieve the content of the parentheses as a specific
group. Groups can even be named and are then called **named capturing groups**.
We can then retrieve a group by its name. Various programming languages include
different ways of defining and searching for capturing groups in their matching
libraries. In the regex presented in this chapter, I will indicate with <F> the *Film*
capturing group and with <A>, the *Actor* capturing group. For example, the regular
expression below will extract single words lowercase as movie titles or actor's names.

```
The film (<F>\b[a-z]+\b) stars (<A>\b[a-z]+\b).
```

But we require more than single words, since both movie titles and actor's names
can be compound nouns. Let us define a few short regular expressions that will
become reusable lexical components, such as words and multi-words, to be used in
larger patterns. Table 11.2 shows the regex corresponding to each component (column 2) and examples of coverage (column 3). I use the surrounding dollar signs to
indicate a defined component. In a programming language, you would define variables to refer to the components and then create larger regular expressions using
a string concatenation operator (+) to combine them. But for the sake of presentation, I will simply include the components (W, MW or any other defined
component) within the regular expression of the larger pattern, as shown in the second line of Table 11.2.

Table 11.2 Regular expressions of lexical components

Component	Lexical pattern	Example
word (W)	\b[A-Z|a-z]+\b	Burn
multi-word (MW)	(W){0,2}W	Burn After Reading George Clooney George

We can now use the components to rewrite more general regular expressions.
Remember how regex expressions are good at representing lists, alternatives, and
optionality. These three possibilities become part of the lexical patterns which capture
the actor-in instances from ACTORCORPUS.

```
1. [T|t]he film (<F>$MW$) star[s|red] (<A>$MW$)
2. (<F>$MW$) stars (<A>$MW$) in the [main|secondary] role
3. [T|t]he movie (<F>$MW$) revolves around ($W$ ){0,8}$W$, portrayed by
   (<A>$MW$)
4. (<F>$MW$)( also){0,1} features (<A>$MW$)
5. (<F>$MW$) produced by $MW$ and starring (<A>$MW$)
6. [I|i]n (<F>$MW$), $W$ \((<A>$MW$)\) is
```

As we see, we are able to define components and larger regular expressions to
capture various expressions of the relation actor-in. It is not necessarily easy to

define these patterns, and our manual attempt allowed us to reflect on pattern specificity issues and level of desired generalizations with respect to precision and recall. We will later discuss the idea of semi-automatic pattern definition (see Sect. 11.5) and examine where and how human effort can best be combined with algorithmic effort in a Relation Extraction process.

For now, we continue our manual exploration, as we now turn to lexico-syntactic patterns.

11.3 Lexico-Syntactic Patterns

To define lexico-syntactic patterns, we require a few processing modules in the NLP pipeline (see Chap. 8): tokenization, lemmatization, and part-of-speech tagging. We will see that introducing **lemmas**, and **part-of-speech information** in patterns, can play both ways by sometimes making them more generic and some other times making them more precise. In any type of pattern representation, issues of precision/recall will come up.

Let us look at the example sentences from ACTORCORPUS, after tokenization, lemmatization, and POS tagging using the Penn Treebank.[1] As a representation of each sentence, let us use the symbol '/' to divide a lemma from its POS, and the symbol ';' to separate tokens.

1. the/DT;movie/NN;burn/VB;after/IN;read/VBG;star/NNS;George/NNP;Clooney/NNP;./.;

2. the/DT;big/JJ;Lebowski/NNP;star/NNS;John/NNP;Turturro/NNP;in/IN; the/DT;main/JJ;role/NN;./.;

3. the/DT;movie/NN;unbroken/JJ;revolve/VBZ;around/IN;the/DT;life/NN;of/IN; Louie/NNP;,/,;portray/VBN;by/IN; .....Jack/NNP;O'Connell/NNP;./.;

4. Fargo/NNP;also/RB;feature/VBZ;Frances/NNP;McDormand/NNP;./.;

5. true/JJ;grit/NN;produce/VBN;by/IN;the/DT;Coen/NNP;brother/NNS;and/CC;star/VBG; Jeff/NNP;Bridges/NNP;,/,; open/VBD;in/IN;2010/CD;./.;

6. in/IN;inside/IN;Llewyn/NNP;Davis/NNP;,/,;Llewyn/NNP;-lrb-/-LRB-;Oscar/NNP; Isaac/NNP;-rrb-/-RRB-;be/VBZ; .....a/DT;struggle/VBG;folk/NN;singer/NN;./.;

The new representation captures word variations as it generalizes from words to lemmas. For example, *feature/VBZ* (Sentence 4) would capture verb tense variations (*e.g., features, featured*). Notice, however, that POS tagging, such as any linguistic processing, is unfortunately not perfect. For example, the word *stars* is not correctly tagged in both sentences 1 and 2. This means that a pattern requiring *star* to be a verb will miss these examples. Ambiguous words, especially ones with high a priori probabilities for a particular part of speech, such as noun for *star* or verb for *cook*, are hard for POS taggers. We had already experienced this difficulty in Chap. 8 as we tried POS tagging to perform disambiguation between *to cook*, *a cook*, and *Mr. Cook*, with limited success.

---

[1] For an introduction to the tags in Penn Treebank, and POS tagging, see Chap. 8.

That being said, POS-tagged sentences do have nice features, and not all words are as ambiguous as *stars*. Let us explore these features as we define the lexico-syntactic patterns necessary to mine information from POS-tagged sentences, again through the use of regular expressions.

11.3.1 Regular Expressions for Lexico-Syntactic Patterns

By concatenating (linking together) all the lemma and part-of-speech information for each words, in the examples above, we actually obtain a long string representation which we can look into with regular expressions. We must adapt the regular expressions to work with these formatted strings. Let us look at an example.

```
[a-z]+/DT;([a-z]+/[JJ|NN];){0,2}[movie|film]/NN;
```

The regex above would allow all variations *a great film*, *the nice movie*, *the movie*, *a funny film*, combining a determinant (DT), followed by zero to 2 words tagged as either adjective (JJ) or noun (NN) followed by either the word *movie* or *film* tagged as noun.

Similarly to lexical patterns (see Table 11.2), let us define reusable components for lexico-syntactic patterns. Given knowledge of part-of-speech information, we can provide a slight refinement to the previous lexical components (word, multi-word) and define **lexico-syntactic components** as shown in Table 11.3. For example, we define NO to represent any word tagged as a noun, and CN to represent any compound noun, which we define as made of zero or one determiner (DT), followed by zero, one or two adjectives (JJ), or nouns (NN), finishing with a noun (NN). Still, sometimes we might want sequences of words regardless of their POS, and we also define those components in Table 11.3.

Table 11.3 Regular expressions of lexico-syntactic components

Component	Lexico-syntactic pattern	Example
determinant (D)	`[a-z]+/DT;`	the/DT;
noun (NO)	`[a-z]+/NN;`	movie/NN;
compoundNoun (CN)	`$D$([a-z]+/[JJ|NN];)` `{0,2}$NO$`	a/DT;funny/JJ;movie/NN; the/DT;film/NN; film/NN;
any Word (W)	`([a-z]+/.{2,3};)`	burn/VB;
sequence of 1–3 words (MW)	`$W${1,3}`	burn/VB;after/IN;reading/VBG;

We can now use the components in the patterns for our 6 examples, including named capturing groups identified as <F> and <A> as we discussed for lexical patterns in Sect. 11.2.1.

```
1. the/DT;movie/NN;(<F>$MW$)star/.{2,3};(<A>$MW$)
2. (<F>$MW$)$star/.{2,3};(<A>$MW$)in/IN;the/DT;[main|secondary]/[JJ|NN];
   role/NN;
3. the/DT;movie/NN;(<F>$MW$)revolve/VBZ;around/IN;$W${1,8},/,;portray/VBN;
   by/IN;(<A>$MW$)
4. (<F>$MW$)([a-z]+/RB;){0,1}feature/VBZ;(<A>$MW$)
5. (<F>$MW$)produce/VBN;by/IN;$CN$and/CC;star/VBG;(<A>$MW$)
6. in/IN;(<F>$MW$),/,;$CN$-lrb-/-LRB-;(<A>$MW$)-rrb-/-RRB-;be/VBZ;
```

In Exercise 11.1, you will get a chance to compare the lexical and lexico-syntactic patterns we have developed for the extraction of instances of the actor-in relation. Let us learn how to perform such comparative evaluation for a different relation, the synonymy relation, in the next section. A shift from the actor-in relation to the synonymy will also provide further examples of the variability of relations' surface forms, even within a contrived context of searching for synonyms in Wikipedia pages.

11.4 Experiment — Pattern-Based Synonymy Relation Extraction

Let us define our goal as the automatic acquisition, using a textual resource, of synonyms for a predefined set of terms. The purpose of the experiment is to evaluate the performance of lexical patterns and lexico-syntactic patterns, in achieving this goal. To perform our experiment, let us go through the following steps:

1. Establish a development set, representative of the task at hand.
2. Devise a pattern-based search strategy for synonym acquisition.
3. Establish a test set and a corresponding gold standard for performance evaluation.
4. Perform synonym search on the test set using our defined strategy.
5. Analyze the results.

11.4.1 Development Set

Wikipedia is an encyclopedic text, an informative text, providing definitions and descriptions of entities as well as other historical facts about them. In such a resource, we are likely to find synonyms, listed as equivalent surface forms to be used for referring to an entity. We can confirm this statement by looking at Table 11.4 which provides examples of the first sentences in randomly selected Wikipedia pages (page titles are indicated in bold).

An initial observation after reading through these examples is that their sentences do contain multiple synonyms. Table 11.5 provides a list of these synonyms, which have been manually extracted from the definition sentences.

The Wikipedia sentences and the extracted synonyms will be used as our **development set**. A development set is a dataset used to develop and refine algorithms, so as to maximize their performances on that set. In this experiment, we will not go as far as trying to maximize performances of our lexical and lexico-syntactic patterns on the development set, but rather simply use it as an inspiration for the development of patterns, which we look at next.

Table 11.4 Presence of synonymy in Wikipedia

No.	Definition
1	A **mobile phone** (also known as a cellular phone, cell phone, hand phone, or simply a phone) is a phone that can make and receive telephone calls over a radio link while moving around a wide geographic area.
2	A **prison cell** or holding cell or lock-up is a small room in a prison.
3	A **database administrator** (DBA) is an IT professional responsible for the installation, configuration, upgrading, administration, monitoring, maintenance, and security of databases in an organization.
4	**Tetragonia tetragonioides** is a leafy groundcover also known as Botany Bay spinach, Cook's cabbage, kōkihi (in Mōaori), New Zealand spinach, sea spinach, and tetragon.
5	**Cymbopogon**, commonly known as lemongrass is a genus of Asian, African, Australian, and tropical island plants in the grass family.
6	The **tomatillo** is also known as husk tomato, Mexican husk tomato, or ground cherry.
7	A **bicycle**, often called a bike or cycle, is a human-powered, pedal-driven, single-track vehicle, having two wheels attached to a frame, one behind the other.
8	A **train station**, railway station (in Commonwealth English), railroad station (in American English), depot (in North American English), or simply station, is a railway facility where trains regularly stop to load or unload passengers or freight (often freight depot).
9	**Rapid transit**, also known as metro, subway, underground, or colloquially as "the train," is a type of high-capacity public transport generally found in urban areas.
10	**Carpooling** (also car-sharing, ride-sharing, lift-sharing, and covoiturage) is the sharing of car journeys so that more than one person travels in a car.

Table 11.5 Synonyms found in Wikipedia

No.	Term	Synonyms
1	mobile phone	cellular phone, cell phone, hand phone, phone
2	prison cell	holding cell, lock-up
3	database administrator	DBA
4	tetragonia tetragonioides	Botany Bay spinach, Cook's cabbage, kōkihi, New Zealand spinach, sea spinach, tetragon
5	Cymbopogon	lemongrass
6	tomatillo	husk tomato, Mexican husk tomato, ground cherry.
7	bicycle	bike, cycle
8	train station	railway station, railroad station, depot, station
9	rapid transit	metro, subway, underground, "the train"
10	carpooling	car-sharing, ride-sharing, lift-sharing and covoiturage

11.4.2 Defining a Synonym Search Strategy Using Lexical and Lexico-Syntactic Patterns

For our pattern development, we will make use of previously defined lexical and lexico-syntactic components from Sects. 11.2 and 11.3, more specifically the multi-word component, MW, and the compound noun component, CN. We see the use of these components in Table 11.6, as part of six patterns for two search strategies, which we refer to as Lexical Strategy and Lexico-Syntactic Strategy. The first column provides a pattern number. The second column provides an approximate "readable" pattern, in which the variable X is inserted to represent the position of the word to be extracted. Then, third and fourth columns show, respectively, for lexical and lexico-syntactic patterns, a regular expression associated with the readable pattern.

Note that since we already know one of the synonyms (the page title), we only require one capturing group, <S>, for the information to be extracted through the regular expression.

Table 11.6 Set of lexical and lexico-syntactic patterns for test

PId	"Readable" pattern	Lexical Pattern	Lexico-syntactic pattern
1	also X	also (<S>MW)	also/IN;(<S>CN)
2	or X	or (<S>MW))	or/CC;([a-z]+/RB;){0,1} (<S>CN)
3	also known as X	(also){0,1} known as (<S>MW))	(also/RB;){0,1}know/ VBN;as/IN;(<S>CN)
4	called X	called (<S>MW)	([a-z]+/RB;){0,1}call/ VB.?;(<S>CN)
5	as X	as (<S>MW)	as/IN;(<S>CN)
6	X, or X	((<S>MW),){1,2} or (<S>MW)	((<S>CN),/,;){1,2}or/ CC;(<S>CN)

Compared to the lexical and lexico-syntactic patterns we developed in Sects. 11.2 and 11.3 for the actor-in predicate, the synonymy patterns presented here are not as much centered around verbs as we had before (e.g., *stars, features, portrayed by*). In general, synonymy is a very difficult relation to search for through a pattern-based approach, as its patterns tend to be very generic. Such generic patterns are likely to have a very high recall, but a low precision, if not used within a controlled environment, explaining our choice of Wikipedia's first sentence as our controlled textual setting.

Notice that the lexico-syntactic patterns are more specific in their definition than the lexical patterns. I included adverbs, such as in Pattern 2, to allow variations (e.g., *or X* and *or possibly X*). I encourage the reader to spend a bit of time trying to understand the patterns. As mentioned in Chap. 3, when we first introduced regular expressions, those *regex* are quite uninviting, and we need to read them over and over, and play with them (make small changes and evaluate the impact), to finally grasp their power.

Let us move on to defining a gold standard on which we will test these two strategies.

11.4.3 Defining a Gold Standard and Evaluation Method

As our test set for this experiment, we will use the sentences from Table 11.7. These sentences do resemble the ones in Table 11.4, as they also come from the first sentences of diverse Wikipedia pages. It would actually be unfair to suddenly test our extraction patterns on completely different sentences, coming from unknown sources. Although we might, in future experiments, wish to test the level of adaptability of our patterns, and for doing so, we would require text from different sources.

Table 11.7 Synonymy test sentences from Wikipedia

1	A **laptop** or a notebook is a portable personal computer with a clamshell form factor, suitable for mobile use.
2	A **system administrator**, or sysadmin, is a person who is responsible for the upkeep, configuration, and reliable operation of computer systems; especially multi-user computers, such as servers.
3	**Solanum quitoense**, known as naranjilla in Ecuador and Panama and as lulo in Colombia, is a subtropical perennial plant from northwestern South America.
4	The **onion**, also known as the bulb onion or common onion, is a vegetable and is the most widely cultivated species of the genus Allium.
5	An **insect repellent** (also commonly called bug spray) is a substance applied to skin, clothing, or other surfaces which discourages insects (and arthropods in general) from landing or climbing on that surface.
6	A **bus** (archaically also omnibus, multibus, or autobus) is a road vehicle designed to carry many passengers.
7	A **taxicab**, also known as a taxi or a cab, is a type of vehicle for hire with a driver, used by a single passenger or small group of passengers, often for a non-shared ride.
8	**Yogurt**, yoghurt, or yoghourt is a food produced by bacterial fermentation of milk.
9	**Maize**, known in some English-speaking countries as corn, is a large grain plant domesticated by indigenous peoples in Mesoamerica in prehistoric times.
10	**Watercolor** (American English) or watercolour (Commonwealth and Ireland), also aquarelle from French, is a painting method.

Starting from the chosen test set, we manually extract the synonyms found in the sentences. The extracted list of synonyms becomes our gold standard. Table 11.8 shows the gold standard. For each sentence in the test set, the table shows the word being defined (column 2), and its synonyms. There are from one to three synonyms for each entry, for a total of seventeen synonyms among the ten sentences.

Table 11.8 Gold standard — manually extracted synonyms

No.	Term	Synonyms
1	laptop	notebook
2	system administrator	sysadmin
3	Solanum quitoense	naranjilla, lulo
4	onion	bulb onion, common onion
5	insect repellent	bug spray
6	bus	omnibus, multibus, autobus
7	taxicab	taxi, cab
8	yogurt	yoghurt, yoghourt
9	maize	corn
10	watercolor	watercolour, aquarelle

As for our evaluation method, we will use precision and recall. Notice how this evaluation will be biased. Why? Our gold standard lacks negative examples. It will therefore not allow us to get a clear picture of how many false positives the patterns would bring back if applied on sentences not containing synonyms. Recall will not be affected as it does not rely on negatives, but precision will. Our precision measure will be very optimistic as it will be based only on false positives found within sentences containing synonyms. Exercise 11.1 will revisit this issue.

11.4.4 Testing Lexical and Lexico-Syntactic Patterns

Now, we apply the patterns defined earlier in Table 11.6 onto the sentences of the test set shown in Table 11.7. Doing so will generate a set of candidate synonyms which are shown in Table 11.9.

Since there is a lot of result information to capture in little space, Table 11.9 is a compact representation of the results which includes the pattern id (column 1), a readable form of that pattern (column 2), the sentence number in which a synonym was found using that pattern (column 3), and the actual synonym found either with a lexical pattern (column 4) or a lexical-syntactic pattern (column 5). To emphasize the comparison between lexical and lexico-syntactic patterns, their results are put side by side (columns 4 and 5).

From this table, we see how the Lexical Strategy, not having any notion of part of speech, can consider any group of words as possible synonyms. This is what happens with the first pattern (also X), which leads to candidates such as *known as the*. This is definitely a false positive for that strategy. On the other hand, the Lexico-Syntactic Strategy, requiring synonyms to be noun compounds, rightly rejects *known as the* as a possible synonym. The Lexico-Syntactic Strategy, by imposing particular part-of-speech sequences, will be very susceptible to the results of the tagger. For example, *omnibus* is tagged as an adjective (JJ) and *aquarelle* is tagged as an adverb (RB),

Table 11.9 Synonym Candidates extracted by a Lexical Strategy and a Lexico-Syntactic Strategy

PId	"Readable" pattern	Sent	Lexical Strategy	Lexico-Syntactic Strategy
1	also X	4	known as the	–
		5	commonly called bug	–
		6	omnibus	–
		7	known as a	–
		10	aquarelle from French	–
2	or X	1	a notebook is	a/DT;notebook/NN;
		2	sysadmin	sysadmin/NN;
		4	common onion	common/JJ;onion/NN;
		5	other surfaces which, climbing on that	–
		6	autobus	autobus/NN;
		7	a cab, small group of	a/DT;cab/NN; small/JJ;group/NN;
		8	yoghourt is a	yoghourt/NN;
		10	watercolour	watercolour/NN;
3	also known as X	3	naranjilla in ecuador	naranjillum/NN;
		4	the bulb onion	the/DT;bulb/NN;onion/NN;
		7	a taxi or	a/DT;taxi/NN;
4	called X	5	bug spray	bug/NN;spray/NN;
5	as X	2	servers	–
		3	naranjilla in ecuador, lulo in colombia	naranjillum/NN; lulo/NN;
		4	the bulb onion	the/DT;bulb/NN;onion/NN;
		7	a taxi or	a/DT;taxi/NN;
		9	corn	corn/NN;
6	X, or X	5	applied to skin, clothing	–
		6	archaically also omnibus, multibus	multibus/NN;
		8	yoghurt	yoghurt/NN;

explaining why they are not found in the Lexico-Syntactic Strategy, which requires nouns (NN) as synonyms.

Let us now compare the synonyms found using the pattern search to the synonyms from the gold standard.

11.4.5   Result Analysis

We compare the pattern search results found in Table 11.9 to the gold standard of Table 11.8, which leads to the results presented in Table 11.10. The first column gives the sentence number, the second column lists the synonyms to be found, the third and fourth columns give the number of correct and incorrect synonyms found by the Lexical Strategy, and the fifth and sixth columns give the number of correct and incorrect synonyms found by the Lexico-Syntactic Strategy.

Table 11.10 Comparative results for synonym search

	Gold standard synonyms	Lexical Strategy		Lexico-Syntactic Strategy	
		Correct	Incorrect	Correct	Incorrect
1	notebook	1	0	1	0
2	sysadmin	1	1	1	0
3	naranjilla, lulo	2	0	2	0
4	bulb onion, common onion	2	1	2	0
5	bug spray	1	4	1	0
6	omnibus, multibus, autobus	3	0	2	0
7	taxi, cab	2	2	2	1
8	yoghurt, yoghourt	2	0	2	0
9	corn	1	0	1	0
10	watercolour, aquarelle	2	0	1	0
	All	17	8	15	1

Summarizing the results even further, we find in Table 11.11 the precision, recall, and F1 measures for both types of patterns.

Table 11.11 Performance evaluation for the Lexical and Lexico-Syntactic Strategies

	Found	Correct	Precision	Recall	F1
Lexical patterns	25	17	68.0 % (17/25)	100 % (17/17)	80.9 %
Lexico-syntactic patterns	16	15	93.8 % (15/16)	88.2 % (15/17)	91.0 %

We notice, even on our tiny dataset, how the Lexical Strategy has a lower precision but higher recall than the Lexico-Syntactic Strategy. This was expected given the way patterns were defined. The lexical patterns were written with less restrictions than the lexico-syntactic patterns and therefore retrieved instances which are false positives. Still, notice how the results are quite good, particularly when using the lexico-syntactic patterns, which is certainly due to the fact that the test sentences (Table 11.7) are taken from the same source (Wikipedia) and therefore are written in the same style as the development sentences (Table 11.4). So, in this case, the human effort put in pattern development, as inspired by the development set, was effort well spent, knowing that we can now apply our strategy to all Wikipedia pages in the hope of automatically finding synonyms.

But pattern development, especially through the use of regular expressions, is a hard task for humans. Domain experts will prefer to annotate at the level of instances. They will find it much easier to validate that *insect repellent* is a synonym of *bug spray* than to write a regular expression to find it. A semi-automatic system, as we will see in the next section, would allow for various combinations of human and algorithmic efforts.

11.5   Toward a Semi-automatic Process of Knowledge Acquisition

Overall, through this chapter, we have seen that the development of patterns was far from trivial. Pattern development is part of the challenging task of knowledge acquisition, which contains many non-trivial steps. An interesting approach to knowledge acquisition is an **iterative approach**, also called **bootstrapping approach**. Algorithm 10 shows the typical steps of an iterative approach for a single relation R.

Define a corpus C.
Define a relation R.
Define a set of seed instance pairs S_{seed} for R
Initialize $S = S_{seed}$
Initialize P, the set of patterns, to the empty set.
while S and P keep expanding **do**
  (a) Find a set of sentences K, in corpus C, which contain any pair from S.
  (b) Extract a set of patterns P' from K.
  (c) Filter the incorrect patterns, to reduce P'.
  (d) Perform generalization patterns in P' to increase recall.
  (e) Use P' to discover a new set of instance pairs S' in C.
  (f) Filter the discovered instance pairs, to reduce S'.
  (g) Add S' to S, and add P' to P.
end

Algorithm 10: Iterative Relation Extraction Algorithm

The main problem of the iterative approach is called **semantic drift**. Semantic drift occurs when the filtering steps (c) and (f) in Algorithm 10 have kept incorrect patterns or instances, which then impacts the following iteration, and the next, and the next, leading to more and more incorrect patterns and instances. If the iterative approach is meant to be semi-automatic, human annotation would be very beneficial to these filtering steps.

I put forward ten questions that should be asked before embarking on a knowledge acquisition task, as these questions will orient our path toward the development of a semi-automatic system and make us consider the interaction between human and algorithmic efforts, within the iterative approach presented above.

1. What are the relations of interest? Which relation instances we hope to find in text is entirely dependent on our initial motivation for performing an extraction task. By motivation, I mean, why do we want to perform Relation Extraction and how do we plan to use the extracted instances? As an example, let us assume we have an interest in the medical domain, and our motivation is to *"populate a medical knowledge base."*

If we start from an already-existing medical knowledge base (e.g., UMLS or other), it will already contain multiple relations in its ontology (e.g., `may_treat`, `contraindicated_drug`, and `has_body_location`). The extraction task does not need to cover all of them, and we can zoom in on a few of these relations.

For our discussion, we will work with `may_treat`. And, at times, we will also go back to our earlier motivation to *"populate a movie knowledge base"* with `actor-in` as our relation of interest.

I point the reader to Appendix C for exploring other types of relations which could correspond to different motivations. We can even challenge the prerequisite of having relations of interest, as is done in Open Information Extraction (see Sect. C.9) based on a breadth-coverage discovery motivation. Open Information Extraction does not start with a particular relation list, but rather assumes that any frequent verb in a corpus can serve as a predicate.

2. What is our apriori knowledge about the instances? If we focus on the `may_treat` relation, the medical knowledge base might already contain valid instances. For example, the pairs *cimetidine/heartburn*, *clonidine/hypertension*, and *clozapine/schizophrenia* could be part of our medical knowledge base. If these pairs are to be used to gather a development set (as we have done in Sect. 11.2) or start a bootstrapping process (S_{seed} in Algorithm 10), it is crucial for them to be valid pairs. Seed pairs found in curated knowledge bases published by recognized organizations (such as the National Library of Medicine (NLM) publishing UMLS) can be trusted. Seed pairs found in collective-based, non-curated knowledge bases should further be validated through other sources.

Knowledge of even just a few instance pairs is quite useful, as it provide the starting point (S_{seed}) to search for explicit information in text. But that brings a related question. What are the known surface forms for the instance pairs? This question takes us back to the beginning of this book, to our first exploration of surface forms in Chap. 2. Knowledge of variations in surface forms is important when searching for entities in text. For example, knowing that *hypertension* and *high blood pressure* are synonyms will allow to search for either one in text, in relation to *clonidine*.

We hope for various forms to be provided in the knowledge base. And if not, then we might need to embark on another knowledge extraction process, one of synonym search, as we performed in our experiment in Sect. 11.4.

3. What is our apriori knowledge about the semantic types? In step (f) of Algorithm 10, we filter instance pairs just retrieved by our set of patterns. A good filtering approach, to limit semantic drift, is to restrict these instances to particular semantic types.

For example, UMLS predefines different semantic types in its ontology, such as ANATOMY, DEVICE, DISORDER, DRUG, GENE, and PROCEDURE. Among these semantic types, the relation `may_treat` is restricted to occur only between a DRUG and a DISORDER. We can then filter the instance pairs which are not of these types. But that would suppose that we can actually recognize those types. This is exactly the type of semantic processing we hope to have access to, as we will discuss in Question 8.

4. What are the available and/or appropriate textual resources? In Sect. 11.1, we discussed the interdependence between relation type, degree of explicitness expected, and textual resources. The choice of corpus is sure to impact the output of the system, as it provides the raw material for the knowledge acquisition process. Our motivation and our set of relations should guide our choice of corpora.

Hopefully, to search for instances of may_treat, we would have access to a corpus of medical texts. The medical domain is quite important and does contain numerous scientific publications. But we might be tempted to just try the Web-as-Corpus (see Chap. 5) approach, since, for sure, we will find medical information among such large amount of data. Perhaps, but such choice will come at a cost. A larger and more diverse corpus implies more ambiguity and more noise, meaning that generic patterns will likely be unusable. For example, imagine how the pattern *is indicated for* would be a good indicator of the may_treat relation if applied to drug-related information, but it would become useless in a corpus covering all kinds of information. Unless we have access to other semantic processing tools (see Question 8) able to correctly identify the semantic type of the instance pairs to filter out the ones that do not correspond to the required DRUG and DISORDER types.

Another issue with the Web-as-Corpus is trust. The Web will contain many non-expert opinions on medical topics. It is certainly a good place to discover may_treat instance *candidates*, but human validation will be required before including any of the extracted information into a knowledge base.

5. What is the a priori knowledge about the patterns? As we worked through the actor-in example earlier in this chapter, to manually identify which part of a sentence would constitute a pattern, we had to rely on our a priori knowledge of word meanings. For example, knowing that the words *role* and *stars* have semantic significance in the world of movies and actors is a priori knowledge which suggests that we should keep these words as part of the patterns. For example, knowing that *role* is a trigger word would justify the following pattern *F has A in the role*, rather than simply taking the middle context *F has A* which is overly ambiguous.

Without this a priori knowledge, it is very hard to delimit which part of a sentence should be kept as part of a pattern. That explains why it is common to simply take the middle context, already delimited on each side by the entities from the instance pair. To this middle context, we might arbitrarily add one or two words to each side of the entities.

As for the actual set of patterns, Algorithm 10 starts with an empty set and will use the seed pairs to find its first patterns. Assume our corpus C is Wikipedia, and our seed pairs S_{seed} are *cimetidine/heartburn, clonidine/hypertension, clozapine/schizophrenia*. The following sentences are found:

> *Cimetidine* is largely used in the treatment of *heartburn* and peptic ulcers.
> *Clonidine* is a medication used to treat *high blood pressure*.
> *Clozapine*, is mainly used for *schizophrenia* that does not improve following the use of other antipsychotic medications.

Notice the synonym *high blood pressure* is found, as an alternative to *hypertension* (see information about surface forms in Question 2). Taking the middle context provides our first patterns in which instances are replaced by their required semantic types (Question 3).

> DRUG is largely used in the treatment of DISORDER
> DRUG is a medication used to treat DISORDER
> DRUG, is mainly used for DISORDER

6. What linguistic tools are available for analyzing the textual resources? We have seen through our pattern development that the choice of pattern representation will directly influence the search capacity of a pattern. Our first patterns for the may_treat relation, shown in the previous question, are simply lexical patterns, requiring no linguistic processing at all. In this chapter, we have also seen lexico-syntactic patterns, relying on the output of a few modules in the NLP pipeline: tokenization, lemmatization, and POS tagging. POS taggers are available for English, but that is not true of all languages. The simpler we keep the representation, the more language independent it is.

Furthermore, a knowledge extraction process relying on linguistic processing should take into consideration the tools performance and typical mistakes. We saw, in Sect. 11.3.1, how the POS tagging of *stars* can be mistaken from verb to noun, impacting the results of search patterns requiring the POS of *stars* to be a verb. The same could happen with the verb *treat* useful to find may_treat relations, but possibly mistaken for the noun *treat* which conveys a very different meaning.

Still, lexico-syntactic patterns can be quite powerful for Relation Extraction, and I would suggest that if you have access to linguistic tools, then you could compare them to lexical patterns to evaluate their relative performances before making a decision.

7. What generalization can be performed on patterns? Pattern generalization is a complex step which is entirely dependent on the pattern representation chosen. Assume we decided on a lexical representation, then the possibility of generalization through parts of speech is just not possible. Each representation brings with it some possible generalization operators. For lexico-syntactic patterns, we can generalize a word to its lemma, or its part of speech. For lexical patterns, generalization operators can be wildcards for the replacement of a word in a pattern, or a set of words, or just a word ending. For example, inserting two wildcards in the first pattern from Question 5 allows a newly generalized pattern to cover examples it has never seen before, increasing its recall.

> Starting pattern: DRUG is largely used in the treatment of DISORDER
> Generalized pattern : DRUG is * used * the treatment of DISORDER
> Possible sentence coverage :
> DRUG is largely used in the treatment of DISORDER
> DRUG is mostly used in the treatment of DISORDER
> DRUG is largely used for the treatment of DISORDER
> DRUG is often used for the treatment of DISORDER

But unfortunately, the same generalization now also allows:

DRUG is not used for the treatment of DISORDER
DRUG is never used in the treatment of DISORDER

Negation words (*not, never*) are problematic in generic patterns and will for sure decrease precision, leading to semantic drift. Human validation of instances can prevent this semantic drift. In Exercise 11.4, you will have a chance to program and test generalization operators.

8. What are the other semantic processing modules available? A Relation Extraction system will best perform if it can work in tandem with other semantic processing tools, especially tools focusing on entity search. As we mentioned in Question 3, relations such as may_treat have specific restrictions on their participants. The relation may_treat requires a DRUG and a DISORDER. Our previous example of actor-in requires a PERSON and a MOVIE.

Named Entity Recognition (NER) aiming at recognizing instances of particular entity types in text is quite a popular task and NER software does exist. NER software usually targets common types such as PERSON, DATE and ORGANIZATION. More specialized Named Entity Recognizers would be required for entity types such as DRUG, DEVICE, PROCEDURE, or GENE defined in UMLS.

We will further explore the difference between various entity types in Chap. 13, and we will discuss the use of NER software and gazetteers to find particular entity types in text.

9. What human annotation effort can be used in the process? To prevent semantic drift, human annotation is very valuable for filtering both patterns and instances, corresponding to steps (c) and (f) of Algorithm 10. Depending on their expertise, they might feel more at ease filtering instances than patterns.

Many research publications address this question of semantic drift and propose methods to counter it without human intervention. Notice that the human can do the validation without negative examples, but an automatic process could not, as it requires false positives for evaluating precision measure. We have not yet discussed the use of negative examples in this chapter, and that is left to Exercise 11.1(b) for you to explore.

10. What are the evaluation criteria for measuring the success of our process? At the end of our Relation Extraction process, how would we measure its success?

Our typical recall, precision and F1 measures are based on the capability of an algorithm to retrieve what we know should be found (what we put in the gold standard). But in a discovery task, such as Relation Extraction, we do not know ahead of time what we are looking for. One evaluation approach is to simulate discovery by "hiding" part of our knowledge, and measuring how good the algorithm is at retrieve this hidden information.

Assume we have a set of 100 valid instances of the relation may_treat. Then we take a random set of 10 instances, as our seed set S_{start} required by the algorithm. We allow the algorithm to perform its iterations, and then validate whether it found the other 90 instances.

Following the idea of cross-validation (see Chap. 3, Sect. 3.4.3), we repeat our experiment 10 times, varying the seed set each time, and measuring the performance. At the end, we average the results over the 10 experiments.

Such evaluation strategy is not entirely satisfying as it does not account for the algorithm's capability at discovering instances not included in the initial set. Yet, we forecast that an algorithm with high precision/recall on the initial set will be likely to bring valid new instances, certainly more so than an algorithm with low results on the initial set.

11.6 In Summary

- Not all forms of text are equivalent from an Information Extraction standpoint. The type of text we should focus on depends on the type of information we are looking for.
- Not all relations are as likely to be discovered through pattern-based approaches. The underlying hypothesis for pattern-based Relation Extraction is that the relation is explicitly stated in text.
- Informative text provides information about a certain topic, whereas narrative text tells a story.
- Wikipedia is widely used as a resource in NLP, due to its encyclopedic nature and widespread availability.
- Performing a manual analysis of data is a good way of getting insight into a problem, and the possible solutions to be explored.
- There is a high degree of variability in the expression of synonymy in text, even in the very restricted setting of the first sentence of a Wikipedia page. We expect even more variability in the language at large.
- Regular expressions are naturally a good tool for lexical pattern search.
- For lexico-syntactic patterns, concatenating results of the lemmatizer and part-of-speech tagger into a large string allows the use of regular expressions for search.
- Lexical patterns will tend to provide higher recall but lower precision than lexico-syntactic patterns.
- Lexico-syntactic patterns results will be dependent on the linguistic tools used to process the textual data to be searched on.
- Bootstrapping approaches to knowledge acquisition suffer from the problem of semantic drift.
- To better define a semi-automatic process of knowledge acquisition, we can go through a set of questions to guide us.

11.7 Further Reading

Survey of relations: A nice overview of different types of relations is presented in Nastase et al. (2013). Appendix C also points to various relation lists.

Pattern-Based Relation Extraction: Given the popularity of this research field, I only provide a few important articles to look at and encourage the reader to find many more, particularly in line with their specific interest. I must acknowledge Hearst (1992) and her much cited work on *Automatic Acquisition of Hyponyms from Large Text Corpora*, and Brin (1998) also much cited for putting forward an iterative approach called DIPRE (*Dual Iterative Pattern Relation Expansion*). For early work on large text collections, see Agichtein and Gravano (2000). The term *rote extractor* was used in Alfonseca et al. (2006). More specific goals, such as working on biographic facts, are presented in Mann and Yarowsky (2005), or attempting Question Answering through the use of surface patterns is presented in Ravichandran and Hovy (2002). For the specific relation of synonymy, exploring Web-as-Corpus, see Turney (2001).

UMLS expansion: UMLS is available at https://www.nlm.nih.gov/research/umls/. For research on instance search for UMLS relations, see Halskov and Barrière (2008) and Barrière and Gagnon (2011).

Text types: I briefly introduced the idea that different types and genres of text will contain different information and be more or less likely to be useful in knowledge extraction. An article by Roussinov et al. (2001) discusses the idea of genre-based navigation on the Web. This article would be a good starting point for the reader interested in this topic and would lead to many other references.

11.8 Exercises

Exercise 11.1 (Lexical and Lexico-Syntactic Patterns)

a. Write a program to test the `actor-in` lexical and lexico-syntactic patterns defined in Sects. 11.2 and 11.3. Write the regular expressions and validate that they retrieve all six instances of the relation from ACTORCORPUS.
b. Think of how to further relax the `actor-in` patterns written in exercise (a) to make them more generic. Write new regular expressions corresponding to your ideas (2–3 new regular expressions for both Lexical and Lexico-Syntactic Strategies). Test your regular expressions on the ACTORCORPUS. Do you still get 100 % recall on the corpus? To evaluate if you are introducing many false positives with the more generic patterns, you must test them on sentences which should NOT lead to instances of `actor-in`. For example, test your patterns on sentences from Table 11.7. Any false positive found in those sentences?

Table 11.12 Small ACTORTESTCORPUS

No.	Sentence
1	*Raising Arizona* is a 1987 American black comedy film starring among others *Nicolas Cage* and *Holly Hunter*.
2	*Miller's Crossing* is a 1990 American neo-noir gangster film, starring *Gabriel Byrne*, *Marcia Gay Harden*, and *John Turturro*.
3	*Barton Fink* written, produced, directed and edited by the Coen brothers, is set in 1941, and stars *John Turturro* in the title role.
4	In the film *The Hudsucker Proxy*, *Tim Robbins* portrays a naïve business-school graduate.
5	*Billy Bob Thornton* stars in the title role of the movie *The Man Who Wasn't There*, which also features *Scarlett Johansson*.
6	The film *Intolerable Cruelty*, directed and cowritten by Joel and Ethan Coen, stars *George Clooney* and *Catherine Zeta-Jones*.

c. As a better source of negative examples, gather ten sentences from biographies, book descriptions, or even symphony descriptions from Wikipedia. Test the original `actor-in` regular expression patterns from exercise (a). Do these patterns extract many false positives? What about your new patterns in exercise (b), do they extract many false positives?

d. Use the ACTORTESTCORPUS shown in Table 11.12 to further test your set of patterns, from exercise (b). What is the overall precision/recall if the test set includes the six sentences from ACTORTESTCORPUS and ten sentences from exercise (c)?

Exercise 11.2 (Synonym resources)

a. To gain an appreciation of the value of Wikipedia as a textual resource for synonym search, go through both Tables 11.5 and 11.8 and identify the synonyms that are already part of Semantic Web datastores, such as DBpedia. To find synonyms, use the label predicates (e.g., `rdfs:label`) or the redirection predicates (`dbpedia:WikiPageRedirects`). Use this information to quantify Wikipedia's contribution to the set of synonyms.

b. What about alternative textual resources? Search for other online textual resources that include the synonyms found in Table 11.5. Do you find any? If so, what are they? Could they be downloaded to be used as corpora?

Exercise 11.3 (Synonym search)

a. Program the regular expression for each of the lexical patterns shown in Table 11.6. Test them on the sentences from Table 11.7. Are the results comparable to those for Table 11.10?

b. Repeat exercise (a), but for lexico-syntactic patterns.

c. Experiment with the POS tagger from the Stanford CoreNLP. Try tagging the sentences from both Tables 11.4 and 11.7. Get a sense of the variability in tagging results. Discuss how this can impact the development of lexico-syntactic patterns.

d. Develop a new dataset for evaluation. First, think of twenty words and write them down, and then gather the first sentence for each word from its Wikipedia page. Manually prepare a test set from these sentences. Using this new test set, test out the patterns you programmed in exercises (a) and (b). How do they perform?

e. In this chapter, we defined patterns for the first sentences of Wikipedia pages. Let us see if these patterns are likely to work on noisier data. First, let us gather sentences from the Web containing the synonyms from Table 11.5 and/or Table 11.8. Using your favorite search engines, search for pages containing each pair (e.g., *insect repellent/bug spray, notebook/laptop*). Explore the documents returned, and manually gather sentences containing both words. Once you have found ten sentences covering at least 5 different pairs, use them as a new "noisy" test corpus. Test out the patterns you programmed in exercises (a) and (b) on this new corpus. How do they perform?

Exercise 11.4 (Pattern generalization)

a. Let us use DBpedia to gather instance pairs and textual information about the `actor-in` relation. Use the following SPARQL query to automatically gather 20 sets of (actorname, filmname, abstract) through the DBpedia SPARQL endpoint.

```
PREFIX dbo:  <http://dbpedia.org/ontology/>
PREFIX rdfs: <$http://www.w3.org/rdf-schema/>
select ?actorname ?filmname ?abstract where {
   ?film  dbo:starring ?actor .
   ?actor rdfs:label    ?actorname .
   ?film  rdfs:label    ?filmname .
   ?film  dbo:abstract ?abstract .
}
```

Use a slightly different query, replacing actor by director (predicate `dbo:director`) to obtain a negative set of 20 sentences. Then, take 20 sentences (10 positive, 10 negative) as your development corpus and hide the other 20 for a later use as test corpus.

1. Manually develop your own lexical patterns and refine them until you obtain good performances on the development corpus. Decide on what you think *good performances* are and justify your decision.

2. Using the same development corpus, automatically develop different sets of patterns. The patterns will range from very specific to more general. Here are different sets of patterns you can automatically build.
   - Set 1 : Lexical patterns "as is" (no changes - full sentences).
   - Set 2 : Lexical patterns from text segments in-between the film and actor.
   - Set 3 : Same as Set 2, but adding two words on the right and left of the film and actor.
   - Set 4 : Same as Set 2, but adding the text segment to the left or right up to trigger words. Automatically find trigger words by calculating word frequency on your development corpus, and assume the top five content words are trigger words.

- Set 5 : Lexical patterns including random one-word wildcards.
- Set 6 : Same as Set 5, but with wildcards included only where 2 patterns from Set 2 differ by a single word. For example, if both *A stars in the funny movie F* and *A stars in the great movie F* are included in Set 2, than generalize to *A stars in the * movie F*.

3. Compare the different sets of patterns on the development corpus using precision/recall measures. How does your manual set compare to an automatically generated set?
4. Same question as 3 but now on the test set.
5. Adapt sets 1 to 6, for lexico-syntactic patterns, and test them. How do the results compare to the lexical patterns?

Exercise 11.5 (Semi-automatic knowledge acquisition)

a. Perform a semi-automatic Relation Extraction experiment for the `may_treat` relation, following the iterative algorithm shown in Algorithm 10. Here are guidelines for your experiment.

1. Start with the three seed pairs *cimetidine/heartburn*, *clonidine/hypertension*, and *clozapine/schizophrenia* presented in Sect. 11.5.
2. As your corpus, use the list of essential medicines from the Word Health Organization. Gather the Wikipedia pages assigned to the Wikipedia category https://en.wikipedia.org/wiki/Category:World_Health_Organization_essential_medicines. You can adapt the code you wrote in Exercise 5.2 (a), in Chap. 5, which was for building domain specific corpora on composers and mobile phones.
3. To automatically generate the patterns from the sentences (step (b) in Algorithm 10), use various methods explored in Exercise 11.4, in which we created various sets of patterns.
4. To filter the patterns and the instances, I suggest to include yourself as a human annotator.

b. Discuss the process, the results obtained and the experience of being a human annotator. Do you think you were essential in the semi-automatic process to prevent the semantic drift?

Chapter 12
From Syntax to Semantics

A language's **syntax** provides a set of **grammar rules** for properly organizing the words in a sentence to make it **semantically interpretable**. A sentence such as *John gives a book to Mary*, because of its construction using proper English grammar rules, is semantically interpretable, as opposed to an arbitrary sequence of words *John Mary a gives to book* which leaves us puzzled as to the underlying interpretation. An example of a grammar rule would state that a verb phrase (*gives a book*) can be constructed by combining a verb (*gives*) and a noun phrase (*a book*).

Note that semantically interpretable does not infer semantically plausible. For example, the sentence *The desk gives a sun to Zoe.* is semantically interpretable, but within our current world, the interpretation of a desk being an animate object able of giving, and a sun being something the desk can give, is, to say the least, challenging. To rephrase this last statement using the terminology introduced in Chap. 9, we can say that the entities (*desk, sun*) in the sentence *The desk gives a sun to Zoe.* are quite difficult to ground to our mental grounding space.

The purpose of this chapter is to understand this gap between syntax and semantics and develop NLP approaches which try to fill it. To do so, we start with an exploration of the syntactic side, then jump to an exploration of the semantic side, and then look at the in-between steps necessary to go from a **syntactic interpretation** of a sentence into a **semantic interpretation** of a sentence.

On the syntactic side, this chapter introduces a common type of grammar used for syntactic processing in current NLP research: **dependency grammars**. Dependency parsers are different in their output than the parse trees generated by **constituency parsers**, which we presented in Chap. 8. Dependency parser results can be shown in predicate-like form, made of a grammatical relation, a source, and a target term. For example, *nsubj(eats,John)* would be obtained from the sentence *John eats.* and express explicitly the dependency between the verb *eats* and its subject *John*. Such representation will be familiar to the Semantic Web audience.

Jumping to the semantic side, we look at a formalism for semantic sentence interpretation, called **semantic frames**. Semantic frames define typical events and the

© Springer International Publishing Switzerland 2016
C. Barrière, *Natural Language Understanding in a Semantic Web Context*,
DOI 10.1007/978-3-319-41337-2_12

semantic roles performed by the participants in the event. For example, a frame describing a *driving* event would include semantic roles such as driver, path, destination, and vehicle used. The resource **FrameNet** contains hundreds of such semantic frames, and it has become a very valuable resource within the NLP community for researchers interested in frame-based sentence interpretation.

We will then provide a link between syntax and semantics, by suggesting a semi-automatic method for the acquisition of **syntactic realizations** of semantic roles. These syntactic realizations are grammatical dependencies likely associated with the expression of a semantic role in a sentence. We will then test our method within a **semantic role labeling** experiment, in which we will process sentences into a frame-based semantic interpretation.

We end this chapter by bridging the gap between frame-based sentence interpretation and **Relation Extraction** which was the topic of Chap. 11. We will show how the syntactic realizations used for semantic role labeling can become **syntactic patterns** for Relation Extraction, providing an alternative to the lexical and lexico-syntactic patterns presented in the previous chapter.

12.1 Dependency Grammars

In Chap. 8, Sect. 8.5, as part of the NLP pipeline, we introduced constituency parsing, which generates as output a phrase-structure tree. These trees are very good at highlighting the actual grammatical rules underlying the structure of a sentence, but they seem remote from semantics. There is a different kind of grammatical representation, called **dependency graphs**, whose purpose, as its name suggests, is to show the different types of dependencies between words. We will see in this chapter that these dependencies bring us a step closer to a semantic interpretation.

When parsing a sentence with a dependency parser, the resulting graph is a set of dependencies, each involving a **head word** and a **dependent word** from the sentence. Let us look at the resulting dependency graph for an example from the COOKCORPUS introduced in Chap. 8, *The cook supervises all kitchen staff.* as generated using the Stanford CoreNLP Dependency Parser.

```
The cook supervises all kitchen staff.
root(ROOT-0, supervises-3)
det(cook-2, The-1)
nsubj(supervises-3, cook-2)
det(staff-6, all-4)
compound(staff-6, kitchen-5)
dobj(supervises-3, staff-6)
```

Important dependencies are *nsubj* and *dobj* which correspond to the **grammatical subject** and **grammatical object** of a verb, not to be confused with the notion of subject and object of predicates familiar to the Semantic Web community. It is better to use the terms **head** and **dependant** to refer to the subject and object of a grammatical dependency.

Within the dependency graph, a number is attached to each word, indicating its position in the sentence. This is necessary as to differentiate between **word forms** and **word occurrences**. For example, the phrase *the cook is in the kitchen* contains two occurrences of a single word form *the*. An explicit numbering, as in *the-1 cook-2 is-3 in-4 the-5 kitchen-6*, allows the two occurrences (*the-1, the-5*) to be differentiated.

Notice in the dependency graph, how words can be both heads and dependants in different dependencies. Notice also the presence of a *root* dependency, providing an entry point into the graph, leading most often to the main verb of the sentence. This is different from the phrase-structure tree in which the root of the tree is the overall constituent S, representing a sentence.

In the example above, we observe that *cook-1* is the subject (nsubj) of *supervises-3* and that *staff-6* is the object (dobj) of *supervises-3*. We also observe that *The-1* is the determiner (det) for *cook-2* and *all-4* is the determiner (det) of *staff-6*. Notice also that compound nouns are made explicit via the *compound* dependency, as with *kitchen staff* becoming *compound(staff-6,kitchen-5)*.

Any dependency grammar will define many types of dependencies. Analyzing sentences from the COOKCORPUS presented in Chap. 8, using Stanford CoreNLP Dependency grammar, provides a good overview of various dependencies available in that grammar. Table 12.1 shows examples of different types of dependencies resulting from that analysis. The first column specifies the identifying number for the sentence in COOKCORPUS which was analyzed. The second and third columns give the short and long names of the dependency. Columns four and five provide the head and modifier for each dependency. The last column gives the sentence segment from which the dependency was extracted.

Table 12.1 is not an exhaustive list of the dependencies found in analyzing COOK-CORPUS. The table rather contains a sample of the dependencies, chosen to illustrate a variety of dependency types. We see that human interpretation of these dependencies is easier than the analysis of phrase-structure grammar results. We move one step away from the actual constituents and part-of-speech tags, and focus on the relation between words. What is highlighted in those dependencies is how words relate and that provides an easier link toward semantic. Below, we compare the constituency tree and the dependency graph for Sentence 10, *The two cooks reflected and found a way out.* from COOKCORPUS.

- Constituency Parsing

```
S --> NP --> (DT The)
         --> (CD two)
         --> (NNS cooks)
   --> VP --> VP --> (VBG reflected)
              --> (CC and)
              --> VP --> (VBD found)
                     -->  NP  --> (DT a)
                               --> (NN way)
                     -->  PRT --> (RP out)
```

● Dependency parsing

```
root(ROOT-0, reflected-4)
det(cooks-3, The-1)
nummod(cooks-3, two-2)
nsubj(reflected-4, cooks-3)
nsubj(found-6, cooks-3)
cc(reflected-4, and-5)
conj:and(reflected-4, found-6)
det(way-8, a-7)
dobj(found-6, way-8)
compound:prt(found-6, out-9)
```

Table 12.1 Types of dependencies with examples from CookCorpus

Sent	Dependency	Name	Head	Dependent	Segment
3	dobj	object	cooked	balls	cooked balls
3	nsubjpass	passive form subject	cooked	dumplings	dumplings are cooked balls
3	nmod:of	prepositional modifier	balls	dough	balls of dough
3	auxpass	passive form auxiliary	cooked	are	are cooked
4	advmod	adverbial modifier	stir	well	stir well
4	conj:and	conjunction	stir	cook	stir well and cook
4	nmod:for	prepositional modifier	cook	time	cook for some time
4	det	determiner	time	some	some time
7	dobj	object	cook	rice	cook rice
7	advcl	adverbial clause	cook	steam	cook by steaming
9	nsubj	subject	continues	she	she continues
9	xcomp	verbal complement	continues	write	continues to write
10	nummod	numeral modifier	cooks	two	two cooks
10	compound:prt	verb compound	found	out	found a way out
11	amod	adjectival modifier	heat	radiant	radiant heat
12	aux	verb auxiliary	cooking	are	they are cooking
12	nmod:for	prepositional modifier	cooking	us	cooking for us
13	nmod:in	prepositional modifier	outside	summer	outside in summer
13	xcomp	verbal complement	helps	keeping	helps keeping
13	compound	noun compound	cool	house	keeping the house cool

Notice in the dependency graph that *cooks* as subject is distributed to both verbs *reflected* and *found*, in the dependencies *nsubj(reflected-4, cooks-3)* and *nsubj(found-6, cooks-3)*. This distribution of conjunctions in individual dependencies renders explicit the fact that *cooks found* as well as *cooks reflected*. Such distribution is valuable when searching for information in text, as it captures long-distance relations which would not be found in sequence models.[1] The conjunction is present in the phrase-structure tree (CC and), but not explicitly distributed. Another type of dependency nicely captured is the compound verb, *found out*, which was hidden within *found a way out*. Again, the phrase-structure tree contains it, but the dependency graph makes it explicit in the dependency *compound(found,out)*.

The dependencies found are still not semantic dependencies. Knowing that a word is the subject of a verb is still a step away from knowing the role that this word is playing in the action. Typical roles can be expressed in semantic frames, which we explore in our next section, as we jump on the semantic side.

12.2 Semantic Frames

We now jump from syntax to semantics. On the syntactic side, we explored dependency graphs, while also revisiting phrase-structure trees as we examined the type of output produced by dependency parsers in comparison with constituency parsers. On the semantic side, the topic of this section, we will focus on one semantic interpretation of sentences, the one provided by **semantic frames**.

There has been interest in frames since the early days of artificial intelligence and knowledge representation. A reference to early work by Fillmore (1968), *The Case for Case*, is required, to pay tribute to his work. He suggested that a sentence is a verb plus one or more noun phrases (NPs) and that each NP has a deep-structure case. Such case can be agentive, instrumental, dative (recipient), factitive (result), locative, or objective (affected object). These early ideas later evolved into **frame semantics** in which deep-structure cases have become frame elements, which have quite diversified and been adapted to the different frames defined.

Also, today, when thinking of frame semantics, we think of the large endeavor of **FrameNet**, developed at the Computer Science Institute of Berkeley, California, being very much active and in use. Exploring FrameNet, we find thousands of frames for events and activities of varied specificities. Each frame contains **frame elements**, which refer to the different semantic roles played by the different elements used to describe the event.

Table 12.2 shows a few frames with some of their frame elements. The first column provides the frame name, and the second column lists a few frame elements for that frame. Frame elements can also be referred to as **semantic roles**. In Table 12.2, we can see a variety of semantic roles, as they vary from being active participants (e.g., *Judge*) to passive locations (e.g., *Location*). As we observe in Table 12.2, we are not any more in the realm of syntax and grammatical relations. We are fully in the

---

[1] For a presentation of sequence models, see Chap. 6.

realm of semantic, where frames are defined to provide **semantic interpretations** of sentences. The last column of the table identifies, in example sentences, the presence of the frame elements (semantic roles).

Table 12.2 Examples of semantic frames

Frame	Frame Elements	Example
Apply_heat	Cook Food Duration	[$_{Cook}$ Helen] cooked the [$_{Food}$ potatoes] for [$_{Duration}$ 10 min].
Being_employed	Employee Employer Location Task	[$_{Employee}$ Paul] is working as a [$_{Task}$ carpenter] at [$_{Employer}$ QW Builders].
Facial_expression	Conveyed_emotion Expression Possessor	[$_{Possessor}$ He] was [$_{Expression}$ smiling] with [$_{Conveyed\_emotion}$ pride].
Fall_asleep	Sleeper	[$_{Sleeper}$ John] fell asleep early.
Growing_food	Food Grower	The [$_{Grower}$ farmer] planted [$_{Food}$ broccoli].
Memorization	Cognizer Pattern	[$_{Cognizer}$ Lucy] learned the [$_{Pattern}$ alphabet].
Use_vehicle	Driver Goal Path Vehicle	The [$_{Driver}$ captain] safely sailed to [$_{Goal}$ Barcelona].

Let us further develop one frame, that of Apply_heat, which is one of the possible frames for interpreting the examples in the COOKCORPUS discussed earlier. FrameNet provides a short definition of the frame elements it contains,[2] as shown in Table 12.3. The table also shows a short form (column 2) which we will later use to refer to

Table 12.3 Frame elements for *Apply_heat*

Frame element	Short form	Definition
Container	Container	The *Container* holds the *Food* to which heat is applied.
Cook	Cook	The *Cook* applies heat to the *Food*.
Food	Food	*Food* is the entity to which heat is applied by the *Cook*.
Heating_instrument	HeatInst	The entity that directly supplies heat to the *Food*.
Temperature_setting	TempSet	The *TempSet* of the *HeatInst* for the *Food*.
Beneficiary	Beneficiary	The person for whose benefit the *Food* is cooked.
Duration	Duration	*Duration* is the amount of time heat is applied to the *Food*.
Place	Place	This identifies the *Place* where the heat application occurs.

---

[2] In FrameNet, the list of frame elements is divided into core and non-core elements. We will not go into this differentiation for our current exploration, as the approach we develop is indifferent to such characterization.

the frame elements. We can see, in this table, how all the elements are explained in reference to the roles they play within the activity of *applying heat*.

This section was a very brief introduction to semantic frames, which provide one possible representation formalism for sentence representation. We now turn to the challenge of processing sentences in order to generate frames.

12.3 From Sentences to Semantic Frames

From a NLP point of view, the frame representation presented in the previous section provides the end-goal of a sentence analysis process. To reach this end-goal, we must go through two challenging tasks, one of **automatic frame identification**, and one of **semantic role labeling**. Let us explore these challenges further.

12.3.1 Automatic Frame Identification

Automatic frame identification is the task of automatically determining which frame to use to interpret a particular text segment. The main obstacle to this task is the many-to-many relation between surface forms and entities, as we have talked about over and over during the course of this book. Again, we face polysemy and synonymy as our challenges.

Let us continue on our earlier example of cooking and look at the possible frames associated with that word. First, we find out that FrameNet contains five lexical units: *cook up.n, cook.v, cook.n, cooking.n, cooking.v*. And these lexical units are linked to five different frames, as we show in Table 12.4. The table provides the name of the frame (column 1), the possible lexical units for each frame (column 2), and then, to complicate things further, other possible lexical units for each frame (column 3).

Table 12.4 Various cooking-related frames and lexical units

Frame	Lexical units	Other possible lexical units
Coming_up_with	cook up.v	coin.v, concoct.v, design.n, design.v, devise.v, improvise.v, invent.v, think up.v
Cooking_ creation	cook.n, cook up.v, cook.v, cook.n	concoct.v, fix.v, make.v, preparation.n, prepare.v, put together.v, whip up.v
People_by_vocation	cook.n	actress.n, architect.n, carpenter.n, clerk.n, engineer.n, farmer.n, journalist.n
Apply_heat	cook.v, cooking.n	bake.v, barbecue.v, blanch.v, boil.v, deep fry.v, fry.v, melt.v, poach.v, simmer.v
Absorb_heat	cook.v	bake.v, boil.v, braise.v, broil.v, brown.v, char.v, grill.v, parboil.v, poach.v, simmer.v

Given these five possible frames, how would we decide which to elicit when the word *cook* appears in a sentence? We described in Chap. 8, a method to perform a coarse-grained linguistic-level disambiguation, using POS tags. This method could provide a coarse-grained differentiation between the verb set (*Coming_up_with, Cooking_creation, Apply_heat, Absorb_heat*) and the noun set (*Cooking_creation, People_by_vocation, Apply_heat*). Unfortunately, the two sets are not disjoint, and further disambiguation is required.

Such disambiguation could perhaps rely on the grounding strategies, presented in Chap. 9, but unfortunately, those are unlikely to perform well here. The BOW-Match algorithm or even the refined BOW-Similarity algorithm[3] we previously explored, aimed at differentiating unrelated entities, such as *Beethoven* (FILM) and *Beethoven* (COMPOSER). The algorithms relied on the fact that the entities in the grounding space would be defined using words pertaining to different topics. In the present case of the many frames for *cook*, the meaning difference between most frames is too fine grain for such algorithms to work. The frames' respective definitions are likely to contain many related words, from the same subject matter, making our BOW-Match or BOW-Similarity algorithms unable to decide which frame can best serve as a semantic interpretation of a contextual occurrence of *cook*.

One possible disambiguation approach is to consider all frames referenced by the lexical unit *cook* as candidate frames and then make an attempt at sentence interpretation with each one trying to perform **semantic role labeling** within each of the possible candidate frames. Since each frame specifies a different set of semantic roles, the result of semantic role labeling on each frame will be different. We can then select the frame for which the semantic role labeling task was most successful. We do not pursue specifically on the disambiguation task in this chapter, but we do focus next on identifying semantic roles.

12.3.2 Semantic Role Labeling

Semantic role labeling is the task of automatically assigning semantic roles to sentence words. Our starting point for tackling this task is to take a closer look at **syntactic realizations** provided in FrameNet. A syntactic realization is a particular grammatical dependency, found in a sentence, which expresses a semantic role.

For many frames, FrameNet contains human annotation of sentences, where syntactic realization of semantic roles is explicitly tagged. In Table 12.5, we see examples of such annotations (column 2). Since we are more familiar in this book with the dependencies listed in the Stanford CoreNLP parser (see Table 12.1), I provide the corresponding Stanford dependencies (column 3), which we will work with in the remaining of the chapter. For example, the first line of the table shows that the *nmod:in* dependency is a possible syntactic realization of the *Container* frame element.

---

[3]See Chap. 9, Sect. 9.6 for an introduction to the BOW-Match algorithm. The BOW-Similarity algorithm was later presented in Chap. 10, in Sect. 10.5.2.

Table 12.5 Syntactic realizations of *Apply_heat* frame elements

Frame Element	Realizations in FrameNet	Stanford CoreNLP Dep
Container	PP[in].Dep	nmod:in
Cook	PP[by].Dep	nmod:by
Duration	PP[for].Dep	nmod:for
Food	NP.Obj	dobj
HeatInst	PP[in].Dep, PP[on].Dep	nmod:in, nmod:on
TempSet	PP[over].Dep, PP[on].Dep	nmod:over, nmod:on

Based on these syntactic realizations, we can discover frame elements. A first semantic role labeling algorithm consists in directly linking each occurrence of a syntactic realization to its corresponding frame element. For example, if we parse a sentence in which a dependency *dobj(cook,potatoes)* is found, we could tag the semantic role of *potatoes* as *Food* since *dobj(cook)* is a syntactic realization of *Food*. Now, what if we find *nmod:in(cook,bowl)*, then do we tag *bowl* as *Container* or as *HeatInst*?

Here is a problem of ambiguity again. Syntactic realizations are polysemous, in the sense that they link to multiple possible semantic roles. In Table 12.6, we highlight this ambiguity. The first column shows the ambiguous syntactic realization, the second column provides two alternative frame elements for each realization, and the third column shows an example of the syntactic realization for each possible frame element.

Table 12.6 Polysemy of grammatical dependencies

Syntactic realization	Frame Element	Example
nmod:in	Container	Cook the vegetables *in a saucepan.*
	HeatInst	Cook the vegetables *in the microwave.*
nmod:on	HeatInst	Cook all these things *on the barbecue.*
	TempSet	Cook all these things *on full power.*
nmod:for	Duration	Cook the rice *for about 5 min.*
	Beneficiary	Cook the rice *for your mother.*

Notice how the example sentences look very similar to each other except for the actual **semantic role filler** they contain. The role filler is the word (e.g., *saucepan*) which can "fill the semantic role" (e.g., *Container*). This is equivalent in meaning to saying that we perform a semantic labeling of a word (e.g., *saucepan*) with a label (e.g., *Container*). That *saucepan* is a possible filler for *Container*, and not for *HeatInst*, is a direct consequence of the intrinsic nature of the filler, which is not capture by the grammatical dependency.

Disambiguation among the possible semantic roles for each dependency will require knowledge of their semantic types. **Semantic types** can be used to constrain the nature of the semantic role fillers. For example, a *Beneficiary* should be a PERSON, whereas a *Duration* should be a TIMELENGTH. Semantic types play an essential role in knowledge representation and knowledge extraction from text, and our next chapter, Chap. 13, is entirely dedicated to that topic.

The next two sections will focus on developing and testing a strategy to extract semantic role fillers, whether they are ambiguous or not. This will provide a set of candidate fillers to be filtered out by semantic type constraints, in the next chapter.

12.4   Semi-automatic Acquisition of Syntactic Realizations

Now that we highlighted the fact that syntactic realizations are on the critical path toward the discovery of semantic roles in sentences, let us look at how we can acquire these syntactic realizations. Let us develop a strategy for the semi-automatic acquisition of syntactic realizations for particular semantic roles, which I refer to as **Dependency-To-Role rules**. I purposely opt for a **semi-automatic method**, as to continue to emphasize the delicate balance between human annotation effort and algorithmic effort toward generating interesting solutions. We first discussed semi-automatic approaches in Sect. 11.5 in connection with the development of semi-automatic Relation Extraction systems targeting different knowledge acquisition goals.

The strategy I suggest can be divided into two steps, the first step requiring human annotation effort and the second step requiring algorithmic effort.

1. A human will write **prototype sentences** illustrating a particular semantic role within a sentence.
2. The prototype sentences will be automatically processed by a dependency parser to generate dependency graphs, which will further be processed to find the **shortest path** between a frame's lexical unit and the semantic role filler word.

It is that shortest path that becomes a possible syntactic realization of the semantic role. Let us go through both steps, in details, as to understand the human annotation effort and the algorithmic effort involved.

12.4.1   Human Annotation Effort — Writing Prototype Sentences

The idea of using prototype sentences to obtain dependency rules comes from the hypothesis that humans would be better at writing short sentences than directly writing dependency rules. For example, assume three possible syntactic realizations for the *Cook* role in the *Apply_heat* frame are as follows:

```
1. nsubj(bake,X)
2. nmod:agent(barbecue,X)
3. nsubj(V,X) + xcomp(V,boil)
```

Our hypothesis is that humans would have an easier time writing the three sentences below than the dependency rules above:

1. John bakes a cake.
2. The fish was barbecued by our guests.
3. They prefer to boil potatoes.

Each sentence contains a lexical unit indicative of the *Apply_heat* frame (see third column of Table 12.4 for examples of such lexical units) and the semantic role *Cook* which we want to capture. But, the information in the above sentences is insufficient to automatically generate the syntactic realizations desired. We actually need the annotator to explicitly indicate three things: the frame's lexical unit, a semantic role, and a semantic role filler. Let us establish a format for specifying this information which is easy to use for annotators and easy to detect for a software program. Let us set the lexical unit to be in capital letters, and the semantic role filler to be directly followed by a '/' and the name of the role. With these requirements, what a human annotator would need to write looks like the following:

1. John/Cook BAKES a cake.
2. The fish was BARBECUED by our guests/Cook.
3. They/Cook prefer to BOIL potatoes.

Now that we have specified a format for how to write prototype sentences, the main issue remains: What sentences should we write?

A first rule is to trust corpus data more than our imagination. That means that the prototype sentences should not just come from the top of our head, but rather, they should be inspired by real corpus sentences in which a frame's lexical unit is present. For example, if we need inspiration for prototype sentences for the *Apply_heat* frame, we would search in a corpus for sentences containing the words *bake, blanch, broil* or any other lexical unit associated with that frame. Remember our **concordancer**, developed in Chap. 5? It can become handy for this exploration. For example, Table 12.7 provides many sentences containing the lexical unit *bake*. And although there is much noise in that data, the set of sentences gives a sense of the expected variability in the surface forms associated with the expression of semantic roles.

Table 12.7 Exploration of frame-related lexical units with a concordancer

```
then plated with sour cherries and baked. During the baking process the cherrie
Murren are coated with eggyolk and baked at 210C (410F) for 20 minutes, until i
to as much as a gram a cookie) are baked into the product in careful steps, so
rench petit four), and popcorn are baked in large batches to serve to guests an
localized to Southeast Asia with a baked rice dish called Curry Zazzle.[23][24]
vegetables and herbs. These can be baked, fried or cooked in wine. Rolitos is a
h powdered sugar. Egyptians either bake it at home or buy it in the bakery. Thu
. Delivering poor results and half-baked ideas, it's my regret to call Aliens v
tly getting into trouble with half baked plans [from which he] is regularly res
or fried, boiled or steamed. It is baked, traditionally, in open-wood-fire to a
he fish is often served steamed or baked.[130] Pork leg cooked with rock candy
00 loaves of bread a day that they bake in their solar-powered bakery, and is b
chili oil. Another variation is to bake the cream and fry it with bacon, which
ne, domesticated girl who likes to bake cakes for her best friend Yumiko. She h
large rootstock (a tuber) that was baked in a fire pit. The spelling is derived
 wine and a hundred cakes of wheat baked in honey. All three stand up to claim
) or wooden barrels where the wine bakes in the sun for several years until it
bati, which are spicy lentils with baked balls of wheat with lots of ghee. The
```

It is worth mentioning that even before relying on concordancers for inspiration, a first place to look is the resource FrameNet itself. FrameNet contains manual annotation of syntactic realizations which provide many example sentences that can be turned into prototype sentences for our purposes.

Let us now move to the algorithmic side of the semi-automatic method, assuming the human effort has been performed, and a set of prototype sentences are ready to be transformed into syntactic realizations.

12.4.2 Algorithmic Effort — Processing Prototype Sentences into Syntactic Realizations

Let us go back to our three prototype examples, written earlier, and repeated here:

1. John/Cook BAKES a cake.
2. The fish was BARBECUED by our guests/Cook.
3. They/Cook prefer to BOIL potatoes.

First, we should write a small program to recuperate from these prototype sentences the information shown in Table 12.8. The format we imposed on human annotators in the writing of the prototype sentences was to allow this automatic step to be done easily.

Table 12.8 Information from prototype sentences

Ex.	Lexical unit	Semantic role	Role filler	Sentence to parse
1	BAKES	Cook	John	John bakes a cake.
2	BARBECUED	Cook	guests	The fish was barbecued by our guests.
3	BOIL	Cook	They	They prefer to boil potatoes.

The sentences in the last column would then be given as input to a dependency parser (here the Stanford CoreNLP parser), which would output the following dependency graphs.

```
(1) John bakes a cake.
root(ROOT-0, bakes-2)
nsubj(bakes-2, John-1)
det(cake-4, a-3)
dobj(bakes-2, cake-4)

(2) The fish was barbecued by our guests.
root(ROOT-0, barbecued-4)
det(fish-2, The-1)
nsubjpass(barbecued-4, fish-2)
auxpass(barbecued-4, was-3)
case(guests-7, by-5)
nmod:poss(guests-7, our-6)
nmod:agent(barbecued-4, guests-7)

(3) They prefer to boil potatoes.
root(ROOT-0, prefer-2)
nsubj(prefer-2, They-1)
mark(boil-4, to-3)
xcomp(prefer-2, boil-4)
dobj(boil-4, potatoes-5)
```

Notice how the resulting dependency graphs contain both the lexical units and the semantic role fillers, but they also contain much additional information corresponding to dependencies involving the other words in the sentence. We must filter out all this additional information and keep only the necessary dependencies required to capture the syntactic realization. Doing this corresponds to finding the **shortest path** in the dependency graph which connects the lexical unit with the semantic role filler. Explaining shortest path algorithms is outside the scope of this book, and we will assume that the dependency parser we use does provide a search for the shortest path within its functionalities. The Stanford CoreNLP dependency parser does provide such functionality.

Below, we show the shortest paths found for the three examples:

```
(1) nsubj(bakes-2, John-1)
(2) nmod:agent(barbecued-4,guests-7)
(3) nsubj(prefer-2, They-1) + xcomp(prefer-2, boil-4)
```

Now, these shortest paths are abstracted to become syntactic realizations, where X corresponds to the semantic role filler for the *Cook* semantic role. The shortest paths are sometimes reduced to single dependencies, but they can include intermediate nodes, as in the third example below.

```
(1)  nsubj(bakes,X)
(2)  nmod:agent(barbecued,X)
(3)  nsubj(Y,X) + xcomp(Y,boil)
```

We now have our strategy for the semi-automatic acquisition of syntactic realizations of semantic roles, which we will put to the test, in the experiment in the following section.

12.5   Experiment — Semantic Role Labeling of *Cooking* Sentences

For our semantic role labeling experiment, we will follow these three steps:

1. Define our gold standard and our evaluation approach.
2. Clearly establish our semantic role labeling strategy.
3. Perform the strategy, evaluate the results, and discuss.

12.5.1   Gold Standard and Evaluation

To generate our gold standard, let us first gather some test sentences which would elicit the *Apply_Heat* frame. Table 12.9 shows sentences about baking. Our dataset is too small to obtain any quantitative results that are significant, but it will be sufficient for discussion and observation of the pros and cons of our strategy.

Now, we must annotate these sentences to obtain our goal standard. We have seen that the *Apply_heat* frame has multiple frame elements, but for our experiment, we will focus on the following subset: Container, Cook, Duration, Food, Heating_instrument, Temperature_setting, Beneficiary, and Location. We therefore take each sentence of Table 12.9, find the semantic roles it contains, and annotate them. Performing manual annotation of sentences is usually very insightful as to the difficulty of the task. If you try tagging the sentences in Table 12.9, is it difficult? Remember, in Chap. 8, we discussed the difficulty of assigning parts of speech to words. Unless they are trained linguists, humans are not used to performing part-of-speech tagging. On the other hand, our current task of assigning frame elements is actually closer to the kind of semantic interpretation that we are doing on a daily basis in conversation, and therefore, it is easier to do.

Table 12.9 Sentences for Gold Standard

No.	Sentence
1	Instead, consumers bake the pizzas at their homes.
2	Italian and Polish bakeries bake fresh bread and various traditional pastries.
3	The scones you baked for me are just delicious.
4	If you overcook, or bake too long you might lose nutrients.
5	Place the muffin tin in the oven and bake for one hour.
6	Nana tried to bake a chocolate cake for Yuichi's birthday.
7	Spread the dough on a square baking sheet, and bake it in a moderate oven.
8	At Zoe's Cafe, the chef bakes the best cheese cake.

Table 12.10 Annotated Sentences Gold Standard

No.	Sentence
1	Instead, [$_{Cook}$consumers] bake the [$_{Food}$pizzas] at their [$_{Location}$homes].
2	[$_{Cook}$Italian and Polish bakeries] bake fresh [$_{Food}$bread] and various traditional [$_{Food}$pastries].
3	The [$_{Food}$scones] [$_{Cook}$you] baked for [$_{Beneficiary}$me] are just delicious.
4	If [$_{Cook}$you] overcook, or bake [$_{Duration}$too long] you might lose nutrients.
5	Place the muffin [$_{Container}$tin] in the [$_{HeatInst}$oven] and bake for [$_{Duration}$one hour].
6	[$_{Cook}$Nana] tried to bake a [$_{Food}$chocolate cake] for [$_{Beneficiary}$Yuichi]'s birthday.
7	Spread the dough on a square [$_{Container}$baking sheet], and bake [$_{Food}$it] in a [$_{TempSet}$moderate] [$_{HeatInst}$oven].
8	At [$_{Location}$Zoe's Cafe], the [$_{Cook}$chef] bakes the best [$_{Food}$cheese cake].

Now, does your tagging match the semantic tagging done in Table 12.10? Most often, there is inter-annotator agreement as to the roles being identified, but there could be many variations, between annotators, as to the boundaries of the textual elements corresponding to the roles. For example, in example 7, is the container a *square baking sheet*, a *baking sheet* or simply a *sheet*? This might seem like a tidious question, but it is not when the results of different algorithms are compared in large-scale quantitative evaluations. In such evaluations, extracted information is automatically compared to gold standard information with pure string matching, and therefore, an answer such as *baking sheet* would not match a gold standard *sheet*. Boundary issues come up in many Information Extraction tasks, as we already experienced in bilingual term search (see Chap. 7) and entity type detection (see Chap. 3), and now in semantic role labeling.

For this experiment, let us consider that if the extracted information is contained in the gold standard information, then the output is deemed correct. This means that we would accept *cake* as a correct answer even if *cheese cake* is the answer found in the gold standard.

Table 12.11 shows the semantic roles present in the tagged sentences from Table 12.10. This constitutes our gold standard, with a total of 24 roles to be identified.

Table 12.11 Expected Semantic Roles

No.	Roles Expected
1	Cook=consumers, Food=pizzas, Location=homes
2	Cook=bakeries, Food=bread, Food=pastries
3	Food=scones, Cook=you, Beneficiary=me
4	Cook=you, Duration=too long
5	Container=tin, HeatInst=oven, Duration=hour
6	Cook=Nana, Food=chocolate cake, Beneficiary=Yuichi
7	Container=baking sheet, Food=it, TempSet=moderate, HeatIns=oven
8	Location=cafe, Cook=chef, Food=cheese cake
Total	24 roles

As for the evaluation method, we will use our usual recall and precision methods.

12.5.2 Define our Semantic Role Labeling Strategy

As to perform Semantic Role labeling, we will define two steps:

1. Define a set of syntactic realizations for each semantic role.
2. Use the syntactic realizations as search patterns into the test examples to extract semantic role fillers.

For our **step (1)**, we use the strategy developed in Sect. 12.4 in which we were trying to balance human annotation and algorithmic effort toward the semi-automatic acquisition of syntactic realizations of semantic roles.

Our human effort is to come up with prototype sentences for each of the semantic roles we wish to cover. In our current experiment, the annotated FrameNet sentences for the lexical units involved in the *Apply_heat* frame served as our development set, being the source of inspiration for the development of prototype sentences. As you have learned by now, we should not use the sentences in Table 12.9 for such development since these sentences are the test sentences. Table 12.12 shows the prototype sentences (column 2) assigned to each semantic role (column 1). For a slightly more concise version of prototype sentences, the specific semantic role is not repeated, but rather shown by the variable X. Notice also that all prototype sentences and their derived syntactic realizations are shown as using the lexical unit *cook* as indicative of the frame, but this lexical unit can be replaced by any other lexical unit (e.g., bake, boil, blanch) that could be used in a *Apply_heat* sentence as well.

Table 12.12 Generated syntactic realizations from prototype sentences

Frame Element	Prototype sentence	Syntactic realization
Container	They cook in a saucepan/X.	nmod:in(cook,X)
Cook	They/X cook their food.	nsubj(cook,X)
	They/X prefer to cook food.	nsubj(V,X) + xcomp(V,cook)
	I ate the pizza cooked by John/X.	nmod:agent(cooked,X)
Duration	It cooks until al dente/X.	nmod:until(cook,X)
	They cook for 5 min/X.	nmod:for(cook,X)
	It cooks about 5 min/X	nmod:about(cook,X)
Food	Potatoes/X are cooked.	nsubjpass(cooked,X)
	They cook their food/X.	nobj(cook,X)
	They cook a lot of pasta/X.	nmod:of(Y,X) + dobj(cook,Y)
	I like the taste of tomatoes/X cooked.	nmod:of(Y,X) + nsubj(cooked,Y)
HeatInst	They cook in the microwave/X.	nmod:in(cook,X)
	I cook on our barbecue/X.	nmod:on(cook,X)
TempSet	Potatoes cook over high heat/X.	nmod:over(cook,X)
	Potatoes cook on full power/X.	nmod:on(cook,X)
Beneficiary	He cooks for his friend/X.	nmod:for(cook,X)
Location	He cooks at home/X.	nmod:at(cook,X)

As for the algorithmic effort, we follow the steps described in Sect. 12.4.2 to transform prototype sentences into syntactic realizations. The extracted syntactic generalizations are shown in the third column of Table 12.12. We have a set of 17 syntactic realizations for our 8 semantic roles.

Step (2) of the strategy consists in parsing the test sentences from Table 12.9 and then using the 17 syntactic realizations as search patterns within the resulting dependency graphs of the test sentences to extract the semantic role fillers.

12.5.3 Result Analysis and Discussion

Table 12.13 shows the obtained results for our strategy, using the 17 syntactic realizations. These roles are compared with the gold standard roles (see Table 12.11) to calculate the recall and precision shown in the second and third columns.

The precision results are already quite high, but could further be improved if we impose some semantic constraints on the semantic roles, as well as rules for non-duplications of semantic roles. In sentence 5 for example, the *Beneficiary* role is not too likely to be associated with the filler *hours*, much less likely than the role *Duration* would. Applying semantic constraints on semantic roles is the topic of the next chapter, Chap. 13.

As for the recall results, Table 12.13 shows that our set of rules is not sufficient for an exhaustive extraction of the semantic roles, as we only obtain 58 % recall. This low recall is somewhat disappointing, but not that surprising giving the limited number

Table 12.13 SRL strategy's output

No.	Roles found (incorrect ones in italic)	Recall	Precision
1	Cook=consumers, Food=pizzas, Location=homes	3/3	3/3
2	Cook=bakeries, Food=bread	2/3	2/2
3	Food=scones	1/3	1/1
4	Cook=you	1/2	1/1
5	Duration=hour, *Beneficiary=hour*	1/3	1/2
6	Food=cake	1/3	1/1
7	Food=it, HeatInst=oven, *Container=oven*	2/4	2/3
8	Location=cafe, Cook=chef, Food=cake	3/3	3/3
Total	14 correct roles found	14/24 (58.3%)	14/16 (87.5%)

of sentence prototypes we have, and the large variety of ways different semantic roles can be expressed. Certainly, the two main parts of our strategy, the definition of prototype sentences and the analysis of prototype sentences with a dependency parser, could be revisited if we were to improve our results, as in their own way, they both contribute to the performance of our strategy. For the prototype sentences, we could expand the list in Table 12.12 by writing more varied sentences. Inspiration could be found with the use of a concordancer, as we had mentioned in Sect. 12.4.1.

As for the dependency parser, our results are totally dependent on its behavior. We will discuss this issue a bit more, as we expand the idea of using syntactic realizations for identifying semantic role fillers into using syntactic realizations as patterns for Relation Extraction.

12.6 Syntactic Realizations as Patterns for Relation Extraction

The use of frame semantics for sentence interpretation may seem remote from the goal of knowledge base expansion, as we presented in Chap. 11. But in fact, the overall process of using syntactic realizations to identify semantic roles is very close to the process of Relation Extraction required for knowledge base expansion.

For example, if we were to think of semantic frames from a Semantic Web perspective, we can imagine transforming frames and frame elements into a more typical `predicate(subject,object)` format, such as:

Frame-like representation
[$_{Cook}$Helen] cooked the [$_{Food}$potatoes] for [$_{Duration}$10 minutes].

Predicate-like representation
```
nlusw:frameInstance(nlusw:f1, frameNet:Apply_heat)
nlusw:cook(nlusw:f1, "Helen")
```

```
nlusw:food(nlusw:f1, "potatoes")
nlusw:duration(nlusw:f1, "10 minutes")
```

Granted, events describing how potatoes are cooked are not the most interesting events to include in a knowledge base, but there are many more interesting events. Within the knowledge bases of the Semantic Web, many entities are events, such as Olympic games or any other sport events, also political events or historical events. One could even argue that almost anything that can be situated in time can be considered an event with various properties (e.g., start date, end date, people involved).

Even the `actor-in(X,Y)` relation, which we looked at in the previous chapter, can be seen as a role in an event. FrameNet defines a frame called *Performers_and_roles* in which various roles are defined: *Performance, Performer, Audience, Script, Performance type* (e.g., dance, theater, movie). With this view, searching for `actor-in(X,Y)` is the same as searching for the two semantic roles *Performer* and *Performance* within the *Performer_and_Roles* frame, assuming the *Performance type* has been restricted to be a movie.

Let us look at an example sentence, very similar to the examples from Chap. 11 used to develop lexical and lexico-syntactic patterns, but now interpreted within the *Performer_and_Roles frame*.

Frame-like representation

[$_{Performer}$ John Turturro] stars in the [$_{Time}$ 1991] [$_{PerformanceType}$ movie] [$_{Performance}$ Barton Fink] as a [$_{Role}$ writer].

Predicate-like representation

```
nlusw:frameInstance(nlusw:f2, frameNet:Performer_and_roles)
nlusw:PerformanceType(nlusw:f2, "movie"
nlusw:Performer(nlusw:f2, "John Turturro")
nlusw:Time(nlusw:f2, "1991")
nlusw:Performance(nlusw:f2, "Barton Fink")
nlusw:Role(nlusw:f2, "writer")
```

Let us even push further the comparison between frame representation and Relation Extraction, and see whether we can also write prototype sentences to capture the Performer/Performance relation. We used to identify a single role at a time in our prototype sentences (see Sect. 12.4.1) but what if we now identify pairs of semantic roles, as in the sentences below.

1. [John Turturro]/Performer STARS IN [Barton Fink]/Performance.
2. [Fargo]/Performance FEATURES [Frances McDormand]/Performer.
3. [The Big Lebowski]/Performance stars [Jeff Bridges]/Performer in the main ROLE.

Notice that I carried over the idea of annotating in uppercase the lexical unit corresponding to the frame, such as *stars in*, *features*, and *role*. Including such a mandatory indicator within a sentence corresponds to the use of *trigger words* within patterns for Relation Extraction. We had discussed trigger words in Sect. 11.5 in the previous chapter.

The prototype sentences can then automatically be processed by a dependency parser. The resulting dependencies for the first prototype sentence are shown below.

```
root(ROOT-0, stars-3)
compound(Turturro-2, John-1)
nsubj(stars-3, Turturro-2)
case(Fink-6, in-4)
compound(Fink-6, Barton-5)
nmod:in(stars-3, Fink-6)
```

From the dependency graph, the last step toward generating a syntactic realization of a semantic role was to search for the shortest path between the lexical unit (or trigger word) and the semantic role. We can extend this idea to be the shortest path between the two roles (Performer/Performance) which includes the trigger word.

For example, the shortest path for the first example sentence would be the following:

```
nsubj(stars-3, Turturro-2)
nmod:in(stars-3, Fink-6)
```

The resulting syntactic pattern will be the following: `nsubj(stars, A);nmod:in (stars, F)`. This patterns requires the trigger word *stars* to provide a link between the actor A (Performer) and the film F (Performance). Three syntactic patterns corresponding to the three examples sentences are shown below.

```
1. nsubj(stars, A);nmod:in(stars, F)
2. nsubj(features, F);dobj(features, A)
3. nsubj(Y, F);dobj(Y, A);nmod:in(A, role)
```

Notice how sometimes, as in the third example, the trigger word (role) is not really on the shortest path, but rather included as an additional dependency constraint. Furthermore, we would in general also need to extend the words found for A and F to their including compounds within the dependency graph. This would allow to retrieve *John Turturro* and not only *Turturro*, as both words are part of the same compound.

At the end of our experiment in the previous section, we concluded by pointing out to limitations associated with the use of dependency parsers. Whether dependency parsers are used as a component in a semantic role labeling task or in a Relation Extraction task, they will for sure make good contributions, but also introduce noise. This reinforces what we often discussed in this book that any use of a linguistic tool within a processing pipeline should come with a warning. Linguistic tools are very useful but also error prone, especially when dealing with ambiguous words.

For example, we should know that the relation `actor-in(X,Y)` will be particularly difficult for a syntax-based approach to Relation Extraction, since movie titles are among the hardest elements to throw at a parser. Movie titles can be made of any combination of parts of speech, and these combinations will be hard to process by parsers. For example, a sentence like *Burn After Reading stars George Clooney.* is very hard to interpret if we do not consider the words *Burn*, *After* and *Reading* as part of a single entity name.

This suggests a strategy in which we should help the parser by recognizing movie titles ahead of time. This idea of recognizing (or validating) the semantic types of entities taking part in semantic relations or frames is the topic of our next chapter.

12.7   In Summary

- Dependency graphs, resulting from an analysis with a dependency parser, show grammatical relations between words, such as subject, object, modifier, determiner, compounding.
- From dependency graphs, we can jump toward semantic interpretation, if we have a set of rules (syntactic realizations) for transforming each dependency into a valid semantic role within the particular sentence at hand.
- FrameNet is an ambitious project, at Berkeley University, California, creating a large resource containing a multitude of semantic frames.
- A frame defines a particular event, action, or state. A frame contains different frame elements, each one playing a semantic role within the frame.
- A semi-automatic approach to writing syntactic realization for semantic roles consists in the following: (1) writing prototype sentences in which semantic roles are explicitly tagged, (2) parsing the sentences with a dependency parser, and (3) finding the shortest path within the result dependency graph which connects the semantic role filler and the lexical unit indicative of the frame.
- The set of prototype sentences for various semantic roles of a frame could be inspired from the use of a concordancer to show occurrences of the frame lexical units in real corpus contexts.
- Since parsing is not perfect, and prone to lexical variations, a semantic role labeling strategy based on parsing will be influenced by the parser's performance and variability.
- Many dependencies, especially prepositional modifiers (*nmod:in*, *nmod:for*, etc.), are very ambiguous, as they can lead to multiple semantic roles.
- FrameNet is a good resource not only to find frame definitions, but also lists of lexical units which are trigger words for each frame, such as *cook* and *bake* for the *Apply_heat* frame.
- Relation Extraction is related to the task of semantic role labeling, most likely looking at the relation between two semantic roles for a unique event.
- Syntactic realizations for semantic roles can be adapted into syntactic patterns for Relation Extraction.

12.8   Further Reading

Dependency parsers: The Stanford CoreNLP software, containing multiple modules, from tokenizer to parser, is available at http://nlp.stanford.edu/software/corenlp.shtml. It allows for both constituency parsing and dependency parsing.

Frames and FrameNet: Early work on frames can be found in *The Case for Case* (Fillmore, 1968). FrameNet, developed at the Computer Science Institute of Berkeley, California, can be explored online at https://framenet.icsi.berkeley.edu and request for full access to the FrameNet database for research purposes can be made as well. I encourage the reader to visit the site and explore the frames to discover the richness of FrameNet.

Annotated semantic roles: The corpus PropBank (Proposition Bank) available at https://github.com/propbank/ is an annotated corpus of semantic roles (Palmer et al. 2005) which could also be very useful as a source of prototype sentences.

Frames and the Semantic Web: Links between frames and the Semantic Web have been discussed in the literature. For example, see Lassila and Mcguinness (2011), Narayanan et al. (2002), or more recently Exner and Nugues (2011) performing event extraction from Wikipedia.

Sentence interpretation and Semantic role labeling: Some early methods on Semantic Role Labeling (SRL) are described in Gildea and Jurafsky (2002). There has been a revival of interest in the recent years. I encourage the reader to look at the tutorial on semantic role labeling from NAACL'2013 (Palmer 2013). To see how SRL is put in relation to Open Information Extraction, see Christensen et al. (2011). For semantic interpretation using not only FrameNet, but also VerbNet (http://verbs.colorado.edu/~mpalmer/projects/verbnet.html) and Wordnet (https://wordnet.princeton.edu/), see the SemLink project described in Palmer (2009). Another large effort into semantic representation is called Abstract Meaning Representation (AMR), with information available at http://amr.isi.edu/. For the development of parsers for AMR, see Vanderwende et al. (2015).

Syntactic patterns for Relation Extraction: In Bunescu and Mooney (2005), shortest paths in dependency graphs are used as Relation Extraction patterns. Sometimes, it is not the shortest path, but rather partial trees (or subtrees) that are used as potential patterns (Sudo et al. 2003; Culotta and Sorensen 2004). Sentences to analyze are compared to the tree-based patterns by measuring their similarity. Although much of the work using dependency trees is within a supervised machine learning view of Relation Extraction, the underlying idea of using dependency parsers to help in pattern definition is similar.

12.9 Exercises

Exercise 12.1 (Dependency parsing)

a. Go back to the CookCorpus introduced in Chap. 8, Sect. 8.6.1. Parse the corpus using the Stanford CoreNLP dependency parser and analyze the results. Do the resulting parses lead to semantically viable interpretations? Try to parse the same sentences using a different parser and compare their output. See Sect. 8.8, Further readings, of Chap. 8 for references to linguistic tools.

b. Go back to the BeethovenCorpus, in Chap. 2 and parse its sentences, using both a phrase-structure parser and a dependency parser. How do the parsers behave? Does the dependency parser provide explicit information not found by the phrase-structure parser? Give some examples.

c. An underlying hypothesis for parsing is that we work with grammatically correct
   sentences. What about the sentences from the ACTORFILMCORPUS introduced in
   the previous chapter (Sect. 11.2)? Are those difficult for parsers? Try replacing
   the movie title in each sentence by "the film" and parse the sentences again. Any
   improvement in the results?

Exercise 12.2 (Exploring FrameNet)

a. Take the time to explore FrameNet, looking at different frames and frame elements. Identify the frame elements which were not included in Table 12.2 given
   the examples of frames provided. Write example sentences in which these other
   frame elements would be present.
b. The best way to become familiar with frames is to try tagging sentences with
   frame elements. First, investigate the *Exporting* frame in FrameNet. Then, look
   at the EXPORTCORPUS in Table 12.14, which gives sentences related to export. Take
   each sentence within the EXPORTCORPUS, and tag it with the appropriate semantic
   roles from the *Exporting* frame.

Table 12.14 EXPORTCORPUS

No.	Sentence
1	The region exports a number of crop products including broccoli, onion, Chinese cabbage, sweet corn, and celery.
2	China, the main supplier of wolfberry products in the world, had total exports generating US$120 million in 2004.
3	They weave out tons of coir carpets, door mats, and jute items every month for exports.
4	A series of successful international business ventures include Champion Pet Foods that exports around the world.
5	Maggi also owns the Amaggi Group, a large company that harvests, processes, and exports soybeans.
6	Until 2000, Nepals' tea exports accounted for only about 100–150 tons per annum.
7	Shock Records distributes, markets, and exports CDs by Australian artists in all styles of music.
8	The house is now successfully headed by Jean-Pierre Cointreau and exports 65 % of its production to more than 70 countries.
9	As a major supplier of fish and crustaceans, its exports reach buyers as far as Hong Kong, Japan, and China.
10	Indonesia and Malaysia both continued to show a trade surplus because of their heavy raw material exports to Japan.

Exercise 12.3 (Semantic role labeling)

a. Go back to the MILLIONCORPUS you built in Chap. 10 (see Exercise 10.1 (a))
   which was a random gathering of a million pages from Wikipedia. Explore that
   corpus using the concordancer you developed in Chap. 5 (see Exercise 5.4 (a)).

Search for sentences containing the word *bake* or *cook*. Is there a large variety of sentences? Do you find many sentences that refer to the *Apply_heat*?

b. From the sentences found using the concordancer in the previous question, choose 10 sentences which match the *Apply_Heat* frame. Then perform the semantic role labeling experiment we set up in Sect. 12.5.

1. Tag the sentences with the semantic roles we explored in Table 12.12 (*Container, Cook, Duration, Food, Heating_instrument, Temperature_setting, Beneficiary, Location*). The sentences become your test data.
2. Write a program that puts in place the semantic role labeling strategy developed in Sect. 12.5.2 to extract frame elements automatically.
3. Test your program using the prototype sentences found in Table 12.12. The program should automatically generate syntactic realizations from the prototype sentences, which can then be applied on the test data gathered in (1).
4. How does the strategy work? Evaluate the recall of the algorithm.

c. Continue on the experiment from question (b) by adding five more prototype sentences. Re-evaluate the results. Any changes? Discuss.

d. Use the five new prototype sentences from question (c) on the sentences from Table 12.9. How do the results compare with the results shown in Table 12.13?

e. Use everything you have learned in this chapter to perform semantic role labeling for the sentences in the EXPORTCORPUS (Table 12.14) using the *Exporting* frame. Use your manual tagging from Exercise 12.2 (b) as your gold standard. Make sure to not use the EXPORTCORPUS for the development of your prototype sentences. Discuss how you will build your development set. Discuss the obtained results on EXPORTCORPUS.

Exercise 12.4 (Relation Extraction with syntactic patterns)

a. Go back to Table 11.1 in Sect. 11.2 and develop syntactic patterns to extract the *Performance* and *Performer* roles in them, as to reconstruct the `actor-in` relations. Test your patterns on the sentences in Table 11.12, in the exercise section of Chap. 11.

b. Compare your newly written syntactic patterns with lexical and lexico-syntactic patterns written in the last chapter. What do you see as advantages and disadvantages of using syntactic patterns? What could be the impact of using syntactic patterns on precision/recall?

c. Develop a dependency-based synonym extraction. Even if the relation cannot be mapped to a frame, you can still use the same ideas of prototype sentences and trigger words to develop your patterns. You can use the sentences in Table 11.4 to develop your patterns, and then test them on the sentences in Table 11.7. Both tables were introduced in the previous chapter, in Sect. 11.4. How do these new syntactic patterns compare to the lexical and lexico-syntactic patterns you had before?

Chapter 13
Semantic Types

Our exploration of frames, in the previous chapter, has pointed at the importance of determining the semantic constraints for particular semantic roles involved in a frame. For example, in the *Apply_Heat* frame we could require the *Cook* role to be a PERSON and the *Heating_instrument* role to be within a *set of possible instruments used for heating food* which we could define as the HEATINSTR type.

The first semantic type, PERSON, is quite generic, and in fact so common that it is part of standard entity types or entity classes normally included in Named Entity Recognizers, along with ORGANIZATION, LOCATION, and DATE. We earlier talked, in Chap. 3, on using regular expressions to automatically search for DATE instances in text. In this chapter, we will explore an open source **Named Entity Recognition (NER)** software to do so.

The second semantic type, HEATINSTR, is on the other hand, very specific and perhaps only useful within a few contexts related to eating and cooking. Standard NER tools do not search for these specific types when analyzing text. Nevertheless, recognizing specific semantic types can be very important for sentence understanding. As we have seen in the previous chapter, dependency grammars can bring us so far as to identify the dependencies between the elements of the sentence, such as *nmod:for(cook,oven)* and *nmod:for(cook,pot)*. But semantic types will be required to determine that these grammatically identical dependencies can be further disambiguated into semantic roles of *Heating_instrument(cook,oven)* and *Container(cook,pot)*.

This chapter will show that definitions of specific semantic types and possible instances of these types can be found in different **lexical and semantic resources**, such as WordNet and FrameNet. Textual resources can also contain instances of semantic types, but we must uncover them through knowledge acquisition methods. To do so, we will revisit pattern-based approaches, both lexico-syntactic approaches (Chap. 11) and dependency-based approaches (Chap. 12) for **automatically building gazetteers from text**.

As we build gazetteers for various semantic types using different approaches, and use these gazetteers within a semantic role labeling task, we will see how they

© Springer International Publishing Switzerland 2016
C. Barrière, *Natural Language Understanding in a Semantic Web Context*,
DOI 10.1007/978-3-319-41337-2_13

individually are noisy and have limited coverage. This will lead us to explore ways of combining their information, and present a **vote combination approach** so as to benefit from multiple resources.

13.1 Common Semantic Types — Exploring NER Systems

Named Entity Recognition (NER) is a very active field of research, aiming at recognizing instances of predefined types of named entities in text. Methods for doing NER vary widely, from pattern-based search, to machine learning approaches, performing sequence learning. In Chap. 3, we focused on a pattern-based approach as we wrote regular expressions in search of DATE instances. We mentioned how the type DATE was a good candidate for regular expressions given the regularity underlying the writing of dates in text. Other entity types would be less detectable through regular expressions and should be helped with gazetteers or even be approached with more refined machine learning methods.

In this section, we explore how we can take advantage of a refined tool, freely available, and included in the Stanford CoreNLP platform, which we have used over and over in this book. A first example of the output of the NER module is shown below, resulting from the analysis of the sentence *John cooked the rice for 6 minutes.* Each line shows the actual word, its lemma, its part of speech and finally its **named entity type**, or O if none can be assigned to a word.

```
John       John      NNP    PERSON
cooked     cook      NN     O
the        the       DT     O
rice       rice      NN     O
for        for       IN     O
six        six       CD     DURATION
minutes    minute    NNS    DURATION
.          .         .      O
```

The example above illustrates PERSON and DURATION. Two other types, ORGANIZATION and LOCATION, are illustrated by the following example: *Ottawa's Diabetes Association collects clothing for people in need.*

```
Ottawa       Ottawa       NNP    LOCATION
's           's           POS    O
Diabetes     Diabetes     NNP    ORGANIZATION
Association  Association  NNP    ORGANIZATION
collects     collect      VBZ    O
clothing     clothing     NN     O
for          for          IN     O
```

```
people          people          NNS     O
in              in              IN      O
need            need            NN      O
.               .               .       O
```

Even if we are not going to dig into the details of the algorithm used in the Stanford CoreNLP NER module, it is a good idea to get an intuition for its strength and weaknesses, by performing small changes in test sentences, and observing the impact on the named entity tagging results. For example, by changing *Diabetes Association* to *Good Hope*, the ORGANIZATION is no longer recognized, whereas changing to a name *Good Foundation* does trigger an ORGANIZATION tag. We can hypothesize that the terms *Foundation* or *Association* are prominent features or patterns use by the NER module.

Also notice, in the example above, how the common noun *people* is not identified as a PERSON. NER usually focus on named entities, meaning specific instances of particular types. Generic words, such as *mother, people, children*, would therefore not be identified, as they are rather subclasses of PERSON and not instances of the class. We hinted at this instantiation versus subclass differentiation earlier, in Chap. 11 (see Sect. 11.1) as we discussed the IS-A relation.

In the next section, we will look into possible resources to help us build gazetteers both for generic types, (e.g., PERSON), as well as more specific types (e.g., CONTAINER). Finding the resources for specific types is especially important since those types are not covered by NER systems.

13.2 Specific Semantic Types — Exploring Lexico-Semantic Resources

Lists of words (gazetteers), corresponding to either instances or subclasses of particular semantic classes, can be found in diverse resources. As we first introduced gazetteers, in Chap. 3 (see Sect. 3.2), we explored the use of DBpedia, as a good source for gazetteers. As an example, we queried DBpedia, to obtain a list of museums instances for the class dbpedia:Art_museum.

In the current section, we will focus on two additional resources from which we can extract gazetteers: **FrameNet** and **WordNet**.

13.2.1 Semantic Types in FrameNet

As part of FrameNet (presented in Chap. 12), some of the semantic roles defined are found in multiple frames, corresponding to the *Who did What When Where How* questions we typically ask when analyzing narrative texts. Among these recurrent semantic roles, some can be assigned semantic constraints corresponding to common named entities (e.g., *Who*/PERSON, *When*/DATE, *Where*/LOCATION).

But other semantic constraints could be much more specific. For some of them, such as *Container*, FrameNet does explicitly define a type CONTAINER[1] to be used. Furthermore, FrameNet also lists over a hundred **lexical entries** corresponding to the type CONTAINER, some of which are given below as examples:

> amphora.n, backpack.n, bag.n, barrel.n, basin.n, bin.n, bottle.n, bowl.n, box.n, briefcase.n, bucket.n, can.n, canister.n, canteen.n, capsule.n, carton.n, cartridge.n, case.n, cask.n, casket.n, casserole.n, cauldron.n, cooler.n, crate.n, creamer.n, crock.n, crucible.n, cruet.n, cup.n, drawer.n, envelope.n, glass.n, goblet.n, jar.n, jug.n, knapsack.n, mug.n, pail.n, pot.n, pouch.n, punch bowl.n, purse.n, ramekin.n, satchel.n, suitcase.n, thermos.n, vase.n, wallet.n, wine bottle.n

This list can very well correspond to our CONTAINER gazetteer. However, we should be aware that no matter how extended this list might be, it is likely incomplete, as any list would be. For example, among the hundred containers listed, *pan* and *saucepan* are not present in the list. I underline this fact simply to show that no matter how much human effort is put into resources (and FrameNet is a good example of this), there will still be information missing, which might just happen to be the information we need for a particular problem.

Another good source of instances of semantic types is the set of **annotated examples**, provided in FrameNet. We discussed these annotated examples in Chap. 12 as sources of syntactic realizations of semantic roles, but let us look at how these annotations can further become part of our gazetteers.

For example, I gathered annotations[2] for a few lexical entries (e.g., *bake, blanch, boil, cook, fry, grill*) corresponding to the frame *Apply_heat*. Table 13.1 shows the annotation found for CONTAINER, HEATINST, and other semantic roles.

Table 13.1 Annotation of semantic roles for *Apply_heat* frame

Semantic Type	Examples
COOK	the patients, they, I, mother and I, Mrs Files, you, Elke, she, the boys, Betty
FOOD	food, pasta, sandwich, duck, beef, potatoes, things, dumplings, rice, onion, aubergines, tart, spanakopita, eggs, cabbage, vegetables
CONTAINER	baking sheet, moulds, pan, saucepan, casserole, dishes
DURATION	until all dente, until thickened, until browned, for 12 minutes, for about 40 minutes, for half an hour, briefly
HEATINST	microwave, pit barbecue, oven, water, camp stove, open fire

---

[1] These types further correspond to frames themselves, but we will not go into such further details within the current discussion.

[2] The annotations were gathered in summer 2015 though the FrameNet online system, and might be different at a different search date.

Notice however, that human annotation, although usually reliable, is not perfect. For example, we can see in Table 13.1 that *water*, was included by mistake in the list of HEATINST. It does not make the data unusable, on the contrary, as any annotated data can be a valuable resource if properly used. We should simply be aware, when using such data, that it could contain a certain level of noise and therefore assess whether that noise will have an impact or not on our task.

As we will see in the next section, a resource content or organization rarely matches our need exactly, but we still make use of it. The resource we present next, WordNet, is a very widely used resource for all kinds of tasks.

13.2.2 Semantic Types in WordNet

WordNet is perhaps the most commonly used lexical-semantic resource within the NLP community. There are a few factors which make WordNet so popular for NLP research. First, its availability. WordNet is free of charge. Second, its design. WordNet is more than a dictionary, since it provides an organization of senses through the clustering of entries in **synsets** (groups of related senses) which are further linked to each other via semantic relations. For example, we show three senses of the noun *green* below.

1. Green (an environmentalist who belongs to the Green Party)
2. green, putting green, putting surface (an area of closely cropped grass surrounding the hole on a golf course)
3. greens, green, leafy vegetable (any of various leafy plants or their leaves and stems eaten as vegetables)

The first sense has only one member in its synset (Green), but senses 2 and 3 each have 3 synonyms in their synset. The list of synonyms is followed by a short definition, called a **gloss**.

Among the semantic relations included in WordNet (e.g., meronym (part-of), similar to, pertaining to, antonym), let us focus on one which is at the core of knowledge organization: **hypernymy**. Hypernymy expresses the relation between a specific entity and a more general entity. For example, *grain* is a hypernym of *rice* or *wheat*. We call the opposite relation **hyponymy**, and therefore can say that *rice* and *wheat* are hyponyms of *grain*.

The three senses of *green* would each have their list of hypernyms, as we go up to more and more generic classes.

1. Green → reformer → disputant → person
2. putting green → site → piece of land → geographic area → region → location
3. greens → vegetable → produce → food

The opposite relation, hyponym, is likely to help us gather gazetteers for semantic types, using our class of interest as a starting point. For example, if we go back to our semantic role *Container*, we're happy to find a WordNet lexical entry

with that same label. Gathering the hyponyms of the lexical entry *Container* provides
a possible gazetteer.

> bag, bin, bowl, box, can, capsule, case, cup, cylinder, dish, drawer, glass, mailer, package,
> pot, receptacle, shaker, thimble, vessel, watering can, workbag

Unfortunately, many other specific roles do not have such a direct mapping. For
example, the *Heating_Instrument* role is perhaps best mapped to the lexical entry
kitchen appliance, which is the hypernym of both *microwave* and *oven* in WordNet.
Two lexical entries having the same hypernym are called **sister terms**. Investigating
other sister terms of *microwave* and *oven*, under the hypernym *kitchen appliance*,
leads us to the following list:

> coffee maker, garbage disposal, food processor, hot plate, ice maker, microwave, oven, stove,
> toaster, toaster oven, waffle iron.

The list contains appliances not possibly involved in *heating* food, such as *garbage
disposal*, *food processor* or *ice maker*.

This example shows that although a resource has been well thought of, being
manually created following solid knowledge organization principles, it might not
'fit' our own knowledge organization needs for the task at hand. Even our earlier list
of CONTAINER did not quite fit the set of food containers we need to constrain the
semantic role *Container* in the *Apply_heat* frame. The list contains containers that
are totally unrelated to food usage (e.g., *drawer, thimble, watering can*).

This means that we must be wise in how we use resources, since they are likely
to suffer from both limited coverage and noise. Textual resources are another place
to explore in search of instances of semantic types, as we see next.

13.3   Building Gazetteers from Textual Resources

In Chap. 11, we saw how we can search in text for explicit mentions of semantic
relations. That chapter investigated three quite different relations, the actor-in, the
synonym and the may_treat relations. In this chapter, we look yet at another relation,
the IS-A relation, that we hope to find through a pattern-based approach. Searching
for instances or subclasses of semantic types to build a gazetteer can be reframed as
a IS-A relation search task.

Remember that an underlying hypothesis for pattern-based search is the explicit
presence of the relation in text. Let us look at a few **explicit markers** for the IS-A
relation in text:

> (1) A gazpacho *is a kind of* soup.
> (2) She made pilafs *and other types of* food.
> (3) They caught pike *and other* fish.
> (4) The soup contains many vegetables *such as* carrots.

From these sentences, we could extract pairs of related entities, within our own
space (nlusw):

(1) `nlusw:isa(nlusw:gazpacho,nlusw:soup)`
(2) `nlusw:isa(nlusw:pilafs,nlusw:food)`
(3) `nlusw:isa(nlusw:pike,nlusw:fish)`
(4) `nlusw:isa(nlusw:carrot,nlusw:vegetable)`

I purposely mention this mapping from textual information to our own nlusw space, since the actual mapping to another resource is far from trivial. As we discussed earlier, each resource defines knowledge through their own organization, and for sure, new information found in text is not likely to 'fit' within these organizations.

In the current example, the mapping to WordNet is quite close, but the level of generalization varies, as we see in following the hypernymic chains:

gazpacho → soup
pilaf → dish → nutriment → food
pike → percoid fish → spiny-finned fish → teleost fish → bony fish → fish
carrot → root → plant organ → plant part → natural object

As expected, the match is not exact, since different sources of information will define their knowledge organization based on different properties. Not being able to find correspondences between resources does not mean we cannot use the resources in combination, as we will do in Sect. 13.4, for our experiment.

To build gazetteers from textual resources, we should perform knowledge acquisition on **trusted sources** of the appropriate genre. The explicit markers presented earlier are likely to be stated in **informative texts**, such as dictionaries, encyclopedia, and textbooks[3]. Those would be good sources of information for our current endeavor.

Let us see how we can perform the extraction of information from the textual resource.

13.3.1 Lexico-Syntactic Patterns

In Chap. 11 we had looked at purely lexical patterns, but also at lexico-syntactic patterns which required tagging of the sentences and concatenating the resulting information into a long string (see Sect. 11.3). As a review, let us look at the result of this process for the example sentences presented earlier.

(1) a/DT;gazpacho/NN;be/VBZ;a/DT;kind/NN;of/IN;soup/NN;
(2) she/PRP;make/VBD;pilaf/NNS;and/CC;other/JJ;type/NNS;of/IN;food/NN;
(3) they/PRP;catch/VBD;pike/NN;and/CC;other/JJ;fish/NN;
(4) the/DT;restaurant/NN;serve/VBZ;dish/NNS;such/JJ;as/IN;spicy/NN;noodles/NNS;

The resulting lexico-syntactic patterns will be highly dependent on the POS tagger. We continue using the Stanford CoreNLP platform for the current exploration. In Table 13.2, we show four patterns, as possible abstractions of the sentences above.

---

[3]In Chap. 11, Sect. 11.1, we discussed the interdependence between semantic relations and text types.

Notice how the first line of the table defines a regular expression representing a compound noun, which we call *CN*, and which is further used within the four patterns[4].

Let us now present different patterns for the same task, which would more deeply rooted in syntax.

Table 13.2 Lexico-syntactic patterns for the IS-A relation

No.	Readable form	Lexico-syntactic pattern
–	Compound noun (CN)	`([a-z]+/DT;)0,1)([a-z]+/[JJ|NN];)0,2[a-z]+/NN;`
1	X is a kind of Y	`($CN$)be/VBZ;a/DT;kind/NN;of/IN;($CN$)`
2	X and other type(s) of Y	`($CN$)and/CC;other/JJ;type/[NN|NNS];of/IN;($CN$)`
3	X and other Y	`($CN$)and/CC;other/JJ;($CN$)`
4	Y such as X	`($CN$)such/JJ;as/IN;($CN$)`

13.3.2 Dependency Patterns

In Chap. 12, we introduced dependency grammars to highlight grammatical dependencies in sentences. We also introduced the idea of using syntactic realizations, as search patterns for Relation Extraction (see Sect. 12.6). Let us revisit this idea of transforming grammatical dependencies into relation search patterns, and adapt it for the is-a relation. For example, the dependency graph for the first example sentence *A gazpacho is a kind of soup.* would look like:

```
root(ROOT-0, kind-5)
det(gazpacho-2, A-1)
nsubj(kind-5, gazpacho-2)
cop(kind-5, is-3)
det(kind-5, a-4)
case(soup-7, of-6)
nmod:of(kind-5, soup-7)
```

In the example above, the words *gazpacho* and *soup* are linked by the fact that *gazpacho* is the subject of *kind* (*nsubj(kind-5, gazpacho-2)*) and *soup* is a modifier for *kind* (*nmod:of(kind-5, soup-7)*). What we just expressed is the syntactic realization of a hypernym relation between *gazpacho* (the hyponym) and *soup* (the hypernym). The shortest path between them in the dependency graph corresponds to the syntactic realization of their hypernymic relation.

Let us write, for each of the four sentences, the shortest path between the hyponym and the hypernym words in the sentence

---

[4]In Sect. 11.3, we had previously defined reusable components for regular expressions.

(1) nsubj(kind-5, gazpacho-2) nmod:of(kind-5, soup-7)
(2) conj:and(pilafs-3, types-6) nmod:of(types-6, food-8)
(3) amod(fish-6, other-5) conj:and(pike-3, fish-6)
(4) nmod:such_as(dishes-4, noodles-8)

In Table 13.3, we show a generalization of these patterns, so as to capture any IS-A relation, expressed in a similar way. The dependency patterns in Table 13.3 provide an alternative to the lexico-syntactic patterns defined in Table 13.2, and both could be tested side by side on the same task.

Table 13.3 Dependency patterns for the IS-A relation

No.	Readable form	Syntactic realization (dependency pattern)
1	X is a kind of Y	nsubj(kind, X) nmod:of(kind, Y)
2	X and other type(s) of Y	conj:and(X, type) nmod:of(type, Y)
3	X and other Y	amod(Y, other) conj:and(X, Y)
4	Y such as X	nmod:such_as(Y, X)

13.3.3 Comparing Approaches

At this point, we should definitely perform a baseline experiment, and test our two search methods, lexico-syntactic patterns and dependency patterns, on a corpus. For doing so, I did prepare a small corpus, as shown in Table 13.4.

Table 13.4 Examples of explicit IS-A relations

No.	Sentence
1	Sub-irrigated **planters** (SIP) are a type of container that may be used in container gardens.
2	When cool, the meat can be transferred to a canning **jar** or other container.
3	Use a **tub**, trough, or other container for water.
4	An appropriate solvent is poured into a glass **beaker** or any other suitable transparent container.
5	Honeypot is literally: A **pot, jar** or other container used to store honey.
6	Growing plants in **pots** or other containers, rather than in ground.
7	There are a total of 168 **jars, cups** and other containers in the mural of various sizes and colors.
8	Later witch bottles were made from glass **bottles**, small glass **vials**, and a variety of other containers.
9	The tribe produces excellent winnowing **baskets**, rattan **hammocks**, and other household containers.
10	This requires good containers such as **pottery, baskets**, or special **pits**.

In the corpus of Table 13.4, notice how I highlighted the sentence elements that
we hope for our methods to find, our gold standard, against which we will measure
precision, recall and F1 of the two search methods. The resulting list would contain:

planter, jar, tub, beaker, pot, jar, cup, bottle, vial, pottery, basket, hammock, pit

This list would represent a small gazetteer for CONTAINER as automatically
extracted from text. It is debatable whether we really want *pottery* or *pit* to be
included, but that would be making a judgment on whether these elements are actually containers or not, and it would not be a judgment on whether our search approach
performs adequately.

Our exploration into textual data would provide, yet another list of containers,
different (but with overlap) with the lists of WordNet and FrameNet. Still, it could
be automatically built, starting from a single word *container*, using NLP techniques.
As previous lists, it has limited coverage and is noisy, which means we should use it
with care and evaluate the impact of its noise on our task.

At this point, you have everything needed for pursuing the current knowledge
extraction task, which I leave to do as Exercise 13.2.

The IS-A relation pattern-based extraction process presented in this section is general enough to be used for any of the seven semantic roles in the *Apply_heat* frame:
Cook, Food, Container, Location, Duration, Beneficiary, Heating_instrument. However, this process might not be the best approach for all of them. Before embarking
on a knowledge acquisition task, we should investigate the presence of entity types
in available resources, and take advantage of the human effort which was put into
constructing them. Also, some entity types are best found through NER systems,
such as DATE and PERSON, and again, we should take advantage of the effort put into
their design. Let us pursue this exploration in the experiment of the next section.

13.4 Experiment — Using Semantic Types to Filter Semantic Roles

The purpose of the experiment suggested in this section is to explore the **combined
use of resources and algorithms** as providers of semantic constraints to apply on
semantic roles. We will explore how to combine the different resource and algorithms
output through a **voting system**. Let us go through our steps:

1. Define our task.
2. Define a gold standard for testing and an evaluation method.
3. Define our strategies to be tested.
4. Evaluate our strategies.
5. Discuss diverse issues highlighted by the results.

13.4.1 Task Definition

Let us go back to the semantic role labeling task, performed in the previous chapter. Using various syntactic realizations of frame elements, we were able to generate a set of candidates for the semantic roles extracted from different sentences. The semantic role candidates are shown in Table 13.5. The sentences from which these roles were extracted are shown in Table 12.9 of the previous chapter (see Sect. 12.5), but we do not require them to pursue the current task.

Table 13.5 Candidate roles

No.	Candidates
1	Cook=consumers, Food=pizzas, Location=homes
2	Cook=bakeries, Food=bread
3	Food=scones
4	Cook=you
5	Duration=hour, Beneficiary=hour
6	Food=cake
7	Container=oven, HeatInst=oven
8	Location=cafe, Cook=chef, Food=cake

Our starting point is a set of candidate semantic role fillers (Table 13.5), and our task is to establish the semantic validity of each candidate semantic role filler, so as to filter out the improbable ones. This would mean that for each candidate semantic role, we want to evaluate how plausible it is from a semantic point of view. Let us write out the question explicitly for a few examples.

Can *consumers* be *Cook*?
Can *pizzas* be *Food*?
Can *homes* be *Location*?
Can *hour* be a *Beneficiary*?
Can *oven* be a *Container*?

Now, let us see how we will define our gold standard, in relation to these questions.

13.4.2 Defining a Gold Standard

Since the questions asked (e.g., Can *consumers* be Cook?) in our current task lead to Yes/No answers, we should define the gold standard also as Yes/No answers, as shown in the last column of Table 13.6. The table shows each possible role (column 1), followed by a short explanation of the meaning of that role (column 2), followed by the instance to validate (column 3) which we will refer to as the **candidate filler**, and the Yes/No annotation (column 4).

Table 13.6 Candidate roles defined in a gold standard

Role	Definition	Filler	Gold
Cook	the entity doing the cooking	consumer	Yes
		bakery	Yes
		chef	Yes
		you	Yes
Food	the entity being cooked	pizza	Yes
		bread	Yes
		scones	Yes
		cake	Yes
Container	the entity to hold the food while cooking	oven	No
Location	where the cooking happens	cafe	Yes
		home	Yes
Duration	how long the cooking lasts	hour	Yes
Beneficiary	the entity benefiting from the cooking	hour	No
HeatInst	the entity providing heat for the cooking	oven	Yes

Evaluation will be done through the usual recall, precision, and F1 measures.

13.4.3   Combining Resources and Algorithms within Voting Strategies

For our problem solving strategy, we will gather a set of **voters** who would have an opinion on questions such as 'Can *oven* be a CONTAINER?'. As gazetteer building from text extraction (Sect. 13.3) was introduced but left as an exercise to complete, we will not make use of the results of this approach as a voter.

We will actually limit ourselves to three voters, based on the resources WordNet and FrameNet, explored in Sect. 13.2 and the NER algorithm explored in Sect. 13.1. The voters will output a Yes/No vote to the question. We will further allow the voters to remain silent on the questions for which they have no opinion. For example, a NER module would only know about generic types (e.g., PERSON, LOCATION), so it will remain silent on questions involving other semantic types. This means that voters will output **Yes**, **No**, or **Silence**.

Let us introduce our voters.

- Voter 1—Stanford CoreNLP NER module
- Voter 2—FrameNet human annotations
- Voter 3—WordNet hyponyms of predefined types

Let us specify how each voter will arrive at a Yes/No/Silence decision, and that on each of the 7 semantic roles: *Cook, Food, Container, Location, Duration, Beneficiary, Heating_instrument.*

Voter 1 – *Stanford CoreNLP NER module*: This voter uses the NER module described in Sect. 13.1. This module will be able to say Yes/No on four roles only: *Cook, Location, Duration*, and *Beneficiary*. For each of these roles, we pre-assign a particular named entity type. *Cook* must be a type PERSON, *Location* must be a type LOCATION, *Duration* must be type DURATION, and *Beneficiary* must be of type PERSON. This voter will process the test sentence using the NER module to tag all the candidate fillers. Then, for each candidate filler, the voter will verify if the tag assigned by the NER module is of the required type. If so, then the vote is Yes, and if not, the vote is No. For the three more specific types: *Food, Container*, and *HeatInst*, this voter remains silent.

Voter 2 – *FrameNet human annotations*: This voter uses an explicit gazetteer for five possible semantic roles: *Cook, Food, Container, Duration* and *HeatInst*. These five roles were the ones annotated by FrameNet human annotators as shown in Table 13.1 (see Sect. 13.2.1). The lists shown in Table 13.1 would be the only knowledge available to this voter. For each candidate filler, this voter verifies if it is listed in the gazetteer for the role it aspires to. If so, the answer is Yes, and otherwise (not in the list), the answer is No. For the two remaining types: *Location* and *Beneficiary*, this voter's answer is Silence.

Voter 3 – *WordNet hyponyms of predefined types*: This voter relies on information within WordNet. It first requires for each semantic role, the WordNet lexical entry which would best capture the semantic constraints to apply on it. As we mentioned in Sect. 13.2.2, the matches are only approximate. Let us manually assign the following (semantic role / lexical entry constraint) pairs: (*Cook*, PERSON), (*Food*, FOOD), (*Location*, BUILDING), (*Duration*, TIME UNIT), (*Container*, CONTAINER), (*HeatInst*, KITCHEN APPLIANCE). In WordNet each lexical entry leads to a set of hyponyms. So, for each candidate filler, this voter verifies if it is a hyponym of the lexical entry corresponding to the role it aspires to. If so, the answer is Yes, and otherwise (not in the list), the answer is No. Since we assigned a lexical entry for each of the seven possible roles, this voter is never silent.

Let us take a few examples, to illustrate the decision of each of the three voters. In Table 13.7, we show 4 questions (column 1), and for each voter (column 2), we give its decision (column 3), as well as a short explanation of how the voter arrived at that decision (column 4). For the FrameNet vote, we refer to the lists from Table 13.1.

Table 13.7 Candidate roles

Role/Entity	Voter	Decision	Explanation
Can *consumer* be *Cook*?	NER tagger	No	*consumer* is not tagged as a PERSON
	FrameNet	No	*consumer* is not in COOK gazetteer
	WN hypo	Yes	hypernym(consumer,person) is true
Can *pizza* be *Food*?	NER	Silence	not knowledgeable about this type
	FrameNet	No	*pizza* is not in FOOD gazetteer
	WN hypo	Yes	hypernym(pizza,food) is true
Can *oven* be *Container*?	NER	Silence	not knowledgeable about this type
	FrameNet	No	*oven* is not in CONTAINER gazetteer
	WN hypo	No	hypernym(oven,container) is false
Can *cafe* be *Location*?	NER	Yes	cafe is tagged as LOCATION
	FrameNet	Silence	not knowledgeable of this role
	WN hypo	Yes	hypernym(cafe,building) is true

Provided we have three voters, each giving a Yes/No/Silence answer, we must further combine these votes into a single decision. For doing so, we must decide on three issues which will impact the final results. Let us first understand the issues, and then devise voting strategies.

1. **Vote combination**: By vote combination, we mean the actual mechanism to generate a vote from the multiple ones provided by the voters. A first option is to simply opt for a majority vote. A second option is to consider that Yes answers have a different value than No answers. For example, as soon as a voter says Yes, we consider that sufficient for the overall vote to be Yes. These are only two possible options, but we could imagine different options adapted to the nature of the voters.
2. **Silence interpretation**: We can choose to ignore the silence or to assign it a Yes or No default value. If we decide to ignore silent votes, this means that the number of votes is reduced, and the vote combination strategy will be performed on the reduced number of voters.
3. **Tie solving**: Even though we start with three voters, given that some remain silent for some decisions, we might end up with only two voters, and then have the likelihood of a tie. Ties can be treated different, by either providing a default answer (Yes or No), or allowing the overall vote to be silent.

Let us define two different strategies, which are likely to lead to quite different results and give rise to later discussions.

1. **Voting Strategy 1 (VS1)**: The vote combination will be a majority vote. A silent voter will be removed from the majority vote. A tie will lead to an overall silent vote.
2. **Voting Strategy 2 (VS2)**: The vote combination will take a single Yes as sufficient to generate a Yes final vote. A silent voter will not be taken into account. Given the chosen vote combination strategy, ties will not be possible.

The voting strategies decided upon are somewhat arbitrary, and as usual, I encourage the reader to challenge them, by trying to come up with different strategies and ideas.

13.4.4 Evaluation of Voting Strategies

We gather the decisions from each voter into Table 13.8, as well as the overall votes, as obtained by the two voting strategies. Silences are indicated by '−' in the table, for easier reading.

Table 13.8 Results of applying semantic constraints on semantic roles

Role	Entity	Gold	NER	FrameNet	WordNet	VS1	VS2
Cook	consumer	Yes	No	No	Yes	No	Yes
	bakery	Yes	No	No	No	No	No
	chef	Yes	No	No	Yes	No	Yes
	you	Yes	No	Yes	No	No	Yes
Food	pizza	Yes	−	No	Yes	−	Yes
	bread	Yes	−	No	Yes	−	Yes
	scones	Yes	−	No	Yes	−	Yes
	cake	Yes	−	No	Yes	−	Yes
Container	oven	No	−	No	No	No	No
Location	cafe	Yes	Yes	−	Yes	Yes	Yes
	home	Yes	No	−	No	−	No
Duration	hour	Yes	Yes	No	Yes	Yes	Yes
Beneficiary	hour	No	No	No	No	No	No
HeatingInst	oven	Yes	−	Yes	Yes	Yes	Yes

In Table 13.9, we summarize the precision, recall and F1 measures for each individual voter and for the two voting strategies.

Table 13.9 Precision, Recall and F1 measures for semantic constraints voters and voting strategies

Voter	Name	Nb Voted	Precision	Recall	F1
1	NER module	8	37.5% (3/8)	21.4% (3/14)	27.2%
2	FrameNet annotations	12	33.3% (4/12)	28.6% (4/14)	30.8%
3	WordNet Hyponyms	14	71.4% (10/14)	71.4% (10/14)	71.4%
VS1	Voting Strategy 1	9	55.5% (5/9)	35.7% (5/14)	43.4%
VS2	Voting Strategy 2	14	85.7% (12/14)	85.7% (12/14)	85.7%

The second voting strategy (VS2) provides much higher precision and recall than the first voting strategy (VS1). We also notice that the voter relying on WordNet hyponyms alone is better than the first combination strategy. As we often mentioned throughout this book, the actual numbers in our small experiment are not significant to provide a proper evaluation of our strategies. Nevertheless, these number are sufficient to trigger discussion on various issues. It is the understanding of those issues which allow researchers to adapt systems (individual voters, voting strategy) to various different tasks.

13.4.5 Result Analysis and Discussion

There are two types of issues to discuss, first, voting strategy issues and second, issues related to language and knowledge representation.

Let us start with the **voting strategy issues**:

- **Vote combinations**: Although a majority vote seems like a good intuitive choice, such strategy relies on the underlying assumption that Yes and No decisions should equally pull the vote in one direction or another. For algorithms, that is not always the case. For example, Voter 2 (FrameNet annotations) relies on a very small list of annotated examples, which are provided by humans, and are therefore very likely correct. This voter is able of high precision on the Yes side only. A Yes, based on these small but highly reliable gazetteers should be considered of greater value than a very likely No answer, based on the fact that the word was never seen by annotators. A majority vote will not take this into account. Another voter might on the other hand, have a different behavior, and be certain of its No answers. We should consider the voter's strengths and the respective trust of their Yes/No to devise a proper voting combination approach.

- **Parallel versus sequential vote**: We presented the idea of combining votes, meaning that all voters are considered in parallel. A different approach is to ask a first voter, and then based on their decision, decide to move on to a second voter, and so on. For example, assume we think the NER module is very reliable on its Yes answers (precise but prone to silence), then we try it first, and only when it says No do we move on to another voter. Again, knowledge of the actual voters will allow to decide on whether we should combine their votes or use them in sequence.

Besides many variations possible as to our voting strategies, the results also highlight **issues related to language and knowledge representation** which we discuss below:

- **Class correspondence**: In order to use WordNet in our task, we had to assign a lexical entry to correspond to a particular semantic constraint. For example, we decided that the *Location* role would be best represented by the *Building* entry in WordNet. That decision allowed for a Yes decision as to the candidate entity *cafe*, since *cafe* is a hyponym of *Building*, but it generated a No decision for *home*, since *home* is not a hyponym of *Building*. On the other hand, *home* is an hyponym of the entry *Location*. We might have added *Location* as another lexical entry, but then, would we have generated a set of possible hyponyms that is too large to properly constrain the semantic role *Location*? This question relates to the difficulty of making resources and tasks, or even resources among themselves, correspond in terms of their organization of knowledge. This is a very hard problem, dealt with since the days when researchers were doing knowledge acquisition from machine readable dictionaries, at the time discussing how difficult it was to match entries provided by different dictionaries. Matching classes in different ontologies is difficult, the same as matching any knowledge resource to each other.

- **Type constraint specificity**: Although it is important to make use of semantic constraints in order to find semantically plausible roles in a sentence, it is also possible that these constraints prevent interpretation that are less probable but still possible. People use a lot of **metaphorical construction** in their language, and strict semantic constraint will not allow for that. One specific language construction of interest is the **metonymy**, in which we replace one entity by another related one. Such a metonymy construct was used in our example of *bakery* as agent of cooking (example 2, in Table 13.5), where as the interpretation assumes that it is the people working in bakery doing the cooking and not the actual bakery itself. With a semantic constraint imposing PERSON as the required semantic type for the role *Cook*, we then prevent restaurants, or bakeries, to be assigned to this role. But then, loosening the semantic constraint too much would allow for too many candidate entities to become plausible role fillers, when they should not be.

These last two issues touch on fundamental difficulties in language understanding and knowledge representation, emphasizing that there is always subjectivity in the organization of knowledge, and that humans are quite good at making inferences and navigating through a bit of ambiguity in text. Humans are quite good at Natural Language Understanding, but algorithms, as we have seen throughout this book, must just keep trying to get better at it. I count on the readers of this book, to help the NLP research field in taking on that challenge.

13.5   In Summary

- Semantic types are important for semantic role validation and disambiguation in sentence understanding.
- NER modules can be used to recognize common semantic types such as DATE, DURATION, PERSON, ORGANIZATION, and LOCATION.
- More specific semantic types, e.g., CONTAINER, can also be useful in semantic interpretation.
- Human annotation of FrameNet semantic role fillers can be used to build gazetteers corresponding to these roles.
- We can use WordNet to gather gazetteers for various semantic types.
- Textual presence of IS-A can be expressed by explicit markers, for example *X is a kind of Y*, or *Y such as X*.
- Both lexico-syntactic patterns and dependency patterns can be used in searching for IS-A relations in text.

- When we have access to various algorithms with limited coverage, and/or noise, we can try to combine them within a voting system.
- The parameters used within the voting strategy (voter's weights, combination strategy, decisions on ties and silences) can largely influence the final result.
- Metonymy allows for changes in semantic types which are likely to render invalid previously assigned semantic constraints.

13.6 Further Reading

Gazetteer construction from text: Early work on gazetteer construction can be found in Riloff and Jones (1999). For gazetteer construction within the Open Information framework (see Appendix C, Sect. C.9), see Etzioni et al. (2005). For a focus on Wikipedia to build gazetteers, see Toral and Mu (2006) and Kazama and Torisawa (2007). Related work is found under taxonomy expansion (Ponzetto and Strube (2007)) or learning of domain knowledge (Yangarber et al. 2000). As this field is very rich and active, the reader could further find multiple articles, inspired from the early work by Hearst (1992) by following citations to her work.

Semantic types in patterns: Some authors have presented the use of semantic types as restriction on the patterns themselves, by including named entities in the patterns (Yangarber (2003)), or semantic categories (Stevenson and Greenwood (2005)).

Named Entity Recognition: By providing an evaluation of multiple systems, Marrero et al. (2009) indirectly provide a survey of tools. Nadeau and Sekine (2007) provide a survey of Named Entity Recognition and classification. An overview is also part of the *Design challenges and misconceptions in NER* by Ratinov and Roth (2009). As the field of NER is booming, there will continue to be many articles describing various systems.

WordNet: The online version, "About WordNet", Princeton University, is available at http://wordnet.princeton.edu. See Fellbaum (1998) for a book reference.

Resource mapping: Since the early days of knowledge extraction from machine readable dictionaries have researchers highlighted the difficulties of mapping information from one resource to another (Ide and Véronis 1990). The current field of ontology matching is dedicated to this task, extending the mapping to the relational knowledge between entities as well (Otero-Cerdeira et al. 2015).

13.7 Exercises

Exercise 13.1 (Named Entity Recognition)

a. Set up an experiment to test the Named Entity Recognition module from Stanford CoreNLP. Ideally, search for another NER system to be able to perform a comparative study. The comparative study would require the following steps:

1. Gather a dataset, by using the three following corpora: the BEETHOVENCORPUS, in Chap. 2, the COOKCORPUS, in Chap. 8 and the EXPORTCORPUS, in Chap. 12.
2. Generate a gold standard of named entities to be found by performing a manual annotation of a set of types ahead of time, PERSON, DATE, DURATION, ORGANIZATION, LOCATION.
3. Perform the NER using your different modules.
4. Perform the evaluation using the precision, recall, and F1 measures.
5. Analyze and discuss the results. For example, how do you deal with word boundaries in the evaluation? Are some types of entities more prone to errors than others, and why?

b. The EXPORTCORPUS from Chap. 12 contains many country names and company names. Write your own NER module which would find these two types in the corpus. You NER module will include a gazetteer for the COUNTRY type and regular expressions for the COMPANY type.

1. To build your gazetteer of country names, you can perform a DBpedia SPARQL query. Write the query and perform it at the DBpedia endpoint. How many countries are part of your gazetteer? How would you include all alternate names for the countries? How many surface forms do you have?
2. To help you build regular expressions for COMPANY, think of words which would be part of company names such as *Org., Inc., Association, Cie., etc.* Include those in your regular expressions.
3. Test your NER modules on the EXPORTCORPUS. How does it perform?
4. Gather a new test corpus on import/export. To do so, use the concordancer you built in Exercise 5.4, Chap. 5, to search for sentences containing the words *export* or *import* in them. As a corpus to search on, you can use the MILLIONCORPUS (or a smaller version) you built in Exercise 10.1 in Chap. 10, containing a random sample of a million Wikipedia pages. Gather 20 new sentences for your test corpus, and evaluate your NER modules on them. What are the results?

Exercise 13.2 (Gazetteer acquisition from text)

a. Using the knowledge acquisition strategy developed in Sect. 13.3, program your own IS-A pattern-based extraction system to test both dependency patterns and lexico-syntactic patterns. Test both approaches against the gold standard shown in Table 13.4. What are the results?
b. Set up an experiment to further test IS-A pattern-based extraction from text. Assume we wish to automatically build a gazetteer of book authors from text. The following steps would be required.

1. Write a Sparql Query to gather 20 book abstracts from DBpedia. One idea is to use the predicate `rdf:type(X,yago:Novel106367879)` to search for novels for which you could find the abstract.

2. Develop your set of both lexico-syntactic patterns and dependency patterns using a development set of 10 abstracts (choose 10 and do not look at the others). Within that development set, you will annotate the author names.

3. Then take the 10 abstracts left aside, and annotate them for the right answers.

4. Evaluating your patterns on this test dataset.

c. Based on the experiment you performed above, and the slightly different experiment you performed in Exercise 12.4 from last chapter, reflect on the following question: is there a difference between searching for the relation `author-of(X,Y)` and searching for the relation `isa(X,author)`? Discuss.

d. Assume you wish to automatically build gazetteers from text for the other semantic roles of the *Apply_heat* frame: *Cook, Food, Container, Location, Duration, Beneficiary, Heating_instrument*. Which roles are more likely to have their instances expressed through explicit markers in text? Notice how I said explicit markers, and not IS-A explicit markers, as sometimes gazetteers are easier built through other relations (see question (c) above). Choose two roles and set up an experiment to find them in text through dependency patterns. You can be inspired by Exercise 12.3 from the previous chapter and combine ideas from the last chapter and the present one for your knowledge acquisition task.

Exercise 13.3 (Semantic role constraints through semantic types)

a. Go back again to the ExportCorpus, in Chap. 12. In Exercise Sect. 12.9, Exercise 12.2, you had annotated this corpus with frame elements from the *Exporting* frame. This can be considered your gold standard, given that all identified roles are correct.

1. Go through the voters (see Sect. 13.4) we presented in this chapter, and adapt their behavior to best be useful for each possible semantic role within this *Exporting* frame.

2. Use each voter to decide on the semantic viability of each semantic role. What is their individual precision/recall on your gold standard?

3. Combine your voters within different vote combination strategies which you should define and justify based on the voter's individual performances as measured in the previous question.

4. Analyze and discuss the voting strategy results.

Appendix A
A Look into the Semantic Web

The official view on the Semantic Web is provided by W3C (World Wide Web Consortium),[1] and I encourage the reader to visit the W3C Website to gather information about the Semantic Web.

In this appendix, I suggest a simple perspective on the Semantic Web as that of a large structured knowledge resource. In this book, Natural Language Processing algorithms will make use of this resource to help analyzing textual data. Natural Language Processing can also enrich the Semantic Web through the structuring of extracted information from text.

A.1 Overview of the Semantic Web Structure and Content

In the Semantic Web, we can think of the most basic unit of knowledge as a URI (Universal Resource Identifier). URIs uniquely define the existence of entities, predicates, or classes (all which can be seen as resources) by assigning to each one a unique identifier on the Web. For example, here are two URIs:

http://dbpedia.org/resource/Eiffel_Tower
http://dbpedia.org/resource/Paris

Each URI is made of two parts: the name of the resource provider and the resource's reference. Our example above shows a single resource provider, DBpedia, and two entities, the *Eiffel Tower* and the city of *Paris*. The resource provider DBpedia makes its entities available at the address http://dbpedia.org/resource/.

To avoid repeating the long string corresponding to the name of the resource provider, we use a PREFIX allowing further references to the site name through an abbreviated form, as shown below. From this point on, to make the examples in this appendix more concise, I will assume any PREFIX defined in an example to

---

[1] https://www.w3.org/standards/semanticweb/.

© Springer International Publishing Switzerland 2016
C. Barrière, *Natural Language Understanding in a Semantic Web Context*,
DOI 10.1007/978-3-319-41337-2

be available in later examples and will only write the prefixes of newly introduced
resource providers.

PREFIX dbr: http://dbpedia.org/resource/
dbr:Eiffel_Tower
dbr:Paris

As much as the URIs above are readable, meaning that they correspond to English
words, it is not required of a URI to be readable. For example, a research group at the
University of Mannheim (http://wifo5-04.informatik.uni-mannheim.de/drugbank/)
makes drug-related information available, such as the drug below referenced by
DB00280.

PREFIX drugbank: http://wifo5-04.informatik.uni-mannheim.de/drugbank/resource/drugs/
drugbank:DB00280

Without further information, it is hard to know what *drugbank:DB00280* is about.
For human consumption of the Semantic Web, the actual naming of entities is very
important. One predicate, the rdfs:label predicate, allows such naming. This predicate is part of the RDF-S (Resource Description Format Schema) standard defined
by the W3C. Another fundamental aspect of an entity's definition is to specify which
class it belongs to. This is possible to represent through a predicate called rdf:type,
which is part of the RDF (Resource Description Format) standard of which RDF-S
is an extension. Anything published on the Semantic Web must minimally follow
the RDF standard.

The example below introduces two prefixes for the W3C as a resource provider
for both RDF and RDFS. It also introduces the triple format for encoding structured
information. A triple is composed of a subject, a predicate, and an object.

PREFIX rdf: http://www.w3.org/1999/02/22-rdf-syntax-ns#
PREFIX rdfs: http://www.w3.org/rdf-schema/
(drugbank:DB00280, rdf:type, drugbank:drugs)
(drugbank:DB00280, rdfs:label, "Disopyramide")

Predicates can express relations between entities (*drugbank:DB00280*), classes
(*drugbank:drugs*) and literals (*"Disopyramide"*). In a triple, predicates and subjects
must be URIs, but objects can be literals. A literal is a string, an integer or another
simple data type. The above two triples tell us that the entity *drugbank:DB00280* is
an instantiation of the class *drugbank:drug* and that it is named *"Disopyramide."*

As much as drugbank is specialized in medical drug information, it will provide
many classes of entities, such as enzymes, drug interactions, and dosage forms.
The definition of these classes and their interrelations will be part of the medical drug domain ontology which defines how "the world is organized" within that
domain. Ontologies can be used to organize knowledge in any domain. For example, in the world of human-made constructions, the DBpedia ontology states that a
dbo:Building is a subclass of an *dbo:Architectural_Structure* which is itself a subclass of a *dbo:Place.*

Below, we go back to the example of the *Eiffel Tower*. The first triple defines
dbr:Eiffel_Tower as an instantiation of a *dbo:Building*. The other two triples use the

predicate `rdfs:subClassOf`, part of RDF-S standard, to state the relation between *dbo:Building*, *dbo:Architectural_Structure*, and *dbo:Place*.

```
PREFIX dbo: http://dbpedia.org/ontology/
(dbr:Eiffel_Tower, rdf:type, dbo:Building)
(dbo:Building, rdfs:subClassOf, dbo:ArchitecturalStructure)
(dbo:ArchitecturalStructure, rdfs:subClassOf, dbo:Place)
```

Now let us introduce a few more facts about the *Eiffel_Tower* in the example below.

```
PREFIX dbp: http://dbpedia.org/property/
PREFIX yago: http://dbpedia.org/class/yago/
PREFIX umbel: http://umbel.org/reference-concept/

(dbr:Eiffel_Tower, dbp:height, "300"(xsd:integer))
(dbr:Eiffel_Tower, rdfs:label, "Eiffel Tower"@en)
(dbr:Eiffel_Tower, dbo:location, dbr:Paris)
(dbr:Eiffel_Tower, rdf:type, yago:Skyscraper)
(dbr:Eiffel_Tower, rdf:type, umbel:Skyscraper)
```

The first triple states that the *dbr:Eiffel_Tower* is 300 meters high. Notice how the predicate `dbp:height` comes from yet another ontology, one which defines various properties of entities. The object of the predicate `dbp:height` is not a URI, but rather a literal of a predefined type integer. The object in the second triple is also a literal, providing the label *"Eiffel Tower"*, in English (@en). From an NLP perspective, this label information will be very useful for mining entity mentions in text.

The third triple establishes the location of the *dbr:Eiffel_Tower* in *dbr:Paris*. This time *dbr:Paris* is provided not as a literal, but rather as a URI uniquely identifying the city of Paris and not other possible entities with that same name. URIs, contrarily to words, are disambiguated, as they represent a single entity. That is why, when providing structured information as triples, objects of predicates should be provided as URIs as much as possible. Before writing an ambiguous literal (e.g., "Paris"), we should choose, if it exists, the appropriate disambiguated URI (*dbr:Paris*) corresponding to the desired entity.

The last two triples assign the *dbr:Eiffel_Tower* as an instance of two new classes, the *yago:Skyscraper* class defined in the YAGO ontology and the *umbel:Skyscraper* class defined in the UMBEL ontology.

Why two Skycraper classes? Well, different providing sites actually contain information on similar domains, and each one defines its own ontology, according to its view of the world. Given that the Semantic Web is not a normalization place (it does not force any view of the world), it rather allows various views and provides mechanisms to establish equivalence links between them. Two type of equivalence links exist, one between entity classes, using the predicate `owl:equivalentClass`, and one between instances using the predicate `owl:sameAs`.

```
PREFIX schema: http://schema.org/Place
PREFIX owl: https://www.w3.org
PREFIX geodata: https://www.geonames.org
(dbr:Eiffel_Tower owl:sameAs geodata:Eiffel_Tower)
```

(dbr:Eiffel_Tower, rdf:type, dbo:Place)
(dbo:Place, owl:equivalentClass, schema:Place)

In the example above, the first triple states that the entity *dbr:Eiffel_Tower* defined in DBpedia is the same entity as the *geodata:Eiffel_Tower* part of yet another resource provider. Such a simple link is quite powerful. We now not only have access to the information about the *Eiffel Tower* from the perspective of DBpedia, but we also have additional geo-localization information about the same entity stored in the geodata knowledge base. This possibility of connecting entities across providing sites opens to the gathering of information kept in a distributed manner.

The third triple in the example above shows that linking can also happen at the class level, as the *dbo:Place* class defined in DBpedia ontology is said to be equivalent to the *schema:Place* class defined in another important vocabulary resource provider called Schema.org.

A.2   Querying the Semantic Web through SPARQL Endpoints

One way of accessing Semantic Web resources is through the use of SPARQL end-points, which "expose" to the Web the actual resource from the resource provider. Those endpoints can be queried using a particular query language, which we refer to as SPARQL queries. The full specification of SPARQL queries can be found at http://www.w3.org/TR/rdf-sparql-query/. There are also various tutorials about SPARQL queries on the Web, which go well beyond the basic knowledge provided in this appendix.

If you are familiar with database queries, you will see a resemblance with SPARQL queries. Imagine that the Semantic Web triples we described in the previous section are a set of rows in a long table of rows, each having three columns: subject, predicate, and object. Using SPARQL queries, you will be able to specify restrictions on the elements contained in these rows so as to return only a subset of them.

To define a basic query, the important parts are as follows:

- Define the prefixes of the resources used.
- Use "select" to define which element(s) (which column(s)) you wish to retrieve.
- Indicate restrictions through the use of a "where CONDITION."

For example, the following query would search for all buildings in the city of Paris. The query says that the information searched for (?X) must be of type *dbo:Building* and must be located in *dbr:Paris*. The resulting replacement for the variable ?X must satisfy both constraints.

```
PREFIX dbr:    <http://dbpedia.org/resource/>
PREFIX dbo:    <http://dbpedia.org/ontology/>
PREFIX rdf:    <http://www.w3.org/1999/02/22-rdf-syntax-ns#>
```

```
select ?X where   {
   ?X rdf:type dbo:Building .
   ?X dbo:location dbr:Paris .
}
```

Now, suppose you wish to submit this query to the DBpedia SPARQL endpoint to actually obtain the list of buildings in the city of Paris. First, using your favorite browser, access the DBpedia SPARQL endpoint, at http://dbpedia.org/sparql and second enter the query defined above in the Query Text space of the Virtuoso SPARQL Query editor. Then, submit the query using the Run Query button. You are done. Here are 10 among over 70 results returned by the query.

dbr:Hôtel_de_Ville,_Paris
dbr:Bridgeman_Art_Library
dbr:Carrousel_du_Louvre
dbr:Les_Mercuriales
dbr:Stade_Bergeyre
dbr:Castille_Paris
dbr:Les_Échelles_du_Baroque
dbr:Opéra_Bastille
dbr:Les_Halles
dbr:Petit_Luxembourg

SPARQL queries can be quite complex, but in this book, we will only make use of very simple queries, such as the one above.

Appendix B
NLP Tools, Platforms and Resources

This appendix lists a few software tools, platforms, and resources we encounter in the NLP literature. This is far from an exhaustive list, and I encourage the reader to search online for additional resources. As the interest in NLP and the Semantic Web grows over the years, there will be for sure additions to this list. Additional references to corpus exploration tools and corpora resources were provided in the Further Reading section (Sect. 5.10) of Chap. 5, *Exploring Corpora*.

NLP Pipeline: Toolkits and platforms usually allow to perform a series of tasks, sometimes referred to as the NLP stack (tokenization, sentence splitting, lemmatization, POS tagging, parsing).

- Stanford CoreNLP: A pipeline containing multiple modules, from tokenizer all the way to Named Entity Recognition and coreference analysis.
  – http://nlp.stanford.edu/software/corenlp.shtml.
- OpenNLP: An Apache project. A machine learning based toolkit for text processing.
  – https://opennlp.apache.org/
- LingPipe: A toolkit for text processing.
  – http://alias-i.com/lingpipe/

Information Annotation Platforms: Platforms with a more general view than the NLP pipelines, sometimes allowing multiple NLP tasks, but presented and used within an annotation framework.

- GATE: A General Architecture for Text Engineering.
  – https://gate.ac.uk/
- UIMA: A platform for Unstructured Information Management.
  – https://uima.apache.org/

Information Extraction: Platforms and APIs dedicated to the ongoing extraction of information from the Web or large corpora.

- Ollie: Open Information Extraction Software.
  – https://knowitall.github.io/ollie/

© Springer International Publishing Switzerland 2016
C. Barrière, *Natural Language Understanding in a Semantic Web Context*,
DOI 10.1007/978-3-319-41337-2

- NELL: Never-Ending Language Learning, a Read the Web research project at Carnegie Mellon University.
  - http://rtw.ml.cmu.edu/rtw/

Indexing: For efficient storage and retrieval of locally stored large corpora.

- Lucene: indexing and search technology
  - https://lucene.apache.org/

Lexical, Linguistic, and Semantic Resources:

- WordNet: From Princeton University, a lexical-semantic resource widely used in the NLP community, mostly for semantic processing. It organizes information into synsets which are groups of synonyms put together to form a single entry for which a small definition, called a gloss, is provided.
  - https://wordnet.princeton.edu/
- Wikipedia: A large collectively created encyclopedia, free of charge, and frequently used in NLP. Wikipedia is an amazing textual resource exploitable in language processing. It provides a category system (see bottom of Wikipedia pages) to tag pages. The Wikipedia dumps are the set of files made available by Wikipedia, containing all the information (articles, titles, categories, etc.) found in Wikipedia. These files combined form a large corpus widely used in NLP.
  - https://dumps.wikimedia.org/.
- FrameNet: A large frame semantics project from the Computer Science Institute in Berkeley, California.
  - https://framenet.icsi.berkeley.edu/fndrupal/
- VerbNet: A large verb description project, initiated and managed by Martha Palmer, University of Colorado at Boulder.
  - http://verbs.colorado.edu/~mpalmer/projects/verbnet/downloads.html.
- BabelNet: A large multilingual project, integrating multiple other resources, such as WordNet, Wikipedia, VerbNet, and GeoNames.
  - www.babelnet.org
- UBY: A large-scale unified lexical-semantic resource, from Technische Universität Darmstadt, merging various resources.
  - https://www.ukp.tu-darmstadt.de/data/lexical-resources/uby/
- Lemon UBY: A Semantic Web version of UBY, collaborative work with John McCrae (CITEC, Universität Bielefeld) and Christian Chiarcos (ACoLi, Goethe-University Frankfurt am Main).
  - http://www.lemon-model.net/lexica/uby/
- Linguistic Linked Open Data: There is growing interest in formalizing linguistic information as part of the Linked Open Data cloud. There are various developments for representation and interoperability formats (e.g., NIF Natural Language Processing Interchange Format).
  - http://linguistic-lod.org/

Appendix C
Relation Lists

This appendix offers a classification of relations with some examples of relation lists provided by different authors, for different tasks, for use in different contexts, or to represent different types of knowledge. The purpose of providing this classification is to supplement Part IV of this book, on knowledge acquisition, and encourage the reader to reflect on appropriate methods for finding occurrences of these different types of relations in text, taking into account the likelihood of finding explicit expressions of such relations in various types of textual resources.

C.1 Lexical Relations

Lexical relations aim to describe relations between lexical units. For example, in UMLS (Unified Medical Language System),[1] lexical relations allow to explicitly express the relation between the different surface forms of the same concept. Table C.1 shows some examples of lexical relations in UMLS.

Table C.1 Examples of lexical relations in UMLS

Lexical relation	Subject	Object
has_expanded_form	Abdmnal pain unspcf site	Abdominal pain, unspecified site
has_permuted_form	2-Acetolactate Mutase	Mutase, 2-Acetolactate
has_alias	immunoglobulin heavy locus	IGH
has_translation	tidylcholine	tidilcolina
has_adjectival_form	heart	cardiac

---

[1] The Unified Medical Language System (UMLS), published by the US National Library of Medicine, is available at https://www.nlm.nih.gov/research/umls/.

© Springer International Publishing Switzerland 2016
C. Barrière, *Natural Language Understanding in a Semantic Web Context*,
DOI 10.1007/978-3-319-41337-2

C.2   Web Content Metadata Relations

Although Web data could basically be anything, it is important to highlight a major development of classes and properties done in Schema.org[2] to try to represent the major contributors of actual Web presence: organizations. This initiative was started in 2011, by large commercial search engine companies (Google, Microsoft), to allow webmasters to mark up their pages and improve the display of there results. Describing organizations leads to almost infinite ramification in the schema, and the number of classes and properties defined is quite large. There are different types of organizations (health organizations, government organizations, restaurants), they create different things (products, creative work, events), they reside in different places, they behave in different ways (opening hours, types of operations), they have different internal structures, they hire people, etc.

As Schema.org evolves, there is a parallel effort to map all the classes and properties of Schema.org to Linked Open Data ontologies used in recognized LOD datasets, such as DBpedia[3] and Dublin Core.[4] Examples of mappings, which are not necessarily one-to-one, are shown in Table C.2.

Table C.2 Examples of mappings between different ontologies

Ontology	Property	Property in Schema.org
Dublin Core	dct:issued	schema:datePublished
Dublin Core	dct:extent	schema:duration
Dublin Core	dct:contributor	schema:musicBy
		schema:director
		schema:actors
DBpedia	dbpedia:club	schema:team
DBpedia	dbpedia:albumRuntime	schema:duration
	dbpedia:filmRuntime	
	dbpedia:runtime	
DBpedia	dbpedia:restingDate	schema:deathDate
DBpedia	dbpedia:language	schema:inLanguage

---

[2]Schema.org is found at http://schema.org.

[3]DBpedia is found at http://dbpedia.org.

[4]Dublin Core is found at http://dublincore.org.

C.3 People and Social Interaction Relations

As much as Schema.org was developed for structuring the Web content of organizations, there is now a larger presence of individuals on the Web, and one particular vocabulary, named FOAF (Friend-of-a-Friend),[5] was developed to capture information about people's Web presence, social networks, friendship, and associations (link to university or work). Table C.3 shows some of its relations.

Table C.3 Examples of FOAF relations

Relation	Domain/Range	Description
foaf:familyName, foaf:firstName	Person/literal	Provide a name to the person
foaf:knows	Person/Person	Link a person to other people they know
foaf:homepage	Thing/Document	Link a person/organization to a homepage
foaf:mbox	Agent/Thing	Provide an e-mail address for a person/organization
foaf:group	Group/Agent	Link a group (such as a group of employees) to a person/subgroup/organization part of that group
foaf:depiction	Thing/Image	Provide a link to a representative image for anything

C.4 Domain-Specific Relations

Many relation lists are domain specific. Any domain's ontology requires careful definition of classes and properties to provide the best model for expressing the knowledge found within that domain. One only has to look at the Datahub site[6] to see the diversity of ontologies and datasets published around the world. Table C.4 shows a few examples of properties within domain-specific ontologies.

---

[5]FOAF is found at http://xmlns.com/foaf/spec/.
[6]Datahub is found at http://datahub.io/.

Table C.4 Examples of domain-specific properties

Domain	Properties
Wine http://www.w3.org/TR/owl-guide/wine.rdf	madeFromGrape, hasSugar, hasMaker, hasColor, hasBody
Museum Art http://collection.britishmuseum.org	curatorial_comment, is_documented_in, has_current_keeper, has_dimension
Teaching http://linkedscience.org/teach/ns/	courseTitle, teacherOf, weeklyHours, grading, academicTerm
Music http://www.musicontology.com/specification/	genre, origin, imdb, interpreter, performed_in
Medical http://www.nlm.nih.gov/research/umls/	has_physiologic_effect, may_inhibit_effect_of, has_finding_site
E-commerce http://www.heppnetz.de/projects/goodrelations/	hasInventoryLevel, hasManufacturer, hasOpeningHours
Geo positioning http://www.w3.org/2003/01/geo/wgs84_pos#	latitude, longitude, altitude

C.5   General Knowledge Organization Relations

Some relations are useful to describe and organize knowledge, independently of a particular domain. A very useful vocabulary, containing multiple relations aiming at organizing knowledge, is SKOS (Simple Knowledge Organization System).[7] Some examples of types of relations are shown in Table C.5.

Table C.5 Examples of relations in SKOS

Purpose	Examples
Grouping concepts	skos:Collection, skos:OrderedCollection
Matching between concepts	skos:exactMatch, skos:closeMatch, skos:broadMatch
Naming concepts	skos:prefLabel, skos:altLabel
Express a semantic relation between two concepts	skos:related, skos:broaderTransitive, skos:broader, skos:narrowerTransitive, skos:narrower
Documenting concepts	skos:definition, skos:example, skos:editorialNote, skos:scopeNote

[7]See http://www.w3.org/2009/08/skos-reference/skos.html for SKOS Schema description.

C.6   Definitional Relations

A good example of the design of a set of relations, for the purpose of defining words and relating word senses, is the one found for EuroWordNet, a European project, completed in the summer of 1999, which aimed at designing a multilingual database on a similar model as WordNet. From information found in Vossen (1998), Table C.6 gathers a list of definitional relations. Although not illustrated in the table, relations have a corresponding inverse relation, e.g., *isCausedBy* and *Causes*.

Another example of a set of definitional relations is from the influential work by Pustejovsky (1995) on the Generative Lexicon. In his work, he divides in four important parts the content of a definition: formal relations, constitutive relations, telic relations, and agentive relations. Influenced by such work, the EU-project SIMPLE (Semantic Information for Multi-functional Plurilingual Lexica) (Lenci et al. 2000) defined a list of definitional relations. Some examples are shown in Table C.7 (taken from Madsen et al. (2001)).

Table C.6 Examples of relations in EuroWordNet

Group	Relation	Example
synonymy	near_synonym (not same synset)	tool/instrument
antonymy	antonymy	good/bad
hyponymy	has_hyponym	vehicle/car
part-whole relations	has_mero_part	hand/finger
	has_mero_member	fleet/ship
	has_mero_made_of	book/paper
	has_mero_portion	bread/slice
	has_mero_location	desert/oasis
cause relations	results_in	to kill/to die
	for_purpose_of	to search/to find
	enables_to	vision/to see
subevent relations	is_subevent_of	to snore/to sleep
involved/role relations	involved_agent	to bark/dog
	involved_patient	to teach/learner
	involved_instrument	to paint/paintbrush
	involved_location	to swim/water
	involved_source_direction	to disembark/ship
	involved_target_direction	rincasarse/casa
	involved_result	to freeze/ice
	involved_manner	to shout/loudly

Table C.7 Examples of relations in SIMPLE

Pustejovsky's role	Relation in SIMPLE	Example
formal relation	is_a	yacht/boat
constitutive relations (to express the internal constitution of an entity)	is_a_member_of	senator/senate
	has_as_member	flock/bird
	has_as_part	airplane/wings
	instrument	paint/brush
	resulting_state	die/dead
	is_a_follower_of	marxist/marxism
	made_of	bread/flour
	has_as_colour	lemon/yellow
	produced_by	honey/bee
	concerns	hepatitis/liver
	contains	wineglass/wine
	quantifies	bottle/liquid
	measured_by	temperature/degree
	successor_of	two/one
	has_as_effect	storm/thunder
	causes	measles/fever
telic relations (to express the typical function of an entity)	indirect_telic	eye/see
	purpose	send/receive
	object_of_the_activity	book/read
	is_the_habit_of	smoker/smoke
	used_for	crane/lift
	used_against	chemoterapy/cancer
	used_as	wood/material
agentive relations (to express the origin of an entity)	result_of	loss/loose
	agentive_prog	pedestrian/walk
	agentive_experience	fear/feel
	created_by	book/write
	derived_from	petrol/oil

C.7 Noun Compound Relations

Noun compounds are intricate lexical units since they capture semantic relations, which are non-stated and implicit, yet understood by readers based on their a priori knowledge. For automatic text analysis tools, they are difficult, since their underlying syntactic property is simple, usually noun–noun, and sometimes adj–noun, but their underlying semantics can only be captured by world knowledge.

For example, compound nouns such as *laser printer* or *tea pot* hide different implicit relations of *uses-technology(printer, laser)* or *contains(pot, tea)*. The order is important, as we would know the difference between a *dance school* and a *school dance*.

One early proposal of a relation list, especially for noun compounds, is the one of Levi (1978). Levi's recoverably deletable predicates, as she calls them, are shown in Table C.8 with a few examples taken from her list.

Other lists of relations for noun compound analysis include those of Vanderwende (1994), Girju et al. (2005), O Seaghdha (2008), and Kim and Baldwin (2005), as cited in Nastase et al. (2013). Some of the relations presented in this section overlap with relations presented in Sect. C.6.

Table C.8 Levi's relations

Relation	Examples
Cause$_1$	tear gas, growth hormone, disease germ
Cause$_2$	drug deaths, heat rash, laugh wrinkles
Have$_1$	apple cake, fruit tree, lace handkerchief
Have$_2$	lemon peel, government land, enemy strength
Make$_1$	song bird, music box, sap tree
Make$_2$	water drop, glass eye, worker teams
Use	steam iron, hand brake, milieu therapy
Be	soldier ant, cactus plant, canine companion
In	field mouse, adolescent turmoil, childhood dreams
For	horse doctor, coke machine, cooking utensils
From	olive oil, cane sugar, coal dust
About	price war, abortion vote, budget speech

C.8   Event-Based Relations

A lot of work has been done and is currently done on event-based relations, or what is more recently called *semantic role labeling*. Looking at FrameNet (https://framenet. icsi.berkeley.edu), there are thousands of frames, for events and activities of varied specificities. For example, a more general frame would be *Activity_stop*, where as a more specific frame would be for *Attending* and an even more specific would be *Bail_decision*.

As FrameNet was covered in Chap. 12, I refer the reader to Sect. 12.2, for further information.

C.9   Infinite Relation List

The following quote from Etzioni et al. (2006) captures the research endeavor to try to extract from text, an infinite list of relation, by which I mean a list that has not been decided in advance and that is discovered along the way.

Yet Machine Reading is not limited to a small set of target relations. In fact, the relations encountered when reading arbitrary text are not known in advance! Thus, it is impractical to generate a set of handtagged examples of each relation of interest.

In a large Information Extraction project, called Open IE (Banko et al. 2007; Etzioni et al. 2011), the purpose is to develop methods for discovering relations between any pair of identified entities, by using weakly supervised methods of knowledge discovery. Given that it has no other a priori information, one underlying hypothesis of this Open IE approach is the notion that redundancy is a good filter.

This recent proposal does not define any list of relations, but rather assume that any verb found (or particular syntactic structure) can act as a predicate. Still, if we gather the verbal predicates per entity to which they pertain, we can compare them to other lists of relations having these same entities as their subject. In Table C.9, we show examples (taken from Banko (2009)) of relations found in DBpedia ontology, in Yago, and in TextRunner (OpenIE ran on the Web) for three types of named entities.

Table C.9 Examples of OpenIE relations

Entity (Domain)	DBpedia Ontology	Yago	TextRunner (Web)
Politician	occupation, birthPlace, birthDate, children, residence, title, knownFor	bornIn, livesIn, isLeaderOf, influences, interestedIn, hasWonPrize, isCitizenOf	has headed, ran for seat in, has been critic of, served as Z with, married Z in:date, campaigned in
Country	currency, capital, language, anthem, governmentType, latitudeNorthOrSouth, largestCity	participatedIn, establishedOnDate, hasCapital, hasOfficialLanguage, hasCurrency	has embassy in, has not ratified, welcomed, has rate of, acceded to, is ally of, intervened in
Company	location, products, industry, type, revenue, locationCity, parentCompany	established on:date, has website, has number of people, created, has motto, has product, is of genre	has shipped, should buy, has licensed, introduced version of, has announced that, acquired Z in:date, should make

Glossary

This glossary contains brief, sometimes informal definitions of all the terms that have been introduced in this book. It is meant to be used as a quick reference for the reader.

Abbreviation   A *surface form* corresponding to a shortened form of a word. For example, *Ont* is the abbreviation of *Ontario*, and *b/c* is the abbreviation of *because*.

Acronym   A *surface form* made up of a series of letters taken from a *compound*. The acronym is usually constructed from one or more letters of each component word of the compound. For example, *AKA* means *also known as*, and *CEO* means *chief executive officer*.

Abbreviation/Acronym expansion   The process of automatically disambiguating an *abbreviation* or *acronym* into its expanded *surface form*, appropriate to the context of occurrence. For example, the acronym *NLP* has at least two possible expansions: *neuro-linguistic programming* and *Natural Language Processing*. In the context of this book, the second expansion is the appropriate form.

Ambiguity   A phenomenon that arises when words appear in a context that allows for more than one possible interpretation. Although the terms *ambiguity* and *polysemy* are often used interchangeably in NLP, there is a subtle difference in meaning between the two. A word can be intrinsically *polysemous* (it can have many possible meanings), whereas *ambiguity* arises only when a word is used in a sentence. A word is ambiguous when there is insufficient contextual information to make a decision about its possible interpretations. For example, the interpretation of the polysemous word *bank* is clear in a sentence such as *He took money out of the bank.*, but ambiguous in the sentence *I love that bank.*

Anaphora   A pronoun used to refer to a particular concept or entity already mentioned in text. For example, in the sentence *Ann cooked a delicious <u>meal</u>, and all the guests loved <u>it</u>.*, the pronoun *it* is the anaphora.

Anaphora resolution   The process of automatically linking an *anaphora* to the earlier mention of the concept or entity to which it refers. For example, in the

© Springer International Publishing Switzerland 2016
C. Barrière, *Natural Language Understanding in a Semantic Web Context*,
DOI 10.1007/978-3-319-41337-2

sentence *Owen bought a new <u>car</u> and drove <u>it</u> home.*, the pronoun *it* can be resolved to the previously mentioned *car*.

Annotated text   (also *annotated example*) Any segment of text to which human annotation is added. This annotation could be of a linguistic nature such as *part-of-speech tags*, or a semantic nature such as *word senses*.

A posteriori evaluation   An evaluation of the results of an experiment that requires running the experiment first, in order to later evaluate the output of the system manually. This is in contrast to using a predefined *gold standard*.

Automatic frame identification   Within *frame semantics*, the process of automatically determining the appropriate *frame* for the interpretation of a sentence. For example, the sentence *John rides his bicycle.* would be best understood under the *Operate_vehicle* frame.

Bag-of-words (BOW)   (also *BOW representation*) The representation of any segment of text by the set of all the words it contains, with no consideration of the sequential order of those words. For example, the sentence *John works from home.* generates the bag-of-words {*John, works, from, home*}.

Bag-of-words overlap   A simple algorithm which will find the set of common words between two *BOWs*.

Baseline algorithm   (also *baseline approach*). A naïve or simple method used to solve a particular NLP task. Its outcome is used for setting a minimum performance value. Outcomes of newly developed algorithms are compared to this minimal value to estimate their gain in performance. Sometimes, a random guess is used as a baseline approach.

Bigram   A unit commonly used in NLP of two consecutive words occurring in text. A bigram can also refer to two consecutive letters in a word. For example, the sentence *John works from home.* generates 3 word bigrams: *John works*, *works from*, and *from home*. The same sentence generates many letter bigrams: *"Jo"*, *"oh"*, *"hn"*, *"n "*, *" w"*, *"wo"*, *"or"*, and so on.

Bigram model   In *probabilistic sequence modelling*, using a bigram model would involve conditioning the probability of a word purely on the word that precedes it. $P(w_n|w_1...w_{n-1})$ is thus reduced to $P(w_n|w_{n-1})$.

Bilingual corpus   A corpus containing documents in two languages. It can be a *parallel corpus* or a *comparable corpus*.

Binary decision   A Yes/No decision, with only two choices.

Boiler plate removal   The process by which all metadata information in Web pages is removed to output solely its actual textual content.

Boundary detection   Certain NLP tasks such as *term extraction* or *Named Entity Recognition* require determining *surface form* boundaries for the terms or entities of interest. For example, the boundaries of the entity in the sentence *The color* *laser printer is not functioning.* should be defined as either *color laser printer*, or simply *laser printer*.

Breadth coverage   A way of exploring a set of ideas or problem solutions by investigating the basic elements of each one before exploring a single one in more detail. This is in contrast to **depth coverage**.

Cataphora   A pronoun used to refer to a particular concept or entity mentioned later in text. This is an uncommon phenomenon in language, rarely used in text. It is studied less often in NLP than the **anaphora**.

Cataphora resolution   The process of automatically linking a **cataphora** to the later mention of the concept or entity to which it refers. For example, in the sentence <u>It</u> *is always leaking, this new <u>garden hose</u> we bought.*, the cataphora *it* can be resolved to *garden hose*.

Category   In certain contexts, a category can refer to a **semantic type** or **entity type**. It can also refer to **Wikipedia categories**, or any class used in a **classification task**. *Note: This word is so polysemous that its usage should be avoided whenever possible.*

Categorization task   (also **Classification task**) The task of assigning one class from a set of predefined classes to some data. In NLP, this data may take the form of a word, a sentence, a document, or any segment of text. There are many classification tasks in NLP, such as assigning a domain (medicine, sociology, farming, etc.) to a document, or assigning a sentiment (positive, negative, neutral) to a review.

Coarse-grained representation   A representation that merges many elements into a single **equivalence class**. For example, if all part-of-speech variations of nouns (proper noun, common noun, singular noun, plural noun) were merged into a single equivalence class called *noun*, we would say that the *noun* class provides a coarse-grained representation. This is in contrast to **fine-grained representation**.

Collocation   A sequence of words whose probability of appearing together in text is higher than what would be expected by chance. Such probability is usually calculated relative to semantically equivalent alternatives. For example, the bigram *fast car* is much more frequent in text than *rapid car*, making *fast car* a collocation.

Communicative setting   The various elements that influence the nature of a communication, including the message support (spoken versus written), the message intention (inform versus influence), and the characterization of interaction between the writer/speaker and the reader/listener. For example, the communicative setting of a textbook is written support, informative, with expert/novice as the writer/reader relation.

Comparable corpus   A corpus containing documents in two or more languages. Documents are not translations of each other but often have certain properties in common, such as subject matter (medicine, environment etc.) and writing style (news stories or encyclopedia pages).

Compositionality The property of a *compound* which makes its meaning derivable from the combination of the meanings of its components. Compounds can have varying degrees of compositionality and can hide certain implicit *semantic relations* between their components. For example, a *floor lamp* is a lamp that is placed on the floor, a *reading lamp* is a lamp used for reading, and a *projector lamp* is part of a projector.

Compound A group of words that makes up a single *lexical unit*. We most often refer to compounds by specifying their grammatical nature, such as a *noun compound* (e.g., *computer keyboard*), or a *verb compound* (e.g., *take off*).

Computational Linguistics A *quasi-synonym* of the term *natural language processing*, with an emphasis on computational aspects of the field.

Concept This term is used rather loosely in NLP and is highly ambiguous. It may refer to a *word sense* in a *lexicographic resource*, to a class in an *ontology*, or even to a unique entity in a *knowledge base*.

Concordancer A tool often used by language learners and translators to better understand particular word usages (such as *collocations*, which are difficult to grasp for non-native speakers). The concordancer is used to search for a target word in a *corpus* and generate a list of *context windows*, which include the word of interest at the center of each context. Using this tool, these contexts can also be sorted based on the word appearing to the right or to the left of the target word.

Conjunctional attachment problem A main source of ambiguity for *parsers*, this refers to the fact that conjunctions are not explicit in what they link. For example, in the sentence *They use large plastic containers and boxes.*, there is ambiguity as to what the noun *boxes* is coordinated with. Is it *plastic [containers and boxes]* or *[plastic containers] and boxes*?

Constituency parser See *Phrase-structure parser*.

Content word A word that conveys subject matter, usually a verb, noun or adjective. In the sentence *The bottle dropped to the floor.*, the words *bottle*, *drop* and *floor* are all content words. This is in contrast to a *function word*.

Context window A fixed-size segment of words or characters. In *distributional similarity*, context windows form the text segments that are used for finding *co-occurrences* of words. They are also used in *concordancers*, to show words in fixed-size text segments.

Contingency table A method of reporting results that summarizes the results of a certain system in relation to a *gold standard*. In the case of a binary classification (true/false), the table contains four possibilities:

- True Positive (TP): Both system and gold standard say true.
- False Negative (FN): System says false, but gold standard says true.
- False Positive (FP): System says true, but gold standard says false.
- True Negative (TN): Both system and gold standard say false.

Co-occurrence   The joint occurrence of two words within a particular segment of text, whether it be a sentence or simply a *context window*. Within the *The dog barks constantly.*, the words *dog* and *barks* co-occur.

Co-occurrence vector   A representation of words in which each word is represented by its set of co-occurring words and their respective frequencies, as measured in a corpus. This is useful in *distributional semantics*.

Coreference chains   Ordered sets of various mentions in a text relating to the same entity.

Coreference resolution   The task of automatically linking different references to the same entity within a document, or sometimes across documents. For example, a text might refer to *Paris* using the references *Paris*, *the city of Paris*, *the capital of France*, *La Ville Lumière*, as well as through multiple anaphoric references (*it*). Linking all these by their reference to a common entity is coreference resolution.

Corpus   (plural *corpora*). A group of texts brought together along some selection criteria, and usually intended for a particular type of study. Note: This definition has loosened over time. Today, the term *corpus* can simply refer to any group of texts.

Corrective annotation   An annotation task that is performed by humans, and is based on the output of a software system rather than performed directly on the raw text data. Humans must approve or correct the system's output. This type of annotation is used for tasks that are difficult for humans, but which systems perform reasonably well, such as part-of-speech tagging. It shortens the correction time as compared to a human performing the full annotation from scratch. This is in contrast to *full annotation*.

Data sparseness   See *sparse data*.

Datastore   See *knowledge base*.

Dependency pattern   A type of pattern used in *Information Extraction* for the acquisition of knowledge (relations or entities) that is based on the dependency representation provided by a *dependency parser*. A pattern could take the form *obj(eat, X)*, which would be used when looking for objects of the verb *eat*. Dependency patterns are an alternative to *lexical patterns* and *lexico-syntactic patterns*.

Dependency parser   A type of parser that describes dependencies between words in a sentence. Typical dependencies include subject-of, object-of, modifier-of, and so on. Dependency parsers have become quite popular in recent years, as opposed to the more traditional *phrase-structure parsers*.

Depth coverage   The approach of exploring a set of ideas or problem solutions by pursuing each one in detail before moving on to the next one. This is in contrast to *breadth coverage*.

Derivation   (also *derivational variation*). A *lexical relation* which not only creates a variation in the form of the word, but also a change in its part of speech. For example, *complaint* (noun) becomes *complaining* (verb), or *phrase* (noun) becomes *phrasal* (adjective). This is in contrast to *inflection*.

Design of experiment   See *experimental setting*.

Development set   A set of *annotated examples* used in the development and refinement of an algorithm. In the case of parametrized algorithms, the development set is used for the optimization of their parameters.

Diachronic study   A study that takes into account the time at which events occurred, in order to investigate their evolution over time. For example, one could compare the change in frequencies of various surface forms of a word from 1950 to 2000.

Dice coefficient   In the context of corpus statistics, a measure of the strength of co-occurrence of two words. Similar to *Point-wise Mutual Information*, this measure takes into account the joint and individual frequencies of the words in question.

Discovery   See *Knowledge discovery*.

Distributional semantics   A take on semantics which views the meaning of words in terms of their behaviour within large corpora. It is assumed that the way in which words behave is important to the understanding of their nature and relations to each other.

Distributional similarity   Within *distributional semantics*, similarity is measured either in terms of the strength of co-occurrence between words (first-level similarity), or through comparison of their co-occurrence vectors (second-level similarity).

Document characterization   The process of characterizing a document using a set of different features, such as genre, domain, purpose, and so on.

Domain   In NLP, this term often refers to the subject matter of a text (medicine, environment, arts, etc.) Contrarily, in the SW, it refers to the class to which the subject of a predicate belongs.

Domain experts   Specialists within a domain (such as geology, medicine, and the like), who would be qualified to develop a *terminology* or an *ontology* of that domain (subject matter).

Dual Iterative Pattern Relation Expansion (DIPRE)   An approach presented in Brin (1998) for developing a set of patterns for Relation Extraction. Relation instances known as *tuples* are used as the starting point. For example, the tuples *(Paris, France)* and *(Berlin, Germany)* could be the starting points of the DIPRE process for a relation *city-in*. The process discovers patterns in text that express the relation between the known tuples and then uses these patterns to extract further tuples, which are then used to find more patterns, and so on.

Dynamic Programming A method of programming whose approach is to solve a large problem by splitting it into its subproblems and optimizing the solving time by solving each subproblem only once. This method is used in the *Edit Distance* algorithm.

Edit Distance A measure of the orthographic distance between two words or text segments, in which basic operations (insertion, deletion, substitution) are assigned a cost. For example, the Edit Distance between *car* and *chat* is two, since we require one insertion ("h" between "c" and "a") and one substitution ("r" becomes "t") to transform *car* into *chat*.

Entity A general term designating a common word (e.g., *mobile phone*) or a *named entity* (e.g., *Mozart*) that is defined within a *grounding space*.

Entity class See *entity type*.

Entity Linking The *grounding* of a mention of an entity in text to its unique identifier within an external resource (e.g., word sense or URI).

Entity resolution See *Entity Linking*.

Entity type A designation of a semantic category for an entity. Certain entity types are most commonly targeted in *Named Entity Recognition* tasks, such as (PERSON, ORGANIZATION, LOCATION, and DATE)

Equivalence classes When two classes are merged as if they represented a single class, they become equivalent classes. For example, if all numbers in a text were replaced by the symbol NUM, we would consider all occurrences of NUM as forming a single equivalence class, and individual numbers would no longer be differentiated.

Evaluation method The method defined before running an experiment for the evaluation of the performance of a system.

Experimental setting An important aspect of NLP work is to perform studies using real data. The experimental setting refers to the preparation of these studies, including elements such as the choice of data, the choice of algorithm to be tested, and the evaluation method.

Explicit mention Information that is given explicitly through words found in text. For example, *a branch is a part of a tree* explicitly expresses a part-of relation through the explicit mention *is a part of*. This is in contrast to *implicit mention*

Extrinsic evaluation The evaluation of an algorithm through a measure of its impact on a subsequent task or application. An example of this would be evaluating a *dependency parser* based on its impact on the subsequent task of *Relation Extraction*. This is in contrast to *intrinsic evaluation*.

False negative See *contingency table*.

False positive See *contingency table*.

Fine-grained representation   A representation of information which allows for a higher degree of differentiation between classes within a given category. For example, a fine-grained representation of the *noun* category would distinguish between different types of nouns (plural, singular, common, proper). This is in contrast to *coarse-grained representation*.

Frame   (also *semantic frames*) A knowledge structure that allows for the representation of an event (e.g., *cooking a meal*), in which different entities are assigned various *semantic roles* (e.g., *Cook, Food, Beneficiary, Heating Instrument, and Container*)

Frame semantics   A semantic representation framework which organizes information around *frames*.

FrameNet   A large semantic representation project based on *frames*.

Full annotation   An annotation task in which human annotators are provided with raw textual data and must perform the annotation without any help from a system. This is in contrast to *corrective annotation*.

Function word   A word which provides the "glue" between *content words*. Determinants, conjunctions, and prepositions are all function words. For example, in the sentence *The screen and the keyboard are both old.*, the words *the*, *and*, and *both* are all function words.

Gazetteer   A list of surface forms corresponding to a particular *semantic type*. For example, a CITY gazetteer would be a list of many city names (*Paris, New York, Montreal, London,* etc.), and a MEASURE gazetteer would list all possible units of measurement (*kilogram, centimeter, liter,* etc.). Today, gazetteers are often used for the task of *Named Entity Recognition*.

General language corpus   A corpus made up of texts that contain everyday language on various topics. This is in contrast to a *specialized language corpus*.

Generative rule   A rule that generates various surface forms from a single one. For example, a rule for obtaining the variations (e.g., *L.V. Beethoven* and *L. van Beethoven*) from the single form (*Ludwig van Beethoven*). This is in contrast to a *normative rule*.

Generic entity   An entity that, for *knowledge acquisition*, is usually of most interest at the class level (e.g., a generic *maple tree*) rather than the instance level (e.g., *the maple tree in Mr. Black's garden*). This is in contrast to a *specific entity*.

Gold standard   A dataset which has been annotated with correct answers, against which algorithms are compared for evaluation of their performance.

Grammar rules   A set of language-dependent rules that define the ways in which words can be combined to form correct sentences.

Grammatical subject/object   A *dependency parser* provides the dependencies *subj-of* and *obj-of* of a verb, which express the grammatical subject and grammatical object of that verb. For example, in the sentence *Amy eats an apple.*, *subj-of(eats,Amy)* expresses that *Amy* is the grammatical subject of *eats*. Note: This is not to be confused with a predicate's subject and object as defined in the Semantic Web.

Grounding   The task of linking surface forms to the entities to which they refer, as represented in a ***grounding space***. Grounding encompasses both ***Word Sense Disambiguation*** and ***Entity Linking***.

Grounding space   A representation of the real world in which entities are defined. At a minimum, a grounding space includes descriptions of entities (a dictionary) and sometimes also relations between those entities (a knowledge base).

Hapax   An event that occurs only once. For example, when running corpus statistics, a hapax is a word with a single occurrence in the corpus.

Hit count   The number of Web pages a search engine returns in response to a particular query.

Hypernymy   The semantic relation that exists between a specific concept (*dog*) and a more general concept (*animal*). We say that *animal* is the hypernym of *dog*. This is the antonym to ***hyponymy***.

Hyponymy   The semantic relation that exists between a general concept (*animal*) and a more specific concept (*dog*). We say that *dog* is the hyponym of *animal*. This is the antonym to ***hypernymy***.

Idiom   A group of words which meaning is not at all ***compositional***. Typical examples of idioms are *bite the dust* or *kick the bucket*.

Implicit mention   Information that is given implicit mention is assumed to be known by the reader and is therefore not stated explicitly in text. For example, in the sentence *With a flat tire, Erika couldn't drive to work.*, there is no mention of the fact that a tire is part of a car. Although this information is necessary for the understanding of the sentence, it is not explicitly provided. This is in contrast to ***explicit mention***.

Inflection   (also ***inflectional variation***) The change that is made to the form of a word in order to express a linguistic phenomenon, such as plural (*cat/cats*), or gender (*actor/actress*). In inflection, the transformed word maintains the same part of speech as the original word. This is in contrast to ***derivation***.

Information Content (IC)   A measure that has been suggested within the field of information theory, to express the level of surprise attached to a piece of information. The IC of a word is inversely proportional to the logarithm of its frequency.

Information Extraction   An important subfield of NLP, whose main area of interest is the uncovering of information in text. The information being sought usually involves *entities* and the *relations* between them and often corresponds to answers to the typical questions of "Who did What, When, Where, and Why?"

Information retrieval   The task of finding the most appropriate documents among a large collection of documents, in response to a particular user query.

Informative text   A text whose purpose is to inform, such as a textbook or an encyclopedia entry. This is in contrast to *narrative text*.

Interpolation model   In *probabilistic sequence modelling*, the idea of creating a complex model through the linear combination of several simpler ones. Simple models could include *bigram models* and *trigram models*.

Intrinsic evaluation   An evaluation of an algorithm that is performed on the actual task for which the algorithm was devised. This is in contrast to *extrinsic evaluation*.

Iterative refinement process   A process involving various steps, repeated in a loop. For example, the steps involved in an iterative refinement of an algorithm would be to devise the algorithm, evaluate it, test it, refine it, re-evaluate it, retest it, and so on. Each iteration is aimed at bringing the results one step closer to what a *development set* has defined as perfect performance.

Keyword in context (KWIC)   To show a word in context, a *concordancer* places its multiple occurrences in the middle of a text window. The expression KWIC is used to describe this type of presentation.

Knowledge acquisition   The process of extracting knowledge from text to create, enhance, or augment a *knowledge base*, an *ontology*, or a *lexical-semantic resource*.

Knowledge base   Sometimes called *datastore*. The actual instantiations of classes and relations as defined in an ontology. A knowledge base can be seen as a repository of information structured by an *ontology*.

Knowledge base expansion   See *ontology population*.

Knowledge discovery   A process involving the quest for information that is not known ahead of time. It is implied that such information will emerge from text with the application of statistical discovery approaches. For example, *term extraction* is a process of knowledge discovery aimed at finding important domain terms in text. In the context of text analysis, knowledge discovery is in contrast to a *search*.

Knowledge pattern   (also *knowledge probe* or *rote extractor*) A pattern that is defined to search for particular information in text, most often instances of a relation. For example, *is also known as* is a knowledge pattern used to find of instances of the *synonymy* relation in text.

Knowledge probe   See *Knowledge pattern*.

Knowledge representation   A general term that refers to the study of how to best represent knowledge for automatic processing, so as to make it as explicit as possible, as well as accessible in a standardized and structured form.

Language dependent   (also *language specific*) Algorithms, methods, or processes are said to be language dependent when they require modification or adaptation each time they are applied to a different language.

Language identification   The process of automatically identifying the language used in a text (e.g., English, Russian, and German).

Language independent   Algorithms, methods, or processes are said to be language independent when they can be applied to different languages without having to be modified. This is in contrast to *language dependent*.

Language level   When it comes to *document characterization*, language level can refer to both the formal/informal distinction and the scientific/layman distinction.

Language model   (See also *probabilistic sequence modelling*) A statistical view (model) of word sequences. The term *language* model is used because these sequences are usually measured within a specific language and are representative of the kinds of sequences that are found in each language.

Language understanding   See *Natural language understanding*.

Laplace smoothing   In order to compensate for the *sparse data problem* in *language modeling*, Laplace smoothing suggests adding 1 to the corpus frequencies of every element of the vocabulary, regardless of whether or not a given element was present in the corpus.

Lemma   The base form, or root of a word. For example, the lemma of the past tense verb *went* is the infinitive form *go*.

Lemmatization   The process of automatically finding the *lemma* of a word. For example, transforming *studying* into *study* or *carrots* into *carrot*.

Levenshtein Distance   A popular variation on *Edit Distance*, in which the cost of a substitution is increased to 2. For example, the Levenshtein Distance between *car* and *chat* is 3, since the transformation from one to the other requires one insertion ("h") at a cost of 1, and one substitution ("r" for "t") at a cost of 2.

Lexical pattern   Patterns aimed at finding instances of relations, defined solely using lexicalized surface forms. For example, *is used to* is a lexical pattern possibly indicative of an instrument relation. If applied to the sentence *A saw is used to cut wood.*, the pattern could retrieve an instance of an instrument relation between *saw* and *cut wood*. Lexical patterns are an alternative to *lexico-syntactic patterns* and *dependency patterns*.

Lexical unit   Any designation (word, compound, term, phrase) that refers to a concept and could be included in a dictionary. Note: Notice the use of *could* rather than *would* in this definition. The criteria for inclusion in dictionaries are debatable and sometimes depend on the focus of the particular dictionary.

Lexical resource   Any resource that is organized around *lexical units*.

Lexical-semantic resource   Any resource which contains information about both words (lexical information) and senses (semantic information). *WordNet* is a typical example of a lexical-semantic resource.

Lexicographer   A person interested in the study of words as *lexical units*, their definitions, meanings, surface forms, usages, and so on.

Lexico-syntactic pattern   Patterns aimed at finding instances of relations, defined using lemmas and parts of speech. For example, *be/VBZ;use/VBZ;to/IN* is a lexico-syntactic pattern possibly indicative of an instrument relation. This kind of pattern should be applied to sentences that have already been processed with *lemmatization* and *part-of-speech tagging*. Lexico-syntactic patterns are an alternative to *lexical patterns* and *dependency patterns*.

Linked open data   The *open data* which is available using the Semantic Web format, within the Semantic Web linked datastores.

Machine Learning (ML)   A field of study with a focus on creating algorithms that automatically build predictive models from data.

Machine Translation (MT)   A field of study with a focus on developing algorithms meant for the automatic translation of language. Statistical MT relies largely on *language models*.

Meronymy   The semantic relation between an entity and the larger entity of which it is a part. We would say that *tire* is a meronym of *car*, since it is part of the larger entity *car*.

Metonymy   A linguistic phenomenon which makes it possible to refer to an entity using a related entity and assume the reader will be able to reconstruct the missing link. A typical example of metonymy is *The ham sandwich left without paying the bill.*, in which *the ham sandwich* actually refers to the related entity of *the person eating the ham sandwich*.

Multi-word expression (MWE)   A general term that refers to a *compound*, a *collocation*, or an *idiom*. This includes any group of words which refers to a concept, with no stipulation regarding syntactic category. For example, *skin care*, *well aware*, and *bite the dust* are all multi-word expressions.

Mutual Information   See *Point-wise Mutual Information* for an explanation of the type of mutual information presented in this book.

Named entity   A *lexical unit* which refers to a uniquely identifiable entity that has a particular name. Examples of named entities are *Dublin* (CITY), *Coca-Cola* (COMPANY), *International Monetary Fund* (ORGANIZATION), and Max Bruch (COMPOSER). Use of this term is often expanded to include dates, numbers, and other entities that belong to identifiable classes.

Named Entity Type   The *semantic type* of a named entity. Common types include PERSON, LOCATION, and ORGANIZATION.

Named Entity Disambiguation (NED)   The process of linking the *surface form* of an entity found in text to its conceptual description found in a *grounding space*.

Named Entity Recognition (NER)   The process of identifying in text the mentions of particular predefined *named entity types* (e.g., ORGANIZATION, LOCATION).

Narrative text   A text, such as a novel, whose purpose is to tell a story. This is in contrast to *informative text*. Note: A news story is usually partly narrative and partly informative.

Natural Language Processing (NLP)   A field of study with a focus on the automatic processing of text. This automatic processing could be intended for various purposes, including *Information Extraction*, text summarization, text classification, *Machine Translation*, and others.

Natural Language Understanding (NLU)   A subfield of NLP that focuses specifically on the processing of text toward the generation of a *semantic interpretation* of that text.

NLP stack   (also *NLP pipeline*) A series of NLP analysis modules through which data are run sequentially for the purposes of text analysis. The stack (or pipeline) could include modules such as a sentence splitter, a tokenizer, a part-of-speech tagger, and a syntactic parser.

N-gram   (also written *ngram*) A sequence of N consecutive tokens. These tokens are usually words in NLP, but can also be letters. *Language models* may concern bigrams (2-grams), trigrams (3-grams), as well as 4-grams and 5-grams.

Nominalization   The transformation of a verb (or verb phrase) into a noun (or noun phrase). For example, *constructed a house* becoming *the house's construction* or *takes off* becoming *the taking off of*.

Non-deterministic algorithm   An algorithm that includes a degree of probability-based random decision making. The output of this kind of algorithm may differ from one application to the next, even if it is applied on the same input.

Noun compound   (also *complex noun*, *multi-word noun*, and *nominal compound*). A group of words forming a noun that refers to a single entity. An example of a three-word noun compound is *skin care cream*.

Normalization rules   Rules designed to reduce the various surface forms of entities found in text to a set of normalized forms found in a resource (e.g., dictionary). These are in contrast to *generative rules*.

Ontology   A formal representation of a domain that includes concepts, relations, and logical descriptions. For example, a wine ontology would encode knowledge about grape varieties, soil types, wine-making processes, perhaps wine producers, and so on.

Ontology expansion   A *knowledge discovery* process aimed at automatically expanding the set of entities and relations in an *ontology*.

Ontology population   A *knowledge discovery* process aimed at automatically expanding the set of class instances and relation instances in a *knowledge base* structured according to an *ontology*.

Out-of-vocabulary (OOV)   Words encountered during a corpus analysis task which had not already been seen during the development phase.

Open Data   Data that is freely available and which can be reused and redistributed freely. Such data could be published by organizations and governments of all levels (e.g., municipal, federal).

Open Information Extraction   An approach to relation extraction which does not presuppose an existing list of predicates, but rather explore all verbs as possible predicates. Predefined *entity types* are sometimes used so as to gather verb predicates around these entity types.

Optimistic evaluation   An evaluation that is favorable to the algorithm. For example, an evaluation that attributes a success to any correct answer found among the top 20 results of an algorithm is a more optimistic evaluation than one that only considers the top 1 or 2 results. This is in contrast to *pessimistic evaluation*.

Orthographic error   An error which comes from the misspelling of a word, such as *choroegraphy* instead of *choreography*. This is in contrast to a *typographic error*.

Parallel corpus   A *bilingual corpus* (or *multilingual corpus*) in which the documents are translations of each other. This type of corpus is widely used for the development of statistical *Machine Translation* models.

Paraphrase   A text segment (sentence or *phrase*) which, although written differently, expresses the same meaning as another segment. For example, *He left the door open.* is a paraphrase of *He didn't close the door.*

Parser   See *phrase-structure parser* or *dependency parser*.

Parse tree   An explicit representation of the grammatical structure of a sentence, expressed as a tree. The processing of a *phrase-structure parser* on a sentence results in a parse tree.

Part of speech (POS)   The grammatical role a word takes on in a sentence (e.g., verb, noun, adjective, adverb, determinant, preposition, and conjunction).

Part-of-speech tagger (POS tagger)   The process of assigning a *part of speech* to each token in a sentence.

Pessimistic evaluation   An evaluation setting which puts the model or algorithm that is being tested at a disadvantage. An example of this would be to take a *probabilistic sequence model* whose learning was done on a corpus of scientific articles and evaluate it on a corpus of blogs, where the language is quite different. This is in opposition to *optimistic evaluation*.

Phrase A group of words within a sentence that plays a particular syntactic role. For example, a determiner (*the*) and a noun (*glass*) together form a noun phrase (*the glass*), which can play the role of subject in a sentence (*The glass broke*). *Phrase-structure parsers* divide sentences into their various phrases, including noun phrases (NP), verb phrases (VP), prepositional phrases (PP), and others.

Phrase-structure parser (also *constituency parser*) A method of sentence analysis designed to uncover the constituents (*phrases* or simple words) of a sentence, as well as the grammatical rules that were applied during the construction of the sentence to bring together those constituents.

Phrase-structure tree See *parse tree*.

Point-wise Mutual Information In the context of corpus statistics, a measure of the strength of co-occurrence of two words. Similar to the *Dice coefficient*, this measure makes use of the words' joint and individual frequencies, as found in a corpus.

Polysemy The ability of *surface forms* to refer to multiple *word senses* or *entities*. A typical example of a polysemous word is *mouse*, which can refer to either a small animal or a computer device.

Precision (also *precision measure*). A common method of evaluation in NLP, which involves comparing an algorithm's classification results to a *gold standard*. Precision relies on the measures found in a *contingency table*: true positive (TP) and false positive (FP) and is defined as $\frac{TP}{TP+FP}$. It is often used along with *recall*.

Predicting capability The ability of a *language model* to accurately predict sequences. When evaluating models against each other, we want to measure their predicting capabilities for a given sequence of words in an unseen *corpus*.

Prepositional attachment problem A main source of ambiguity for *parsers*, this refers to the fact that prepositions are not explicit in what they link. For example, in the sentence *He made a soup with vegetables.*, the prepositional phrase *with vegetables* modifies the noun *soup* (prepositional attachment to the noun), whereas in the sentence *He made a soup with his friend.*, the prepositional phrase *with friends* modifies the verb *made* (prepositional attachment to the verb).

Probabilistic language model See *language model* or *probabilistic sequence modelling*.

Probabilistic sequence modelling The use of probabilities for the interpretation of words in sequence. The underlying hypothesis is that the order of words in text is to some degree predictable.

Qualitative result analysis A method of analyzing the results of experiments that does not include any measure, but is instead based on observing and describing results (e.g., finding similarities between examples and noting special cases). This is in contrast to *quantitative result analysis*.

Qualitative exploration   A method of exploring data (most often a corpus, in NLP) without quantitative measures, but with tools, such as a *concordancer*, that facilitate observation of the data. This is in contrast to *quantitative exploration*.

Quantitative result analysis   A method of analyzing the results of experiments that compares a system's output to a *gold standard*, using quantitative measures such as *recall* and *precision*. This is in contrast to *qualitative result analysis*.

Quantitative exploration   A method of exploring data (most often a corpus, in NLP) using quantitative measures, such as *word frequencies*, *co-occurrences*, and others. This is in contrast to *qualitative exploration*.

Quasi-synonym   A lexical unit whose meaning is almost equivalent to that of another lexical unit. Quasi-synonyms are not always interchangeable in text, since they can have subtle variations in meaning based on language level, intensity, and other factors.

Ranking   Although a general word, in NLP it often refers to the process of sorting the results of an experiment in decreasing order of correctness.

Raw text   A text in its original, untouched form. This is often used in contrast to *annotated text*, which has been annotated by humans for a particular task.

Recall   (also *recall measure*) A common method of evaluation used in NLP, which involves comparing an algorithm's classification results to a *gold standard*. Recall relies on the measures in a *contingency table*: true positive (TP) and false negative (FN) and is defined as $\frac{TP}{TP+FN}$. It is often used along with *precision*.

Reference   Although highly ambiguous, this word is used frequently in NLP. Its most common use is for the designation of a *textual reference*, meaning a mention of an entity or concept in a text. However, it can also designate the entity that is referred to by a surface form.

Regular expression   (informally, *regex*) An artificial formal language developed for searching in text. Regular expressions have a broad expressive power. They allow the search of particular characters, ranges of characters, particular sequences, negations of sequences, and so on. They include operators for defining lists, optionality, and disjunction, which can be applied to characters or sets of characters.

Related words   Words that appear to be semantically close, but whose relation has not been specified. Related words could have the relation of *meronymy* or *hypernymy*, but could also simply occur together frequently in text, or be topically-related (e.g., *teacher* and *homework*).

Relatedness measure   A measure of the strength of the connection between *related words*.

Relation   The general term used to designate a named association between concepts or words.

Relation Extraction   The process of mining corpora in search of instances of *semantic relations*.

Resource   Any source of information that can be used when analyzing a text. A resource in NLP can take the form of a *lexical resource*, a *gazetteer*, a *knowledge base*, or a *corpus*, among others. Note: This term takes on quite a different meaning within the Semantic Web, where it can mean an entity, class, or predicate referenced with a Uniform Resource Identifier (URI).

Rote extractor   See *Knowledge pattern*.

Search   Searching in a text assumes we know ahead of time what we are looking for. For example, using a *gazetteer* of car names would allow us to search a corpus for sentences about cars. In the context of text analysis, this is in contrast to *discovery*.

Semantic drift   An iterative *Relation Extraction* approach, which at each iteration, extracts instances less and less semantically related to the seed instances used at the start of Relation Extraction process. Semantic drift is due to cumulative errors both on extracted patterns and on instances.

Semantic frame   See *frame*.

Semantic interpretation   The process of automatically uncovering the semantic information that underlies the surface form of a sentence. Certain knowledge representation formalisms, such as *frames*, can be used to express this semantic interpretation.

Semantic relation   A relation between two word senses that is used to describe a semantic phenomenon, such as *meronymy* or *hyperonymy*.

Semantic role   A role that is defined in relation to an event, most often used in representation formalisms such as *frames*. Certain semantic roles, such as *Location*, *Agent*, and *Beneficiary*, are valid in multiple frames (e.g., *cooking, giving, and working*).

Semantic role filler   A word that can fulfill a particular *semantic role* within a *frame*. For example, in the sentence *John drives his car.*, *John* can serve as a semantic role filler for the semantic role *Driver* in the frame *Operate_vehicle*.

Semantic role labeling   The process of analyzing a sentence to automatically assign its *semantic role fillers* within a *frame*.

Semantic type   See *entity type*.

Semantic type restriction   The *entity type* that is required for an entity to take part in a semantic representation, either a *frame* or a *semantic relation*. For example, the semantic type restriction for the entities X and Y in the relation works-for(X, Y) would be PERSON and ORGANIZATION, respectively.

Semantically interpretable   The description of a sentence from which a particular meaning can be extracted. Some sentences are only semantically interpretable with the help of imagination, as they might not be semantically plausible within our current world. For example, the sentence *The flowers are swimming in the arms of the terrace.* is not semantically plausible, but it is interpretable.

Semantics   A field of study that focuses on the senses of words, phrases, or any other kind of representation or expression of ideas.

Sentence alignment   The process of automatically finding the sentences that correspond to each other in a *parallel corpus*.

Sentence splitter   An NLP module used to find sentence boundaries within a text. A sentence splitter is usually part of an *NLP pipeline*.

Separator   Within the context of *tokenization*, a separator is one of the many possible characters (e.g., space, comma, and period) that can be used for boundary detection between tokens. The positions of separators in a string are used to split that string into tokens.

Short form   In a text, a short form is often used for referencing an entity previously referred to by a longer surface form. For example, the short form *Beethoven* in the second sentence of *Ludwig van Beethoven composed many symphonies. Beethoven was quite prolific.* comes after the long form used in the first sentence. Given that the short form is more polysemous, the previous use of the long form provides the information necessary for disambiguation.

Sister terms   (also *co-hyponyms*). Two terms which have the same *hypernym*. For example, *car* and *bicycle* are sister terms under the hypernym *vehicle*.

Smoothing   In *language models*, we refer to smoothing as a method of distributing a portion of the probability mass onto unseen events. Smoothing is made necessary by the *sparse data* problem.

Soundex   An algorithm that measures the similarity of words based on established *equivalence classes* for sounds of consonants and vowels. For example, "b" and "p" are considered part of the same equivalence class, making words such as *pat* and *bat* similar from a sounding point of view.

Source language   In translation, the source language is the language of the original document that is to be translated. This is in contrast to *target language*.

Sparse data   The fact that in language, most sequences will never be found in a particular corpus. For example, a vocabulary of V words would generate V^3 different possible trigrams. We encounter the sparse data problem when using a particular corpus to estimate trigram probabilities, since the corpus is likely to contain only a subset of these possibilities, and the size T of that subset is bound to be much smaller than V^3. *Smoothing* techniques are used to attenuate this problem.

Spearman correlation   A measure of correlation based on ranked values. This type of correlation can be used to compare the results of two *ranking* algorithms, such as algorithms that establish *relatedness* between pairs of words.

Specialized language corpus   A corpus made up of texts that contain language particular to a specific domain, such as medicine, agriculture, or computer science.

Specific entity   Most often referred to in the literature as an instance of an *entity class*, or as a *named entity*, such as a specific city (e.g., Minneapolis) or building (e.g., Empire State Building). This is in contrast to *generic entity*.

Spelling correction   The task of automatically correcting a word that contains a *typographic error* or an *orthographic error*. For example, correcting *computr* to *computer*.

Stop words   Usually short, common words such as conjunctions, prepositions, and determiners. For example, in the sentence *The dogs bark at each other in the yard.*, the words *the, at, each, other,* and *in* are all stop words.

Surface form   A *word*, *compound*, *abbreviation*, or *acronym* used in text to refer to a particular entity.

Synonymy   The relation that exists between *surface forms* that have the same meaning. For example, *car* and *automobile* are synonymous surface forms.

Syntactic analysis   (also *syntactic interpretation*) A type of sentence analysis that is performed in order to uncover the syntactic structure of the sentence. *Phrase-structure parsers* and *dependency parsers* are used for syntactic analysis.

Syntactic realization   The syntactic manifestation of a particular *semantic role* in a *frame*.

Syntax   The set of grammar rules of a language which stipulate how sentences should be constructed in order to be *semantically interpretable*.

Target language   In translation, the target language is the language of the translated document. This is in contrast to *source language*.

Taxonomy   A type of knowledge organization in which concepts are related to each other through *hypernymic* links.

Term   A term is a *lexical unit* that refers to a particular meaning within a specialized domain. This word is often used more loosely, to refer to any *lexical unit*, but the stricter definition requires the contextualization of a lexical unit within a domain. For example, the lexical unit *nanotube* is a term within the domain of nanotechnology. A word such as *dog*, even if it is a common lexical unit, could also become a term if it is considered within the domain of *zoology*.

Term equivalent   Given a term in a particular language (e.g., *ordinateur*, in French), a term equivalent would be a term in another language (e.g., *computer*, in English) which refers to the same concept.

Terminology   The terminology of a domain is the set of concepts and their associated terms (possibly provided in different languages) that are important to the definition of that domain, whether it is mechanics, law, geology, or music.

Test dataset   A set of *annotated examples* that is used after the development of an algorithm, to evaluate it. A fair evaluation of an algorithm would be performed on a test set that is similar in nature to the *development set*, but novel to the algorithm, so that its performance could not have been optimized on it.

Text cohesion   The extent to which a text contains sentences which are related to each other by the fact that they contain information on the same subject matter.

Text corpus   See *Corpus*.

Text genre   The characteristic of a text which describes the way it is written and its intended readership (e.g., police report, brochure, film review, and blog).

Text mining   The process of searching in text for information and rendering it explicit or making use of it for a particular task (e.g., sentiment analysis and *Relation Extraction*).

Text type   See *text genre*.

Token   A string of arbitrary size, resulting from the process of *tokenization*. Tokens can correspond to words, parts of words, punctuation symbols, numbers, and other strings.

Tokenization   The process of splitting a text segment into *tokens*, using a list of *separators* which indicate token boundaries. The space is the default separator in tokenization, meaning that a phrase such as *a large bird* would result in three tokens *a*, *large*, and *bird*.

Tokenizer   The implementation of an algorithm used for *tokenization*. The tokenizer is the first module in the *NLP pipeline*, and variations in its implementation are therefore likely to influence the results of the whole pipeline.

Trigram model   In *probabilistic sequence modelling*, a trigram model conditions the probability of a word on the two words that directly precede it, meaning that $P(w_n|w_1...w_{n-1})$ is reduced to $P(w_n|w_{n-2}, w_{n-1})$.

True negative   See *contingency table*.

True positive   See *contingency table*.

Typographic error   An error in a word that results from a typing mistake (e.g., *tempersture* instead of *temperature*). Errors of this kind often occur between two letters that lie close together on the keyboard.

Unigram model   In *probabilistic sequence modelling*, a unigram model conditions the probability of a word only on the word itself, excluding the context in which it appears. This means that $P(w_n|w_1...w_{n-1})$ is reduced to $P(w_n)$.

Voting strategy   (also *voting system*, or *voting scheme*) An approach to problem solving in which we first develop different modules to provide independent solutions to a problem and then combine their solutions to form a single solution. We say that the algorithms "vote" for their solution as they put it forward to be considered along the other solutions. As part of the voting strategy, we must develop a *vote combination approach*, to determine how the votes will be considered toward the final solution.

Vote combination approach   The method used to combine the votes in a *voting strategy*. For example, a combination approach based on majority voting would take as the final solution to problem, the solution put forward by the majority of "voters" (algorithms).

Web as corpus   An expression meaning that the whole Web becomes a very large corpus, to be searched and used for *Information Extraction* or other NLP tasks.

Weighted Edit Distance   An *Edit Distance* algorithm in which the cost of deletions, insertions, and substitutions is weighted according to some criterion (e.g., consonants versus vowels and close keyboard keys).

Window size   Although a fairly general term, in *distributional semantics*, this refers to the size of the *context window*. Given that we study the behaviour of words within *context windows* in order to find their *co-occurrences*, the size of these context windows will have a major impact on the results.

Word   The word *word* has become imprecise within the field of NLP, although most often it refers to a token that exists within a particular language. Words are also sometimes referred to as tokens, terms, or labels. To avoid ambiguity and more precisely represent the language unit we wish to describe, it is best to refer to various surface forms encountered in text as a *token*, *term*, *lexical unit*, *compound*, or *phrase*.

Word boundary   The boundary of a word determines where it starts and ends in a sentence. This becomes problematic for surface forms of entities with various spellings. For example, *half-baked ideas* and *half baked ideas* could be seen as two or three words, depending on the *separators* used for *tokenization*.

Word frequency   The number of occurrences of a word in a particular *corpus*. Finding word frequencies in a given corpus is a very simple but effective *quantitative approach* to getting a sense of its content.

Word sense   A possible meaning (sense) of a lexical unit.

Word Sense Disambiguation (WSD)   The process of *grounding* a surface form found in text to its appropriate meaning (word sense) in a dictionary or other *lexical resource*.

References

Agichtein E, Gravano L (2000) Extracting Relations from Large Plain-Text Collections. In: Proceedings of International Conference on Digital Libraries, vol I, pp 85–94

Agirre E, Alfonseca E, Hall K, Kravalova J, Pas M, Soroa A (2009) A Study on Similarity and Relatedness Using Distributional and WordNet-based Approaches. In: Human Language Technologies: The 2009 Annual Conference of the North American Chapter of the ACL, Boulder, Colorado, June, pp 19–27

Alfonseca E, Ruiz-Casado M, Okumura M, Castells P (2006) Towards Large-scale Non-taxonomic Relation Extraction : Estimating the Precision of Rote Extractors. In: Proceedings of the second workshop on ontology learning and population, Coling-ACL'2006, 1999, pp 49–56

Banerjee S, Pedersen T (2002) An Adapted Lesk Algorithm for Word Sense Disambiguation Using WordNet. Computational Linguistics and Intelligent Text Processing 2276:136–145

Banko M (2009) Open Information Extraction for the Web. Doctoral thesis, University of Washington

Banko M, Cafarella MJ, Soderland S, Broadhead M, Etzioni O (2007) Open Information Extraction from the Web. In: International Joint Conference on Artificial Intelligence (IJCAI'2007), pp 2670–2676

Barrière C, Gagnon M (2011) Drugs and Disorders : From Specialized Resources to Web data. In: Workshop on Web Scale Knowledge Extraction, 10th International Semantic Web Conference, Bonn, Germany

Bouamor D, Semmar N, Zweigenbaum P (2013) Using WordNet and Semantic Similarity for Bilingual Terminology Mining from Comparable Corpora. In: Proceedings of the Sixth Workshop on Building and Using Comparable Corpora, pp 16–23

Brin S (1998) Extracting Patterns and Relations from the World Wide Web. In: The World Wide Web and Databases, pp 172–183

Budanitsky A, Hirst G (2006) Evaluating WordNet-based Measures of Lexical Semantic Relatedness. Computational Linguistics 32(1):1–35

Bullinaria Ja, Levy JP (2007) Extracting semantic representations from word co-occurrence statistics: a computational study. Behavior research methods 39(3):510–26

Bunescu RC, Mooney RJ (2005) A Shortest Path Dependency Kernel for Relation Extraction. In: Proceedings of Human Language Technology Conference and Conference on Empirical Methods in Naural Language Processing (HLT/EMNLP), Vancouver, Canada, October, pp 724–731

Chen SF, Goodman J (1999) An empirical study of smoothing techniques for language modeling. Proceedings of the 34th annual meeting of the Association for Computational Linguistics pp 310–318

© Springer International Publishing Switzerland 2016

C. Barrière, *Natural Language Understanding in a Semantic Web Context*,
DOI 10.1007/978-3-319-41337-2

Christensen J, Soderland S, Etzioni O (2011) An analysis of open information extraction based on semantic role labeling. Proceedings of the sixth international conference on Knowledge capture (K-CAP'11)

Church KW, Hanks P (1990) Word association norms, mutual information and lexicography. Computational Linguistics 16(1):22–29

Crowston W, Williams M (1997) Reproduced and emergent genres of communication on the World Wide Web. In: Proceedings of the 13th Annual Hawai International Conference on System Sciences, pp 201–205

Culotta A, Sorensen J (2004) Dependency Tree Kernels for Relation Extraction. In: Proceedings of the 42nd Annual Meeting of the Association for Computational Linguistics (ACL'04)

Dagan I, Church K (1994) Termight: Identifying and translating technical terminology. In: Proceedings of the 4th Conference on Applied Natural Language Processing (ANLP'94), pp 34–40

Dagan I, Lee L, Pereira FCN (1999) Similarity-Based Models of Word Cooccurrence Probabilities. Machine Learning 32:43–69

Dai Hj, Wu Cy, Tsai RTH, Hsu WL (2012) From Entity Recognition to Entity Linking : A Survey of Advanced Entity Linking Techniques. In: The 26th Annual Conference of the Japanese Society for Artitifical Intelligence, pp 1–10

Drouin P (2003) Term extraction using non-technical corpora as a point of leverage. Terminology 9(1):99–115

Elango P (2006) Coreference Resolution: A Survey. Tech. rep., UW-Madison

Ell B, Vrandečić D, Simperl E (2011) Labels in the web of data. Lecture Notes in Computer Science 7031 LNCS:162–176

Etzioni O, Cafarella M, Downey D, Popescu AM, Shaked T, Soderland S, Weld DS, Yates A (2005) Unsupervised named-entity extraction from the Web: An experimental study. Artificial Intelligence 165(1):91–134

Etzioni O, Banko M, Cafarella MJ (2006) Machine Reading. In: AAAI'06 Proceedings of the 21st national conference on Artificial intelligence, pp 1517–1519

Etzioni O, Fader A, Christensen J, Soderland S (2011) Open Information Extraction : the Second Generation. In: International Joint Conference on Artificial Intelligence (IJCAI'2011)

Exner P, Nugues P (2011) Using Semantic Role Labeling to Extract Events from Wikipedia. In: Proceedings of the Workshop on Detection, Representation, and Exploitation of Events in the Semantic Web (DeRiVE 2011), at ISWC'2011, CEUR-WS.org

Fellbaum C (1998) WordNet: An Electronic Lexical Database. MIT Press, Cambridge, MA, USA

Fillmore CJ (1968) The Case for Case. In: Universals in Linguistic Theory, pp 1–88

Firth J (1957) A synopsis of linguistic theory 1930-1955. In: Studies in Linguistic Analysis, pp 1–32

Francis WN, Kucera H (1982) Frequency analysis of English usage: lexicon and grammar

Fung P (1998) A Statistical View on Bilingual Lexicon Extraction : From Parallel Corpora to Non-Parallel Corpora. In: AMTA'98 Proceedings of the Third Conference of the Association for Machine Translation in the Americas, pp 1–17

Gale W, Church K (1993) A Program for Aligning Sentences in Bilingual Corpora. Computational Linguistics 19:177–184

Gildea D, Jurafsky D (2002) Automatic Labeling of Semantic Roles. Computational Linguistics 28(3):245–288

Girju R, Moldovan D, Tatu M, Antohe D (2005) On the semantics of noun compounds. Computer Speech & Language 19(4):479–496

Gurevych I, Kim J (eds) (2013) The People's Web Meets NLP. Springer

Gurevych I, Eckle-Kohler J, Hartmann S, Matuschek M, Meyer CM, Wirth C (2012) UBY – A Large-Scale Unified Lexical-Semantic Resource Based on LMF. In: Proceedings of the 13th Conference of the European Chapter of the Association for Computational Linguistics (EACL 2012), pp 580–590

Halskov J, Barrière C (2008) Web-based extraction of semantic relation instances for terminology work. Terminology, Special Issue on Pattern-based Approaches to Semantic Relation Extraction 14(1):20–44

Hearst M (1992) Automatic Acquisition of Hyponyms from Large Text Corpora. In: Proceedings of COLING-92, Nantes, pp 539–545

Hellmann S, Lehmann J, Auer S, Brümmer M (2013) Integrating NLP using linked data. Lecture Notes in Computer Science 8219:98–113

Ide NM, Véronis J (1990) Mapping dictionaries: A spreading activation approach. 6th Annual Conference of the Centre for the New Oxford English Dictionary 12601:52–64

Jurafsky D, Martin JH (2007) Speech and Language Processing. In: An introduction to speech recognition, computational linguistics and natural language processing

Kageura K, Umino B (1996) Methods of Automatic Term Recognition. Terminology 3(2):259–289

Kazama J, Torisawa K (2007) Exploiting Wikipedia as External Knowledge for Named Entity Recognition. Proceedings of the 2007 Joint Conference on Empirical Methods in Natural Language Processing and Computational Natural Language Learning pp 698–707

Kilgarriff A, Rosenzweig J (2000) Framework and Results for English SENSEVAL. Computers and the Humanities 34:15–48

Kim SN, Baldwin T (2005) Automatic Interpretation of Noun Compounds Using WordNet Similarity. In: IJCNLP 2005, pp 945–956

Koch GG, Landis JR (1977) The measurement of observer agreement for categorical data. Biometrics 1:159–174

Lassila O, Mcguinness D (2001) The Role of Frame-Based Representation on the Semantic Web. Tech. rep., Knowledge Systems Laboratory, Stanford University

Lee H, Peirsman Y, Chang A, Chambers N, Surdeanu M, Jurafsky D (2011) Stanford ' s Multi-Pass Sieve Coreference Resolution System at the CoNLL-2011 Shared Task. Proceedings of the Fifteenth Conference on Computational Natural Language Learning: Shared Task pp 28–34

Lehmann J, Isele R, Jakob M, Jentzsch A, Kontokostas D, Mendes PN, Hellmann S, Morsey M, Van Kleef P, Auer S, Bizer C (2012) DBpedia - A large-scale, multilingual knowledge base extracted from Wikipedia. Semantic Web 6(2):167–195

Lenci A, Busa F, Ruimy N, Gola E, Monachini M, Calzolari N, Zampolli A, Guimier E, Recourcé G, Humphreys L, Rekovsky UV, Ogonowski A, Mccauley C, Peters W, Peters I, Gaizauskas R, Villegas M (2000) SIMPLE Work Package 2 - Linguistic Specifications. Tech. rep.

Lesk M (1986) Automatic Sense Disambiguation Using Machine Readable Dictionaries: How to Tell a Pine Cone from an Ice Cream Cone. In: SIGDOC'86: Proceedings of the 5th annual international conference on Systems documentation, New York, NY, USA, pp 24–26

Levi JN (1978) The Syntax and Semantics of Complex Nominals. Academic Press, Inc, New York

Lin D (1998) Automatic retrieval and clustering of similar words. In: Proceedings of the 36th Annual Meeting of the Association for Computational Linguistics and 17th International Conference on Computational Linguistics, pp 768–774

Ling X, Weld DS (2012) Fine-Grained Entity Recognition. Proceedings of the 26th AAAI Conference on Artificial Intelligence doi: 10.1.1.431.8777

Ling X, Singh S, Weld DS (2015) Design Challenges for Entity Linking. Transactions of the Association for Computational Linguistics 3:315–328

Madsen BN, Pedersen BS, Erdman Thomsen H (2001) Defining Semantic Relations for OntoQuery. In: Proceedings of the First International OntoQuery Workshop, pp 57–88

Mann GS, Yarowsky D (2005) Multi-Field Information Extraction and Cross-Document Fusion. In: ACL'05 Proceedings of the 43rd Annual Meeting of the Association for Computational Linguistics, June, pp 483–490

Marrero M, Sánchez-Cuadrado S, Morato J, Andreadakis Y (2009) Evaluation of Named Entity Extraction Systems. Research In Computer Science 41:47–58

McCrae J, Aguado-De-Cea A, Buitelaar P, Cimiano P, Declerck T, Gomez-Pérez A, Gracia J, Hollink L, Montiel-Ponsoda E, Spohr D, Wunner T (2012) Interchanging lexical resources on the Semantic Web. In: Language Resources and Evaluation (LREC), vol 46, pp 701–719

Mehler A, Sharoff S, Santini M (eds) (2010) Genres on the Web - Computational Models and Empirical Studies. Text, Speech and Language Technology Series, Springer

Mihalcea R (2007) Using Wikipedia for Automatic Word Sense Disambiguation. In: HLT-NAACL, pp 196–2003

Mikolov T, Sutskever I, Chen K, Corrado G, Dean J (2013) Distributed Representations of Words and Phrases and their Compositionality. In: Advances in Neural Information Processing Systems 26 (NIPS 2013)

Miller GA, Charles WG (1991) Contextual correlates of semantic similarity. Language and Cognitive Processes 6(1):1–28

Mitkov R (1999) Anaphora Resolution: the State of the Art. Computational Linguistics pp 1–34

Moro A, Raganato A, Navigli R, Informatica D, Elena VR (2014) Entity Linking meets Word Sense Disambiguation : a Unified Approach. Transactions of the Association for Computational Linguistics 2:231–244

Nadeau D, Sekine S (2007) A survey of named entity recognition and classification. Named Entities: Recognition, classification and use Special Issue of Lingvisticae Investigationes 30(1):3–26

Narayanan S, Fillmore CJ, Baker CF, Petruck MRL (2002) FrameNet Meets the Semantic Web: A DAML+OIL Frame Representation. In: Proceedings of the Eighteenth National Conference on Artificial Intelligence (AAAI-02), September 2000

Nastase V, Nakov P, Séaghdha DÓ, Szpakowicz S (2013) Semantic Relations Between Nominals. Morgan & Claypool, Toronto

Navigli R (2009) Word sense disambiguation: A survey. ACM Computing Surveys 41(2):10

Navigli R, Informatica D, Ponzetto SP (2010) BabelNet : Building a Very Large Multilingual Semantic Network. In: Proceedings of the 48th Annual Meeting of the Association for Computational Linguistics, Uppsala, Sweden, July, pp 216–225

Norvig P (2009) Natural Language Corpus Data. In: Beautiful Data: The Stories Behind Elegant Data Solutions, pp 219–242

O Seaghdha D (2008) Learning compound noun semantics. Ph.d. thesis, University of Cambridge

Otero-Cerdeira L, Rodríguez-Martínez FJ, Gómez-Rodríguez A (2015) Ontology matching: A literature review. Expert Systems with Applications 42(2):949–971

Palmer M (2009) SemLink - Linking PropBank , VerbNet, FrameNet. In: Proceedings of the Generative Lexicon Conference (GenLex-09), pp 9–15

Palmer M (2013) Semantic Role Labeling Tutorial - Part 1

Palmer M, Gildea D, Kingsbury P (2005) The Proposition Bank: An Annotated Corpus of Semantic Roles. Computational Linguistics 31(1):71–106

Pennington J, Socher R, Manning CD (2014) GloVe: Global Vectors for Word Representation. In: Proceedings of the 2014 Conference on Empirical Methods in Natural Language Processing, pp 1532–1543

Pereira B (2014) Entity Linking with Multiple Knowledge Bases : An Ontology Modularization Approach. In: Proceedings of the 13th International Semantic Web Conference, Springer, pp 513–520

Poesio M, Ponzetto SP, Versley Y (2010) Computational Models of Anaphora Resolution : A Survey The Linguistics of Anaphora. Tech. Rep. 1

Ponzetto SP, Strube M (2007) Deriving a Large Scale Taxonomy from Wikipedia. In: AAAI, pp 1440–1445

Pustejovsky J (1995) The Generative Lexicon. MIT Press

Ratinov L, Roth D (2009) Design Challenges and Misconceptions in Named Entity Recognition. In: Proceedings of the Thirteenth Conference on Computational Natural Language Learning (CoNLL), Boulder, Colorado, June, pp 147–155

Ravichandran D, Hovy E (2002) Learning Surface Text Patterns for a Question Answering System. In: ACL'02 Proceedings of the 40th Annual Meeting of the Association for Computational Linguistics, pp 41–47

Resnik P, Diab M (2000) Measuring verb similarity. Proceedings of the 22nd Annual Meeting of the Cognitive Science Society pp 399–404

Riloff E, Jones R (1999) Learning Dictionaries Ellen Riloff for Information Bootstrapping Extraction by Multi-Level. In: Proceedings AAAI '99/IAAI '99, American Association for Artificial Intelligence, Menlo Park, CA, USA, pp 474–479

Roussinov D, Crowston K, Nilan M, Kwasnik B, Cai J, Liu X (2001) Genre Based Navigation on the Web. In: Proceedings of the 34th Hawaii International Conference on System Sciences, pp 1–10

Sekine S, Sudo K, Nobata C (2002) Extended named entity hierarchy. In: Third International Conference on Language Resources and Evaluation (LREC 2002), pp 1818–1824

Silber HG, McCoy KF (2002) Efficiently Computed Lexical Chains as an Intermediate Representation for Automatic Text Summarization. Computational Linguistics 28(4):487–496

Smadja F (1993) Retrieving Collocations from Text : Xtract. Computational Linguistics 19(1):143–178

Smith JJR, Quirk C, Toutanova K (2010) Extracting parallel sentences from comparable corpora using document level alignment. In: Human Language Technologies: The 2010 Annual Conference of the North American Chapter of the Association for Computational Linguistics, pp 403–411

Stevenson M, Greenwood MA (2005) A Semantic Approach to IE Pattern Induction. In: Proceedings of the 43rd Annual Meeting of the ACL, pp 379–386

Strube M, Ponzetto SP (2006) WikiRelate ! Computing Semantic Relatedness Using Wikipedia. In: AAAI, February, pp 1419–1424

Sudo K, Sekine S, Grishman R (2003) An Improved Extraction Pattern Representation Model for Automatic IE Pattern Acquisition. In: ACL'03 Proceedings of the 41st Annual Meeting of the Association for Computational Linguistics, pp 224–231

Sundheim BM (1995) Overview of results of the MUC-6 evaluation. Proceedings of the 6th conference on Message understanding - MUC6'95 pp 13–31

Tkachenko M, Simanovsky A (2012) Named Entity Recognition : Exploring Features. In: Proceedings of KONVENS, Vienna, Austria, pp 118–127

Toral A, Mu R (2006) A proposal to automatically build and maintain gazetteers for Named Entity Recognition by using Wikipedia. In: Proceedings of the Workshop on New Text, EACL'06, pp 56–61

Turney P (2001) Mining the Web for Synonyms : PMI-IR Versus LSA on TOEFL*. In: Twelfth European Conference on Machine Learning (ECML'2001), Freiburg, Germany, pp 491–502

Usbeck R, Ngomo AcN, Michael R, Gerber D, Coelho SA, Both A (2014) AGDISTIS - Graph-Based Disambiguation of Named Entities Using Linked Data. In: Proceedings of the 13th International Semantic Web Conference, Springer, pp 457–471

Vanderwende L (1994) Algorithm for the automatic interpretation of noun sequences. In: Proceedings of the 15th International Conference on Computational Linguistics, Kyoto, Japan, pp 782–788

Vanderwende L, Menezes A, Quirk C (2015) An AMR parser for English, French, German, Spanish and Japanese and a new AMR-annotated corpus. In: Proceedings of the NAACL-HLT 2015 Conference, pp 26–30

Vasilescu F, Langlais P, Lapalme G (2004) Evaluating Variants of the Lesk Approach for Disambiguating Words. In: Language Resources and Evaluation (LREC), pp 633–636

Vossen P (1998) EuroWordNet : Linguistic Ontologies in a Multilingual Database. Communication and Cognition for Artificial Intelligence, Special Issue on The creation and maintenance of electronic thesauri pp 1–33

Yangarber R (2003) Counter-Training in Discovery of Semantic Patterns. In: Proceedings of the 41st Annual Meeting on Association for Computational Linguistics - ACL '03, pp 343–350

Yangarber R, Grishman R, Tapanainen P, Huttunen S (2000) Automatic Acquisition of Domain Knowledge for Information Extraction. In: Proceedings of the 18th ICCL

Printed in the United States
By Bookmasters